FROM FACT TO JUDGMENT

THE MACMILLAN COMPANY
NEW YORK • CHICAGO
DALLAS • ATLANTA • SAN FRANCISCO
LONDON • MANILA
BRETT-MACMILLAN LTD.
TORONTO

FROM FACT TO JUDGMENT

HAROLD F. GRAVES
BERNARD S. OLDSEY
The Pennsylvania State University

THE MACMILLAN COMPANY—*New York*

Printed in the United States of America

First Printing

Library of Congress catalog card number: 57-6716

PREFACE

From Fact to Judgment offers a program for helping college students make better use of facts in a variety of writing situations—all the way from simple reporting to defending a complex judgment. We emphasize facts because so often the lack of them makes student writing superficial, unconvincing, and dull. At the same time we make it clear that facts are only a means to an end; to be worth a writer's attention they must lead somewhere, serve a clear purpose, have significance. We intend this book, with its illustrative readings, to help students develop the accuracy in observing, the critical sense, and the analytical skill they will need for the kind of writing our society expects of them.

As the title implies, *From Fact to Judgment* begins with the study of factual statements and proceeds to kinds of writing that involve increasing reliance on judgments. Learning is to be cumulative: the student must apply principles from earlier chapters to the more complex assignments that follow.

The first chapter is introductory. It outlines the writing process: stating a clear purpose, based on a recognition of the writer's background and his readers' needs and interests; limiting the subject; getting materials; organizing; and writing. The chapter points out the varieties of informative and critical writing the modern world requires, and proposes that students practice writing for "real" needs and audiences beyond the classroom.

Chapters 2, 3, and 4 introduce principles of informative and explanatory writing: the simple report that "just sticks to the facts"; definition and classification, not for mental exercise but as means to clear and orderly communication; and explanation of "a complex unit" (such as a mechanism, process, or organization), which must use facts in the analysis of principles, relationships, and descriptive detail. These three chapters provide an understanding of expository elements from which judgments may evolve.

The last four chapters constitute a second unit, a kind of Part II: how to analyze a "problem," reach sound judgments about it, and defend the judgments. Specifically, Chapter 5 is concerned with defining and analyzing a problem, determining the issues or criteria upon which reliable judgments must depend, and explaining a problem for readers. Chapters 6 and 7 introduce principles of critical thinking: the tests of sound inference, the evaluation and interpretation of evidence. Chapter 8, "Defending a Judgment," explains how all the elements combine when a writer marshals evidence and logic to support conclusions.

The expository defense of a judgment, the most complex writing assignment we discuss in this book, is different from propaganda or even debate. While recognizing the readers' wants and interests, it avoids appeals to prejudice and passion; it encourages an objective examination of premises and evidence. Such expository defense has wide application—in evaluating books, plays, symphonies, or jazz; in judging houses, laws, machines, or institutions; and in recommending courses of action. It varies widely too in scope and method, from book review to consumer report to the research of scientists and scholars. In this book we remind the student of the great range of possibilities. In his writing practice we ask him to recognize both his limitations and his opportunities.

From Fact to Judgment introduces numerous contributions of semantics and logic, as well as those of rhetoric. We have translated the language of specialists into terms the student can readily understand and adapt to the ends of his own writing. We have concentrated attention on those principles that the student can apply directly to his own thinking and writing.

The readings selected to illustrate methods and principles in the text represent a wide range of subjects, purposes, styles—even levels of significance. We prefer not to call them "models" because we hope the student will approach them critically: we want him to analyze, study, and evaluate rather than merely imitate.

The exercises and assignments will, we hope, suggest to both students and instructors many other problems and subjects to use for practice writing. We suggest a direction; we do not intend to lay out a course in detail.

We recognize how much we owe to scores of predecessors and

contemporaries who have written about problems of observing, thinking, and writing. Unfortunately we do not know which ones to single out for special acknowledgment.

We have had the benefit of years of informal discussion with colleagues about the problems of teaching expository writing. Our fellow English instructors at The Pennsylvania State University deserve and have our gratitude. We want to thank Professor John S. Bowman particularly, because he helped us plan the experimental program from which this book evolved, and he gave us genuinely useful advice about the manuscript itself.

CONTENTS

Chapter

Chapter

CHAPTER 1

Writing for a Purpose

Why Write?

We live in an age of radio and television, movies and comic strips, committees and conference rooms, yet you are being told that an educated American—even more than in the past—must know how to write. Our schools and colleges teach English composition to the millions. Why?

The truth is we need far more writing today than ever before in history. Of course one reason is that more people read books, newspapers and magazines; we need more writers to satisfy the demands of general readers. But only a few of the millions studying expect to write professionally for publication. The wider demand for writing arises from the greater complexity of our society. Our corporations, state and federal governments, technical and professional societies, labor unions, foundations, public and private agencies—all are larger and more complicated than they used to be. Hence all need more written records. To function effectively, our civilization needs a staggering quantity of letters and memoranda, reports, directives, agreements, and written interpretations. We need millions of competent writers.

That picture of the demand for writing may seem a rather discouraging one if you like to think of writing as a personal means of self-expression. Who can find inspiration in a hundred tons of corporation or government reports with the prospect of someday adding a few pounds to the total? But of course that's not the way it is. Good writing is not measured by the pound. It is not made by machines. It is still produced by living, thinking human beings with something to say to particular readers. The doctor writes for his colleagues in the County Medical Society, the architect for his clients, the engineer for his general manager, the teacher for the PTA. As an educated American you will some day have real readers to inform, enlighten, interest, and convince through what you write. You will find subjects related to your work or community interests, and though some of the writing may be compulsory and not exactly fun, it will be important.

Now practice can never be quite the real thing. A paper you write for practice may find no readers except yourself, an English instructor, or a friendly critic; it will never reach the citizens of Reedville or a board of directors. But if you always practice with a definite purpose and a definite group of readers in mind, you will find greater interest and come closer to the situations of real life.

This doesn't mean that all your practice should be concentrated on one favorite subject and one kind of reader. You cannot predict accurately the exact writing problems you will face a decade from now; our world changes fast. The right kind of practice, then, must be varied. Think about your probable future needs, of course; but remember too that your writing practice should help you develop abilities to think, judge, and adapt to new and unforeseen conditions. Like good education in general, the best kind of writing practice will help you to adjust to a changing environment.

About What?

A writer's subject generally comes out of his experience and immediate needs. Unless he is a reporter just looking for news, a novelist, or a free-lance writer searching for "an interesting angle," the writer is likely to find his subject thrust upon him. Your employer asks you to investigate reasons for low production and to give him a report. The mayor appoints you to a committee to study parking conditions and submit recommendations for improving facilities. Or perhaps you need something done about trash removal in your neighborhood, or you don't like what the schools are teaching your children, or you want to tell your customers how to assemble the Hi-Fi equipment you are selling them. Under these circumstances you do not look for a subject. The subject is right there.

Unfortunately, the subjects you use for practice are not so obvious. Perhaps you have a very wide choice and don't know where to start. You might begin by asking yourself:

1. What subjects have special interest for me? How long and varied a list can I make?
2. How much do I know about those subjects? How can I learn more?
3. What readers could I hope to reach? What can I tell them they don't already know?
4. What effect do I want to produce? What definite purpose shall I set for each piece of writing?

Our concern in this book is not with imaginative or creative writing: not with verse, fiction, or the personal essay. We shall concentrate our attention on the facts of our surroundings and the uses we can make of such facts in writing. Three broad purposes will be apparent:

1. We may want only to report the facts themselves, without comment or interpretation. The broad purpose is *to inform.*

2. We may want to explain meanings and relationships, to show cause-and-effect connections, to analyze complex conditions or problems. The broad purpose is *to explain.*

3. We may want to use facts and explanations as a basis for value judgments or recommendations. What merits and defects do we find in this book, machine, system, law, society, candidate, or activity? What policy or action do we want to recommend? The broad purpose is *to support a judgment.*

It is important to decide upon one broad purpose at a time. If your aim is to tell students in a Driver Training course how the automobile engine works, you give them facts; but your ultimate, controlling purpose is *to explain.* And if you want to show the Student Council why rules applying to freshmen ought to be repealed, you tell them what has happened, and you explain the effects of the rules; but your ultimate, controlling purpose is *to support a judgment.* Distinguish the means you use from the end you want to reach.

One good way to express your purpose before you write is to state both the effect you want and an epitome (a brief summary) of what you will say:

1. Purpose: To inform readers of the Belltown *Gazette.*
   Epitome: Borough Council's new budget includes $30,000 for a variety of services not included in past years.
2. Purpose: To explain to students in a reading clinic how they can increase their reading speed.
   Epitome: You must train your eyes to take in more words for each movement they make along a line of print.
3. Purpose: To show members of the Cooperative the value of the Dent Wythe TV sets.
   Epitome: While the sound is better than in most sets and the picture good, the price is too high.

The purpose ought to control the selection of facts and ideas, the form and method, and the style of what you write. The purpose will come from your experience, knowledge, needs, and the kind of readers you expect to reach. You cannot express purpose and epitome in final terms until you have all your material together and understand your whole writing problem.

Who Will Read It?

Writing is for readers. To succeed it must be adapted to their interests and wants, their education and background, and their attitudes and beliefs. That doesn't mean, of course, that good writing merely restates what readers already know and think. Quite the contrary: it gives them something new, it stimulates interests, adds to knowledge, clarifies, interprets, or changes opinions.

Suppose you are writing about a new machine. If you hope to sell it, you study the motives of prospective buyers and try to find impressive evidence that will influence them to buy. If you are explaining the machine for engineers, you emphasize engineering principles and tests of efficiency; your language is appropriately objective and technical. If you are writing for unskilled operators, you give the simple instructions they need to run the machine properly.

To write for readers, try to answer these questions:

1. What are my readers' interests? (You cannot expect them to care much about *your* financial problems unless *their* problems are related to yours.)

2. How much do my readers already know? (If they know as much as you, why write at all? If they are acquainted with the general field but know little about your specific topic, you can omit elementary principles and go directly to new details. If they know little about either general field or specific topic, you must patiently fill in the missing background.)

3. What is their reading level? (The better educated readers naturally expect a more sophisticated style. The less educated need a simpler style—not childish or condescending, but less complex, with more definition and examples.)

4. What are their attitudes and beliefs? (Social, political, religious, occupational, and sectional differences influence people's response to names, words, facts and ideas. Will your readers look favorably or unfavorably at "General Motors," "Christian Science," "Republican policies," "United Mine Workers," "athletic scholarships," "progressive education"? Reader attitudes may affect considerably the success of your examples and evidence. They take on added importance when your aim is to influence opinions or behavior.)

Know Your Limitations

Consider your subject, readers, and purpose. Now how fully are you prepared to write what you have in mind? You may discover that you have little more than some vague ideas about political corruption in your city, the uselessness of courses in economics, or how to direct a school play. You will need more facts, examples, evidence—and thinking too—before you begin to write.

This may be the time to limit the scope of your subject. If "Political Corruption in Buxton" is more than you can handle in five hundred words, perhaps you can do full justice to "How the Ex-Water Commissioner Went to Jail." If you find "Great Books Reading Courses" too broad for the half column your local editor allots you, why not concentrate on "How the Great Books Course Works in Danville"?

Besides limitations of time and space, every writer has limitations of knowledge and experience. For example, you might find you could write authoritatively on "The Small Town Drugstore Clerk's Responsibilities" because you have worked three summers in your uncle's drugstore and have numerous observations and experiences to draw on; but to broaden the subject to "The Modern Drugstore" takes you far beyond what you know. You might, of course, talk with your uncle and other druggists; you could visit scores of drugstores; you could read widely, too. But it would be some time before you could write with any authority on so broad a subject. A good writer will not pretend to be more than he is or to know more than he knows. The ex-Marine who wrote miserably about "The U.S. Marines" produced a wonderfully informative piece called "What I Saw of the Marines."

If everything you know about your subject comes from somebody else, what do you have to offer? Perhaps you have read widely. You have listened to authorities. But what can justify your writing from second-hand materials? Certainly you must make some contribution of your own. Here are possibilities:

1. You may save your reader time by digesting or summarizing what in the original form (a book, a long article, or perhaps numerous articles) would take him hours to read. But of course you tell your reader what you are doing.
2. You may be able to simplify or explain rather difficult or technical statements for readers who would have trouble with the originals. You ought to tell your reader what you are interpreting.
3. You may apply what you read or hear to your reader's particular needs and interests. For example, you read about a plan for improving interreligious understanding in Exeter; you use the Exeter experience to show how the same plan might be adopted in Winchester.
4. You arrive at your own conclusions or interpretations about things you read. You defend those conclusions with evidence drawn from various sources.
5. You may add personal experiences or new facts to support ideas presented in books or articles you have read.

Remember that all writing is expected to make some fresh contribution to its readers. Even the least ambitious composition ought to offer *something* that the reader could not get as well elsewhere.

The Writing Process

The writing process, you can see, involves more than sitting down to write. Usually, if the problem amounts to much, the process takes this kind of path:

1. Deciding subject and tentative purpose
2. Jotting down initial thoughts
3. Collecting needed materials
4. Restating purpose and arranging major ideas
5. Selecting details
6. Writing—and Rewriting

The first step we have already discussed; it may end with a tentative statement of the controlling purpose that serves to guide your investigation and thinking. This purpose (including intended readers, medium, and an epitome of what you expect to say) influences everything that follows.

2. Jotting down initial thoughts. With your main purpose in mind, suppose you list on paper all the ideas, examples, witnesses, experiences, and so on that come into your head. Don't undervalue your own experiences. Include questions you need to answer as well as items of information; such questions will suggest things to "look up."

If you were preparing a report to American Airlines urging that your town be put on a regular passenger route, you might jot down something like this:

Pop. of borough—10,345 (How many within fifty-mile radius?)
Main occupations of area: farm equipment plant, farming, cannery, merchants, lawyers . . . (what else?)
How many would be regular patrons? (salesmen . . . who else?)
How many women?
Present facilities: NYC four stops daily; Greyhound; pvt cars
Average distance of business trips: Plant salesmen cover U.S., main office Chicago . . . (Others?)
Area attracts some tourists, vacationers: lake, fishing
Local interest in all-year air service: Quote *Tribune* editorials; committee by Council; Chamber of Commerce statement (talk to Burgess, editor . . . others?)
Location of airport: five miles to west, main highway 625

Condition of airport: dimensions?—needs hard-surface runways, lights (see Gorman, Witt . . . who else?)

How many would use American for shopping trips to Indianapolis? Chicago? (Shows? vacations? . . . ?)

Get quotations from citizens who say they'd use planes at least four times a year (Guinness, Fitts, O'Brien, Perez . . . more?)

See editor about newspaper poll

And so forth, at random. Don't worry yet about a logical order; that can come later. Don't think too much either about the relevancy and importance of everything you put down; evaluation and selection will come later too.

3. Collecting needed materials. The preliminary list of ideas should suggest fairly well what you already know and what you need to learn. The kind and amount of necessary research ought to become apparent. You may need:

1. Facts: names, dates, dimensions, cases, statistics, etc.
2. Explanations: definitions, classifications, directions, analysis of machines or organizations, etc.
3. Opinions of experts or specialists
4. Reasons or arguments supporting certain judgments

Your potential sources include:

1. *Interviews* with friends and acquaintances, experts or specialists in your neighborhood. You might even decide to take a poll of a representative sample of people.
2. *Correspondence,* letters of inquiry to your congressman, public agencies, companies, and others who might answer particular questions.
3. *The local newspaper office:* Editor, reporters, and the newspaper files may help you find things you need about local matters especially.
4. *The library:* Generally begin your library search by going to indexes that list books or articles under a given subject. For example:

The Library card catalog of books

Reader's Guide to Periodical Literature (a subject index of articles in general magazines)

New York Times Index (a subject index of all news and comment in the *Times*)

Agricultural Index, Industrial Arts Index, and many other special indexes for special fields

And of course you will not overlook the possibility of further direct investigations of your own. If you want to write about the parks and playgrounds in your town, go look at them again, walk through them, study them. Farms, machines, factories, streets, classrooms, restaurants, book stores—all kinds of subjects are available to first-hand observation. You may even conduct informal experiments, like making comparative tests with two cameras, or several different gasolines in your car, or different golf clubs. Your own investigations may be limited in scope and scientific controls, but if you try to be accurate and intelligent about them they can give added interest and definiteness to what you write.

It is a good idea to take notes of what you hear, read, and see to guarantee accuracy and prompt your memory. Record the source on every note and put quotations in quotation marks: you don't want to forget who said what. Cards or half-sheets of ordinary typewriter paper will serve well for ordinary notes; you want them in a form that you can shuffle and arrange for any future purpose.

4. Restating purpose and arranging major ideas. Your tentative purpose may, of course, have to be modified as the result of the materials you collect and the thinking you do about them. Now you are ready to express it in final form with a sentence epitome of what you will try to say.

If you expect to write at much length, you will need some kind of plan or outline. For clarity, the fewer major divisions the better; supporting points belong logically in subordinate positions. But the plan you decide to use must suit your purpose, readers, and the kind of details you have available to use.

5. Selecting details. The details include illustrations, examples, sources, quotations—evidence of all kinds that good writing must have to hold interest and support the generalizations. If you go back to your preliminary jottings and then run through your notes, you will probably find that many notes do not fit your latest outline; some you reject, and some may suggest a change in the outline itself. You may find duplications, or very similar examples of the same point; you can now select the most interesting and significant, and put the others aside.

Sometimes you can work effectively from the original list of ideas that you jotted down before you began to investigate. You cross out, add, and number items in the order you now intend to use them—like this:

1. Who is for the change over?
1a. Mr. Noyes' statement
~~Watson's~~
3c. IBM data
4. What are the main arguments against the plan?
3. What main points in favor of the plan?
~~Philips~~
4a. Mercer
~~Nichols~~
5. Is there any chance for a compromise plan?
6. What's the possible outcome?
2. What is the vital issue?
3a. Cunliff's idea
3b. Tests at Briarton
4b. Cost estimates

No outline should be used as a straitjacket. After you begin writing you often find your plan less effective than it seemed. You modify it in any fashion that results in improvement. Sometimes you even decide to throw it away and try another.

6. **Writing—and rewriting.** Now, with a controlling purpose fixed in your mind, a plan to go by, and notes arranged as you think you want them, you are ready to begin writing.

What's the best method? (1) Write as fast as you can for a first draft? (2) Think through, polish, and revise each sentence and paragraph as you get to it? (3) Take a middle course? Nobody can answer with certainty for you. Since you are in a period now of practicing for future needs, it may be sensible to experiment with all three until you find the system that seems best adapted to your own temperament and abilities. Most writers probably get best results with the first method: they write rather fast in order to get the spirit and movement of their thinking down on paper. After that, they correct, rearrange, and edit with painstaking care. Other writers find it difficult to write anything fast; they need to do most of their revising before they go on to the next sentence or paragraph. Some writers can, with experience, learn to "think in paragraphs" or longer units; with them the words really flow. Other writers find they must do most of their thinking on paper; it is a painful and expensive process because it uses up great quantities of paper and typewriter ribbon, and it does take time, but eventually writers do get excellent results that way.

Newspaper writers must learn to write fast because their deadlines permit little time for rewriting. But even they know they could write much better if they had time for more drafts. Some creative writers, like Flaubert and Hemingway, have written as many as forty drafts of a paragraph or page. Practical engineers and accountants say they have made over a dozen drafts of a single report before it satisfied their needs.

Probably you will, for now, adopt a program somewhere between Hemingway and the newspaper reporter. You will write fewer than forty drafts but certainly more than one.

Eventually you must learn to become your own critic, and a good time to start is now. Before you give a paper to an instructor or to a friend for criticism, try being your own audience. Learn a few simple proofreading symbols (see the *American College Dictionary* or Webster's *New Collegiate Dictionary* for proofreading marks) and edit your copy while you read it. Use question marks to indicate doubtful expressions and statements not quite clear or of doubtful accuracy. Underline awkward expressions. Add words for transition. Clear away deadwood. With arrows, circles, and marginal notations, shift whole sentences or paragraphs for more effective organization.

Then rewrite.

EXERCISES

I. List subject, readers, medium, and purpose for each of six pieces of writing that you think you are likely to be doing ten years from now.

II. (a) List twelve subjects that you consider good for writing practice now, half of them related to the work you hope to be doing in the future, half of them concerned with something else.

(b) Limit each subject for development in 500 to 700 words to suit your own knowledge and potentialities.

(c) For each of these subjects, state a definite purpose for such a paper (proposed effect on what readers in what medium, and a one-sentence epitome of what you would say in each paper).

III. (a) Choose one of these subjects:
Who should go to college?
The ____________ curriculum
Social democracy in a college community

(b) Choose one of these reader groups to address on that subject:
Readers of a high school paper
A college board of trustees
A PTA in a small town

(c) Write a concise analysis of the reader group you choose. Consider: interest in the subject, knowledge of the subject, reading level, and attitudes.

IV. (a) How could you limit the following subjects so that you, yourself, could write on them effectively in about 500 words:

What's Wrong with American Politics
How to Get Ready for College
Modern Automobiles
Modern Television
Religion in the Twentieth Century
The Influence of the Atomic Bomb
Editing a Paper
Athletic Conditioning
Juvenile Delinquency
What Is Patriotism?
The Modern American Novel
Race Relations in America
What Foreigners Think of America
Love and Marriage
Traffic Problems

(b) Jot down ideas that occur to you as possibilities for use in preparing to write a paper on *one* of these subjects. (State tentative controlling purpose first.)

(c) Make a list of potential sources for such a paper.

ASSIGNMENTS

Before you go further in this book it will be useful to make preliminary plans for a comparatively extensive writing assignment that you will complete a month or two later.

Choose a subject for a series of four related papers (500 to 1000 words each). State a tentative purpose and epitome for the series, and a topic for each paper of the series. For example:

Series of articles in hometown newspaper about a proposed Driver-Training course in the high school

Purpose: To show citizens the need for such a course.
Epitome: This course is a practical and feasible way to teach our teen-agers how to drive safely and well.

Article 1: To create interest ("How Teen-agers Learn to Drive"—account of similar course in another town)
Article 2: To show that something needs to be done ("Driving Is Dangerous"—evidence of teen-age accidents)
Article 3: To convince readers that the course will pay ("Driver Training Really Pays"—evidence of its success in various places)
Article 4: To show citizens how to get it started ("How We Can Establish Driver Training in Tanville")

Chapters in a pamphlet for freshmen in the pre-legal curriculum

Purpose: To inform freshmen of what lies ahead in college, law school, and the legal profession.
Epitome: For one who likes to delve into problems affecting man's relations to his society, the law offers a great variety of opportunities.

Chap. 1. What Do Lawyers Do?
Chap. 2. What It Takes to Be a Lawyer
Chap. 3. Getting Ready: College and Law School
Chap. 4. Opportunities Ahead

If you have a subject that interests you, readers in mind who can profit from what you can tell them, and a tentative plan of development, we believe you will find the chapters that follow interesting and useful.

CHAPTER 2

Reporting the Facts

What Good Are Facts?

A writer must respect facts. Our age, more than any in the past, puts much store in them. Of course they have different values for different people, but scientists, reporters, statisticians, lawyers, and numerous fact-finding committees of industry and government are constantly searching for facts. No successful writer can ignore their importance.

Yet facts have no value by themselves. A village eccentric once memorized the height of every mountain listed in his atlas and got nothing for his trouble except local notoriety as a freak. "The temperature in Allentown at 10:30 a.m., June 7, 1943, was 69°F" may be verifiable fact, but who cares? All of us observe, read, and hear thousands of things that are not worth remembering or reporting because they mean nothing to us. They don't help explain, illustrate, or amuse; they lead to no judgment. Fortunately we forget most of the facts that do not count.

The facts that do count are those that help answer meaningful questions. The *who, what, where, when,* and *how many* are just means to something more important to us. They are only preliminary to answering further questions:

What makes it work? How is it done?
How can we get there?
Why? What made it happen?
Is this related to that? If so, how?
What is it worth?
What will happen if . . . ?
What shall we do about it?

Thinking from the facts is what makes facts worth collecting and reporting. Man, unlike the lower animals, can use facts as a basis for classifying, explaining, predicting, and advising. But because he can think, he is also capable of thinking in a vacuum if he chooses to escape reality. Constant reference to the facts is a protection against futile thinking.

Sane men must avoid the extreme. Vast collections of unrelated, unassimilated facts can lead to nothing until thinking men use them for a purpose. (Collecting odd information with the hope of winning quiz programs is a very hazardous occupation indeed.) At the same time, constructive thinking cannot proceed from guesses, rumors, and unsubstantiated assumptions; efficient thinking about jobs, crime, accidents, machines, politics, or human relations must be based upon some knowledge of realities—upon solid facts.

The writer uses facts for various purposes. He needs illustrations and examples—of centrifugal force, the "half nelson," or how to design a house. He needs evidence to support his judgments—the governor's record, what happened before the explosion, the actual costs of building in Colorado. Finally, the writer needs facts to add interest. Most dull writing is vague and abstract; most interesting writing is sprinkled with names, instances, and specific details. Of course not all interesting writing is strictly factual, and not all factual writing is interesting. The facts have to be used in proper proportion and for a useful purpose. But sensibly used, they are invaluable.

Just Sticking to the Facts

Before we go any further into the problems of reporting the facts we had better stop and consider what we mean. If you happen to be an ordinary witness in a courtroom you will generally be expected to "stick to the facts." Or someday on a job the boss will say, "Here's the situation—see if you can dig up the facts on it." Just what is it you are expected to stick to? Just what are you supposed to dig up?

"The light turned green," you say. "Mr. Curry, who was driving my car, started across the intersection. Mr. Johnson's car, on our right, struck my rear fender." Now even Mr. Johnson's lawyer is likely to accept that as a statement of fact. He may question your veracity; he may ask questions to bring out more, or to show inconsistencies. But he is not likely to ask what you mean by "green," "my car," "Mr. Curry," "intersection," and so on.

Suppose, on the other hand, you say, "This Johnson is a pretty reckless driver anyway. He was going far too fast for conditions, and I suppose his car got out of control. He just barged right into us." Of course Johnson's lawyer will cry "Objection!" and the judge may be expected to concur. You are no longer telling what happened but are stating what you *think* of Johnson, his habits, and his behavior. You are far beyond the matters of fact.

A statement of fact is confined to matters capable of observation; that is, it reports something that everybody agrees *could* have been observed. Its language is precise and unambiguous; it will not get us into disputes over meanings. It is impersonal and objective, and it includes no feelings or judgments. It may be a lie, but if so the author can hardly plead, "Well, that's my opinion." It permits of no differences of opinion.

Statements of Fact	*Statements of Judgment*
Jack Rourke played 43 minutes at left halfback Saturday against De Soto and scored two touchdowns.	Jack *set up* two other touchdowns and played a *magnificent* game.
New Orleans is south of Memphis.	New Orleans is a *livelier, more interesting* town than Memphis.
The Morse property, 394 Linden Street, has a lot 75 x 172 ft.	The Morse property, in a *good* neighborhood, is *attractively* landscaped.
Mary Linfeldt belongs to the Players, Women's Glee Club, the Junior Honor Society, the Poets' Retreat, and Gamma Chi Pi.	Mary is *certainly* one of the *most active* and *popular* girls in her class.

The language of science is ideally suited to factual reporting because the terms are so precise. Our common units of measurement, most proper names, and official records of births, marriages, and so on are usually quite unambiguous. But it takes at least a sentence to make a statement of fact. Scientific terms applied loosely to "the best families," or "pretty girls" will not produce factual reports.

The most acceptable statements of fact are verifiable. Not only will everybody agree pretty well what the statement says: it is also possible to check its accuracy. "Heather Heights is seven miles from Wilton" can be verified by your speedometer. "The President said at his press conference . . ." can be verified by the many reporters who were there. But, "Stalin told me in strictest confidence just before he died . . ." cannot very likely ever be verified. Of course we cannot afford to reject all statements that are incapable of verification, but their credibility is naturally reduced no matter who the witness.

You aren't likely to be asked to stick to the facts at all times, and that's a good thing. The best writing must add meanings to the facts through interpretations and judgments. Much writing needs the subjective elements of personal feeling to give it warmth.

But a little rigid discipline in reporting the facts is good for all of us. More than anything else, it will remind us just where facts end and our thinking begins. It will make us more careful writers; it can make us better observers.

Accurate Observing

Whenever you go after facts for yourself—not through reading but through seeing, listening, and using your other senses—a few guiding principles are useful:

1. *Discount Your Own Preconceptions.* Experience leads to habits of thinking, as it should; but these habits produce stereotypes or pictures in our heads that may affect the accuracy of what we actually see. If, for example, you were told to "observe that room of morons," the very word *moron* would pretty surely suggest characteristics you'd expect to find. Unless you take care you will see nothing else. These stereotypes, or pictures in your heads, will prevent your looking at things honestly and with open eyes—unless you take some precautions. Can you observe "Harvard men," "Southern California," "unskilled labor," "New Englanders," or "Cadillacs" without permit-

ting prejudice and preconceptions to do the observing for you? The only protection is to recognize your own stereotypes and tell yourself "perhaps that's not the whole picture." Prepare yourself for surprises —not to be shocked, but just to see things straight.

2. *Postpone Judgments.* The first things you observe may be misleading; if you jump to conclusions you may not see the whole picture. For example, one hour in a restaurant doesn't prove it a "teen-age hangout"; perhaps you need several more visits before you judge. What looks after an hour's inspection like "a well-organized office" may not seem that way if you continue looking. Quick generalizations hurt your ability to get the facts.

3. *Observe for a Purpose.* It isn't likely you'll often be expected "to observe" without knowing why. "All" the facts about a street, a game, or a building is an absurd assignment. Only the significant, useful facts are worth attention. An insurance investigator visiting the scene of a fire is not concerned with the taxi ride to get there, the cars parked across the street, or the way curious neighbors are dressed. Some of these things might be interesting enough for other purposes, but not for getting the relevant facts about the fire.

To summarize:

1. Don't know what you will see before you see it. Discount your stereotypes.
2. Don't jump to conclusions before you get all the pertinent facts.
3. Don't bother with facts that aren't related to your main purpose.

Effective Reporting

Whenever somebody says "Here's the problem," the first need is to get pertinent facts before anybody looks for solutions. Medicine, psychology, and various social sciences need important case studies to provide accurate information about specific patients, delinquents, alcoholics, unemployed miners, the handicapped, and the gifted. Scores of different fields need good factual reports of a similar kind.

An effective factual report meets certain demands:

1. It confiines itself to matters of fact. It excludes the writer's guesses, signs of approval or disapproval, feelings, and conclusions. It is objective.

2. It selects the facts that point somewhere. The selection fits the purpose. An engineer reporting tests of road materials omits mention of the singing of the birds and the joking of his assistants.

3. It selects the facts fairly and impartially. It will not stack the cards in favor of one judgment over another. It will not leave out facts that point "the wrong way" or give undue emphasis to other facts that point "the right way."

4. It uses words that will mean the same thing to readers that they mean to the writer. It omits "loaded" words with emotional connotations. It seeks the precise term.

5. It makes the sources of information apparent: what the writer himself directly observed, what he read and who wrote it, what he heard and who said it. The factual report may include opinions and expressions of feeling *if they are properly labeled*: "J. S. Kunyngham told me he considered MX 'absolutely the meanest stuff I ever handled' " is in the language of a factual report because it states what the man said—not what the writer thinks himself.

6. Finally, the best reports are verifiable. If another writer is quoted, is his statement published where the reader can look it up? If a speaker is quoted, did others hear him say it? Is he alive to substantiate the quotation himself? If direct observations are reported, did anybody else observe the same things? Or would it be possible for anybody to *re*-observe what is reported—just go see for himself?

Remember that a dozen concurring statements of opinion by different witnesses do not produce a statement of fact. If a dozen neighbors agree that "George Witham is mean to his son," we have strong opinion arrayed against Witham; but we still have none of the facts on which the opinions were based.

If a report of fact is verifiable it *can* be checked in one of several ways: by obtaining corroborating testimony concerning what was seen or heard; by going to official or other reputable records; by direct observation. And if a report *can* be verified, it is much more credible to readers even if they have no intention of going to the trouble of verifying for themselves.

Writing a Summary

The summary of an article, report, document, table, book, or lecture is one kind of factual report. All a true summary does is condense.

It adds no ideas, feelings, criticisms, or opinions to the original. A genuine summary is nothing but a report of what somebody said in fewer words than he used to say it.

When, where, and why will you ever need to write such summaries? One use is for evidence or illustration in your own writing. You refer to an authority and state in brief what he said. After you have summarized his statement, you may want to evaluate it, criticize it, even attack it; but first, you must be able to present it objectively.

Another kind of summary may stand by itself as an "abstract" or "digest" intended for readers who may never see the original. *Chemical Abstracts,* for example, is a periodical that is read widely by specialists in chemistry and related fields who need to be informed of new developments that concern their work. Such abstracts include no critical comments about the original. Another example is the digest prepared for the use of busy executives who must have essential information from reports, contracts, and other documents but cannot afford the time to read them in full. And of course the general reader finds in such periodicals as *Science Digest* readable summaries of much longer articles or even books, presented in simplified form that he can read in limited time.

When you try writing a few summaries you begin to realize the difficulties. One problem is to keep out your own feelings and opinions. You like something—and want to emphasize it. You dislike something—and want to attack (or omit) it. So this is a test of objectivity. Keep yourself out of it.

Another difficulty is to find the right synonyms for words that are too technical or academic for your readers. Sometimes you must simplify as well as condense.

Another problem is in deciding proportion and emphasis. Perhaps you need to summarize 25,000 words in about 350. That's quite a task. An honest summary must not omit any major idea or development of the whole. One possibility is to determine the comparative space that the original gives to Point A, Point B, and so on, then give the same proportionate space to each in the summary. But you cannot be too mathematical about it. The force of ideas can seldom be measured by lines of print. You must try to give the kind of emphasis in your summary that the original gives its major and minor points.

You will note the important difference between a *topical* summary that provides a sort of table of contents of the original, and an *informative* summary that reports what the original actually says. For example:

> This book gives a brief history of the American labor movement from the Civil War to the late 1930's. It includes accounts of strikes at Haymarket, Homestead, Pullman, and other places, and includes the author's interpretations and opinions of causes and effects.

This informal summary is factual enough, apparently objective, but it tells nothing about what the book says. The following summary, on the other hand, is *informative*:

> This history of the American labor movement, from Civil War to the late 1930's, tells stories of strikes and lockouts at Haymarket, Homestead, Pullman, and elsewhere—almost all "lost" by the unions—which the author views as temporary defeats for "justice" but important influences in the development of "a vigorous and mature labor movement."

The topical summary provides no useful information except to tell the reader where he can go to read something for himself. The informative summary, on the other hand, contributes at least some of the contents of the original.

When you include informal summaries as part of your own writing, it is important to distinguish carefully between any opinions of the author and opinions of your own. For example, the informative summary above says "the author views" and uses several quotation marks ("lost," "justice," "a vigorous and mature labor movement") to tell the reader clearly whose judgment terms these are: they belong to the original, not to the writer who presents the summary.

If your summary stands by itself and is labeled "Digest" or "Abstract" or the like, then it may use the exact phrasing of the original without quotation marks. In fact, the original language may do much to preserve the spirit and sense that a good digest tries to carry to its readers. But be sure your reader understands what he is getting.

Learning to summarize efficiently takes practice, but a few suggestions may help:

1. Read through the original rapidly to get the sense and movement of the whole thing first.

2. State in a sentence what the entire work says.

3. Pick out the major divisions and conclusions. If you find good summarizing topic sentences, copy them down.

4. If the original is very long, make a rough outline, possibly incorporating topic sentences. If it is not very complex, make the necessary plan in your head, but get everything in the right order. (The order needn't always be the same as that in the original, though usually that is best.)

5. Go back over the original, copying key words and phrases that you may be able to use.

6. Now try to write your summary without worrying too much yet about brevity. Include everything you consider important.

7. Cut out deadwood, reduce clauses to phrases and phrases to words, and eliminate everything that is unnecessary.

8. Now try a "final draft"—which may, of course, need to be revised and rewritten several times before you have what you want.

One of the best preparations for writing good summaries is practice in writing informative epitomes, one-sentence summaries of numerous things you read. To make it informative you begin: "This article *says that* . . ."—NOT "This article is about young racketeers."

READINGS

The first three selections that follow are essentially reports of facts. What purpose do you think each might serve?

Do you find words or expressions that go beyond reports of direct observations?

Can you state a conclusion or judgment that you think might be warranted from the facts given in each?

1

BACKGROUND INFORMATION: George F.

The Hearing Clinic referred this ten-year-old boy to the Psychiatric Service after deciding to obtain an evaluation of him as a behavior problem before recommending a hearing aid. The patient's mother, Mrs. F, provided the following information:

Now thirty-three, she never lived with her husband after her son's birth. She was divorced when the patient was nine months old. The father is a dentist now practicing in another state.

She took the boy to live with her widowed mother immediately after his birth. Others living in the same house were her older, married sister, and an aunt. Two of her brothers visited occasionally, never more than a day at a time, but no man lived in the house permanently. The grandmother fed the boy till he was five, put him to bed, dressed him, and gave him his bath. Mrs. F reported frequent "quarrels" with her mother and said "George always took his grandma's side."

Until a year ago Mrs. F told the patient frequently: "Daddy will come someday"; but then she explained that his father would never return. She said he "cried hard" when he learned the truth.

In kindergarten the boy had been called "uncooperative" and "unsocial" by his teachers, and his mother had threatened to put him in a "home" unless he did better.

In first grade he crushed his finger in a closing door and his mother took him to a doctor who gave him a local anaesthetic and took several stitches. Mrs. F said he "yelled" and "was hard to control." On the way home he told her "You did it on purpose, you did."

When he was seven he was given ether for a tonsillectomy. He fought the doctor until forced to give up the struggle. Shortly after that operation his mother noticed that he no longer spoke clearly. Then he "seemed not to notice" when somebody spoke to him. "At first," she said, "I thought he was just dreaming. He always was a kind of dreamer."

A month after this operation, Mrs. F announced to the family that she intended to marry Mr. K, a man her son had never seen. She told the patient that they would move "from Grandma's" to another town.

Since that time, she reported, "He doesn't seem to hear at all. So I took him to the clinic."

2

INSPECTION OF GREENWICH BOYS' CAMP

During the past camping season, on July 17, I spent eight hours at the Greenwich Boys' Camp, where the director, Mr. Thornton, and his assistant, Mr. Kent, answered my questions and showed me the camp.

The camp occupies ten acres on the east shore of Lake Elmore, five miles from the village of the same name. It has a sandy beach about twenty-five feet long and about twenty feet wide. There is a diving raft with two springboards. Depth poles show the water to be not quite five feet deep at a distance approximately twenty yards from shore.

I examined the twelve rowboats and four outboard motors. I had the opportunity to see instruction being given in the handling of oars and motors. Mr. Thornton said that classes at specified hours are held six days a week in swimming, life-saving, woodcraft, tennis, and various handicrafts. A schedule board announced a hike of five hours' duration for each week of camp, and two over-night hiking trips into the mountains to be made during the eight-week session.

Five buildings—four cabins used for sleeping quarters and one larger central building including recreation and dining room—are located in the wooded area fifty yards back from the lake shore. A baseball diamond and three tennis courts are in an open field immediately behind the woods.

A register showed that at the time of my visit the camp had enrolled seventy-two boys ranging in age from eight to sixteen. The director and his assistant plus four counselors supervise all camp activities. Three of the counselors are college undergraduates who spent at least two years at the camp as boys. Mr. Thornton, Mr. Kent, and the remaining counselor are all high school teachers who have been at the camp from three to twelve years. The staff is rounded out by a cook, two women employed for cleaning and general work, and a general handyman.

The boys are expected to care for their own bunks and do an hour's work each day either in the kitchen or keeping the camp "clean and orderly," as Mr. Thornton expressed it.

3

DAWN OVER ZERO *

William L. Laurence

[This is a report of events on the day "the atomic age began," July 16, 1945, when the first atomic bomb was exploded.]

* Reprinted from *Dawn Over Zero*, by William L. Laurence, by permission ot Alfred A. Knopf, Inc. Copyright 1946 by Alfred A. Knopf, Inc.

The bomb was set on a structural steel tower one hundred feet high. Ten miles away to the southwest was the base camp. This was "G.H." for the scientific high command, of which Professor Kenneth T. Bainbridge of Harvard University was field commander. Here were erected barracks to serve as living-quarters for the scientists, a mess hall, a commissary, a post exchange, and other buildings. Here the vanguard of the atomists, headed by Professor J. R. Oppenheimer of the University of California, scientific director of the Atomic Bomb Project, lived like soldiers at the front, supervising the enormously complicated details involved in the epoch-making tests.

Here early that Sunday afternoon gathered Major General Leslie R. Groves, commander in chief of the Atomic Bomb Project; Brigadier General T. F. Farrell . . ., General Groves's deputy; Professor Enrico Fermi, Nobel Prize winner and one of the leaders in the project; President James Bryant Conant of Harvard; Dr. Vannevar Bush, director of the Office of Scientific Research and Development; Dean Richard C. Tolman of the California Institute of Technology; Professor R. F. Bacher of Cornell; Colonel Stafford L. Warren, University of Rochester radiologist; and about a hundred and fifty other leaders in the atomic bomb program.

At the Base Camp was a dry, abandoned reservoir, about five hundred feet square, surrounded by a mound of earth about eight feet high. Within this mound bulldozers dug a series of slit trenches, each about three feet deep, seven feet wide, and twenty-five feet long. At a command over the radio at zero minus one minute all the observers at Base Camp lay down in their assigned trenches, "face and eyes directed toward the ground and with the head away from Zero." But most of us on Compania Hill remained on our feet.

Three other posts had been established, south, north, and west of Zero, each at a distance of 10,000 yards (5.7 miles). These were known, respectively, as South-10,000, North-10,000, and West-10,000, or S-10, N-10, and W-10. Here the shelters were much more elaborate—wooden structures, their walls reinforced by cement, buried under a massive layer of earth.

S-10 was the control center. Here Professor Oppenheimer, as scientific commander in chief, and his field commander, Professor Bainbridge, issued orders and synchronized the activities of the other sites. Here the signal was given and a complex of mechanisms was set in motion . . . No switch was pulled, no button pressed, to light this first cosmic fire on this planet.

At forty-five seconds to zero, set for 5:30 o'clock, young Dr. Joseph L. McKibben of the University of California, at a signal from Professor Bainbridge, activated a master robot that set off a series of other robots, until, at last, strategically spaced electrons moved to the proper place at the proper split second.

Forty-five seconds passed and the moment was zero.

4

The following article was written by a resident of the city where all the events he reports took place. He was rector of the Episcopal Church of the Ascension in Montgomery, Alabama, at the time.

How objective is the writer; that is, how impartial? How careful is he to separate rumor from authenticated report or what he observed from what he read or heard?

From the report can you, without prejudice of your own, reach any conclusions or judgments? If you had to defend such judgments, what additional information would you have to add for:

Montgomery whites?
Montgomery Negroes?
People in your own town?

ALABAMA'S BUS BOYCOTT *

The Rev. Thomas R. Thrasher

Montgomery, Alabama

The facts of our local situation are essentially simple. Yet various members of our community, both white and Negro, believe things that make it enormously complex.

Last December 1 in the early evening, one of the busses of the Montgomery City Lines passed through Court Square, in the heart of town, and headed for the stop in front of the Empire Theatre. On board the thirty-six-passenger bus twenty-four Negroes were seated, in the traditional manner from the rear forward, and there were twelve whites seated in the front. Some people of each race were

* Reprinted by permission, from *The Reporter*, March 8, 1956.

standing in the aisle. The bus driver has since testified that there were no empty seats. Yet today, many weeks later, there are many who believe that the bus was substantially empty, while others believe that four Negroes were asked to get up in order to allow one white person to sit down.

At the Empire Theatre stop a number of white passengers were waiting to board the bus. The driver of the bus, as was the practice when in his judgment it was necessary to "equalize facilities," requested four Negroes, including Mrs. Rosa Parks, to give up their seats. No charge of discourtesy has been made against the bus driver. Three of the Negroes rose and moved toward the rear. Mrs. Parks, a seamstress at a local department store and a highly respected member of the Negro community, refused. She said later that she acted on a sudden impulse, probably arising from the fact that she was tired. There are substantial numbers of people here in Montgomery who believe that she was a willing participant in a trumped-up plot.

The driver, seeing that Mrs. Parks was adamant, called a policeman, who led her off the bus and escorted her to the police station. There she was booked on a charge of violating the city's segregation law and the trial was set for the following Monday, December 5. She was released on bond.

At this point the facts become somewhat less precise. On Saturday, December 3, a number of mimeographed and typed circulars were distributed in the Negro sections of the community calling on citizens to stage a one-day protest by not riding the city busses the day of the trial. I have never been able to determine just who initiated this planned boycott, and there are innumerable conflicting rumors about it. But on Sunday, the day before the trial, there was a news story in the local paper that carried the information far more widely than the original circulars had. A number of Negro ministers, it is known, referred to it in their sermons that day.

On Monday three-quarters or more of the usual Negro riders stayed off the busses. The extent of the protest was noticeable, for the fifty thousand Negroes who live in Montgomery constitute about forty per cent of the population and made up nearly seventy-five per cent of the bus passengers. This was an act of passive resistance on a monumental scale, which could not be passed off as simply a product of outside interference, agitation, or intimidation. There was no widespread absenteeism from work that day; the protesters went to their jobs by Negro taxis, wagons, or by foot over long distances.

That same day, Mrs. Parks appeared at the city court with her lawyer. The city prosecutor asked that the charge against her be based not on the city segregation ordinance but on a state law giving bus drivers authority to assign or reassign passengers in accordance with segregation practice. Mrs. Parks was found guilty and fined ten dollars and costs, a total of fourteen dollars. (The law permits a maximum fine of five hundred dollars.) She appealed her case.

That night, according to a newspaper account, approximately five thousand Negroes overflowed the protest meeting at the Holt Street Baptist Church. Forty-seven Negro ministers are said to have been present. There was a good deal of hymn singing and speechmaking, none of it inflammatory, according to the newspaper report, but all of it defiant. From the story it appears that there was a general welling up of grievances in which the specific case of Rosa Parks was all but forgotten. But those members of our community who believe that the whole thing was staged by outside influences generally do not believe that the local press has given an accurate reporting of the facts.

The meeting accomplished three things. First, a resolution was adopted to continue the bus boycott indefinitely and calling on "every citizen of Montgomery regardless of race, color, or creed to refrain from riding busses owned and operated in the city of Montgomery, by Montgomery City Lines, Incorporated, until some arrangement has been worked out between said citizens and the Montgomery City Lines." Second, those present were urged to make their cars available in assisting others to get to work. An organization was formed on the spot—the Montgomery Improvement Association—and a board of directors was named. Its chairman was Dr. Martin Luther King, the twenty-seven-year-old Negro minister of the Dexter Avenue Baptist Church. Dr. King, though Southern born, holds a Ph.D. degree from Boston University. The board of directors included several other Negro ministers.

Finally, the meeting addressed three proposals to the Montgomery City Lines as the basis for ending the boycott:

More courteous treatment of Negro passengers.

Seating on a first come, first served basis, with Negroes continuing to sit from the rear of the bus and whites from front to rear.

Negro bus drivers to be employed on predominantly Negro runs.

By the next day the boycott was close to ninety-five per cent effective, a figure that has been maintained with remarkable consistency ever since. A car pool began to take shape. On telephone poles and in other public places, unsigned and unidentified schedules were posted. For a time the police didn't know what they were. Actually, they listed the forty pickup points at which some two hundred and fifty cars were operating from 6 to 8:30 a.m. and from 3 to 6:00 p.m. To avoid violating city regulations governing taxis, this rather sizable carlift charged no fares but collected funds for gas at the churches and at rallies, which have been held with regularity. Other funds undoubtedly came in from outside the South, a fact that some members of our community choose to dwell upon. Some also believe that the Negroes secretly pay ten-cent fares to the drivers and won't admit it when the police question them.

By Wednesday, December 7, neither side had made any contact with the other. The Alamaba Council on Human Relations, a biracial organization of which I am a member and which was holding its semiannual meeting that day, decided to offer its "good offices" to bring about a meeting between the Negro leaders and bus-company and city officials. The mayor accepted our suggestion and a meeting was set for the next day at the City Hall. There the Negro group presented its three demands. The attorney for the bus company replied that the company would always investigate formal complaints of discourtesy but asserted that the discourtesy was often provoked. He rejected the other proposals as contrary to city law and inappropriate. The mayor called on the bus-company officials and the Negro leaders to work their problems out. Everyone else withdrew and these two groups continued the discussion for a time—but without success.

Though their meeting adjourned without even an agreement to meet again, I feel that at least two good effects stemmed from it. It was the first proof, small but significant, that the parties to the dispute could sit down together. Further, it helped to ease the pent-up frustrations which in the first days of the boycott had provoked several cases of stoning and even firing upon the busses. After this first meeting there was only one further incident of that nature.

Again at our request, the mayor arranged a meeting for Saturday, December 10, so that the Negro leaders could meet the representative of the National City Lines of Chicago, owner of the local bus company. This representative had come to Montgomery to look into the trouble, we learned, but had not approached the boycott leaders. To this meeting the mayor invited a larger number, including a prominent leader of the local white Citizens' Council. After again listening to a recital of the grievances and to a statement disclaiming authority under city and state laws by the National City Lines representative, the mayor appointed a committee to try to reach a solution.

The committee failed in its purpose. The Negro group felt that some of the members, including the white Citizens' Council leader, were not appointed in good faith; the white group felt that the Negroes were not ready to negotiate in good faith. Not being a member of the committee, I can only report what I have read in the press regarding its deliberations. The voting was reported to have been eight white against eight Negro on matters where they disagreed. Unanimous concurrence was achieved on the proposal that more courtesy on the busses was in order. On this note the committee broke up after only two meetings.

Montgomery returned to a state of affairs in which there was no communication between the two groups—only mounting tension and the grim, ever-present fact of the boycott.

The Christmas season passed and there were reports that some businesses were off by thirty per cent or more. But this was rumor, not confirmed fact, and there were other stories that some businesses were booming. The bus company had raised its fare by fifty per cent. Negro leaders hailed this as evidence of the boycott's success, while white leaders pointed out that local rates had been below those elsewhere. The bus company had long since suspended routes going into predominantly Negro neighborhoods. A number of bus drivers were furloughed. On January 6, the police commissioner dramatically entered a meeting of the white Citizens' Council and announced that he was paying his $3.50 membership fee. "I wouldn't trade my Southern birthright for one hundred Negro votes," he declared.

There were false hopes on January 21, when the city commission announced that after a conference with unidentified "prominent Negro ministers" a plan had been reached for ending the boycott. Next day the hopes were dissipated. The leaders of the boycott announced that they had not been present at the City Hall meeting and didn't know who had. Subsequently, there were recriminations between the three Negro ministers who had been present and the city commissioners. The ministers said that they had gone there on other business and had not entered any agreement. The commissioners, in turn, accused them of double-dealing. It was at any rate clear that the three ministers had not been prominent in the boycott movement. And the boycott continued.

On January 24 the mayor issued a statement: "We have pussyfooted around on this boycott long enough and it is time to be frank and honest . . . The Negro leaders have proved they are not interested in ending the boycott but rather in prolonging it so that they may stir up racial strife. The Negro leaders have proved that they will say one thing to a white man and another thing to a Negro about the boycott . . . [They] have forced the boycott into a campaign between whether the social fabric of our community will continue to exist or will be destroyed by a group of Negro radicals who have split asunder the fine relationships which have existed between the Negro and white people for generations . . . What they are after is the destruction of our social fabric . . . The white people are firm in their convictions that they do not care whether the Negroes ever ride a city bus again if it means that the social fabric of our community is destroyed so that Negroes will start riding the busses again." He called on white citizens to refrain from carrying their domestic servants to and from work in their cars and thus contributing to the boycott.

That same day it was announced that the mayor and the remaining city commissioner had joined the white Citizens' Council. On the following day there were reports that a "get tough" policy was being initiated. Scores of Negroes driving volunteer cars were given tickets for minor traffic violations. On Thursday, January 26, Dr. M. L. King, the boycott leader, was arrested for going thirty-five miles an hour in a twenty-five-mile zone. His case is on appeal. The following day King's house was bombed, causing minor damage. Neighbors said the explosive had been thrown from a passing car. Some members of the white community believe firmly that the incident was staged by the Negroes themselves. Both the mayor and the police commissioner went promptly to the scene, and stated firmly that the culprit would be caught and prosecuted. Dr. King exhorted the Negroes who had gathered not to resort to violence.

"We believe in law and order," he said. "Don't get panicky. Don't get your weapons. He who lives by the sword will perish by the sword. Remember that is what God said. I want it to be known the length and breadth of this land that if I am stopped this movement will not stop."

Two days later, a dynamite cap exploded in the front yard of a Negro who had not been prominent in the boycott but who was active in the local N.A.A.C.P. For a time the whole community realized the grim possibilities of the situation, and reason held back emotion. The arrests and issuing of tickets by the police slacked off as suddenly as they had started. The white Citizens' Council added five hundred dollars to the reward offered by the city commissioners for information leading to the arrest and conviction of the bomb throwers.

On February 1, the whole dispute moved into the courts. That day five Montgomery Negroes filed suit in the U.S. District Court asking that state and local segregation laws pertaining to transportation be declared unconstitutional. This, of course, is a far broader challenge than had been posed by the boycott itself.

Subsequently, the grand jury indicted the Negro lawyer who had brought the cases to court because one of the five plaintiffs, a young Negro woman, testified that she had not known what he was asking her to do. If convicted, the lawyer can be disbarred for false representation.

This same grand jury on February 21 indicted about one hundred Negroes for participating in the boycott. The indictment cited a state anti-conspiracy act passed in 1921 to deal with coal-mining strikes in Birmingham. While the anti-conspiratorial features of the act have never been tested in the courts, its anti-picketing provisions have been declared unconstitutional. Among those indicted was Mrs. Parks, who had refused to pay the fourteen-dollar fine and was sentenced to serve a jail sentence instead for the incident that led to the boycott.

As these legal battles went forward, it was announced that secret efforts at a compromise in the dispute by a businessmen's organization, the Men of Montgomery, had been unavailing. There are some who believe that they might have succeeded if these court indictments had not been threatening.

As the painful weeks have passed, the facts of the situation have become more rather than less obscure. There is, for example, the recurrent rumor of goon squads operating among the Negroes to force them to obey the boycott. Thus far only one arrest has been made on this count—a Negro youth picked up for preventing a Negro woman from boarding a bus. She testified in court that he was helping her cross the street and the charge was dropped. If there has been widespread intimidation among Negroes, the police have been unable to get evidence of it.

There have been rumors in the Negro community that white employers were going to discharge them on a certain day, and rumors in the white community that all Negroes were going to quit on a certain day.

Businesses have been damaged severely by rumors circulated among white people that they had contributed to the N.A.A.C.P. or rumors among Negroes that they had contributed to the white Citizens' Council. In a few cases businesses have been caught in a crossfire of rumor. Some say that competitors have been starting these rumors.

If there is anything universal in our community it is fear. The businessman's fear lest his business be destroyed by some false move or baseless rumor. The Negro's fear for his safety and his job. The clergy's fear that their congregations may be divided by the tense feelings generated by our situation. The politician's fear that he may do something disapproved by the majority of voters. And finally the whole community's fear that we may be torn asunder by a single rash act precipitating interracial violence . . .

5

Study the following summaries of the preceding article. How adequately do they meet the tests of informative summaries?

DIGEST

ALABAMA'S BUS BOYCOTT

BY The Rev. Thomas R. Thrasher—
(Rector, Episcopal Church of the Ascension, Montgomery, Alabama)
—from *The Reporter*, March 8, 1956

Montgomery, Alabama

Thursday, last December 1, Mrs. Rosa Parks, a Negro seamstress, refused a bus driver's request to give up her seat to a white passenger.

She said she was tired. Many think it was a trumped-up plot. She was arrested and booked for violating the Montgomery segregation law. Trial was set for the next Monday.

On Saturday somebody distributed circulars urging a Negro boycott of city busses the day of her trial. On Monday most Negroes stayed off the busses. Mrs. Parks was found guilty and fined fourteen dollars.

That night thousands of Negroes, including forty-seven ministers, overflowed a protest meeting in their Baptist Church, where, newspapers said, they sang hymns and made non-inflammatory but defiant speeches. They voted to continue the boycott, organize a car pool, and call upon the bus company to permit first-come, first-served seating with Negroes continuing to fill seats from the rear and whites from the front. They asked that Negro drivers be placed on predominantly Negro runs.

The boycott has been ninety-five per cent effective ever since. The car pool provides rides to thousands. Attempts to disrupt it have failed.

The biracial Council on Human Relations got Negro leaders and bus officials to sit down together. Other meetings followed, but with no success. Both sides charged the other with bad faith. Through the Christmas season conflicting rumors spread: that business was seriously affected, that business was better than ever. Bus fares were raised, but opinion differs regarding the boycott's influence.

The white Citizens' Council enrolled new members. In January the mayor accused Negro radicals of trying to destroy "the social fabric of our community." Rumors spread of a new "get tough" policy by mayor and Citizens' Council. Scores of Negro drivers were charged with minor traffic violations. The house of Dr. King, Negro clergyman, was bombed, with slight damage. A dynamite cap exploded in another Negro's yard. Arrests of Negro traffic violators suddenly slacked off.

A grand jury indicted a hundred Negroes for participating in the boycott, citing an act passed in 1921 to deal with coal-mining strikes.

Facts become more obscure as conflicting rumors spread: that, for example, white employers will discharge Negroes on a certain day; that all Negroes will quit on a certain day. Fear is universal—for business, for Negroes, for the clergy, for politicians. The whole community fears that it may be torn asunder by a single rash act precipitating interracial violence.

AN INFORMAL SUMMARY

In "Alabama's Bus Boycott" (*The Reporter,* March 8, 1956) the Rev. Thomas R. Thrasher, Montgomery Episcopal rector, shows how a simple incident has led to interracial tension and fear. It all began when a Negro woman refused to give up her seat on a local bus to a white passenger. Her arrest led to a widespread Negro boycott of all busses, "ninety-five per cent effective" ever since. Rumors have spread among whites of "a trumped-up plot," outside agitation, goon squads to force Negroes to obey the boycott. Rumors have spread equally among Negroes of a white conspiracy against them, threats to their jobs, threats to their lives.

After several meetings of white and Negro leaders, all negotiations broke down. Mutual distrust has existed since that time. "If there is anything universal in our community," says Mr. Thrasher, "it is fear . . . that we may be torn asunder by a single rash act precipitating interracial violence."

EXERCISES

I. Evaluate the following statements as factual reporting (How objective, impartial, free from judgments or "loading," and how verifiable? What apparent purpose, if any, does each serve?):

1. After interviews with the four applicants we chose Kulp. He made a better impression on us than any of the others because he has had seven years' experience at similar work, five of them in this state. He is 31 years old, married, and father of two children. He had recommendations from three previous employers.
2. McCorkle has set a price of $1350 for his two-door Plymouth convertible which he bought from us 26 months ago. The speedometer reads 26,456 miles. It has radio and heater. Mills, chief mechanic, drove it five miles and gives it his OK.
3. Three clerks and two delivery boys quit within the past five weeks. Both delivery boys said the work was too hard, hours too long. These boys are 24 and 26 years old respectively, unmarried,

and neither had finished eighth grade in school. Our records show that both had held seven previous jobs in the past five years.

The clerks range in age from 26 to 30. All are unmarried. One is a high school graduate; the others finished ninth grade. Our records show they had held from five to nine jobs in the past five years. One clerk gave "more pay" as his reason for leaving. The other two simply said "dissatisfied."

4. Dear Doctor:

I wish to ask advice about what to do with our boy, age five, who causes us much worry.

He climbs onto everything. Once he climbed onto bathroom sink and opened medicine cabinet. He ate several aspirins before being discovered and punished. Another time he climbed onto kitchen table, stood on the bottom shelf of the cupboard and reached cookies he had been forbidden to touch. Again he was severely punished. Another time he climbed over the backyard fence and kept going till he was six blocks from home. He was gone four hours and we were nearly frantic before the police found out who he was and we went after him at the Police Station.

He won't eat anything but soft cereals and mush. We have to feed him. He doesn't like to chew, though he has good enough teeth. He wakes up at five in the morning and raises such a rumpus nobody else can sleep.

He doesn't mind very well. He likes his father better than he likes me, though I am always kind and considerate.

What shall we do to calm him down?

Mrs. Y

5. As a concrete example, Tom Jones, to give him any name at all, was the son of a onetime seaman who had given up the sea because of some incurable complaint, and who now worked, when he could, in a local mattress factory. His mother used to come and clean for us. Could I get their Tom a job? I could and did. A port captain I knew had a summer home near-by, and when I mentioned Tom, he said he would take him up with him in his car and start him on a ship. All fell out as he promised.

But one voyage was enough for Tom. When the ship docked, he got his mother on the telephone and said he was coming home. Mrs. Jones and her husband hurried to New York and implored Tom to stay. Tom was adamant. The work was too hard and too dirty. There were furriners on the ship. He wanted to come home, and the three of them returned.

Tom is still around town. What he missed at sea was the thrill of walking up the street Saturday night, the exquisite joy of standing at the corner and watching the local bus push off for Danbury. He wanted his game of pool at the local 'Y.' In fact, he wanted the way of life he had always had. He wanted to be surrounded by all the familiar sights and sounds of his native town . . .

—William McFee, "Why Boys Don't Go to Sea,"
The Yale Review, Summer 1939

6. This is what happened Friday at 10:10 a.m. as an illustration of the way parking laws are enforced:

   On 15th Street, between Arch and Cherry, seven cars were parked illegally, including two in the area plainly posted, "No parking from here to corner."

   Between Cherry and Race Streets, seven cars were parked illegally, including two in the area marked "No parking from here to corner."

   Between Race and Vine Streets, four cars were parked illegally.

   Between Vine and Callowhill streets, eight cars were parked illegally.

   Thus in a four-block stretch of 15th street, 26 cars were parked illegally at one time.
7. Within a period of three weeks during the late winter and early spring of 1940, sitting by the little four-pane window, Oché Toné celebrated six anniversaries—the eightieth of his birth in the village of Ajdovec, near the town of Zuzemberk, in Lower Carniola, then a province of Austria; the fiftieth of his arrival as an immigrant in the United States; the fiftieth, too, of his beginning to work for, and getting on the payroll of, the American Steel and Wire Company on Fortieth Street in Cleveland; the forty-eighth of his marriage to Karolina Novinec, who had come to America a year and a half after him from the village of Veliki Lipovec, also in Lower Carniola; the forty-seventh of the birth of the first of his eleven children, a son; and the twenty-fifth of his retirement on a monthly pension from his job, when he had decided that he had done his bit in the world and sat down in that chair (then new and free of squeaks) by the

kitchen window, to gaze out and smoke and think from daybreak until nightfall every day of the week, week after week, month after month, year in and year out; and to wait for his pension check, which the postman brings him once a month without fail.

As Oché Toné sees his life, now that it is tightly wrapped in old age, these anniversaries cover or suggest its high spots. Among them roam all his thoughts and talk. There is only one other important fact in his career, as he sees it: he is not a citizen of the United States, because he did not want to become one—a fact closely linked, however, to his notion that he is *neke vrste Amerikanec vse eno,* a kind of American anyhow.

He understands some English but does not speak it. His medium of expression is a Slovenian peasant dialect, but he uses many American-English words twisted into Slovenian form to fit his tongue. In his speech, for instance, a "house" is a *gauz,* "shoes" are *shukhi,* "street" is *shtrit,* and "beer" is *pir.*

—"The Old Alien by the Kitchen Window," a selection from Louis Adamic's *From Many Lands.* Copyright 1940 by Louis Adamic. Published, 1940, by Harper & Brothers.

II. In the following paragraph, delete every work or phrase that is not a "matter of fact." Where possible substitute specific fact terms for any that you delete. Revise sentences when necessary.

Mudtown, popular shopping center and county seat, has a larger population than any other town in Log County—4630 by the latest census. A few descendants of first settlers, who arrived in 1748, still live there; but 56% of the residents are foreigners of first or second generation. The Americans have the better homes, usually north of Elm and west of Fig Streets. The foreigners usually live south of Elm in unpainted shacks and they have a high illiteracy rate, yet they are generally law-abiding, hard-working, and thrifty. Some own retail stores. A few have considerable influence. Mudtown voters are highly conservative: registered Republicans outnumber Democrats two to one, and no Democrat or other liberal has had any luck in Mudtown elections for over fifty years. The taxes are high because the town has no large industries (one plant employs 112, but no other business hires more than 19) and yet people insist on good clean streets, excellent schools, a fine library, splendid playgrounds, and a good police force.

III. Rewrite the following sentences, eliminating judgments and generalizations and substituting statements of fact (not more than fifty words for each):

1. He was very active as a freshman, but after that he didn't do much.
2. Prices in this town are too high.
3. That was one of the dullest courses I ever had.
4. He's anything but popular.
5. A book that small shouldn't cost so much.
6. He was punished severely for his dishonesty.
7. Student leaders are almost always conservative.
8. The play failed miserably on Broadway.
9. The administration has made a sorry mess of our foreign policy.
10. Everybody agrees that the Governor, whatever his faults, is a deeply sincere and honest man.
11. The people voted for the amendment because propagandists had completely misrepresented the situation.
12. Labor never seems to like laws that give consumers a decent break.
13. We really had hard luck on that trip.
14. Undergraduates know hardly anything of events that occur off the campus.
15. During the past year he has done considerable reading.
16. The president has plenty of noisy critics.
17. The strike was the most costly for labor in the past twenty years.
18. He is one of the most cultured men in the city.
19. She's a typical grade school teacher.

ASSIGNMENTS

1. Faculty advisers want information to help them schedule students most effectively. Write a factual report about a specific course you have taken. (The advisers want no opinions yet; they will ask for those later.)
2. An employer to whom you have applied for a position asks for a letter "simply giving me the facts about yourself."
3. Assuming an acquaintance of yours has been suspected of a crime, write a report of what you know about his activities for a two-day period. (You are strictly a "fact witness.")
4. A business man who wants to buy a house asks you to make a brief inspection and report on what you find.

5. You are a member of a committee responsible for deciding which students deserve scholarship aid. Make a factual report of what you have observed about a certain student that would be pertinent information for this committee to have.
6. An administrative committee is studying the efficiency of registration procedures. You, as one of a hundred students selected as a representative sample, are asked for a report of your own experiences during the last registration period.
7. The Dean's office is making a study of factors leading to academic failure and success. You are asked for a factual report of the study habits of two students—one on probation or otherwise in academic difficulties, the other on the Dean's List.
8. For a survey of traffic conditions, report on traffic at a particular intersection for a one-hour period.
9. A Committee on Undergraduate Activities is studying the kind and amount of work that students do in various undergraduate competitions. Write a factual report for this committee about your own experiences (what you did, how much time you spent, etc.) on an athletic squad, in managership competition, dramatics, student publication, or the like—any *one* activity.
10. The Committee on Student Expenses wants information about the cost of textbooks and supplies for students in various curricula. You are one of several hundred students selected to write a factual account of your own expenditures for two semesters:

    What you purchased
    How much you paid for various items
    What you sold
    How much you received for resales

    Present this in the simplest form possible.
11. Summarize, in 400 words, a fifteen-minute radio or TV news or discussion program.
12. Summarize, in 400 words, the most important business and financial news for a two-day period. Make this a readable digest for a busy executive.
13. Summarize, in 400 words, a chapter from one of your textbooks so that a student unfamiliar with the subject can read it with understanding. Bring the book to class and discuss matters of selection, proportion, emphasis, and simplification.
14. Cut out a newspaper or magazine article. Select what you consider its five most important paragraphs, those containing the most significant information. Then analyze all the statements in those five paragraphs and place words, phrases, clauses, or full sentences under the appropriate heading as follows:

Verifiable matters of fact	Unverifiable assertions from other sources	Assertions with sources named	Writer's opinions
________	________	________	________

15. Read different stories of the same events in two different newspapers.

    (a) Write an informative summary comparing the two stories.
    (b) Write an evaluation of the two stories:
        How objective?
        How much verifiable fact? how much of the writer's opinions or attitudes?
        Do the stories differ in the information reported? If so, can you infer any reasons for the differences?

CHAPTER 3

Defining and Classifying

Why Define?

A writer obviously cannot communicate with readers who do not understand the language he is using. He cannot communicate in Russian to readers who know no Russian, nor in English to those who know no English. The scientific or specialized language of electronics, entomology, or psychiatry carries no meaning to readers who have no acquaintance with the field. No writing can be effective for everybody; it is the writer's responsibility to make himself clear to the particular readers he wants to have understand him.

The first approach to clarity is to find words that are familiar to your readers. If they understand the vocabulary of baseball or meteorology you can use such a vocabulary in writing to them—without apologies or definitions. If they lack such a vocabulary you ought to try first to translate technical or special terms into everyday language your readers know. Translating or paraphrasing is better than extensive defining when it works. Much popular writing on rather technical subjects does that successfully.

But of course translation is not always feasible. You may really need some terms that your reader never even saw before. You may also want to introduce your reader to some of the language of a new field so that he can continue the study for himself. Every textbook in botany, sociology, or music appreciation introduces the student to a new vocabulary. The most elementary explanations of yachting or glassblowing likely need at least a few special terms that readers will not know. So one need of definition is to explain meanings of new and strange words.

But the difficulty in writing clearly may be less with handling special technical terms than with very common words that have different meanings. Words like *politics, race, science, education,* and *agriculture* are all common enough; yet they sometimes block real communication because the writer means one thing and the reader understands another. Words like *employables, income, textbooks,* and *athlete* have more meanings than you may suppose. If you want to use such a term for a special purpose, you may have to define.

For example, suppose the dean of an engineerng college asks faculty advisers to "schedule more nontechnical courses for seniors." Unless he says more precisely what he means he is likely to find the advisers scheduling everything from Business Letters to Optics to Math. 464. He will have to indicate the boundaries of "technical" and "nontechnical" if he wants them to understand what he means.

Or suppose a big corporation wants to find out whether it is a good idea to hire college graduates who have engaged in extra-curricular activities in preference to those who have not. A study is in order. But first it will be necessary to define exactly what belongs under the name *extra-curricular activity*. Is it to include fraternity membership, or not? Is it to include jobs as waiter or furnace tender, or not? What about week-end dancing? hiking? going to church? Before trying to reach any conclusions somebody will have to decide exactly what to include and what to leave out—that is, make a definition that will serve the purpose.

The Amateur Athletic Union has its own precise definition of *amateur athlete* that it applies in determining eligibility for amateur competition. The Bureau of Internal Revenue has its own precise definition of *benefit* in determining whether proceeds from a so-called "benefit performance" shall be tax free or not.

With adequate definition it is possible to transform matters of opinion into matters of fact. A table showing the number of "Successful Farmers in Leghorn County, 1946–1956" is just a compilation of somebody's opinions; but once you define *successful farmer* arbitrarily as "owner or entrepreneur of a farm from which the net profit derived from dairy, poultry, vegetables, grain, fruit, and/or meat combined amounts to at least $3,500 a year exclusive of products consumed by the farm family," then everybody knows pretty well who was counted and the table reports matters of fact. Let people quarrel all they wish about whether this use of the word *successful* is appropriate, fair, or "correct"; at least they all know what the table *says*.

In arguments, definition can save a surprising amount of needless controversy. A defender of "religious education" in the public schools was surprised at all the opposition he met. All he meant was "moral training" and everybody else wanted to talk about religious dogmas, separation of church and state, Quakers, and the Spanish Inquisition. A simple process of changing the word *religious* to *moral*, and then explaining what he wanted to include in the program, might have saved everybody's time and temper.

Some words carry such emotional connotations that using them always creates more heat than light. "Is the Governor *playing politics*?" "Is the TVA *creeping socialism*?" "Is the Chamber of Commerce *anti-liberal*?" These are not profitable questions for discussion because they demand too much energy and emotion for the definition of terms. Better find other terms—and then get full agreement on what they mean before the argument starts.

To make your meanings clear in writing it is often better to find other words than to take the time to define those that first occur to you. Perhaps "Successful Farmers" is not the best word to use because *successful* arouses too many varied feelings, and it is also too ambiguous. Perhaps "Farmers with Above-Average Incomes," though it must be defined, will escape the emotional conflicts. "Happy marriages" may suggest more than the facts can justify and only increase the threat of futile disputes over who is "really happy." You might try "stable marriages" and then define that.

It is well to think of definition as a necessary evil. If you can avoid it by changing some words, that's better for everybody than taking time out to define. If you believe your language will be clear and intelligible to your readers, you won't need to detain them with explanations of meanings. Never define a term that is entirely clear as it stands. If you must define (and often, certainly, you must), do the job as quickly and efficiently as possible.

How to define a Term. The job of defining is essentially a matter of drawing clear boundary lines around a subject: the lines must show what belongs inside and what doesn't. So an adequate definition meets two tests:

1. It is broad enough to include everything you want the term to include.
2. It is narrow enough to exclude everything you want to exclude.

In very simple situations you can meet these tests by simply listing everything covered and saying "that's all." For example:

The School of Natural Science at De Soto University includes only the departments of Physics, Chemistry, and Biology.

There you have a definition that distinguishes this school in this university from the others: it names all the departments that belong in the school; it excludes (by the word "only") departments of Mathematics, Astronomy, Psychology, and everything else.

Of course many terms are too abstract or inclusive to define that way. It would be impossible to list all they encompass. But it may still be possible to define in a single sentence. To do that we need some rules:

1. First assign the term to a definite *genus*—a category or family of things to which it belongs. This procedure at once eliminates all other categories or genera from consideration and limits the possible meanings accordingly. For example, if you say "engineering is a *curriculum* . . ." you have already eliminated many other possible meanings of your term; you have told your reader that you are not here referring to engineering as a *profession*, an *applied science*, or an *art*.

A *phosphate* is a *carbonated drink* . . . (so far, with this genus, you have eliminated the chemical and agricultural meanings of the word)

Gas is an *explosive mixture in the mine* . . . (this restriction has eliminated gasoline, the meanings of gas in physics, and others)

Sometimes you will find it helpful to say that a term is "colloquial," "slang," "a medical term," or the like to let your reader understand where and by whom the term is commonly used. But you make no headway whatever by assigning a term to the class of *words, terms,* or *expressions*. "Garrote is a term . . ." makes no progress towards definition because everybody already knows it's a term. But "garrote is a Spanish means of capital punishment . . . ," or "garrote is a strangling device . . ." would be a useful beginning to a definition.

Of course the more limited the genus, the more you exclude from your meaning by this first step. *Citizen* is more limited than *person*, and *registered voter* is more limited than *citizen*.

2. Differentiate your subject from everything else in the same genus. If engineering is a profession (genus), you must show how it is distinguished from other professions like architecture, medicine, and the rest. If it is to be viewed as a curriculum (another possible genus), you must explain the characteristics that differentiate it from other curricula like Natural Science.

3. Don't define in a circle; that is, don't use derivatives of the term itself or synonyms that need the same defining as your subject. "Geniality is the quality of being genial" is hardly more helpful than saying a shim is a shim. For most readers, "cowardice is fear" does not help because they are about as familiar with one term as the other—and both may need definition equally in a certain context. On the other hand, "prejudice is pre-judgment" does make progress by giving emphasis to an essential characteristic of prejudice that might not be immediately apparent.

4. Define in words your reader will understand in the way you mean them. "A rib is any one of the arched bones attached posteriorly to the vertebral column" hardly carries meaning to ordinary readers for ordinary uses. The writer who said "propaganda is organized public persuasion" found that his readers missed his meaning because they did not know that by *organized* he actually meant "directed by some organized group" and by *public* he meant "addressed to all the people affected by a given controversial question." Too much compactness sometimes loses the reader.

5. Eliminate all statements that are irrelevant to genuine definition. For example, "Mormons, many of whom live in Salt Lake City, . . ." interjects a clause that, however true or interesting, serves no purpose in definition because many Mormons do not live in Salt Lake City. "Most psychiatrists are themselves maladjusted personalities" is not a criterion for distinguishing psychiatrists from other persons; it gets in the way of real definition.

Extending a Sentence Definition. Putting a definition in a single sentence is one way to develop preciseness and accuracy in thinking and writing. Even if the one-sentence definition never actually appears in the final composition intended for readers, it is still often a guide and discipline for the writer himself. Often, too, the single sentence will provide the clearest and most economical definition any reader could want.

Frequently, however, readers require considerably more explanation of meanings than they can get from one sentence. Extended definition sometimes takes pages; sometimes, in fact, it takes whole books.

Typical methods of developing definitions follow:

1. *Examples* can be especially useful, even indispensable. Especially for abstract terms like *retarded children* or *state agencies,* it is often necessary to take the reader closer to the referents—the actual things for which the term stands. To give any real conception of what a "pressure group" is like it is necessary to have names and examples of their behavior—perhaps quite a variety of them.

2. *Contrast* is the right device for showing distinctions between words likely to be confused. Perhaps "general," "liberal," and "special" education all need to be contrasted if the reader is to understand your meaning for any one. You may need to distinguish *fraternities* from *honoraries, T-formation* from *Wing-T* and *Split-T,* engineering *design* from *research.*

Of course it is a waste of time to contrast things that have little similarity anyway. The method serves its purpose best when it points out differences among things enough alike to cause confusion.

3. *Obverse iteration* is the method of stating first what a thing is not, then what it is. The method has special value in eliminating elements that do not belong:

> Scientific thinking is not the same thing as practical thinking. It does not lead directly to useful inventions. It provides no quick cures. Because it is not fast thinking it doesn't fit the immediate needs of businessmen or congressmen. Rather, scientific thinking is critical, skeptical, and very slow in getting to conclusions. It often seems to raise more questions than it answers. . . .

4. *Origins* is the method of explaining meanings by showing the etymology or history of the term:

Robot, coming from the Czech word *robotnik,* meaning serf, or *robota,* compulsory service, was first used in Capek's play *R. U. R.* for the man-like machines he used as characters who did the routine work of humans.

It has since been applied to an apparatus with concealed mechanism that can move and work by itself.

And finally, back to man himself, the term is applied to a human being who acts mechanically, without thought.

Knowing the earliest use of a word does not always help us understand its current meaning, but sometimes the historical development does serve a useful purpose.

5. *Authority* is the method of citing specialists or experts who have defined a word as you want to use it. Standard texts, encyclopedias, and dictionaries are possible authorities. Of the dictionary we had better say more.

Using the Dictionary. A good dictionary provides us with an amazing variety of information about the language: spelling, pronunciation, derivation, usage, and—most important—meanings. One business of a dictionary is to define words; and since a dictionary is the most widely recognized general authority on meanings that we have, we can all get help from it.

You don't need a dictionary everytime you want to define, and often it can provide no help whatever. "The downtown section of McKeesport," "eligibility for Little League play," and "XY quality thread" are terms no dictionary will define for you. In fact, a dictionary can seldom do all your work in defining. Usually it is simply an excellent starting point.

Although the making of dictionaries requires exceptional judgment and the final product represents thousands of conclusions, the dictionary's reputation depends upon how well it reports the way people actually use the language. The editors of a good dictionary (like the Merriam-Webster dictionaries or the *American College Dictionary*) do not invent words or the meanings they ascribe to words. They do their best to report meanings that writers and speakers have given to words; and when a word begins to get new meanings, or when older meanings no longer apply, the alert editors report the change.

So the help you get from a good dictionary in defining words is the record of the way other people, for various purposes and in all kinds of situations, are using a given term.

One important aid in defining is the labels you find with certain entries in your dictionary:

1. Labels of time (*archaic*, meaning *antiquated; obsolete*, no longer used at all) tell whether you can appropriately use a word in your writing now.

2. Labels of place (*U. S., Brit.*, restricted to a country; *dial.* or *local*, restricted to a section or locality) suggest where or with what readers a term may be fitting.

3. Labels of level (*colloq.*, colloquial, appropriate as a very informal, conversational expression, not in formal writing; *slang; illiterate*) point to the degree of formality.

4. Labels of trade, profession, or field (*engineering, physics, medicine, basketball, military*) point out the technical or specialized uses of a term.

One thing a dictionary will show most emphatically is the number of different meanings the same word can have in different contexts. When you read or hear a word you don't understand and look it up in your dictionary, you may find several different definitions, listed 1, 2, 3, etc. You must then find the single definition that fits your context.

The context of a word is its immediate environment—the sentence or paragraph, place or situation in which it is used. Because the same word will change its meaning in different contexts, you as a writer have to be sure your readers understand your terms in the context of your writing. Sometimes you need to use a term for a definite, limited situation, like the problem of maintaining or not maintaining an "open shop" in road construction by the Butley Construction Company in Weirly County. Suppose you had to write a report on the labor problems involved, and the terms *open shop* and *union shop* seem appropriate because the men there are using them. Will the dictionary help?

You might try the *American College Dictionary*:

open shop. 1. a nonunion shop which may or may not employ union members together with nonmembers, but which does not recognize or deal with a union as the representative of the employees . . . 2. an anti-union shop in which union members are not knowingly employed. 3. a shop in which a union, because chosen by a majority of the employees, acts as representative of all the employees in making agreements with the employer, but in which union membership is not a condition of employment.

Now of course these three meanings are quite different, the second and third even irreconcilable with each other. So your first question is "Which of the three kinds of open shop applies to the Butley Construction Company?" Suppose you decide that number (3) comes closest. Local 1326 of the Roadworkers International has won an election and has been negotiating with the management, but membership in that local is not "a condition of employment." Number (3) in the dictionary, then, is a good basis for a working definition. But what about the confusing word *shop*? Butley has no "shop" in the usual sense of that word. Why not just call it "an agreement under which . . ." (genus) and proceed with the third dictionary definition?

Your dictionary may save hours of pain and time, but no dictionary can foresee every possible context for a given word. Neither can it include definitions that will fit the vocabulary of every specialist. Always remember that the language you use in writing is intended to carry *your* meaning to *your* readers.

Why Classify?

When we assign a term to a genus as the first step in a formal definition, we are relying on a classification or division of the genus into which the thing we are defining can fit. If we say "the jib is a sail . . . ," we have in mind other kinds of sail; to distinguish the jib clearly from all the others we do well to have in our mind a logical classification of all sails. So an understanding of general classifications is a basis for defining. On the other hand, you can hardly make a classification or logical division of a broad subject without giving attention to defining. The two processes are inter-dependent.

Suppose, for example, that you want to discuss "basic courses" for industrial psychology. You will need to define your term, and that requires clear distinctions between what you call "basic" and all the other courses. A classification of all courses in the curriculum is needed. You might decide on three main divisions:

General courses
Basic courses
Professional courses

Now, can you define each of these three groups so that you (and your readers) will understand where every single course properly belongs?

Scientists, of course, give more attention to strictly logical classifications than is demanded in most other fields. Geologists, botanists, and astronomers, for example, need exact classifications and precise definitions of the phenomena with which they deal. Most of us do not require anything quite so complete.

In writing, classification often provides a framework for extended analysis. For instance, to write about "The Industries of Zenith" you would need to make a broad classification first—according to capital investment, or number of employees, or location in the city, or some other basic principle that suited Zenith and your purpose in writing. The classification itself is nothing but an outline or diagram. In writing it serves to keep things in order and show significant relationships.

A logical classification should follow these rules:

1. Limit and define the subject of classification. Your purpose, the uses to be made of your classification, will determine the limits. Do you want to classify *all* books published in 1940, or only all "books published in the United States," or only all "books about Germany published in the United States in 1940"? The subject of a classification must be clearly in mind before you begin.

2. Select one basis for division at a time. You could classify students in a school according to age, sex, class, curriculum, religious preference, height, weight, or a hundred other bases. If you mix the bases you get confusion:

Freshmen
Baptists
Top fifth
Fraternity members
Coeds
Pre-med

A logical classification would have to use one basis at a time:

By sex:	male	By class:	freshmen	By residence:	dormitory
	female		sophomores		fraternity
			juniors		private home
			seniors		

3. Choose a basis that means something for your purpose. You could, if you wished, classify people according to the diameter of the ear or length of the index finger, but you will hardly find it profitable. In writing you should not classify just for the fun or the mental exercise. Always ask yourself before you begin classifying: Why? Is this a basis that matters? What is it good for?

4. Avoid overlapping. For a logical classification of books in a library you must have just one place (or class) for each book. If you find you don't know where to put Mr. Dunne in your classification of citizens because he fits into both "Professional" and "Clerical" classes, then there is something fundamentally wrong with your division; you need to start again.

5. Cover the whole field. Your classes must include everything that belongs to the subject you are classifying. If you classify occupations as "Agricultural, Manufacturing, Trade," you apparently have no place for lawyers, physicians, postal clerks, and so on. If you classify religions in America as "Catholic, Protestant, Jewish," you must add at least an "Etcetera" or "Miscellaneous" to provide a place for Mohammedan, Greek Orthodox, and others.

6. Be sure your classifications fit realities. Men once classified the "humours" of the human body, but since nobody ever really found any such humours the idea was properly abandoned. Many classifications that once seemed important, even in science, have been discarded as unrealistic.

David Riesman in *The Lonely Crowd* made an interesting classification of people as "Tradition-directed," "Inner-directed," and "Other-directed," with extensive definitions of each. But since few actual persons fit clearly into any one of those categories, it is important to recognize that this is not so much a classification of actual human beings as it is of tendencies. It is a classification of human motivations rather than of men. Once that is clear the division and the definitions are significant; if it is not clear the classification merely disturbs and confuses.

If you are classifying things or persons, look closely and be sure you have a place, and only one place, for each. But if you are classifying ideas, principles, abstractions, be sure your reader understands what you are dividing.

1. *Dividing on a Scale*. You will recognize the difficulty in dividing

some phenomena into clear-cut, separate classes. For example, the heights, weights, and IQ's of millions of people do not fall into neat classes but spread over a wide scale. If you arbitrarily draw a line between "IQ's 100–110" and "IQ's 111–120," etc., you somewhat falsify the facts because the difference between 110 and 111 is much less than that between 111 and 118. Suppose you divided cities by population:

Under 50,000
50,000–99,999
100,000–499,999
500,000 and over

This kind of classification may sometimes be necessary, but it is quite arbitrary and it tends to lose sight of the truth that a city of 95,000 has more similarity to one of 105,000 than the latter does to a city of 450,000.

Where things really spread out on a scale, therefore, it may be better to stay with the scale and not attempt to set apart particular areas as arbitrary classes. At least remember that the individuals in any "class" maintain their individual characteristics.

2. *Informal Classifications—Enumeration.* Logical classifications are necessary in science and in many practical situations where we need a place for everything and everything in a proper place. But it is absurd to try to fit every division of every subject into the rigid pattern of formal classification. For example, you may want to discuss "typical basketball players" in this order:

The rebound experts
The playmakers
The scoring stars
The defensive specialists

Your purpose here is not dividing actual players of an actual squad, but only emphasizing the various skills needed by a successful team. It is a useful division even though one player might belong in two or three of the classes. It emphasizes what you want to emphasize.

An informal enumeration need not always be complete. "Principal causes of the Spanish Civil War" does not pretend to name every cause, only those the author calls the "principal" ones. "Students who fail" may discuss representative failures; it need not include every single student who ever failed.

"Job Opportunities in Idaho," "Some Good Books for Summer Reading," and "Qualities of a Good Actor" are all subjects calling for some classification or enumeration; but they would hardly demand strict application of all the rules.

Always use the rules with common sense.

READINGS

Selections 1, 2, and 3 that follow are examples of extended definition.

Which of the methods discussed in this chapter do they exemplify? How well does each meet the tests of clear and adequate definition?

1

WHAT IS SCIENCE *

Anthony Standen

What exactly is this "Science" that is so highly regarded? Buckets of ink have been used up in defining it, but the simplest way is to say "Science is any knowledge that is arrived at by the Scientific Method"—and then to define scientific method. Many more buckets of ink have been used in explaining this method, but its essentials can be described rather easily as a series of definite steps, roughly as follows. The first step is observation. Usually what is observed is the result of a deliberately contrived experiment (but not necessarily, for astronomy is a science, and it is impossible to do any experiments with the stars). A number of observations are collected, and then the scientist goes into a huddle with himself and forms a hypothesis, that is, a suggested explanation, of some sort or other, of the facts that have been observed. A hypothesis is, if you like, a sort of guess. . . . In the next step the scientist says, "If my hypothesis is true, then when I do such and such an experiment, so and so ought to happen." The final step is to do the appropriate experiment, and see

* Reprinted from the book *Science Is A Sacred Cow* by Anthony Standen. Copyright, 1950, by Anthony Standen. Published by E. A. Dutton & Co., Inc.

if the hypothesis is substantiated. If the result of the experiment is different from what was expected, the hypothesis is rejected at once, it's wrong. If the experiment agrees, the hypothesis is accepted tentatively. As further experiments are done, perhaps by other scientists, the hypothesis is continually put to the test of experiment, and if it survives a large number of experiments, and can explain them all, it is promoted to a "theory." A theory is simply a well-tested hypothesis, but there is no sharp dividing line. Even the very best of theories may turn out to be wrong, for tomorrow an experiment may be done that flatly contradicts it.

2

ARE THEY ANTIQUES? *

A permanent display of old automobiles has been opened on Broadway . . . nostalgically driving us back to the days of the duster and the cry, "Get a horse!" But all is not placid and serene. For in and around the 1895 one-seater runabout and the others swirls a semantic fury over the question, Are they or are they not antiques? The rigidly formal antiquarian turns up his nose at old cars. To him nothing is antique unless it was created more than 124 years ago, the year 1830 serving as the dividing line. Under that restriction, obviously there could be no such thing as an antique automobile, since motor cars didn't see the light of day until the Eighteen Eighties.

Our formal antiquarians fall back on no less an authority than the United States Government in setting 1830 as the date to drop this historical Iron Curtain. The Government faced the problem of definition during the first days after World War I, when tariff talk was in the air. In determining what was an antique for tax purposes, the year 1830 was selected. By decree, anything made before that year is an antique, anything after is not. There is nothing capricious in the choice. It was chosen because it represents roughly the date of the start of the Industrial Revolution and of machine-made products.

On the other hand, there is a vocal school of antiquarian thought that is much less formalistic in its approach. It uses as authority one Noah Webster, himself an antique under any definition, since he

* Reprinted by permission from "Topics of the Times," *The New York Times*, July 28, 1954.

arrived in this world in the year 1758. And his great work, the two-volume "An American Dictionary of the English Language," the foundation of all modern Websters, also slipped under the ban, its first edition having been published in 1828. According to the learned Noah, an antique is, "in general, anything very old." More specifically, he calls an antique "a piece of furniture, tableware or the like, made at a much earlier period than the present. . . ."

All signs point to the formal antiquarians fighting a losing battle, with Webster winning out over Washington. Victorian furniture, from a period of French revival that lasted through the end of the nineteenth century, is already being collected. So are such post-1830 objects as druggist jars, business catalogues, inkwells, match boxes, Confederate memorabilia, barbershop mugs, decoys, toy banks, and magic lanterns, to name a few.

It stands to reason that the things to collect must be added to with the passing years. . . . If we try to restrict ourselves to collecting what was made before 1830, when our population was a fraction of today's 160,000,000, we would stifle collecting. . . . Today we are already collecting Stanley Steamers and cigar-store Indians, which only yesterday were commonplace. And somewhere among today's commonplaces lurk the antiques of tomorrow.

3

The following definitions introduce a debate between Senator Byrd and Senator Douglas on the question:

ARE WE HEADED TOWARD 'COLLECTIVISM'? *

1. *What is your definition of collectivism?*

Senator Byrd . . .

Collectivism is a system of government which subordinates individual freedom and initiative to an all-powerful state in which the government supports the people rather than the people the government. But for the sake of those who wish to be academic, the Library of Congress has supplied this definition of collectivism:

"A political or economic doctrine which maintains that the owner-

* From *The New York Times Magazine*, December 18, 1949.

ship of property, especially land and capital, should reside in the community as a whole or in the state as the designated agent of the people. Collectivism is a broader term than communism in that revolutionary methods are not necessarily advocated. Moreover, the term is to be distinguished from socialism in its advocacy of broader controls over property rights."

Senator Douglas . . .

Collectivism is the public ownership of the means of production and distribution. Under it, the state would own and operate the railroads, mines, manufacturing establishments, banks, and insurance companies. Under the most sweeping definition of collectivism, the state would also own and operate farms, retail stores and wholesale establishments; and virtually all members of the professions, such as doctors, dentists, teachers and journalists, would also be employed by the state.

4

What light does the following excerpt throw on the influence of "emotional connotations"? Why was this set of rules drawn up?

Make a similar list of "don't's" about using words for an entirely different situation.

THOU SHALT NOT . . .*

(There is a profitable lesson for all who would use words in the most diplomatic fashion to be found in the rules of the editorial staff of the *United Nations World* magazine.)

There is no place in the world "distant" or "far" (from where?).

No place, culture, custom or people is "strange" (to whom), "exotic," "queer," or "bizarre."

People can be "illiterate" but never "ignorant"; they can be "simple" but never "backward."

There are no "heathen," no "pagan cultures," no "Christian ideals" (except in direct discussion), and no "chosen people."

Avoid "we," "ourselves," etc. when referring to citizens of the United States, or to Westerners in general.

* From *Word Study*, G. & C. Merriam Company, May 1948.

"We" are *all* the people.

Give the FACTS. Be objective.

The people will make up their own minds . . . and probably they'll be pretty close to right.

5

The following selection is from Norbert Wiener's *The Human Use of Human Beings*. It is part of an introduction to cybernetics, a new field of science.

Can you select key statements made about the term *cybernetics* and from these write a sentence definition?

Where does Wiener imply that definitions and classifications are part of the purpose of science?

As it is used here in this piece, can you define the word *entropy*?

CYBERNETICS *

Since the end of World War II, I have been working on the many ramifications of the theory of messages. Besides the electrical engineering theory of the transmission of messages, there is a larger field which includes not only the study of language but the study of messages as a means of controlling machinery and society, the development of computing machines and other such automata, certain reflections upon psychology and the nervous system, and a tentative new theory of scientific method. This larger theory of messages is a probabilistic theory, an intrinsic part of the movement that owes its origin to Willard Gibbs. . . .

Until recently, there was no existing word for this complex of ideas, and in order to embrace the whole field by a single term, I felt constrained to invent one. Hence "Cybernetics," which I derived from the Greek word *kubernétēs*, or "steersman," the same Greek word from which we eventually derive our word "governor." Incidentally, I found later that the word had already been used by Ampère with reference to political science, and had been introduced in another context by a Polish scientist, both uses dating from the earlier part of the nineteenth century.

* Reprinted from *The Human Use of Human Beings* by Norbert Wiener. Copyright by Houghton Mifflin Company.

I wrote a more or less technical book entitled *Cybernetics* which was published in 1948. In response to a certain demand . . . I published the first edition of *The Human Use of Human Beings* in 1950. Since then the subject has grown from a few ideas shared by Drs. Claude Shannon, Warren Weaver, and myself into an established region of research. Therefore, I take this opportunity occasioned by the reprinting of my book to bring it up to date, and to remove certain defects and inconsequentialities in its original structure.

In giving the definition of Cybernetics in the original book, I classed communication and control together. Why did I do this? When I communicate with another person, I impart a message to him, and when he communicates back with me he returns a related message which contains information primarily accessible to him and not to me. When I control the actions of another person, I communicate a message to him, and although this message is in the imperative mood, the technique of communication does not differ from that of a message of fact. Furthermore, if my control is to be effective I must take cognizance of any messages from him which may indicate that the order is understood and has been obeyed.

It is the thesis of this book that society can only be understood through a study of the messages and the communication facilities which belong to it; and that in the future development of these messages and communication facilities, messages between man and machines, between machines and man, and between machine and machine, are destined to play an ever-increasing part.

When I give an order to a machine, the situation is not essentially different from that which arises when I give an order to a person. In other words, as far as my consciousness goes I am aware of the order that has gone out and of the signal of compliance that has come back. To me, personally, the fact that the signal in its intermediate stages has gone through a machine rather than through a person is irrelevant and does not in any case greatly change my relation to the signal. The theory of control in engineering, whether human or animal, or mechanical, is a chapter in the theory of messages.

Naturally there are detailed differences in messages and in problems of control, not only between a living organism and a machine, but within each narrower class of beings. It is the purpose of Cybernetics to develop a language and techniques that will enable us indeed to attack the problem of control and communication in general, but also to find the proper repertory of ideas and techniques to classify their particular manifestations under certain concepts.

The commands through which we exercise our control over our environment are a kind of information which we impart to it. Like any form of information these commands are subject to disorganization in transit. They generally come through in less coherent fashion and certainly not more coherently than they were sent. In control and communication we are always fighting nature's tendency to degrade the organized and to destroy the meaningful; the tendency, as Gibbs has shown us, for entropy to increase.

In the following selections, point out the relation of classification to definition.

How logical are the classifications? How clear and adequate are the definitions?

6

INTELLECTUAL DEFICIENCY *

[This is an excerpt from a chapter titled "Intellectual Deficiency," at the beginning of which the authors warn that the "intelligence test is simply one means employed in determining feeble-mindedness" and that it is only "part of the total picture," which includes mental age and other important factors about the individual.]

From the standpoint of intellectual capacity there are five grades of deficiency, or feeble-mindedness: idiot, imbecile, moron, borderline, and dull-normal.

Idiot

The mental age of the idiot is up to three years and his I.Q. ranges between 0 and 25, using the Stanford-Binet test. The lower-grade idiot cannot dress himself, cannot make himself understood, cannot be taught cleanliness, and requires constant attention. The idiot who is somewhat higher in grade may be taught some of the fundamentals

* Reprinted from A *Handbook of Psychiatry* by P. M. Lichtenstein and S. M. Small by permission of W. W. Norton & Company, Inc. Copyright 1943 by W. W. Norton & Company, Inc.

of cleanliness. . . . As a rule, the idiot does not walk or talk until late in life and then only with a limited vocabulary, and some idiots never walk or talk at all. . . .

Imbecile

The mental age of the imbecile ranges from three to seven and his I.Q. ranges from 25–50. He can be taught to bathe and dress himself, and he may even learn to protect himself against danger if he is of the higher grade. Many of these individuals can carry out simple tasks. They begin to talk and walk later than normal children.

Moron

A moron is one whose intellectual capacity falls within the seven-to-twelve-year mental age limit, with an I.Q. of 50 to 70. Morons as a rule are capable of simple tasks, but lack ordinary judgment and discriminative ability. They have difficulty in generalizing from particulars, and are usually quite suggestible and easily led. They have fewer physical stigmata (such as paralyses and bodily deformities) than do imbeciles and idiots. Many of them are capable of performing simple tasks and are adequately adjusted to the less strenuous social levels. . . .

Borderline

In the borderline group we find people with an I.Q. ranging from 70 to 80 and whose success or failure in adjustment depends to a great extent on the complexity of their environment. Proper supervision and training may make the difference between a potentially feeble-minded person and a dull-normal individual.

Dull-Normal

The dull-normal people have an I.Q. ranging from 80 to 90. They can get along independently if their particular inadequacies are minimized, but they show disabilities in certain limited fields such as mathematics, abstract thinking, forming concepts, and so on. In order to make a continuously satisfactory adjustment to life they must try exceedingly hard. Sometimes they refuse to continue their efforts at a maximum, which causes them to become behavior problems at school, at work, or at home. They may even get into difficulty with the law.

7

CLOUDS *

To most people a cloud is just a cloud. They will have words enough and to spare when describing the landscape, but for the cloudscape they have almost none. It has always been so. Even the Ancients, who delighted in giving names to everything and in weaving stories around them, found for clouds neither names nor history. Theophrastus, for all his ingenuity, could do no better than distinguish between "streaks of cloud from the south" and "clouds like fleeces of wool"; and few of us ever get much further. Indeed, it is probable that many of the names by which clouds are known today to meteorologists are quite strange to us; but then meteorologists have had names for clouds—Latin names at that!—for only little over a century.

The cloud classification in general use at the present time is based on one devised by Luke Howard, a London chemist, who specified four types and gave to each a Latin name that its appearance suggested. The high wisps of clouds that reminded him of a lock of hair, he called *cirrus*. The cloud that spread itself like a sheet became *stratus;* the cloud that gathered itself into a heap became *cumulus;* and the shapeless, ragged threatening low cloud that gives us most of our rain and snow he dubbed *nimbus*, which simply means cloud. But any classification limiting us to a lock of hair, a heap, and a sheet quickly involves us in trouble when we come up against clouds "backed like a weasel, or very much like a whale." Ideally, something more elastic and comprehensive is required, yet the International code is based upon the same key words. By combining them variously it does succeed in giving us ten major types instead of four, and is about as satisfactory as any other scheme that has been devised.

For convenience, rather than precision, we can group the ten types under three heads, thus:

* George Kimble and Raymond Bush, *The Weather*. Copyright 1943 by Penguin Books, Inc. Reprinted by permission.

High clouds: cirrus, cirrocumulus, cirrostratus.
Middle clouds: altocumulus, altostratus.
Low clouds: stratocumulus, stratus, nimbostratus, cumulus, cumulonimbus.

The big snag about pegging clouds to altitudes is that high clouds as thus defined are sometimes found below middle clouds, while low clouds like cumulonimbus (= thundercloud) may be low, middle, and high simultaneously. Generally, however, they keep pretty much to their respective levels, as shown in the accompanying table:

Position	*Meteorological Name*	*Abbreviation*	*Height in Feet*
High clouds	Cirrus	Ci	25,000
	Cirrocumulus	Cc	to
	Cirrostratus	Cs	35,000
Middle clouds	Altocumulus	Ac	10,000
	Altostratus	As	to
			25,000
Low clouds	Stratocumulus	Sc	Up to 10,000
	Stratus	St	but mostly
	Nimbostratus	Ns	below
	Cumulus	Cu	7,000
———	Cumulonimbus	Cb	Up to 25,000

EXERCISES

How well do the following statements meet the tests for clear and logical definitions?

1. "In this competition, a short story is simply a work of prose fiction between two and five thousand words long."
2. "Daily Double" is a term used in horse racing indicating that the bettor has selected the winner of both first and second races.
3. A commercial is a part of a radio or television program devoted to the promotion of the sponsor's interests by means of direct statements about them.
4. The Middle Class of Topton, many of whom work in offices in the city, are men of moderate but not high income who live in modest

homes most of which they own, and generally subscribe to middle-class social, political, and religious customs.

5. Style in creative writing is characterized by "a series of tiny, scarcely perceptible surprises."
6. "Cousin" is a slang baseball term meaning that a pitcher is easy to hit.
7. A protective tariff is a schedule of duties imposed by a government on imports for the primary purpose of protection rather than revenue.
8. The clerical force in this company includes all office employees below the rank of Assistant Office Manager.
9. A juke-box is for playing records in a public place.
10. A medical clinic, as we refer to it here, is a class of medical students who receive instruction by observing the treatment of a patient.
11. A "BMOC" is campus slang for "Big Man on Campus."
12. What we call "parity" for farmers means a balance between prices they pay and prices they receive which equals the relationship existing from August 1909 to July 1914.
13. Cribbing is dishonesty in scholastic work.
14. In the United States today a communist is anybody who subscribes to the doctrines of Marx or takes orders from Moscow.

ASSIGNMENTS

I. Define (in about 300–500 words) to fit the context; do not argue:

1. "Too many engineering schools," the committee declared "now emphasize engineering arts rather than science. Courses based on engineering arts result in rapid obsolescence of the methods and information learned, while education based on science and the engineering approach will sustain the engineer for a lifetime." (Define *engineering science* as this committee apparently means it to be understood.)
2. "College fraternities, so characterized by false discrimination, snobbery, and injustice, are the very antithesis of real fraternity." (Define *fraternity* in the latter sense.)
3. "Communism is really less a philosophy, system or form of organization than it is a religion."
   (Define *religion* in this context.)
4. "The freedom to go wrong is essential in a university, where men are learning not to obey, but to choose."
   (Define *freedom to go wrong.*)
5. "Some corporations have found that college graduates who have

engaged in extra-curricular activities are more likely to win advancement than those without such experience."
(Define *extra-curricular activities* for the use of the Personnel Division of a company that wants them listed in applications for positions.)

II. Write an analysis (400–500 words) using a logical classification as your framework:

1. A small city intends to establish a zoning code. There are to be four zones, with building and other restrictions for each: Industrial, Business, Residential A, and Residential B.
   Explain the zoning provisions for readers of the city's leading newspapers.
2. All students of a university are required to schedule several so-called "courses in general education."
   Discuss the possibilities for the information of freshmen.
3. A new enterprise will bring a hundred new families into your town or city.
   Explain the housing possibilities in a statement prepared for these new families.

CHAPTER 4

Explaining a Complex Unit

Mechanism, Processes, Organizations

A map is a kind of pictorial generalization based upon many direct observations; we can verify its accuracy by following it from one place to another. A diagram of a camera is another kind of pictorial generalization—of many cameras; we can verify the accuracy of that diagram by examining the parts of a real camera. Writing may do a similar job: it may provide verifiable generalizations of machines or tools, structures, processes, and organizations.

Exposition of this kind has numerous uses. Anybody who buys an electric razor, a garbage-disposal unit, or a power mower expects a set of instructions telling how to use it efficiently—perhaps also how to assemble, install, care for, or repair. New employees unfamiliar with their work need instructions, even courses of study, to prepare them for what they must do. New members of a club, and especially newly elected officers, often need information about the aims, principles, and methods of the organization.

Sometimes the exposition is less immediately practical though no less important. A textbook in physics explains instruments and mechanisms not always to help students use them, but to illustrate scientific principles. Magazines like *Popular Mechanics* satisfy their readers' curiosity about many things they never expect to use directly. Man's curiosity about this universe extends far beyond the immediately "practical"—all the way from the nature of the blood to the planets of outer space. It may even include the government of Afghanistan.

So the analysis of complex units may prove either immediately useful or broadly educational. It may give essential directions to apprentice plumbers, the nurse who tomorrow must assist in her first major operation, or the newly elected burgess of Newville. It may give important information to students, engineers, or executives. It may also tell the ordinary casual reader how machinery helps modern farmers raise more wheat, the way a congressional investigating committee functions, or the kind of strategy that a successful football coach is using.

In this chapter we arbitrarily limit the study to mechanisms, processes, and organizations. By *mechanism* we mean a device for getting something done. An adding machine is a mechanism; so is the human eye. A *process* is a connected series of operations or changes leading to a certain result. Making soap is a process; so is tooth decay; so are directions for baking a pie or getting from Stormstown to Port Matilda. An *organization*, as we use the term here, is a group of persons formally joined together for some common interest. Congress, General Motors, the University of Illinois, Phi Beta Kappa, and the American Medical Association are examples.

Analysis of this kind seems to treat of tangible and definite things, but it is not the same as specific description. For example, analysis of the Ford V-8 motor is not a description of Harry Cutler's particular Ford motor, but rather a generalized account of hundreds of thousands of motors and what they all have in common. Suggestions on "How to Plan a House," though naturally based on experience and observations, make generalizations about houses not yet built. Such writing is therefore different from the descriptions and anecdotes of fiction or personal reminiscence where the main purpose is entertainment rather than information. "Uncle John's Silo" and "My Initiation into Sigma Zeta Sigma" are topics for personal description and anecdote rather than general exposition. If you want to explain "The Silo" or "Initiation Procedures in Sigma Zeta Sigma," you would use Uncle John's silo and your own initiation as illustrative evidence—not as main subjects for development but as very useful material for explaining broader subjects.

The facts of actual observation, reports of what others have seen and done, here become means to a larger purpose. They help explain general purposes, principles, and relationships.

Another thing: this kind of analysis is more than simple definition (distinguishing one machine from others, one process from other processes), and it is more than a classification of parts, steps, or elements. For example, analysis of a thermostat obviously goes beyond defining *thermostat*; it also goes much beyond a classification of all the parts of a thermostat. A complete list of parts really tells nothing whatever about the device; it is the way all essential parts are connected to function together that makes the unit we call a thermostat. Again, coal mining is one process—not various disconnected activities, but a series of related steps combining to get coal out of the ground and where men want it. Again, our federal government is one government; important as it may be to classify the several divisions, the analysis must also show the interdependence of these divisions in governing our people. Exposition of this kind must always emphasize the relationships that bring unity.

Adapting to Reader Interests

Before you decide your exact purpose in writing it is important to distinguish between readers with *passive* and readers with *active* interest. One with active interest expects to use a mechanism, play some part in a process, or assume a responsible role in an organization. The reader with passive interest, whether an executive, an engineer, or just a curious layman, may have no direct contact with the mechanism, process, or organization; he wants general information, not directions.

Naturally, the way you write ought to depend upon the way your readers will use what you tell them. If, for example, they are expected to assemble a machine, service it, repair it, your analysis should include:

Names of all the parts they need to know
Clear identification of every part (often with accompanying diagrams or pictures)
Directions in an order they can follow
Specific warnings of danger or trouble

On the other hand, if your readers are unlikely to handle the machine themselves, you emphasize its purpose, the principles it applies, and what it accomplishes. Readers with technical interests are especially concerned with theory and principles; business executives may care most about costs and practical results; casual readers may be interested in surprising inventions, the human beings who developed and use them, how they work, and how they may change men's lives. Not all readers need or want the same kinds of information.

Reader interests influence your choice of verbs and pronouns. To give specific directions, for example, you will generally use the pronoun *you* and the imperative mood:

> When you adjust Valve C, be careful to press . . .
> At Danbury, turn left on Route 7.
> If you need to increase the speed, turn the dial F and . . .

On the other hand, scientific and technical writing usually subordinates personalities to objective truth. Hence personal pronouns like *I*, *you*, and even *we* are sometimes unacceptable. Passive voice is much more common than in less formal writing:

> These tests were conducted at Hanover Laboratories . . .
> Oil is poured from the top.
> When this step is completed, the sheet passes . . .

The pronoun *we* is something of a compromise between the totally impersonal passive voice and the highly informal *I* and *you*:

> We find as we adjust our eyes to these bright lights that . . .

The passive voice is often a clumsy construction, and even highly technical writing can be improved by changes that in no way reduce the objectivity:

Awkward, Unnecessary Passive	*Improved*
The boxes are carried by rollers.	Rollers carry these boxes.
It was disclosed during the tests that . . .	The tests showed that . . .

Reader interests also influence the details you include. Illustrative anecdotes, names, homely analogies, and stories of human experiences can give life and clarity to exposition directed at the average layman. Ordinary readers can see an industrial process more vividly if "Jack Conklin, a typical workman," is a part of it. American government seems less remote and abstract when readers see how President Eisenhower, Chief Justice Warren, or Senator Johnson went about specific tasks.

Finally, reader interests ought to determine the kind and quantity of facts and figures you introduce. The data required in technical reports are often too precise to mean anything to casual readers or common workmen. Figures can become unbearable when we get too many to digest, or fail to understand them. But in modest doses, exact dimensions, prices, census figures, and other statistics can be informative and interesting.

Getting Started

An effective introduction does two things: it gets the reader's attention, and it prepares him to understand details that are to follow. A good *introductory summary* may do both; a broad view of the whole subject increases interest and helps a reader fit the later details into place when he gets to them.

Suppose you began reading:

> The essential element of the Powers Automatic System is an electrically controlled machine. Pressing a key closes the circuit which operates the motor running a punch. Cards 2½ by 6 inches in size, of lightweight stock, are placed in a slot at the left of the machine and feed through to the right.

Unless you already know what the system is you have no interest in that paragraph. It is unlikely you understand very much of it either, not because you find any unusual words but because you "don't know what it's all about." Without knowing the purpose of the system or machine you don't care how it works, and without some general idea of the structure and principle of the mechanism you have some difficulty understanding how it works anyway.

To provide the background necessary for understanding details in expository analysis, an introductory summary may include:

For a Mechanism	*For a Process*	*For an Organization*
Purpose	Purpose	Purpose
Physical description: size, shape, etc.	Scope: time, space, persons or materials involved, etc.	Scope: size, nature, distribution of membership and divisions
Working principle	Operational principle (or key to success)	Organizational principle

Of course you will not include information that your readers know perfectly well already. The purpose of a well-digger is, presumably, to dig wells; and the purpose of an oil furnace in a house is to heat the house. You shouldn't tell readers what is quite obvious. "This cigarette lighter is two inches long, one inch wide, and half an inch thick" is superfluous information for the reader who already holds the lighter in his hand.

Remember also that whatever you include in an introduction should be only a summary of the whole analysis—not all the information you have to impart. The summary introduction to a set of directions may require only a sentence or two. Even for a rather extensive discussion you may find a single paragraph adequate.

A common mistake of some writers is to crowd into an introduction long lists of items: all the parts of a complicated device, every major and minor step in a process. Some writers include a glossary of all the unusual terms they intend to use. Now the whole purpose of this introductory summary is to simplify the picture, and too many things for a reader to remember have quite the opposite effect. The best time to define a new term is usually right where you use it. Few readers can grasp the meanings of a dozen new words before they see where and how they apply. So define in the introduction only those terms essential to getting started, and save other definitions till your reader needs them. List the tools and materials necessary for beginning a process, tell your reader everything he is supposed to assemble at once, but don't include details he won't need till later stages.

Summarizing the "principle" of a mechanism, process, or organization is perhaps the most useful thing your introduction can provide a reader. It is also one of the most difficult things to express. Here are some examples:

Intense heat and pressure can change the atomic pattern, or lattice, of ordinary carbon into that of a diamond. Harnessing such pressure and heat is the basis of synthetic diamond making.

The whirling rotor blades of the helicopter combine the function of the airplane's wing ("lift") with the function of the propeller ("thrust").

Early heat-pumps were like reversible refrigerators. Using the heating and cooling properties of expanding and contracting gases, they could pick up heat from the air and put it where it was wanted—outside in the summer, inside in the winter.

Eventually the power in the "National Society" rests with the Board of Directors, which must pass on every order put into effect by the President.

Suggestions for Effectiveness

Here are a few ideas for making the analysis of mechanisms, processes, and organizations, readable, clear, and useful to readers:

1. *Use the Appropriate Pattern.* After an adequate introduction, the details of expository analysis should follow in some clear and definite order.

Chronological order fits a surprising variety of subjects. A set of directions ought naturally to explain each step in the order the reader will follow to carry them out: first step, second step, next step. Since every process has a time sequence, that is usually the pattern to adopt in an analysis. The same order may prove right for explaining a mechanism too: you begin with the source of power and follow the interaction of one part on the next.

Spatial order, the way an observer would actually see the details, is common for descriptions of rooms, buildings, or areas. Sometimes, as in explaining a manufacturing process, the spatial and chronological patterns combine: you conduct your reader around the plant so that he can observe the process step by step, department by department, from raw materials to finished product.

Abstract logical division is necessary for explaining an organization. You might show the "chain of command," for example, from Board of Directors to President to Vice-Presidents and so on down. Or you begin with the sovereign authority (king or dictator, stockholders, or voting citizens) and follow the delegation of authority to representatives (prime minister, the corporation management, Congress and the President) and thence down to lesser positions. Or your main divisions may be already determined by the organization:

Executive	Finance
Legislative	Production
Judiciary	Sales

2. *Use Appropriate Language.* How simple do you want to make it? Or how technical? The language must be clear and informative to its readers—and readers certainly differ.

The language of directions ought to be simple because readers who need directions are always unfamiliar with the things they are to do. The clipped "cookbook style" ("Beat eggs in bowl, add one cupfull milk") is good enough for recipes and very short directions, but a few pages without articles and prepositions demands too much reader concentration; it isn't a readable style for many kinds of subject. You generally get simplicity best not by over-condensation but with common words and simple structure.

Readers with specialized training in your general subject probably expect precise technical language. Exactness and accuracy seem very important to them. They are likely to be impatient of attempts to startle or amuse them; and of course they don't want to waste time reading what they already know.

The readers without much knowledge of your general subject cannot follow highly technical discussion, but a few technical terms in key places can be effective. Professional writers who popularize scientific information have learned to use such terms so that their readers see from the context approximately what they mean, or they give just enough definition to clarify without interrupting the reader's progress.

Examples and analogies are especially useful in this kind of writing. Comparing the heart with a pump, the jet with a toy balloon, or a hill of ants with a human village may seem very trite. They are better than no analogies at all, but fresh comparisons are what you are after. Find those that fit your reader's experience.

3. *Use Pictures, Diagrams, or Charts when Appropriate.* An actual photograph of a tool or machine may do more than many words to

show readers what it is like. A diagram can emphasize positions, principles, and relationships. A map is often a necessary supplement to written directions. Be sure to give clear titles to these pictorial supplements. So far as possible make them understandable even without the accompanying text.

But such devices are almost always supplementary to what you write. They don't take the place of exposition—they aid and support it. For best results you ought to tie the picture, diagram, or chart in with what you write. *Refer* to it, *explain* it, *use* it:

> Fig. 3 shows how this tube (C) is connected to the other chamber (K).
>
> Note on the chart that the Personnel Director is responsible for the administration of four divisions . . .

4. *Show the Relationship of the Parts.* Never forget that you are explaining a unit—not many parts or elements of separate importance but a single organism. It is your responsibility to show how the parts function together for a purpose.

Good transitions can emphasize interdependence and unity:

After the castings are cleaned, the next job includes counting, sorting, and trimming—all done in the so-called Trimming Room.

The "picture" is now on the plate, but that does nobody any good until it is transferred to paper. So the next part of the device to consider is . . .

Although the whole membership is responsible for passing motions that decide general policy, the Chairman has considerable influence in deciding policy as well as executing the will of the majority.

5. *Make Use of Relevant Facts.* If you have operated a machine, or had experience with a process or organization your observations ought to supply facts that you can use for illustration. Reading and listening may have furnished reports of actual incidents, tests and experiments—even statistics—that could provide interest and clarification.

6. *Keep Opinions in their Place.* The first purpose of analyzing mechanisms, processes, and organizations is to inform. However, it is natural to make judgments about these things and of course such analysis may become an essential element in advertising or propaganda. The warning here is to keep judgments in their place. When

your central purpose is to explain, don't let opinions get in the way. Calling a machine "very inefficient," for example, does not inform; it expresses a value judgment that needs reasons and evidence to back it up. If you label an organization "subversive" your reader is naturally curious to know why you think so; you may find yourself arguing rather than explaining.

When your purpose is to *explain* a mechanism, process, or organization, either exclude judgments entirely or use them only incidentally. The judgments shouldn't dominate the discussion. Sometimes, especially in popular writing, they add interest: This device is "a great time-saver"; this route is "the most interesting way to go"; this corporation is "a good company to work for." Judgments that aren't controversial require no special defense and needn't divert attention from your main theme. It is the controversial judgments—"This TV set is the best buy on the market"; "the Democratic Party is the defender of the common man"; "the zone defense isn't really basketball at all"—that threaten the effectiveness of expository analysis. If you don't take time to defend them, your readers may lose confidence in your fairness and reliability. If you do take time to defend them, you have taken time from the main job of explaining your subject.

This chapter, like those before it, concentrates attention on methods of informing and explaining. Later chapters consider the methods of reaching sound judgments about the problems of life, evaluating evidence, thinking logically, and defending the judgments you make. Later you will use facts, definitions, and expository analysis not only to inform but also as information to support your judgments. What you learn now about clear, adequate, and impartial explanation *without* judgments can be of utmost value when you want to array the strongest and most reliable evidence *for* your judgments.

Right now, try writing exposition that excludes all controversial opinion.

READINGS

The following selections all explain a complex unit. Answer these questions about each:

1. Is this selection primarily an explanation of a mechanism, a process, or an organization?

2. Is it written for an "active" or a "passive" reader? What kinds of verb forms and pronouns does it use?

3. Which order does it follow mainly—spatial, chronological, or logical? How would it appear in outline?

4. Does it use an introductory summary?

5. Does it state an underlying principle?

6. How much use does it make of specific factual reporting, definition, and classification?

7. Does the author go beyond objective explanation? That is, does he express or imply opinions or judgments? If so, are they appropriate?

1

JET MUFFLER *

A hush-hush project—reducing nerve-shattering screeches of powerful jet aircraft engines to a muffled roar—was shown here today at the Republic Aviation Corporation airfield.

A graphic demonstration of the new muffler, a steel structure that looks something like an oil tank lying on its side, was witnessed by members of the Institute of Aeronautical Sciences who are attending their organization's twenty-fourth annual meeting in New York City.

Designed to reduce the sound of jets being ground-tested as much as 75 per cent, the $25,000 unit is the first of five to be installed by Republic to eliminate "noise nuisance" in neighboring residential areas. The mufflers can be moved to different positions on the field by power cranes.

Two Republic Thunderstreak fighter-bombers, one with its tailpipe inserted into the noise suppressor, were used in today's demonstration. The Thunderstreak is powered by a Wright Sapphire J–65 turbojet engine that develops 7,200 pounds of thrust.

Observers, standing to one side and 200 feet behind the planes, first heard the unmuffled plane run at full power for sixty seconds. Sound waves vibrated their bodies and conversation was impossible.

When the muffled plane started running, the sound from the short exhaust stack was a dull roar that seemed to come from a great dis-

* From a news item in The New York *Times,* January 26, 1956. Reprinted by permission.

tance. There was no discomfort among the observers and conversation was carried on in normal tones.

Recent tests made in surrounding communities were described by Roland C. Bergh, Chief Staff Engineer at Republic. He said that the muffler reduced the noise of an engine to a level comparable to normal automobile traffic at various points.

These "community type silencers" reduce full-power engine noise by twenty-three decibels in areas of peak intensity. Mr. Bergh said, A decibel is a unit of sound-pressure intensity, and the twenty-three decibel reduction represents a 75 per cent cut in noise, he said.

The muffler was designed and built by the Industrial Acoustics Company of New York, under a contract with Republic.

Republic's study of noise nuisance to the communities was described by Mundy I. Peale, the company's president.

"We are making good progress toward cutting down the noise of engines being tested, but there still is work to be done if the problem is to be completely solved," he said. "We are continuing our research and development work, including development of a muffler to suppress the noise of more powerful engines which are coming."

Other factors involved include the positioning of planes during the ground test, so sound must travel across the widest possible expanse of the 560-acre airfield; flight patterns are planned, when feasible, to avoid populated areas and tests are confined to daytime hours as much as possible.

2

THE GUN THAT PROTECTS YOUR HOME *

You can't beat a calking gun for home defense. Once you've triggered one of these hand tools you'll find it as indispensable as a hammer or a handsaw. Better yet, it's fun to use. It works like Junior's water pistol, but the similarity ends there.

A calking gun fights back at water. Correctly handled, it does a thorough job of squeezing mastic compounds into troublesome cracks that develop, season after season, even in the best-built homes. Whatever the weatherproofing or sealing job, a calking gun does it the neat, professional way.

* From *Popular Science Monthly,* September, 1956. Reprinted by permission.

A calking gun that you can buy for a few dollars will give you a lifetime of service and pay for itself many times over. You have three types to choose from—half-barrel, combination and pressure guns.

Half-barrel guns. A popular homeowner model is the little half-barrel gun, so named because its body is shaped like a semi-circular trough, with a fully cylindrical cap at each end. The forward cap may have a tip attachment. If it doesn't there will be an opening at the center of the cap. You buy compound either in metal or heavy cardboard cartridges.

A tipless gun uses a cartridge that has its own built-in plastic tip. To operate the gun you lay the cartridge in the half-barrel with the tip projecting through the cap opening. Then you press the gun's plunger firmly against the bottom of the cartridge and puncture the seal in the tip. When you trigger the gun you're in business. The trigger ratchets the plunger forward, forcing the bottom of the cartridge into the cylinder like a piston. A smooth ribbon of compound feeds out through the tip.

For a half-barrel gun that has its own tip attachment, you can use the same type of cartridge by cutting off the container's plastic tip. Tipless cartridges are also sold for this type of gun at many hardware and paint-supply stores.

The advantages of the half-barrel gun are its low cost (around $2.50) and, in the case of the tipless type, the fact that the gun never has to be cleaned unless a cartridge ruptures. Guns with tip attachments need a bit of cleaning each time a cartridge is removed. Offsetting this disadvantage, the gun with a tip attachment takes a variety of specially shaped nozzles for unusual calking, glazing and seaming jobs.

Combination guns. Favorite of some homeowners and most professionals is the combination gun, costing from $4 up. This is a full-barreled job that can handle either bulk compound or flexible cellophane cartridges ("loads"). Although it uses the same triggering mechanism as the half-barrel gun, it must have a leather piston washer attached to the face of the plunger. This washer creates a sliding air seal. To load the gun with bulk compound you remove the forward barrel cap, dunk the open end of the barrel in the compound and draw the plunger rod back.

To release the plunger ratchet from the trigger for loading, or to stop the flow of compound through the tip, some guns have a rotating plunger rod. A half turn disengages the ratchet teeth. On other guns, letting the trigger snap back frees the ratchet. Still a third type has a release lever on the handle.

The combination gun is both versatile (you can load it with certain types of compounds that can't be bought in cartridges) and economical, especially on big calking jobs. Bulk compound costs about 12 cents less per gun load than a cartridge. That's why professionals go for combination guns. As a homeowner, however, you may find that the ease and cleanliness of handling cartridges more than make up for the extra dollar or so you'll spend on an occasional calking job.

Pressure guns. Unless you own a paint-spray compressor and have an unusually large amount of calking to do, you can write off this type. Its cost is low (about $8), but it is strictly a production tool. It uses either cartridges or bulk compound, forcing the material out of the tip by backing the plunger with compressed air. A touch of a thumb controls air flow to the rear of the barrel.

Special tips. If your gun has a tip attachment it will probably come with a standard ⅜″ oval nozzle—the most useful type for ordinary calking. For special jobs you can buy extra tips with openings that range from ⅛″ to 2¼″. The openings may be round, oval, flat or triangular. A good bet is an assortment of four tips in a kit that sells for around $1.25. With one of these kits, you can handle practically any home calking job you're likely to run into.

Even with plastic-tipped cartridges, you can vary the shape and volume of a calking bead to some extent by applying more or less side pressure to the flexible plastic nozzle as you trigger the gun. Better yet, soften the tip by soaking it in hot water, then model the plastic to the desired shape. When it cools, it will retain the form.

Choosing the right compound. Your choice of compound can make the difference between a good job and a bad one. Low-grade compound may be lumpy. It may not bond properly. It may also shrink, harden, crack or stain excessively. If the compound is packaged in inferior cartridges, they may break open at the seams. A low-grade cartridge often calls for excessive triggering pressure to produce a flow. When this happens, it is generally because the cartridge has not been lined with wax to make the compound ooze out easily. Top-grade compound is almost always labeled: "Meets Government Specifications."

Choose the right type for a particular job, too. When you walk into a paint store and say, "I want a cartridge of calking compound," chances are you'll get a cylinder of brown-gray goop. That's fine if you plan to paint over it afterward. But if you are doing an inside job around the edges of white tile, you can save a lot of extra fuss by asking the salesman for "pure white" or "brilliant white" compound.

Asphalt calking. For exterior work that calls for a particularly durable and elastic compound, your best bet may be asphalt. Although it will adhere to any surface, wet or dry, its surface loses its tackiness after it is applied. Asphalt calking is especially useful for repairing small roof leaks and for sealing flashing around chimneys, skylights, gutters and the like. If you plan to paint over asphalt calking compound, ask for the "nonbleeding" type.

Suppose you want a batch of compound of a particular shade or color to match adjacent surfaces. You can't buy this tinted compound in cartridges, but if you have a gun that takes bulk compound you can mix your own color blend. A half-pint of coloring solution—pigment ground in oil—is about the right amount for a gallon of compound. After you have added the color—there's usually room for it in the top of a gallon can of compound—close the lid tightly and have your paint supplier put the can in his mechanical shaker for a two-minute session.

How to use a calking gun. Use as much care in preparing surfaces for calking as you do for a good paint job. Remove all loose material—chipped masonry, rotted wood, peeling paint, etc. If you are calking over wood, make sure that it is dry. Do not calk if the weather is damp or the temperature is below 40 degrees. To make calking easier to trigger on cool days, warm it before loading the gun. For the best bond, swab the area to be calked with a rag moistened with turpentine or mineral spirits.

To fill a crack, incline the gun at about a 50-degree angle. The tip should straddle the crack so that the calking is applied equally on both sides of it. Be sure to *fill* the crack—don't just cover it. Also, once you've laid down a bead don't flatten it; its surface should always be convex. When you calk an opening that is wider than ⅜″ or deeper than ½″, pack the area with oakum, rope, mineral wool, plaster, wood or felt before applying compound.

Once you get the knack of handling the gun, you'll find that you can calk a whopping 10′ crack in under 30 seconds. To estimate the amount of compound you'll need for a particular job, figure on from 20′ to 22′ of cracks per standard-size cartridge or gun load.

3

SHIP'S COMPANY *

Jan de Hartog

The first man sailing the first hollowed-out tree trunk alone was a sailor. The first man who had a boy with him was a captain. Captains have not changed since; their vessel is still as flimsy, the sea as perilous, and the boy as hopeless.

Only if the young sailor keeps this elementary state of affairs in mind will he be able to see his captain clearly. This is important, for living as he does among officers who are not yet captains but feel that they should have been long ago, the apprentice may easily be influenced by their talk at the messroom table. It may not even be talk, just raised eyebrows, upcast looks, and shrugs of the shoulders. The young sailor will be led to believe that the ship is sailed virtually by the mate, for that is the way the mate sees it.

It is difficult on a long, long ladder that reaches into the sky to see further than the next rung; it is impossible for the apprentice to identify himself with the captain. The only comfort I can offer is that the captain, despite appearance, can identify himself to an astonishing degree with the apprentice if he should be called upon to do so. It is advisable, however, to postpone this call as long as possible, for captains don't like it. They seem to be quite content with their hermit's existence, remote and godlike in their double cabin, and there will be many days when only a chesty cough or a sneeze from below reminds the apprentice on the bridge of his captain's existence.

In practice, every captain looks like an old fool and never is. His very presence determines the nature of the community that sails the ship. He is the best argument against atheism I can think of, for every quarrel, every tension, even the grimmest conflict among the

* From *A Sailor's Life* by Jan de Hartog, copyright © 1955 by Littra, A. G. Reprinted by permission of Harper & Brothers.

members of his crew is entered into with the underlying knowledge that, if the worse comes to the worst, there always is somebody to give the final verdict. In the case of a conflict, the mate will say, "Take care the captain doesn't notice," and the chief engineer, "You'd better watch out or I'll take it up with the captain." Chief engineers refer to the captain the way self-confident clergymen refer to their private deity.

Should the apprentice be driven to the point of suicide about some personal problem (and apprentices' problems always are personal), he may go and ask the captain for advice, as it is less final. He must realize, however, that by doing so he is inviting mortification. The captain will be quite kind, but the apprentice's problem will take on puny stature in his own eyes on crossing the threshold. The sight of the Old Man writing at his desk with the calm concentration of a silversmith engraving a spoon will so impress the young sailor that the captain hardly need open his mouth. It may be a humane thing to tell the apprentice that the captain is usually writing nonsense at those moments.

Probably, occasions will be rare on which the apprentice will see his captain in his true light. It may be a gale, but then it takes a fairly long time before captains are convinced that there is a gale on. Usually they only show their heads at bridge level, scowling at the officer of the watch as if they suspected him of rocking the boat. Before turning around and vanishing back into their cozy den, they will mutter, "I presume you have looked after hatch number three, Mr. Er," which strikes the junior officer like lightning from Olympus. Captains are rarely noticed at work checking up on hatch number three beforehand.

There is little else I can tell the young sailor about captains, until he is about to be promoted to one himself. For the time being, two basic rules will do: bad captains do not exist, and even the youngest masters are old. On board ship, it is one's sea-days that count, not the years of one's life.

Mates

Mates are basically the unhappiest people at sea, because they are busy becoming captains. As everyone who has been an adolescent knows, not to be something yet is a depressing situation. What's more, every mate is convinced that he is better than his captain, for his captain only tells him what to do, rarely does it himself. The happy mate, quite satisfied with his situation, is for some reason unsatisfactory. A man who wants to remain a mate is a bad mate and a man who is a mate and wants to become a captain is frustrated, so one can easily see that a mate's lot is a hard one.

It is indeed like adolescence. Many secretly long for the happy, simple world of childhood; no man in his senses has any nostalgia for the horrible years in which he was neither child nor man but an awkward, clumsy creature between the two. This is why a mate's philosophy resembles that of the adolescent: nobody understands him, other people are always happier, girls are either too bad or too pure, and he can never do anything right, from shutting a door to packing a bag. The adolescent is supposed to wash up cheerfully, to hum a happy song while mowing the lawn or washing the car, to hop up and down clapping his hands crying, "Goody goody," when he is ordered to take Junior to the zoo.

All these situations, like nightmares from the past, repeat themselves hauntingly once the junior officer becomes a mate. To be an ordinary seaman becomes the lost land of childhood; to become a captain feels like climbing a glacier in gumboots.

Mates soon give up hope of ever becoming captains because their own superiors lose no opportunity of assuring them that, if they carry on in this fashion, they will be a hundred before promotion comes their way. To hear a father talk about his sixteen-year-old son is to hear a captain about his mate: lazy, stupid, unclean, sulky, without interest or sense of duty, as deaf as a mole and as blind as a bat.

Yet I should like to see the ship that sails itself, without a mate shivering and grumbling on the bridge. There is only one hope for heavenly justice as far as the mate is concerned: that the second mate may break a leg and the captain be forced to take over his watch. It is as good as an adolescent's night at the opera when the prima donna loses her bloomers in the high C. I don't know why captains are so often unlucky when taking over a watch in an emergency; perhaps it is a proof of the power of prayer.

But this situation is as rare as a white whale. In the ordinary run of things, the mate does everything. He is the ship's housewife, psychoanalyst, handyman, house painter, plumber, vermin expert, and removal man. If rust shows its bubbles underneath the paint, it is the mate's fault. If the cargo starts to work after a fortnight of gales in the Atlantic, the mate has done it. If the crew is rebellious, the cook sulking, the bridge slippery, and the captain's grog cold, the mate is told he will be a pensioner before he is promoted. On board bigger ships, the mate eats with the second-class passengers and it is hard to describe what this does to a man who has five thousand other things to look after. For whoever is unable to evince a fascinated interest in Mr. Proudfoot's operation during the sweetbreads, and at the same time work out in his mind what error Snark the apprentice can have made in his calculations to put the ship back eighty miles on the chart, will provoke a sour little mouth in the owner's drawing-room when the captain is asked what he thinks of his assistant over a glass of sherry.

There is a poem running into sixteen couplets that describes the fate of a mate, but it is unprintable. The young sailor will soon come to know it by heart, and cherish it until the day he lays his hand on the engine-room telegraph for the first time, three centuries from now.

Engineers

They are the happiest addition to the ship's staff since the advent of steam. The officers of the glorious age of sail may never have felt there was something lacking; who sails on a windjammer now, after having traveled on steam, misses not the engine, but the engineers.

Engineers have one idiosyncrasy: they think about everything in terms of engines. They know the ship is sailed by the deck-officers and that sailors and a captain are necessary, but they consider them as people who profit by the engines. The ship's fate is in their hands.

Engineers are calm in times of gale, soothing in times of stress, and irksome only when the sea is dead calm and a tropical sun turns their dungeon into purgatory. The young sailor will soon be struck by the circumstance that whatever engineers are doing or talking about, they always listen to their engine. In the messroom the Chief, while regaling himself with untidy forkfuls of spaghetti, will hold forth about the advantage of having cabins painted in psychological colors. In the middle of the conversation, with his fork halfway to his mouth, the Chief will freeze. Should anyone ask what is the matter, he will reply, "Sh!" The others will strain their ears, and hear nothing. Motionless silence will reign for seconds, during which the spaghetti dangling from the Chief's fork swings slightly with the swell.

Then the Chief will say, "Damn it! That young ass hasn't tightened the nut on the bilge-pump yet." After that he will continue eating, but the subject of his monologue will have changed from psychological colors to modern apprentices.

Engineers have one supreme quality: patience. It is caused by their secret preoccupation with engines, which makes all other problems seem secondary; also by the professional perseverance of the man who is often called upon to lie on his back in an oil-bath, fiddling with a spanner the size of a toothpick, while a piston strong enough to crush a rock hisses up and down, a quarter of an inch away from his nose. The inner peace they radiate, which goes with a well-oiled and smoothly-running soul, reflects the perfection of their engines. I know of no better cure for inner turmoil, worry, and general nervousness than a visit to the engineroom. There they are, in their greasy overalls, their caps on the backs of their heads, wads of cotton waste protruding from their pockets. On the wall are their tools, neatly lined up according to size; on the workbench some object is clamped in a vise, and with it they are quietly pottering. The colossal racket of their engine makes conversation impossible, so each man thinks, while his eyes rove around his, to him, completely comprehensible universe. To sit down on a three-legged stool, to look at this vast complicated mystery of whizzing, ticking, spinning, and sliding parts, all of them polished like watches, is soothing. For here you are, facing the riddle of your existence and, next to you, stands another man with his back to it, filing away at the workbench, secure in the knowledge that he understands everything.

What a boon it was that with the mechanical monster that mauled the Flying Cloud came so charming and patient a kornak. To those who can't speak whatever language it is, the words means: the boy who rides the elephant.

Cooks

It is impossible to talk about ships, crews, cargoes, foreign parts, or the mystery of the weather without bringing in cooks.

This being a personal record, I am aware of the fact that I have come across many cooks who were almost identical. It is possible that another sailor will have come across quite a different type of cook, but if he gives the subject some thought, he will come to the conclusion that almost all the cooks he has known were practically identical too. This has led me to believe that cooks are like sunsets. Every man has a mood associated with him that changes little during his lifetime.

As in the case of sunsets, I know people who are depressed by cooks and judge them to be the most unpleasant members of the crew. Other people have the same kind of allergy toward wireless operators. Personally, I find cooks delightful, fascinating, and very tricky to get on with.

One could call them the mothers of the ship or the housewives; whatever allegory one hits upon, the feminine element will be dominant. It isn't only the messing around with pots and pans, the talking about menus while tossing back imaginary curls, it is the gossip and the superstition that give every sea cook this touch of femininity. After some time, the young sailor may even come to the conclusion that his cook is a pansy. This is rarely the case. It is just that the job has left its indelible imprint on the man.

No cook can identify himself wholeheartedly with his function without turning at least partially into a squaw. The complaint, familiar to every captain, of the cook the day before leaving, "What on earth am I going to give them to eat this trip?" was heard frequently in our nomad past when whole villages were forever on the move and womankind was harassed by menus that only varied with the seasons. In the North, pea soup and cottage pie are the staple diet on board ship; in the tropics it is nassigoreng, a rice dish with a fried egg on top. By the time the eggs go bad, they are replaced by fancies like stewed onions or canned peaches which the cook has hit upon because of their resemblance to fried eggs. As sea cooks' cooking is visual, each complaint will be met with the question, "What's the matter with it? It looks all right, doesn't it?"

To celebrate the captain's birthday, cooks beat an egg white and crown the day's dish with a wisp of white meringue, suitable or not. The same thing happens when any of the officers becomes a father.

Until he is a captain, the young sailor need not worry about the cook. All he need worry about is to be on good terms with him. To achieve this, there is only one advice I can give: treat him as if he were a beautiful rich young widow.

Bosuns

The bosun is the petty officer in charge of the foc'sle and his personality determines the mood of the seamen. If the bosun is happy in his job, there is a fair chance that the seamen will be too. If he is not, there is sure to be trouble during the trip. Life in the foc'sle is like life anywhere: either enjoyed or borne like a cross. A narrow bunk on board an old-fashioned ship can be either wonderfully snug or a coffin with one side missing—it depends on the mood of the man who lies in it. And that man's mood depends on the bosun's.

Bosuns who are aiming for the bridge are fairly rare. Their job needs such experience, weight of authority, and knowledge of human nature that to become a bosun is enough for one man's life. Whenever a bosun is out to make the grade and studies in his free hours for his examination as a deck officer, the foc'sle will be unhappy, for it upsets his superiority, not toward them but toward the bridge. A bosun who is eager to learn from his captain, instead of thinking that it should be the other way round, is no good at his job. The best bosuns are firmly and sincerely convinced that the ship would sink like a stone but for their benevolent vigilance over the fox-hunters on the bridge. In moments of stress or on entering a harbor, the bosun holds the wheel and he holds it like an old mechanic trying out a fussy customer's car. The bosun is the one man who really knows how to handle the ship, and if he comes across a captain who will handle her as well as he does, he will not be impressed but saddened. He'll mutter, "A body can want to know too much," and ask for transfer at the end of the trip.

The young sailor, if he comes across the right kind of bosun, should watch him carefully and listen to what he has to say. All the solid, relaxed craftmanship of sailing a ship is there under his very eyes, unassuming and given to big hairy yawns. A bosun who yawns a lot is all right; one who, while holding the wheel, breaks wind, shakes his head, and says, "God, I'm over-weight," is even better. The bosun a captain needs always knows where everything is, buys penny notebooks to write the captain's orders in but never has a pencil, smiles when the foc'sle roars with laughter, is feared but loved unreasonably by the ship's dog, and writes a letter to his wife or his mother every week consisting of "Dear Ma," followed by an extract from the log and the meteorological bulletin, signed, "Your affectionate son, Herbert" or "Dad." There is usually, after long scratching of the scalp with the pen, futile cleaning of nails and chewing of matches, a P.S. that runs, "Don't worry" or "Chin up."

A good bosun is as important to a ship as a good captain, if not more so. For the captain is the mind of the ship, and it is commonly known that the mind is a feeble thing of fairly recent date. Bosuns will give advice on anything, if asked or forced by circumstances. Their advice, which comes out after an impressive prelude of chin-rubbing and nose-pulling, usually runs, "Sleep on it," if the problem is personal, and "I'll show you," if it is practical.

If a captain asks a bosun for advice, the answer will start with the phrase: "It's not my place to tell you." The captain can ask for advice without prejudicing his authority as skipper next to God, for the bosun has known all the time that he is a bungler, whatever God may think of him. He will respect the Old Man for making a clean breast of it.

Bosuns traditionally leave sinking ships together with the captains but, in contrast with the latter, they rarely drown. Owing to their intimate knowledge of the order in the chaos of the ship's insides they always get hold of something suitable that will float. The young sailor will probably come across the story of the bosun who, while treading water after a shipwreck, was invited to climb into an already overcrowded lifeboat and answered, "No thank you. I'll wait for the doghouse to come up." He was the only one washed ashore alive.

If there is a life hereafter remotely like ship life, be it heaven or hell, I hope I'll be met at the gangway by a bosun.

Cabin Boys

The smaller the ship, the smaller the urchin. Cargoes that run into thousands of tons have messroom boys, coasters have boys, and everything from a trawler down has a little child who picks his nose, touches his lips with the result, wipes it on the seat of his pants, puts his dirty thumb in the soup tureen, washes up by wiping, sings lurid songs in a choirboy's voice, and occasionally has his scalp inspected by the Captain, after which a liquid called Macnamara's Hunting Water, for sale in harbor drug stores, is applied.

The young sailor will not come across a cabin boy unless he starts as the mate of a fishing smack or a pint-sized coaster owned by its captain. Once cleaned, combed, and taught to leave their noses alone, cabin boys are fascinating. Their one worry is to seem grown-up. They will smoke, smell of gin, whistle from the foredeck at the sight of a woman, swear until smacked, and do anything for a pair of long trousers. They give it all away, however, when they are asleep, for then they look about three years old.

Cabin boys, contrary to what anxious mothers and scoutmasters might assume, run no risk of being perverted in the foc'sle. The presence of a child turns any crew into a Fathers' Union. Men who can hardly write themselves insist on dictating clumsy nonsense to the child to keep up on his education, and quarrels break out among the tutors over a matter of spelling, which make the pupil flee to his bunk. Every week they are stood, stark-naked, in a bucket on the foc'sle table, where they look much thinner than one had assumed, and are scrubbed until they wince.

They are taken to see the sights in foreign harbors, and when their elders go to a bordello, they take the cabin boy with them, to wait for their return in the downstairs parlor, under the care of the fattest of the ladies, dressed like a circus horse, who feeds him pralines and encourages him to talk about his travels. They are taken to bazaars where they are told to pick a present for their mothers, and if they have no mother, for their aunt, and if they have no aunt, for the person that surely must exist somewhere worthy of a filial token of fondness and esteem. Difference of opinion about the suitability of the present may cause the crew to go and look elsewhere under pressure from the manager. Somehow, the quest for the cabin boy's present always ends up with a red glass vase.

The luckiest cabin boys are those who have run away to sea and stowed away on board a small freighter. The captain will telephone the owners at his next port of call; the owners will telephone the parents; the father, angry with relief, will say to the captain, "Keep him on board, sir, I'll pay anything you ask if you can see to it that he will never want to see the sea again when he comes home."

The owner instructs the captain to lead the boy the hard life; the captain will pass the order on to his officers and wash his hands of the matter; the officers will look stern; the foc'sle will rise as one man behind the persecuted infant, and the fortunate cabin boy will find himself surrounded and protected by eleven uncles. Whether he later goes back to sea or not, one thing he will never doubt as long as lives, and that is the essential goodness of man. I know what I am talking about, for it happened to me.

THE POLAR PATH: Where Every Direction Is South *

Wolfgang Langewiesche

Short-cutting across the top of the world is the coming thing in flying. From Tokyo to Europe, from London to New Zealand and Australia, from Paris to Tahiti, from Japan to Brazil—the short way is via the North Pole! Try it with a piece of string on a globe: New York to Shanghai, the United States to India, Moscow to Detroit. The polar route is the shortest route.

It has always been true, but now it is getting real. To the Scandinavian Airlines System goes the credit for breaking the polar barrier. In 1954 they opened their first short-cut route from California to Europe via Greenland; cutting 412 miles off the New York route, and taking nineteen hours. In February 1957, they will open the Japan-Norway route, making one stop in Alaska, and taking from eighteen to twenty hours. The present track from Stockholm to Tokyo (through Asia) requires fifty hours.

Last April, SAS had a crew-training flight going over the polar Stockholm-Tokyo route, and I went along to see how it is done. The air plane was a DC-6, although they will use DC-7s when the line is in operation. It had everything that makes you disregard the country you fly over: four engines, pressurized, muffled cabin, Pullman berths. The Arctic, I thought, will be merely a place where the earth is painted white instead of green or blue. Why go? Why not just read SAS's Polar Navigation Manual?

But your respect for the mysterious region grows as you approach it. We hit the Aleutians at dawn, coming from Tokyo through an afternoon and a night that were shortened, by our eastward-north-

* From *Harper's Magazine,* November, 1956. Reprinted by permission of the author, *Harper's Magazine,* and the *Readers Digest.*

ward motion, into a mere ten hours. In Tokyo, the cherry blossoms had been blooming furiously, and the population had been in the parks, looking at them. Here now a lone volcano stuck up above the clouds, coughing up an occasional puff of black smoke in a performance watched by nobody. It makes a strange, profound difference when you are the only one who sees a thing. This effect started here —this feeling of "Where *is* everybody?"

We came down on a long approach across black lava rock and white frozen bay and some gale-whipped water and landed at Cold Bay in the Aleutians: it was just an airport, no customs, no immigration—in fact no town. When you stepped out of the airplane the wind felt like a blast from an icehouse, which is of course what the Arctic is. Cold Bay is a former military base, once quite a town. You could still see the system of hard-surfaced roads, but where the buildings had been there was now a pool of water, frozen this time of year into a block of blue-green ice. Everybody had gone away, and left a perfectly good town. The refueling crew came out, heavily packed in clothes. If you lived here, you would be thinking all the time a little about keeping warm. We paced back and forth, some of us jumped up and down.

We flew on into Alaska, to "shoot" landings at the various airports which the pilots would have to know well on later commercial flights. Alaska has, of course, everything and you see it. It has several tall buildings, and parking lots crowded with gay-colored cars, a railroad, a highway, a university—even some farms. But from the air you see it the other way round—what vast empty spaces there are in between things, nothing but wilderness.

Late in the afternoon, we took off from Fairbanks and headed north. There were twenty-one of us aboard, including five captains, two crews, two hostesses, a Japanese official, a Norwegian newsreel team, and me. Weather clear, and predicted to be clear all the way. Our flight plan called for fifteen and one half hours to Bodö, Norway.

We crossed the Arctic Circle while still climbing; it's just a line on the map. The real beginning of the Arctic is the northern limit of trees. I was watching for it, expecting a gradual fading out. But in Alaska it comes differently. North of the Yukon River, the country rises into a mountain range—the Brooks Range, 10,000 feet high, steep, alpine. Naturally the trees stay below, and all is ice and snow and rock. The country falls again, but the trees don't come back. You're in the Arctic. You're over a snowy plain, grassy in summer. Last sign of man: a military airport, Barter Island, a snow-plowed runway, some army-type buildings, and on the snow a track made on the surface by some vehicle that runs on caterpillar treads, tank-like. The men were indoors and didn't show as we went over.

Right there, the country changed. It became unnaturally flat, and at the same time rough in texture—a "crackle-finish" you would have called that sort of surface in a hardware store. It wasn't country any more: it was the Arctic Ocean, covered with ice. It's a real, full-size ocean. From here it is 2,750 miles to the opposite shore—the North Cape of Norway, the Finnish Coast, the Murmansk region of Russia. Right in the middle, off somewhere on our left, under 14,150 feet of water, is the Pole. Visible was nothing but blue sky, brilliant sunshine, and the ice.

The Crackle Finish

It is a terrific part of the world to see. Until recently the only way to see it was to walk there, with dog sleds; and the chances were that you would die. Now from the air you could see the "country" on which the polar explorer had to move. In some ways it was good. The frozen sea is a sea, flat, every part like every other part. From the air, it looks as if he could travel straight courses, like a ship. And he had an almost wonderful surface to travel on; almost a skating pond. *But*—that crackle finish: the ice is all broken up into floes. Around each floe is a ridge—maybe five feet high, maybe twenty feet. Polar exploring must have been like having to drag a cart across a London suburb in a straight line: up one garden wall, down the other side, across a garden, up the next wall.

This is the surprising thing about the polar ice—that it is so full of commotion. You would think the ocean would freeze over once, and ever after it would be a dead plain. But no. It looks as if someone were going about with a sledge hammer, breaking up any piece of ice bigger than a couple of hundred feet across. Main breaking force: the ice freezes downward from the surface. New ice forms under the bottom of the old ice: it heaves the ice surface up and cracks it.

Then the wind pushes the pieces about. Fifty billion slight wind forces push on fifty billion ice roughnesses; then whole ice-countries start sliding. The floes bump against each other like heavy barges, slowly, but with enormous weight behind the motion. Where they touch, they crunch, and push up those ridges. Then they freeze together. Elsewhere, the ice field tears apart, and gaps like rivers open up. I saw some that must have been three hundred feet wide and, slightly winding, twenty miles long. In summer, these "leads" are open water. They would stop an explorer with his sled and his dogs. He had to wait till the gap closed again, or he had to ferry across, using ice floes as rafts. In winter, the leads freeze over, making new ice that is smooth and strong, fit to land on. But this runway doesn't last. Presently *it* cracks, breaks up, and the pieces grind against each other.

Into this chaos of slow-grinding millstones Fridtjof Nansen took his ship, the *Fram*, in 1893. For the first time now I understood that famous arctic adventure. Nansen knew that the ice moves in a steady, slow drift across the Arctic. By letting yourself be frozen in the ice at the right spot, you might be carried right across the Pole—if your ship wasn't crushed. The *Fram*, specially built, stood the pressure and got farther north than anyone ever had. Now the *Fram* is in Oslo, with a museum built over her—a sacred thing, like our Liberty Bell.

Then there was Salomon Andrée, the Swede, who tried the air. This was in 1897, before airplanes, and before the dirigible was at all practical. Andrée thought he could control flight direction to some extent, by putting sails on his balloon and trailing drag ropes behind him on the ice. The idea was correct. Andrée might have made a perfectly astounding aerial voyage. Before take-off, his drag ropes had been coiled up on the ground, sailor-fashion. When the balloon rose, the ropes, in uncoiling, twisted themselves off the balloon and fell back to the ground. It was the kind of evil joke—almost ridiculous and often deadly—that still happens almost every time somebody tries something new in the air. That's why there are test flights. That's why a route like SAS is flown dozens of times, at all seasons and under all sorts of conditions, before it is declared open. Even so, Andrée and his partners flew sixty-five hours and made several hundred miles northward. And they walked back, reached Spitzbergen, built a winter camp, lived several months. Then they died. And now it is just an airline ride, complete with hostesses, and no adventure at all.

What is so special about transpolar air routes? It's not the weather. Ours was perfect—a ski holiday in the Swiss Alps. True, April is the best month of the year; the sun is up but the ice still keeps the ocean sealed tight, so there is very little moisture in the air, hence little cloud. Later on, there are more open leads, and hence more cloud. But for the pilot of a high-flying pressurized airplane, the arctic weather is quite okay at any season. There are no thunderstorms. At 20,000 feet you can be on top of all cloud, all turbulence, all wing-icing. There may be icing fog below, but you fly in clear air with sun or stars available for "shooting": while in the tropics at 40,000 feet you may have to pick your way between thunderstorms or through them. As for the cold, it is a problem mostly on the ground. It makes mechanic's work a torture, and it makes engines hard to start. In flight, cold is a help: it makes jet engines more efficient!

The Crazy Compass

The special thing about the Pole is this: it's hard to find your way. The compass goes crazy near the Pole, and the mind, too, suffers a strange kind of dizzy spell. As for the compass, it is a dislikable instrument anywhere: the slightest turn or bump of the airplane makes it swing so that it's hard to get a good reading. It doesn't really point at the North Pole but at the Magnetic Pole, a place in Northern Canada, a thousand miles away from the true Pole, and it doesn't even do that reliably, but has an error in its error! All this gets worse as you go north. There are places in the Arctic where the compass says South when it means North. And when you get within a thousand miles or so of the Magnetic Pole, the compass thinks it is already there, and quits pointing altogether. It turns aimlessly round and round, or it points at the nearest chunk of iron—the airplane's engine. On one SAS survey flight, they had four different compasses point in four different directions.

And the pilot's brain goes dizzy. His whole way of thinking about direction—North, East, South, West—becomes less and less useful as you go north, and finally meaningless. At the Pole itself, *there is no North*. You've gone as far north as there is. East and West don't exist either—at the North Pole, *every* direction is South. And time goes crazy. At the North Pole the sun rises only once a year, on March 21, and goes round and round the sky till September 21. Because every direction is South, the sun is always in the South, and it is always noon! It's also any other time anybody claims it is. All the world's time zones come together at the Pole, so it's your choice.

Suppose now you fly directly across the North Pole. Then at the instant of crossing the Pole, your flight direction changes from North to South; a west wind, at the same moment becomes an east wind; your time jumps twelve hours. All this is not "real": the airplane has not curved, the wind has not shifted, the sun has not jumped. But it's mighty real for the navigator. It turns all his bookkeeping upside down. His pluses become minuses. Confusion has been the biggest source of accidents in arctic flying. The navigator adds an item he should have subtracted; the airplane flies off in the wrong direction and runs out of fuel somewhere over the ice.

If you don't fly directly over the Pole but past it, as we did, all this gets even more confusing. The work load on the navigator becomes fantastic. In military polar flying right after the war, before a way around all this was discovered, it took two navigators to keep track of an airplane. You are flying straight; but the directions wheel around you in a silly way as if you were flying a curve; North moves from almost on your nose over to your wing-tip and then to your tail. On the other side of the airplane, South comes forward from the tail to the nose. Time races; half an hour after nine o'clock, it's 10:30. Time may race backwards! Half an hour after nine o'clock, it may be 8:30. The sun and stars move backward through the sky.

All this we saw . . . we lost track of time first. Our watches were on Greenwich time—the international navigator's time. Our stomachs were still on Tokyo time. But our time sense had been reset at Fairbanks, where at our takeoff it had been, locally, late afternoon, with the sun low in the West. Which time was real? To me, Tokyo time was. I kept wondering when the hostess would come around with the dinner. Meanwhile, the sun was acting wrong. It was off our left wing-tip, slowly going down until it just touched the horizon. There now it stopped. For an hour or so, it sort of rolled along with us, holding position on our left wing-tip. And then it rose! This was the magic moment of the flight. For where the sun rises, that's East; and *when* it rises, that's morning. So, during dinner (steak with peas), West had snapped over into East. Evening had become morning.

There would be no night. Our course was now no longer North—it was now South.

I went forward to the cockpit. All was calm, all the needles steady. The pilots just sat there, quietly alert; the airplane, on auto-pilot, snoring straight ahead. In the navigator's compartment Einar Pedersen, SAS's specialist on polar navigation, was checking out another navigator on polar methods. How do they do it? It turns out that the whole difficulty of polar flying, instead of being a cosmic necessity, having to do with sun and stars on their eternal courses, is strictly man-made. All you have to do is think a little differently, and the whole difficulty disappears.

To keep their thinking straight near the North Pole, navigators don't make some Einsteinian mental effort: they simply don't *have* a Pole. It's, after all, only in the mind or on paper. In reality, it's just a point like any other point on a vast flat ice desert. So instead of drawing (in their minds and on the map) the usual lines of latitude and longitude that all come together in that one whirlpool of confusion, they draw a new pattern. SAS uses a standard American flying map of the polar region, but overprints it with a Polar Grid. This leaves the Arctic covered with lines that are as straight and square as the street plan of an American city.

The main avenue of this Polar Grid is the line that goes from London across the (now abolished) North Pole to the Aleutians and on down the South Pacific. The other lines run parallel to it. You call North, *Grid* North—the direction from Europe to the Pacific—and you call it North even after you've passed the (former) North Pole and are flying down toward the Pacific, *i.e.* in ordinary parlance South. With North thus fixed, Grid South, East, and West fall in place—and *stay* in place. Taking off at Fairbanks, we headed by ordinary reckoning North by East. By Polar Grid directions, we headed Grid South by East and we kept the same grid direction all the way across; the same numbers on our direction indicator, the same numbers in our calculations. No fancy, phony curving of the flight path. No switch-over when passing the Pole: No Pole!

How the Gyro Remembers

The navigators' answer to the compass problem is just as radical: don't use a compass. Polar flying is done by *memory*: an artificial

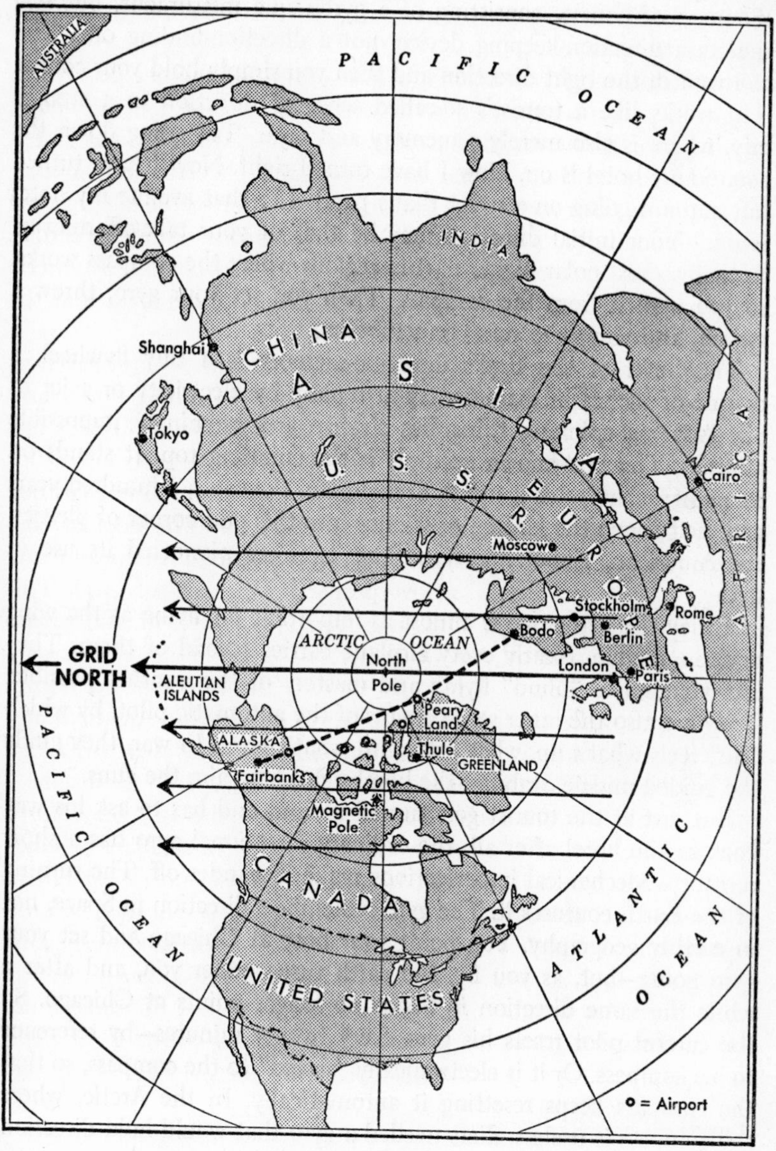
AUSTRALIA
PACIFIC OCEAN
INDIA
CHINA
ASIA
Shanghai
Tokyo
U. S. S. R.
EUROPE
AFRICA
Cairo
Moscow
Stockholm
Rome
Bodo
Berlin
London
Paris
ARCTIC OCEAN
North Pole
GRID NORTH
ALEUTIAN ISLANDS
Peary Land
ALASKA
Thule
GREENLAND
Fairbanks
Magnetic Pole
PACIFIC OCEAN
CANADA
UNITED STATES
ATLANTIC OCEAN
o = Airport

memory, of course, consisting of a gyroscopic instrument, but still merely a direction-keeping device, not a direction-finding one. You start out in the right direction and then you simply hold your course.

It works like a tourist's so-called sense of direction in a strange city, which is also merely a memory and says: "I'm going down the avenue my hotel is on. Now I have turned right. Now I have turned left and am going on a street that's parallel to that avenue my hotel is on." Your initial direction may be that of your take-off runway. Actually, most polar flights start in regions where the compass works, so you take it from the compass. Then you set your gyro, throw a switch, and your gyro starts remembering.

The heart of the gyro's direction-memory is a tiny flywheel, a couple of inches in diameter, spun rapidly by electricity or a jet of air. Any fast-spinning thing has strange and seemingly impossible abilities. The best-known example is the spinning top. It stands on its point: what holds it up? A Frenchman, Foucault, a hundred years ago, first shone the lantern of science into this odd corner of physics. An American, Elmer Sperry, in the 'twenties pioneered its use in flying.

Today the gyroscope is almost as important for flying as the wing and the engine. Nearly every airplane carries several of them. They are what make "blind" flying and mastery of the weather possible. They are also the inner sense organs of the automatic pilot, by which "he" feels what's up, what's straight, what's level. In war, they guide the guided missile, stabilize the bombsight, help aim the guns.

But just as the tourist gets turned around and has to ask his way back to the hotel after all, the ordinary directional gyro has a short memory. Mechanical imperfections make it wander off. The turning of the Earth confuses it. The gyro remembers direction in Space, not in earthly geography. You point your nose at Chicago and set your gyro going—but, as you fly, the earth turns under you, and after a while the same direction in Space no longer points at Chicago. So the careful pilot resets his gyro every twenty minutes—by reference to his compass. Or it is electronically "slaved" to the compass, so that the compass keeps resetting it automatically. In the Arctic, where the compass is useless, fliers needed a gyro that would hold direction not for twenty minutes, but for twenty hours.

When SAS tried to have such a super gyro built, an American firm of instrument-makers took on the job and did it. The Polar Path Gyro is a solid-gold Cadillac of an instrument. Its little flywheel, made of a rare expensive very heavy tungsten, spins fifteen times as fast as an airplane propeller. Its bearings are the most delicate that today's mechanical art can produce. The makers added an electric clock that keeps cranking in small corrections for the earth's rotation; the navigator sets the rate according to the latitude at which he is flying. Result: a directional gyro that remembers straight, not for twenty minutes, but for twenty hours. Price: about the same as a Cadillac.

We carried two (one as a stand-by) mounted above the navigator's desk—just a little black box, slightly warm, slightly buzzing to the touch. A wire from it led to the pilot's direction-indicator in the cockpit. Another wire went to the auto-pilot, which was flying the airplane straight, straight, straight across the ice-flats.

That's the whole secret of polar flying—a mental scheme of directions, and an instrument for holding direction. On top of that, there is of course an overlay of techniques and hard work. The navigator keeps "shooting" the sun, checking the gyros against the sun and against each other; he measures drift and observes the barometric pressure and calculates the winds and takes radio bearings and generally cross-checks everything against everything—but that's just airline perfectionism. Actually a Polar Path Gyro and a map with the grid on it would take you there.

Who Owns the Arctic?

Now the Arctic has become a busy place, even though you don't see anybody else flying around. The U.S. Air Force has for years run a daily weather flight almost to the Pole. The Russians have had a whole series of camps on the ice. They were the pioneers well before the war, in the difficult operation of setting up and supplying a camp by air. Now, polar gossip is that they are supplying some camps by submarine, under the ice. Our weather map which was given us at Fairbanks, showed one, and only one, ground station reporting weather from the Arctic Ocean area itself. This was the Russian camp, Nordpol 5. It was located almost at the Pole, just a little over on the Russian side. Its reports were evidently available at Fairbanks.

Even commercial flying is already a fact. On a charter basis—when somebody hires the whole plane—SAS has flown quite a bit of pay load over, or hard past, the Pole: two hospital staffs of doctors and nurses for the Korean war; a DC-6 full of Scandinavian business big-shots, with ladies, to a world Chamber of Commerce meeting in Tokyo; an airplane load of Japanese cameras to Europe; the Vienna Symphony Orchestra to and from concerts in Japan, trumpets, fiddles, and all.

SAS had lined up six plane-loads of German and Scandinavian Olympic athletes to go to Australia via the Pole. Even that is a short cut. It's not only shorter, but more pleasant than the southern route through the Middle East and Asia: no visas, no cholera and yellow fever shots, no hostile officials. By now, on that southern route, no matter what a passenger's race, religion, nationality may be, somebody in some country is hoping for some legitimate occasion to give him a hard time.

Who owns the Arctic? The question is tactless. Our Canadian government maps showed as Canadian everything north of Canadian land—all the way to the Pole. Our U. S. government maps showed no such Canadian sector and claimed no American sector for the United States north of Alaska. The Russians don't say. Nobody wants a hassle over this question just now, especially because the world's ideas of "high seas" are changing anyway. The classic idea was that a country's sovereignty used to reach three miles out to sea, or maybe seven, or maybe twenty. Everything beyond that used to be high seas, international water. Now, for air-traffic control and air-defense zones, countries reach hundreds of miles out to sea.

And in the Arctic, there's an extra complication: the Ice Islands. These are not the usual floes of sea ice; they are pieces broken off from glaciers in northern Canada—huge icebergs, really. They are much bigger and taller than the sea ice; therefore they resist the crush and stay big. Estimated life: a couple of centuries. It therefore pays to equip them—with airports, houses, radio stations, weather observatories, maybe radar, they may become floating towns. The Americans are known to occupy at least three named T1, T2, T3; the Russians, at least one—Nordpol 6. They move with winds and currents. Where are they now? Nobody's talking.

In the new air geography, Russia is a large block of *nyet*. Other nations let foreign airlines cross their territory, even if perhaps without the traffic rights to pick up and discharge passengers. Russia doesn't. As owner of the Arctic shore almost half around the world, she blocks many possible polar routes. At the same time, as owner of most of Asia, she forces many airlines to detour far to the south. The present standard track from Europe to Japan goes, absurdly, through India! This is what makes SAS's polar route to Tokyo so attractive. Should Russia ever open herself up, that route would be meaningless; you'd fly through Siberia, and many other routes would immediately become possible.

In the air Arctic, Thule, the U. S. Air Force base on Greenland, is the Paris, the City of Light. Most of us think of Thule as the ultimate in northern outposts. It's not. It is one of the most northern points on earth that can be reliably supplied every summer by ship. It therefore has everything—huge runways, all sorts of radio to get you down in almost any weather, all sorts of supplies, all sorts of talent. You can even have your appendix out.

Thule itself is not open to civilian traffic. This is tough on the Scandinavians, who would love to use it as a refueling stop for both the California and the Japan route. But they carefully keep all resentment out of their voices when they mention it. But the mere fact that it's there makes a big difference, for the USAF keeps tabs on the arctic weather, and from here Search and Rescue would come after you if you were forced down on the polar ice. And in an emergency, of course, Thule is open. It may be used as an "alternate" in flight plans—as the place to run to if your intended landing place is closed by weather. Every airline flight requires an alternate airport, and its location affects the fuel load that has to be carried, hence the pay load that may be carried.

Beyond Thule, 400 miles or so farther north, there are now airports all along the northern edge of land. Their names are likely to get into the news: Mould Bay, Isachsen, Eureka, Alert—all RCAF fields on the northern-most Canadian islands—and Nord, Danish, on the north end of Greenland. These fields have radio beacons, so you can find them; men are stationed there, and could give you shelter and heat and food. You can even buy gas and oil there, 400 miles from the Pole! It costs $10 a gallon, because it is flown in from Thule. These fields line up into a polar air route, which is the old Northwest Passage. You feel their presence, and if you were the captain of a transpolar airliner, you would feel it even more, off on your right, only an hour's flight away.

Nine and one-half hours out of Fairbanks, we saw land. Big mountains—up to 7,000 feet. Here we saw something which was not ice or snow: rock. It was the north end of Greenland, Peary Land, Danish—the most northern land on earth. For the Scandinavians this scenery rang all sorts of bells. One captain seriously claimed this was the most beautiful sight on earth. From where we were, above the mountains, we had about the same view, only from higher up, that Peary must have had when he set out to walk to the Pole in 1909. It took him thirty-seven days.

Then all that fell behind, and we were once more over the ice, still four hours from Norway. Forward in the cockpit, still the same cool workmanship, but still no strain, and no elation either. These were veterans of the oceans and far continents, and for them "checking out" over the polar route did not mean proving they could do it. It was as if you or I were getting into a car with an unfamiliar gear shift—I see; that's how it works.

Still brilliant sun, ahead of us now, still in this white glistening desert. I admit if you have seen one ice floe you've seen 'em all—but I kept looking, and the longer you look at it, the more you see. Sometimes the ice looked as if it had laundry bluing in it. Sometimes there were pink regions. Newly frozen-over leads looked the color of concrete highways. Tricks of light, like the rainbow? Tricks of the eye? Painters have seen reds and blues in snow right along. Perhaps the eye up there, where all is white, is like the ear in a very quiet room: it becomes more sensitive, so you see colors only the painters saw before. Where a cloud shadow fell on the ice it looked like earth. Once I dozed off and in the confusion of waking up I thought it was still yesterday and I was looking at a low oriental coast chambered-off into innumerable rice fields.

One nap later we were in cloud. Down through holes in it you saw real liquid ocean, very dark. Then we came out again in the sunshine. The sun was now on our right. On our left stood big, bare mountains, glowing pink in the evening sunlight: the coast of Norway.

There are several airports in northern Norway. But one, Bodö, south of Narvik, is big. It belongs in your list of the world's stepping-stone airports, along with Goose and Gander, Kano, Idris, Entebbe, Shannon. On that last low sweep into the airport we passed low over some small houses—smoke from chimneys, laundry on line: people looked up as we looked down. We were back in the world where what you see is also seen by others. We gassed up here. The sun, which had shone for us for two days and a night, now set in a conventional and orderly fashion. A few hours later we were in Stockholm, where it was snowing. End of flight: passports, customs, hotel. We were sure enough in Europe. For days I could not shake the feeling that I had come in down the chimney, like Santa Claus. But that only shows I'm not a real air-age man. The North is everybody's front door now, and we might as well get used to the idea.

ASSIGNMENTS

I. Write a summary-type introduction for the analysis of one of these subjects:

1. A college organization—club, political clique, fraternity, honorary. (Write for new members.)
2. The workings of a mechanism used in the laboratory. (Write for those who are beginning a lab course.)
3. The way to take an essay-type examination. (Write for members of the course in which such examinations are given.)
4. How an unusual game is played or an unusual athletic feat is accomplished. (Write for those whose interest would not go beyond reading.)
5. The organization of a musical group—symphony or dance orchestra, jazz or marching band. (For listeners.)

II. For one of the subjects listed in assignment I, or for any other subject your instructor may suggest, make a short outline that suggests spatial, chronological, or logical arrangement. Try getting transitional words and phrases—*first, second, next, finally, under the cogs, behind the violins, when the cards have been re-shuffled, this is the last stage,* etc.—into the outline.

III. Write an exposition (400–700 words) of a mechanism, process, or organization. State purpose, readers, and medium.

CHAPTER 5

Analyzing a Problem

Answers to Problems

There are problems that daily test the resources of businessmen, politicians, and community leaders. There are still others that challenge the intellectual powers of historians, mathematicians, and scientists. Any problem worth attention demands constructive thinking. Actually it is only when we try to solve a problem that disturbs or interests us that we really begin to analyze, to think carefully and fully. Such a problem may have very practical importance to us: which course to elect, which job to take, which way to vote. Or it may concern our cultural interests: What is the meaning of *Hamlet*? How much does modern jazz contribute to American music?

How do we deal with the problems that concern us? Here is the common pattern:

1. We recognize a problem that needs answering. Juvenile Delinquency is increasing in Allport. Why? What can we do about it? Or school enrollments are twice what they were a few years ago. What should colleges do to prepare for the estimated increase in applications a few years hence? In this way, problems arise out of observations and reports that puzzle us.

2. We analyze the problem. First we must *state* it—the "perplexing question"—just as we mean to tackle it. Then we must define,

not only key terms but sometimes the complex question itself. And we must pull the problem apart into its various elements, find the issues or criteria we wish to apply, the subordinate questions we have to answer to reach a final judgment.

This chapter concentrates attention on this stage—the *analytical statement of a problem*—which is a necessary preparation for whatever constructive thinking you may do later.

3. We try to reach a satisfactory judgment. To do this we consider various hypotheses, possible answers or solutions. We find evidence that supports the hypotheses or raises doubts, always testing the reliability of the evidence. We apply our criteria and draw inferences or conclusions. We choose the best hypothesis—our final judgment—modified in the light of evidence and reason.

4. We defend our judgment.

The last three chapters in this book show how to reach satisfactory judgments and defend them effectively for readers. But everything we have discussed in previous chapters has uses in this process. In the first place, verified facts and reports of facts lead to recognition of problems:

> "Charlie Jones quit college the month before finals." (Why did he quit? What should he do now? Should the college take steps to help other students like Charlie?)
>
> "Last year 1,242 accidental deaths occurred in coal mines." (What were the causes? How can such accidents be reduced? What legislation should the government consider to make coal mining safer?)

Then, too, facts are the basis of the evidence we use to reach our conclusions: reported or observed cases, aggregates of facts that we call statistics, statements of experts and authorities. We need definitions of problems and of key terms related to them. We need classifications of hypotheses, issues or criteria, sources of evidence, and the people involved. We often need analysis of mechanisms, processes, and organizations either as important evidence in dealing with broad problems, or as essential information leading to judgments about such things. An evaluation of a new typewriter keyboard, for example, naturally ought to include explanations of the mechanism and changes in the process. All of these methods of exposition have useful roles to play when we discuss problems and support judgments.

Setting up the Problem

The way to approach a problem is with an open mind, suspending final judgments till evidence and reasons are appraised. This is not the approach of the propagandist who knows what he intends to advocate even before he finds the arguments he will use. All of his thinking is "intentional"; that is, it is a search for appeals, slogans, facts pointed one way, arguments to support his ready-made conclusions. Constructive thinking begins with questions, not answers. It considers all the relevant evidence, not just the kind that supports one side. It postpones final conclusions till the basis for them is clear.

Setting up a problem objectively so that all your readers can understand it, so that all sides are fairly represented, is one means of preventing premature conclusions of your own. Begin your thinking with questions. Assemble what you already know. Decide what you need to know. Then state the problem as fairly as humanly possible. From this you can later work out valid and reliable judgments that you can defend confidently and with a clear conscience.

How Limited a Problem?

Vague feelings that something is wrong or something might be better are not yet real problems; they develop into problems when you can express them as questions you want to answer. "This whole valley suffers from the destruction from the flood. Property loss amounted to ten million dollars." That is a condition. It is not in itself a problem—but it certainly suggests problems:

(A) What caused the flood?
(B) How can we rehabilitate the valley?
(C) What methods are best to prevent future floods?
(D) Is the Weir-Putnam Flood Control Bill a desirable means of helping the valley?
(E) Should Congress pass the Weir-Putnam Bill?

Which question will you choose for major attention? What you decide to call the "problem" is the one big question demanding immediate attention. There will be numerous subordinate questions, but what is the *main* problem? Look at the list of questions as the people of the valley might look at it:

Question (A) is important and interesting, but it is rather a matter for scientists than for people in the valley right now. It is not their main problem at the moment, though it will be a significant element in questions (C), (D), and (E).

Question (B) is of utmost importance right away. It is not related to other problems directly, however, and the people of the valley may want to dig into (C), (D), or (E) at the same time they give much of their attention to (B).

Question (C) leaves the way open for any number of answers. It is what we call an *unrestricted* question. Questions (D) and (E), on the other hand, are *restricted* questions that must be answered yes or no; they leave no opening for alternatives. Now if the Weir-Putnam Bill is the only one of its kind before Congress, people must make up their minds about it. They must take it or reject it. But if other bills with similar objectives are being considered, or if time is available for investigation of a problem like (C), then it seems wise to give consideration to numerous suggestions for preventing future floods.

You can see that some problems are limited by both subject and the wording itself. (C) is limited to causes. Both (D) and (E) are limited by wording to the single subject of the Weir-Putnam Bill.

The either-or, yes-no type of problem is less complicated, but usually it is a later development of the unrestricted problem that leaves the way open to consider all possible solutions. We may begin with "How can we reduce traffic hazards on Pearl Street?" After we have considered numerous suggestions, we find most of them undesirable or unworkable. We may finally arrive at the restricted problem: "Should we install a traffic light at the corner of Pearl and Main?"

Some problems can never intelligently be reduced to either-or alternatives, and others shouldn't be if we want satisfactory answers. "Is this a great book?" has less chance of being answered than "How great?" or better still "How good?" "Is our public school system the best in the world?" is a less profitable question than "How good is our public school system?"

What Kind of Judgment?

It's good to know what kind of judgment your stated problem requires. Knowing this will keep your thinking in relevant channels. Here are some possible kinds of judgments that may be called for:

1. *Question of Fact.* Of course a "fact is a fact," but many problems arise over exactly what *is* the fact. Thus:

Who fired the first shot?
Did Shakespeare write the plays ascribed to him?
Was Trotsky killed by Communist agents?
How fast was Nichols driving?

The only judgments needed to answer such problems may be decisions about the reliability of witnesses and the consistency of the evidence; but sometimes these tax the minds of experts.

Other questions of fact such as "What is the population of Turkey?" or "How many rooms are there in the Pentagon?" are not "problems" that concern us here. The answers come directly from records or observation, not from analytical thinking.

2. *Questions of Probability.* The answers to some problems come from reasoning that leads not to certainty, but to a high probability of truth:

Does smoking contribute to lung cancer?
Will the Republicans carry the city in November?
How much did the use of alcohol influence Poe's writing?

Such problems go beyond matters of fact; they call for judgments about causes and effects, the reliability of generalizations, and predictions of future events. But the questions ask nothing about values (Is smoking "bad"? Will Republican victory be "beneficial"? Was Poe "immoral"?), and they ask nothing about policy (*Should* we stop smoking? How *should* we vote in November? *Should* children read Poe?)

3. *Questions of Value.* Questions of value involve merits and defects, advantages and disadvantages, good and bad. Usually they are best expressed as unrestricted questions because very few things in life are all right or all wrong:

Which applicant for the job of office manager is most reliable?
How much are the "JayCees" worth to this community?
What are the comparative merits of this year's Fords, Chevrolets, and Plymouths?
How well does *Marjorie Morningstar* accomplish its purpose as a novel when compared to *Anna Karenina*?

4. *Questions of Policy*. Problems of policy concern change or action: What should we *do*? These are the most complex of all problems in the sense that they must rely upon subordinate questions of fact, of probability, and of value. Here are examples:

How should we act to reduce accidents in the plant?
Should the Governor pardon Ed Fulton?
How much life insurance should single men carry?
Should the college allow students to have cars on the campus?

Such problems depend on numerous subordinate questions of various types:

How many stay-home accidents occurred last year?
How reliable is the testimony against Ed Fulton?
How much will life insurance cost the average single man in his lifetime?
How many parking places will the college have to provide to accommodate students?

Thus problems of policy tend to be composite problems of fact, probability, and value.

Phrasing the Question

To express the problem you are considering exactly as you mean it, remember these guides:

1. Distinguish the restricted from the unrestricted problem. The restricted question can be answered yes or no. The unrestricted question—frequently introduced by *what? why? when? who? which? how much? how many?*—leaves the way open for numerous answers.

Unrestricted Question	*Restricted Question*
What, if anything, should we do to improve the water supply?	Should we vote Yes on the watei bond issue?
Which tractor will serve best for hill farms?	Is the Whipley Tractor the best for hill farms?

2. Distinguish clearly by appropriate wording the problem of fact, the problem of probability, the problem of value, and the problem of policy. Doing so is an important step toward getting the problem into focus for you and your reader.

Note that problems of fact are never questions about what will happen, what is desirable, or what should be done. They ask simply *what happened? when did it happen? what exists? where? who did it?* and the like.

Note that only problems of value contain such adjectives as *desirable, economical, efficient, ethical, loyal, convenient, fitting, beneficial, good.*

Note that problems of policy are usually identified by words like *should, shall,* or *ought*: "What should we do . . . ?" "Shall we buy . . . ?" "Who ought to join . . . ?"

3. State restricted problems so that those advocating new beliefs or new policies will answer yes:

a. Can rockets reach the moon? (Since the fact has not yet been established, the burden of proof belongs to those who say it is possible. They are the ones who must answer yes.)

b. Should Congress pass the Intorre-Luxton Bill? (Until the bill is passed, the burden of proof belongs to those who want it passed.)

4. Keep the phrasing impartial. Don't "beg the question":

a. Should Council repeal the *inequitable* wage tax? (If the tax is already admitted to be inequitable, what problem remains?)

b. Are *ineptly devised* examinations a true test of student ability? (If they are actually ineptly devised, no real problem remains.)

As you can see, the fallacy of begging the question consists of assuming the truth about something that needs to be proved.

Criteria for Judgments

After you have set up the problem by expressing it exactly, setting its limits and indicating the type of conclusion it calls for, the major task in analysis is to break it down into parts that can be examined separately. These parts must represent significant, even vital elements of the main problem. The idea is to ask further questions. Out of these we arrive at the issues, standards, and criteria to be applied. Let us see what these criteria might be for the different kinds of problems that have been discussed.

Questions of fact become problems when we lack information or doubt the reliability of our information. Useful criteria for evaluating any hypothesis of fact ("Poe was not in Baltimore on that date";

"About two hundred Arabs crossed the border at midnight") are these:

What records or testimony do we have?
How reliable are the witnesses or sources?
How consistent is the evidence? (Consistent with laws of nature? with other facts? with itself?)

More will be said about testing evidence in Chapter 7.

Questions of probability can be checked by various criteria. The reliability of a generalization we can judge by asking:

How large a sample has been taken?
Is the sample truly representative?

The probability of a causal relationship we can judge by asking:

Did A precede or accompany R (the "result")?
Was A a necessary antecedent to R—or was the connection merely a coincidence?

Chapter 6 considers criteria for testing the various kinds of reasoning that are important in reaching conclusions about nearly any problem.

Problems dealing with value suggest a great variety of criteria, depending on the subject. A classic formula for evaluating literature can be adapted to thousands of things:

1. What is the author trying to do?
2. How well has he done it?
3. Was it worth doing?

Question 1, of course, is not a criterion of value but a question of definition or purpose. Still it is a necessary introduction to the second and third questions, which are real criteria for evaluation. You can modify this list of questions to fit, for example, a machine:

1. What is the purpose of the machine?
2. How well does it fulfill its purpose?
3. Is the purpose worthwhile?

Actually these questions are too general to serve as sole criteria for any final evaluation, but they are excellent starting points that can be utilized in many situations. In reality, for every problem of value we should consider the standards peculiar to the subject, to the time and place, and to other controlling factors. "How well did Shakespeare satisfy the theatre audience of his day?" demands quite different criteria from those applied to the question "How well do Shakespeare's plays fit the theatre of today?" Value criteria may thus be historical (standards for the time in which a book, a ruler, an institution is to be measured); local, national, or world wide (standards for one place or many places); social (standards that interest one group especially); or personal (standards that suit some requirement or preference of your own).

Different problems do demand their own particular criteria for solution. We can learn something, though, from representative examples. Suppose you were faced with this problem: "Shall Delancey Stores grant $2000 credit to Jerome Wingham?" You would have to familiarize yourself with the three main criteria which apply in such situations:

1. Character. What is his record for meeting his obligations?
2. Capital. What are his net assets?
3. Capacity. What is his net income? his position? his potential for future employment and income? his total financial commitments at present?

Or suppose the problem was this: "What courses shall I choose as free electives?" You might list:

1. Liberal values. How will it influence my intellectual development? my acquaintance with new ideas?
2. Practical values. How much will it be worth in my profession? in the daily problems of the future?
3. Interest. How exciting or challenging will it be now? How well will I like it?

You can see that the issues for most problems of policy are *questions of value*. To decide whether we should do something, we want first to decide whether the action is desirable, helpful, ethical, or interesting. Beyond that we need to ask whether it is feasible or possible. Criteria of value are not all of equal weight; you must always decide which ones deserve most attention, and how much.

Note also that these criteria are usually best put as unrestricted questions: not "Is it durable?" but "*How* durable?"—not "*Is* it maneuverable?" but "*How* maneuverable?" The point is that we ought to leave ourselves free to make comparisons, to find things partly good rather than all good—in short, to judge things the way they are in a real world rather than in a utopia.

For problems of policy, authorities long ago suggested a list of "stock issues" that are applicable to many different specific questions. They frequently provide useful suggestions that you can change to suit the particular problem:

1. Is there a definite need for a change? (Is the present law, system, organization, mechanism, etc. seriously unsatisfactory?)
2. Is this proposal a desirable improvement? (Do the advantages, compared to what we now have, outweigh the disadvantages?)
3. Is this proposal feasible? (Can it be done?)
4. Is this proposal better than any alternative proposal?

These are general, and perhaps rather obvious, but they often do provide a framework for the more specific criteria of value that we need to apply to every potential answer to a problem of policy. Assume, for example, you want to analyze the problem "Should Congress reduce American appropriations for economic aid to foreign countries?" You might try the stock issues, with modifications, and list tests of value as subordinate issues:

1. Are present appropriations affecting us adversely?
   a. How do they affect our own economy?
   b. What is their effect on the countries we aid?
   c. What is their influence on American security?

2. Will a reduction in such aid prove desirable?
   a. How will it affect our own economy?
   b. How will it affect the countries we now aid?
   c. How will it affect American security?

Stock issues 3 and 4 appear to be inapplicable here. No question of feasibility seems pertinent: if it is desirable, no question of constitutionality or the like will interfere with the reduction. And no alternative seems pertinent either.

Finding the really important issues, you can see, is a necessary step in holding attention on things that count. It leads us to the kinds of evidence and reasoning we need.

Analyzing Problems for Readers

It is clear why we must understand a problem thoroughly before we can effectively try to reach judgments about it. It is equally clear why we frequently want to explain problems to others so that they will be able to think constructively about them. Analyzing a problem—to inform, to explain, not to advocate or persuade—is a common and important type of exposition.

The judge's charge to the jury is an interesting example. He defines legal terms, explains the proper criteria to apply to evaluating evidence, outlines the essential issues, and emphasizes the jury's responsibilities before it retires to deliberate. He doesn't tell the jurymen what verdict to reach; he helps them to think honestly and intelligently for themselves.

The chairman of an investigating committee often does a similar service. He states the problem demanding investigation, defines its scope, summarizes the information already available and the points about which everybody agrees, and outlines the questions the investigation ought to answer.

Editorials, magazine articles, and sometimes whole books are devoted to stating and analyzing significant problems.

Finally, of course, analyzing a problem is often the necessary introduction to an extensive defense of a judgment. Theses and dissertations require such introductions. So does the formal recommendation report of industry or government. So, for that matter, does the less ambitious "research" or library paper that you write as a student.

What goes into such an analysis of a problem for readers? Here is a list of possibilities; but this is not the outline of a paper. The order varies, and so does the emphasis on given elements:

1. *Significance of the Problem.* It is unfair to ask readers to give time to trivial problems, or those having little real interest in their lives. So the analysis ought to show why this problem is timely, important, interesting—and perhaps controversial. You generally should do this right away.

How can you do it effectively? Not just by saying, "This is a timely, important, and interesting problem." You don't really show importance by the word *important*, nor interestingness by the word *interesting*. If used at all, these are introductory, abstract words; they are promissory notes that must be paid off quickly with news of unusual events, striking quotations, concrete cases, or pertinent statistics.

2. *Definition of Key Terms*. To explain a problem concerning "parity prices" you may need to define *parity*. To analyze a problem regarding "Fair Employment Practices legislation," you may have to define the meaning of the whole term for readers who aren't familiar with this special use of common words. Sometimes, of course, the entire problem may hinge on the meaning of a term, at which time definition becomes not only essential but vital.

3. *Background History*. When was this law first passed? What court decisions relate to this problem? What changes, conflicts, developments have occurred that affect the present situation?

Whatever history you include ought to be strictly relevant to the main problem—and really useful. There is seldom need or time to go back to the Industrial Revolution, Roman highway building, or the Italian Renaissance. Recent developments are usually more to the point. Limitations of time and space, and your common sense, will determine how much history is worth including, and how far back it should go.

4. *Explanation of Alternatives*. Just what are the provisions of the proposed bill? How does it differ from existing laws? What system are we using now, and what changes in the system have been suggested?

If your readers are not fully informed of the various potential answers to the problem, your analysis should provide an adequate, objective explanation.

The analysis of a problem should by all means be impartial and unprejudiced. It does not answer the main question, but simply states it. If controversy exists, such an analysis ought to be satisfactory and useful to all sides. Whatever facts it introduces are not evidence pointing towards a judgment, but expository information needed to understand why there is a problem and what it involves.

Sometimes the best way to show the nature of a controversial question is to summarize conflicting arguments. A fairly balanced account of what opposing sides say, without critical comment, may highlight the major issues. This kind of summary is not easy to write. Each side must get its fair share of attention; the most important arguments, not the trivial ones, must be selected: no suggestion of the writer's own opinions ought to enter.

If you decide that such a summary of opposing arguments is desirable, be sure to label them for what they are—not *your* ideas but the opinions and arguments of partisans. You must introduce each case with appropriate identifying phrases: "Advocates of this measure say that . . . On the other hand, opponents point out that . . ." Of course, well-chosen quotations from opposing sides may be very useful.

5. *Common Ground.* The more matters about which everybody can agree, the less investigation and discussion will be needed. That is why it often pays to remind your readers of things already known, issues already settled, and points that are irrelevant in solving the problem. In other words, explaining common ground is a matter of telling your readers what is important to their understanding of the problem but not important any longer in arriving at a solution.

Let us say, for instance, that you are analyzing a proposal to increase pension payments for hosiery workers, and suppose all parties—workers and management—agree about these points:

> Workers ought to be guaranteed some pensions when they are too old to work.
>
> Size of pensions should be partly dependent upon the worker's years of service.
>
> Retirement should be compulsory and payments should begin at 65.
>
> The company ought to pay part of the cost; the worker also ought to pay part.

It may be helpful to reaffirm these points of agreement in your analysis, first to remind your readers of how much all sides have in common, and also to forestall useless discussion later. But be sure that what you call common ground really is common ground. It is a great disservice to call something settled that is not settled, and if any doubt exists about certain points at issue, then they deserve attention before men reach a final judgment.

It may be useful also to remind readers of common irrelevancies that might divert attention from the real issues. When the problem is arousing heated controversy and rival propagandists are calling each other "leftwingers" and "tools of vested interests" there is particular value in getting your readers back on the track. For example:

The public debate on this bill has become needlessly bitter and sometimes over-personal. After all, a reasonable tax measure is the ultimate objective. Name-calling and personal abuse, of which both sides have been guilty at times, must not distract public attention from the real merits or defects of the bill.

6. *Issues or Criteria.* The most important contribution you can make to your reader's understanding of a problem is to give him the questions he must answer to reach a satisfactory judgment. Sometimes, especially in formal reports, it is well to list these questions in outline form, even with symbols I, A, etc. for easy reference later. More informally, they may be presented something like this:

When the average worker weighs in the balance the comparative merits of an open shop, a closed shop, a union shop, or any variation of these, he may well ask himself: Which system is most likely to add to his income, shorten his hours, and improve his working conditions? Which will give him the most real security? And finally, which one best preserves his personal freedom and self-respect?

7. *Suggestions for Further Study.* The whole analysis of a problem is an introduction to further study, investigation, thinking, and finally judgments. You write to direct your readers towards the best answers. So one function of the analysis may be to suggest where readers can find evidence—a list of all kinds of potential sources. You may suggest surveys, books, observations, even experiments.

The analysis of a problem—stating it in an impartial, expository manner—may be an end in itself. But often it leads to the search for sound judgments, the subject of the next chapters.

READINGS

Selections 1, 2, and 3 are analytical statements of problems.

State the main problem in a sentence. Is it restricted or unrestricted? Is it a question of fact, probability, value, or policy?

Does the author state the problem fairly and impartially? Would all sides find it equally acceptable?

What kind of readers does the author apparently intend to reach?

Which of the elements suggested in this chapter as important in the analysis of a problem (showing its significance, defining terms, providing background history, analyzing alternatives, etc.) does the author include?

How are the issues presented? Are all the important ones included?

1

TV OPTION *

CHARLES MERCER

The general public apathy toward the current series of federal investigations of the television industry is a matter of some surprise.

Conversations with numerous viewers reveal that they understand little of what's going on—and many say they don't care. The fact is that in the long run no one will be more deeply affected by the investigations than individual television viewers.

The most important issue is the extent of control over programing exercised by the chief TV networks. Some say a small group of persons should not be able to decide what the country at large in general sees. Others maintain that the steadily rising standards of TV programs would be destroyed if the networks' wings were clipped.

There is one phrase which you, an individual viewer, would be wise to understand as the key to the situation. That is "option time."

When your local station joined a network it agreed that the network would have "first option" to show its programs over the station during fixed hours of the viewing day and evening. The remainder of the viewing hours are known as "local time," in which the station does its own programing—live shows or films.

Some opponents of the networks would cut or abolish option time. This would vest control of programing with the local station. In option time the network and the station share the revenue. But the station retains the full revenue in "local time" when it sells a program to a sponsor.

The situation has been sharpened recently by the release of huge

* From Mr. Mercer's syndicated column, *Television-Radio,* June 13, 1956. Copyright 1956 by the Associated Press. Reprinted by permission.

backlogs of old Hollywood motion picture films which can be sponsored by local advertisers. It's profitable to both the stations and the movie package firms. In the case of many local stations less option time doubtless would mean more Hollywood movies shown.

The networks say, on the other hand, that option time is the cornerstone on which TV programing as we now know it has been built. Under commercial TV many of the best programs on the air now are sponsored by advertisers who are guaranteed that a certain number of stations throughout the country will show the program.

Take away the guarantee, say the networks, and sponsors will be interested only in those types of programs which they believe would be "popular." The present balance of television programing—which finds a place for excellent dramas and documentaries, as well as big name comedians and popular quiz shows—will be thrown out.

There is great danger of there being some extreme result from the present controversy. There is danger of an "either-or" rather than a "both-and" conclusion. In television programing, as in everything else, a golden mean is possible. Certainly there are enough local stations to show the best in enlightened programing by the networks—and the best in locally sponsored films.

2

HOW BIG SHALL OUR COLLEGES BECOME?

The pressure to increase college enrollments is bound to get greater. Everybody knows that. The questions the colleges must answer are: How many more students shall we accept? If we do accept many more, how are we going to provide the facilities?

Last week the American Council on Education devoted many painful hours looking for solutions. The Council represents 1128 different groups and institutions of all levels—public, private, and parochial. Over six hundred representatives of American institutions of higher learning took an active part. Without exception these influential educators felt the coming pressures and knew that answers would be hard to find.

First come the "war babies" of the early 1940's. They are already close to the college gates. Then there's the birth rate: about 2.5 million during the depression years, more than four million now. Convention speakers emphasized the future academic headaches:

"Present college enrollment of two and a half million, future enrollment of at least five million—by 1970." And to meet the academic program of the future: "Within fifteen years we'll need at least 250,000 additional professors to keep standards at anywhere near the present level." Where are American colleges to get the room and the money? Where can they find a quarter of a million new professors?

This is no ordinary educational crisis. America has never seen its likes before. But the two opposing educational philosophies divide much as they have before. There are, to simplify the whole story rather unfairly, "two sides."

The first side says: "Limit enrollments—reasonably, of course. Accept a few more students than we have now, but use the new pressure to improve the quality of higher education in America. With double the number of applicants we are really in a position to select the best. In this way American colleges and universities can become the envy of the world. We can use this crisis to produce the greatest leaders in science, technology, and the humanities that the world has ever seen. All this is within financial and administrative reason."

The other side says: "America's great contribution has been the extension of democratic opportunity to the many. We must give higher education to a greater proportion of our people, not a smaller proportion. We need vastly more engineers, scientists, and generally educated citizens than we have now. Governments and business corporations must contribute vastly greater funds for higher education. We must find and train the faculties needed."

In general, those who take the first view belong to the privately endowed colleges and universities that have a long tradition of "high standards." Those who take the second position are generally in the land grant institutions, the state universities, and the city universities. The first group objects to any "watering down" of college standards. The second group objects to "intellectual snobbishness" that would deny opportunity to "all those who can profit by" a college education.

It seems that each institution of higher learning must make its own decisions. The questions to be answered are something like these:

1. Is our present enrollment level inadequate for future needs?
   a. How great is the demand of American society for college-trained men and women?

b. How many more students can meet the standards we consider proper?

2. Is expansion of enrollment desirable?

a. How will it affect admission standards?
b. How will it affect standards of instruction?
c. How will it affect social and economic conditions of students and the institution?

3. Is such expansion feasible?

a. How do we get necessary buildings and equipment for such expansion?
b. How do we get the necessary faculty?

Every college and university in America must in the next few years find its own answers to these questions. And no matter what the final answer, the pressures are bound to be uncomfortable. The institution that says "Let's preserve what we have—hold on" will find alumni and public pressing for more liberal admissions policies. The institution that says "Let's increase enrollments" will find untold financial and administrative difficulties in the way. It's safe to say that nobody will be altogether happy.

Nevertheless, now is the time for all kinds of Americans to make up their minds about what they expect from higher education in this country of ours. Do we want to beat Europe and the rest of the world in quality? Or do we want to carry the democratizing of higher education to a new high? And if we want to bring college education to more and more, how do we intend to pay for it?

3

PYFGCRL VS. QWERTYUIOP *

PETER T. WHITE

One of the touchiest experiments of our time is now going on in Washington. There, twelve typists picked from ten Federal agencies are banging away on a scientifically simplified typewriter keyboard

* From *The New York Times Magazine*, January 22, 1956. Reprinted by permission of the author.

that differs radically from the one on some 6,000,000 typewriters in the nation. Some weeks from now, these typists will be "raced" against twelve others using the old keyboard.

It's all being done in the hope of spacing out the taxpayers' money. The inventor of the simplified keyboard insists it can tremendously increase office efficiency and save millions of dollars all over the place. If the test bears out his claim, the Government may gradually adopt the simplified keyboard and industry might follow suit. Quite a few people, however, already suspect that what it would increase most is intra-office argument; the very thought of having to learn typing all over again is enough to make some white-collar workers see red.

Just what, you might ask, is wrong with the standard keyboard everybody uses now? Not much to get keyed up about, certainly, if you're content to hunt and peck with two fingers. But to the motion-study engineer, observing a touch typist's ten fingers fly, the standard keyboard is an affront indeed—a marvel of inefficiency.

The typical typist, he'd say, hits 46,000 letters every day—making her fingertips travel a total distance of twelve to twenty miles. Teach her the simplified keyboard, and she'll reach the same number of letters just as often, but in doing so her fingertips will travel only one mile.

If pressed for details, he'll explain that the standard keyboard requires far more flitting up and down from row to row than is necessary (only 32 per cent of the characters are typed on the "home row," where the typist rests eight fingers). It overloads the weaker fingers and the entire left hand (which must type 56 per cent of the characters). When these faults combine in the cases of 3,300 fairly common words, one of which is "federated," the left hand is forced into a flurry of up-and-down motion, while the right does nothing. Conversely, the right hand must do all the work on 500 words, one of which is "minimum"—a word Government typists are likely to meet often in its Federalese form, "minimize."

All these built-in disadvantages stem directly from the tinkering of Christopher Latham Sholes of Milwaukee. He was probably the fifty-second man to invent a typewriter, but undoubtedly the first to get a successful one on the market in 1873.

The first to try was Henry Mill, an English engineer who got a patent from Queen Anne in 1714, and nobody can say now exactly what his device was. After that, Austrians, Swiss, Frenchmen and an Italian designed typewriters of sorts. A Russian made one that looked like a permanent-wave machine. A New Yorker's model resembled a piano and had twenty-four white and fifteen black keys. A man in Baltimore made one about the size of a baby grand piano, with seventy-eight type bars in thirteen rows. All were ingenious machines, but writing on them was as slow as, or slower than, writing with a pen.

Sholes' machine had a rather sluggish action, too, because the type bars depended on gravity to fall back into place. They clashed and jammed. His first keyboard was laid out alphabetically, but then he moved the letters around to find a pattern which would make the type bars collide least. Finally, he wound up with the letters most frequently joined in words moved as far apart as possible. This is the standard keyboard today.

Sholes' arrangement did not bother the early professional typists, since they used only two fingers at first, and then four. But grumbling arose almost as soon as the touch system caught on, around 1888, after a speed contest in Cincinnati, where Louis Taub, a good four-finger man, was clobbered by F. E. McGurrin, a good ten-finger man. Since then scores of new patterns have been proposed and eighteen have been patented.

Some of the claims made by potential reformers have been hard to swallow, to be sure. The FarFaster keyboard of 1936, for example, featured a home row with two A's—one under the little finger of each hand, to be struck by the finger less busy or tired at the moment. This did not impress the experts. But they did praise a later idea to move the shift key and back spacer into the center of the keyboard, to be handled by the strongest fingers. In 1949 the Minimotion keyboard aroused admiration, too, because so many sentences could be written on its home row alone. (Inventor's sample: "THE SENATOR SITS ON HIS LEATHER SEAT IN THE NATIONAL INTEREST.")

This brings us to the "Simplified" keyboard now up for testing in the capital. It was developed by Prof. August Dvorak of The University of Washington in Seattle, a non-typist who had studied the standard keyboard's disadvantages with the aid of stopwatches, cameras, masses of sample copy and two grants from the Carnegie Foundation for the Advancement of Teaching.

Dvorak patented his keyboard in 1934, and during World War II—when he was a commander, stationed in Washington—the Navy tested it. The published results were sensational. Fourteen typists, after eighty hours of retraining each, averaged 74 per cent more work with a 68 per cent improvement in accuracy.

The Navy never got around to wide use of Dvorak's keyboard. "It's still the only one based on motion study and the mathematical

WHAT TYPISTS ARE SETTING

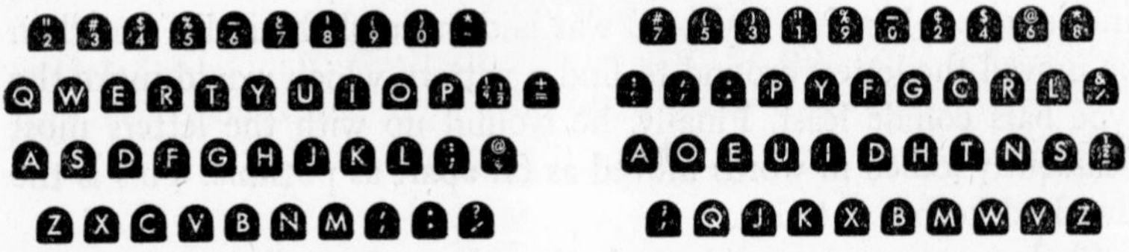

Standard key board, above, burdens the left hand

Key arrangement here is said to be more efficient

approach," he says now. "But I wasn't just out to reduce observable motion. A typist probably can get all the energy she needs for surplus motion she now expends from a slice of toast and a lettuce leaf. A big factor is the energy used up by internal tension. When a girl on a standard keyboard hits words like minimum or exaggerate, she unconsciously tenses up. It's like a hunter watching for a deer to come by. Watching is the most fatiguing part of the hunt."

Even if the new tests should be spectacularly successful, many of the 23,000 public and private schools teaching typing wouldn't be happy about scrapping their textbooks and retraining their teachers. Business men, who employ more than 2,500,000 women to do at least some typing, would think a long time before xxx-ing out, so to speak, a vast amount of skill. It's a safe bet, too, that the majority of office girls would prefer to stick with the keyboard they know rather than try to master a new one, even if that one is more efficient.

"Besides, a girl's efficiency depends on a lot more than her typewriter," insists a lady office manager. "There's the color of the walls, the air conditioning, the frequency of coffee breaks, the company's attitude toward personal phone calls, and the looks and the manners of the men."

The man who ordered the current keyboard test—Edmund F. Mansure, head of the General Services Administration, which holds title to some 800,000 typewriters—already has received neatly typed evidence of feminine disapproval. "This new system would set white-collar people back a hundred years," writes "an irate California girl and taxpayer." And a "57-year-old typist who must work to eat" hopes that "God will punish you fellows who always try to find some new way to take somebody's job."

Mansure insists he isn't trying anything of the kind. "We wouldn't want to retrain girls who are already pretty proficient," he says. "But G. S. A. efficiency experts have saved the Government $320,000,000 in the past two years, and I don't see why we can't save more by rearranging keyboards so that our typists will get more work done. If Dvorak's system doesn't work out, we'll test others. I'm optimistic."

4

In this chapter we have discussed the occasional need for reminding people of irrelevancies that can divert attention from real issues. Here is an example of how the irrelevancies can be cleared away and the real issues brought to light.

MISUSED WORDS BEFOG POWER DISPUTE *

Ralph W. Page

The Philadelphia Bulletin

The controversy between public power and private power is conducted in terms and on assumptions that have no relation to reality.

To begin with, there is no such alternative, nationally speaking. A sound estimate is that the American public will need even more power for its prospective development than the maximum that State, Federal, municipal, and private plants can produce, with all of them going at full capacity.

Branding any source of electric power as a "monopoly" in a deroga-

* By Ralph W. Page from *The Philadelphia Bulletin*. Reprinted by permission.

tory sense is meaningless. Usually an electric power company is, and should be, a monopoly. Communities do not want to be served by a flock of power companies. Hence power producers are regulated. If by monopoly it is meant that Federal power is usurping the entire field, the answer is that it now provides 13 per cent and private companies 83 per cent of the supply.

There is even less validity in the claim that Federal power, based upon the harnessing of the great rivers, is a menace of "Socialism."

The use of the word "socialism" in this and other political connections shows a complete misunderstanding of American capitalism. Socialism, Dictatorship, and Communism are theoretical systems which would attempt to order the economy in a fixed pattern.

Capitalism as developed in this country has no ideology and no blueprint. It is an evolution based squarely upon the pragmatic principle of trial and error. It is the product of endless experiment and discovery. Whatever propositions work in practice, are profitable, and satisfy the people, are adopted. Those that do not are discarded without the slightest regard to what they are called, or what academic, ideological, or theoretical purpose they were supposed to serve.

If Socialism worked—if it in fact produced more goods and distributed them better to the satisfaction of our needs—we would adopt it. The reason we do not is that we have discovered it doesn't.

Applying the American system of trial and error, we discover that the state can develop and control the hydraulic power of a river system to the great advantage of the public. This is because no other agency can do so and at the same time conserve the other necessary uses of the water; and because building dams and generating the juice is one operation the Government can do as well, and cheaper, than anyone else. It isn't an entering wedge for theoretical Socialism, because there are very few businesses in which this is true.

In fact, it is demonstrated that it doesn't take the general organization of corporate management to conduct this business. All over the country farmers' co-operatives have established their own power lines and services with complete success. Municipal plants owned and operated by cities provide cheap power and light to everyone's satisfaction.

This being the case, who cares what you call it?

5

In the following selection Dixon Wecter does not analyze any specific problem. Rather he explains the criteria that he believes the American people apply in choosing their heroes.

How fully do you agree that these actually *are* the standards most Americans apply?

Do you think they are adequate, intelligent criteria for choosing the best leaders?

HOW AMERICANS CHOOSE THEIR HEROES *

DIXON WECTER

The sort of man whom Americans admire, trust, and are willing to follow can be sketched with a few lines. East and west, north and south, his portrait is familiar. At the basic level he must be self-respecting, decent, honorable, with a sense of fair play; no Machiavelli nor Mussolini need apply. He must be firm and self-confident in leadership: Davy Crockett's "Be always sure you're right, then go ahead!" is approved American doctrine, whether in the headstrong and cocksure types we sometimes follow, like Old Hickory and Theodore Roosevelt, or in the great characters of our imagination like Paul Bunyan and Huckleberry Finn. Mother wit and resourcefulness we love. But a reputatation for "genius" is unnecessary and may do the hero harm. Brilliantly clever men like Alexander Hamilton and John Randolph of Roanoke, and pure intellectuals like John Quincy Adams (by the guess of educators given the highest I. Q., 165, of all Americans in the Hall of Fame), are not major idols. An able man must not glory in his cleverness. By our standards one is sometimes allowed to "put over a fast one"—Benjamin Franklin and Abraham Lincoln did, repeatedly—but he must not appear to relish the coup for its own sake. Art must conceal art. A clodhopper politician like Huey Long, boasting "There are not many people in the United States who are smarter than I am, and none in Louisiana," did not understand this restraint. Long's scornful assertion that

* From *The Hero in America* by Dixon Wecter; copyright 1941 by Charles Scribner's Sons and reprinted with their permission.

he could buy votes in his Legislature "like sacks of potatoes," to the country at large was equally bad politics. Uncle Sam allows his favorites to be shrewd in a good cause, but there must be no avowal of cynicism in principle. (In modern movies, the hero may pull a fast one for the sake of his mother, or his girl friend, or some worthy ideal, but not for himself.) The backwoods always has a certain admiration for rustic rascality, and the metropolis loves a flippant wisecrack—but in America at large there is a pretty strong prejudice against the wise guy.

Vanity of personal arrogance in any form is taboo. The dandy in public life—accepted more tolerantly in the England of Disraeli and Lord Curzon—is disliked by Americans. Meriwether Lewis, a great explorer of the West, was handicapped by the nickname of "The Sublime Dandy" and his manners of a Beau Nash. William Pinkney, one of the most brilliant lawyers of a century ago, was ridiculed because of his fawn-colored gloves and corsets, and the vanity that led him to begin a speech all over again when he saw ladies enter the visitors' gallery of the Supreme Court.

Effeminacy is fatal. Martin Van Buren failed of re-election in 1840 after the public had grown tired of his lace-tipped cravats and morocco shoes, and a ribald Whig politician had exposed his use of a lotion called "Essence of Victoria." In the West the dude was a traditional villain. (Ironically, in 1860 Lincoln's campaign manager worked hard to get him photographed in a boiled shirt with pearl studs, to make a better impression in the East.)

The arrogance of caste is equally deadly in American hero-worship. Hancock, Jay, Gouveneur Morris were snobs who never won the sway, with even a seasoning of popular admiration, that some Tory statesmen have enjoyed in England. The public can never forget that Hamilton once exclaimed, "Your people, sir, is a great beast!" (These words, quoted in the second decade of this century in school texts on American history by William B. Guitteau, McLaughlin and Van Tyne, and Albert Bushnell Hart, were omitted after protests from school boards and patrons, from subsequent editions in the 1920's, when the Hamiltonian philosophy was in favor during the era of Republican prosperity.) Harding paid Hamilton the dubious compliment of saying, in 1921, "No man's life ever gave me greater inspiration than Hamilton's"; and bankers have often praised the first

Secretary of the Treasury. But the people at large have repaid his scorn with neglect.

Even Daniel Webster—for all his adoration in New England and among the propertied classes—has failed, for like reasons, to make the upper rungs of hero-worship. All else favored him: a head so noble that it was often said "no man could be as great as Webster looked," a record of success from barefoot boy on a New Hampshire farm to the United States Senate and Cabinet, a superb voice that made the blood pound in men's temples. But he was known as "the pensioner of Wall Street," who spent his days so exclusively around mahogany tables in clubs and directors' rooms—where the smoke of Havana cigars hung blue, and "mountain dew" Scotch regaled his fine palate—that in the end he became not the idol of the People but of the Best People. There are apparent exceptions. The rich man's friend is sometimes elected President—as in the days of McKinley, Harding, and Coolidge—when the voters look upon themselves as potential rich men, but his popularity strikes no roots in the substratum of affection and legend.

Within limits, the mores of the hero may vary with his times. Emerson, living in the day of Old Hickory, Clay, and Webster, remarked that to the great man, "doing for the people what they wish done and cannot do, of course, everything will be permitted and pardoned—gaming, drinking, fighting, luxury . . . everything short of infamous crime will pass." Hadn't Jackson run off with another man's wife? Didn't he and Clay fight duels and bet on race-horses? Weren't Clay and Webster notoriously heavy drinkers—even though Webster was said to concede enough to appearances on the platform to refresh himself with white brandy out of a water-glass? Emerson's conclusion was probably too sweeping: in the first place he forgot that the capital of Puritanism had already moved from New England into insular America, and secondly he failed to reckon with the merely regional popularity of Clay and Webster which even then was fading. Only Jackson endured, a greater democrat as well as a man of higher personal integrity. The hero of a democracy—unlike the Stuarts, Bourbons, and Napoleons of the Old World—cannot invite public opinion to go to hell. He must pay tribute to conformity.

Through most of our cultural history, for the average man sex and religion have been life's two most serious subjects, and irregularity even in the mighty leader must not go too far. Aaron Burr's "one hundred bastards" belong to the legend of villainy, along with Thaddeus Stevens's alleged mistresses white and black; while Tom Paine's agnostic mockery made him in spite of his great patriotic services an object of folk hate. As for the hero, debunkery by sensational writers has usually addressed itself to secret nips at the bottle, failure to attend church, or flirtation with a neighbor's wife—rather than to matters of rightful public concern, like soundness of military strategy, foresight, or statesmanly wisdom.

The great man who wins acceptance as a hero will find his vagaries and skepticisms trimmed down by convention. Nevertheless, it is surprising how few of the American great, in comparison with those of the Old World, have cultivated lush private lives, though their individual views on religion have often shown more independence than orthodoxy. To a man's man, the sturdy profanity of Washington and Old Hickory, like the earthy jokes of Franklin and Lincoln, will be forgiven and, in the main, forgotten. Fundamentally the hero is required to be chaste, loyal, honest, humble before duty and before God. He is apt to have a dash of Puritan conscience, but the beauty of holiness is no more expected than is a sense of poetry.

The people's choice of heroes for America has been prevailingly sound; our major favorites are those any nation might be proud of. They go far toward vindicating the whole democratic theory of careers open to talents. We believe that character is more important than brains. Hard work, tenacity, enterprise, and firmness in the face of odds are the qualities that Americans most admire, rather than originality or eloquence of tongue and pen.

The hero must be a man of good will and also a good neighbor, preferably something of a joiner. Of the solitudes and lonely isolations of a great man like Lincoln the public has little conception. It likes to think of its idol as simple in greatness. Manliness, forthright manners, and salty speech are approved. Love of the soil, of dogs and horses and manual hobbies and fishing, is better understood than absorption in art, literature, and music. (The public distrusts Presidents who are photographed fishing in their store clothes.) The hero must not lose touch with his birthplace and origins, however humble; the atmosphere of small towns and front-porch campaigns, cultivated by so many candidates for President, pays tribute to this demand.

"I really believe there are more attempts at flattering the farmers than any other class," Lincoln as candidate for President remarked at the Wisconsin State Fair, "the reason for which I cannot perceive, unless it be that they cast more votes than any other."

Also, the touch of versatility and homely skill is applauded in a hero. Thomas Jefferson is remembered less as the eighteenth-century virtuoso than as an inventor of gadgets from which he plainly got a great deal of fun. "Tinkering" is American. European lads—like Henrich Steffens growing up in Denmark, and Michael Pupin in a Serbian village—have testified to the fascination that Franklin, "wiser than all the wise men of Idvor," held for them. The hero must do things better than the common folk, but his achievments (unlike those of the artist, philosopher, and pure scientist) must lie open to everyman's comprehension. It is well, too, that the labels of the hero conform to those of the group, so that identification between him and the majority can more easily be made: for example, all of our major idols have been both Anglo-Saxon and Protestant.

Bravery, honesty, strength of character are the stuff for hero-worship. At the boy's level, this worship gravitates toward the door of spectacular deeds; on the average adult level, toward the wielder of power; and in the eyes of a more critical judgment, toward idealism and moral qualities. The most universal hero is he who can fill all these specifications. This, by the many shapes of their courage, integrity, and strength, Washington and Lincoln and Lee are able to do. When the dust of partisanship has settled, another leader in two great crises, economic and military—Franklin D. Roosevelt—will probably join their august company. But Jefferson the sedentary man, Ben Franklin the opportunist, and Andrew Jackson the rough-hewn soldier fail to satisfy everybody. Upon a still lower rank, men like Daniel Boone and Crockett and Buffalo Bill and Edison remain almost juvenile heroes. They do not have all the dimensions of our few supreme symbols. Was it not Emerson who suggested that we Americans were the shattered pieces of a great mould?

Our most powerful hero epics center about our leaders. What, then, in the final analysis do Washington, Franklin, Jefferson, Jackson, Lincoln, and in a provisional verdict Wilson and the Roosevelts have in common? Among them lie many differences. In heredity, economic origins, training, skill, temperament, party affiliations, and attachment to specific policies they may seem as diverse as we could find by sifting the nation from Atlantic to Pacific. All save perhaps Washington were "liberals" by the gauge of their times—and Washington, one must not forget, was an arch political rebel, who even in old age sought to balance his conservatism by an honest effort to be nonpartisan. (And even Washington has slowly waned before the warmer humanity of Lincoln.) What is their common denominator?

All of them, the people believe, loved America more deeply than any selfish consideration. The hero as made in America is a man who has the power and yet does not abuse it. He is the practical demonstration of romantic democracy. Washington is most sublime because, after winning our freedom, he refused a crown, military dictatorship, and every personal reward. Lee is grandest because he did what he thought was his duty, failed under heartbreaking odds, and then with gentleness did his best to repair all hate and malice. Lincoln is most appealing because, in the conduct of that same desperate war which gave him the power of a czar, he never forgot his love for the common people of North and South.

More clearly than the great heroes of Europe, military and political, ours stand for a progress concept. They spring from stock that has bred schemes both wise and foolish—with its talk about the pursuit of happiness, the more abundant life, and the American Dream. None of these epic leaders left the Republic as he found it—although to avoid disturbing a single stick or stone seems to have been the policy of men like James Buchanan, Chester A. Arthur, William McKinley, and Calvin Coolidge. At times, to be sure, the people themselves have wanted no change, felt no urge to take on fresh responsibility in the national sphere. In eras like theirs, nothing is added to the stature of American ideals—such as civil liberty, equality of opportunity, faith in the average man, social justice, respect for the rights of weaker nations and for the good estate of democracy throughout the earth. A Chief Executive may then be called to office who rules as a minor Augustus over a gilded age, or serves as the genial host at a great barbecue. But ten years hence he is not likely to be remembered as a great man, or even as a symbol worth keeping.

Our heroes, we believe, are cast in a different mould. Their ruling passion, as we see it, is a sense of duty, alert to the best among the stirring impulses of their time, and able to make the impulse effective. They translate the dream into act. The supreme leader is he who can hitch the great bandwagon to the star of American idealism.

6

In the following article John W. Campbell, Jr., himself a science-fiction editor, defends a set of criteria that he thinks should be applied in judging this form of literature.

In just what ways do these criteria differ from those you would apply to realistic fiction?

SCIENCE-FICTION AND THE OPINION OF THE UNIVERSE *

JOHN W. CAMPBELL, JR.

In late 1943 a story by Cleve Cartmill reached my desk at *Astounding Science-Fiction*. It had a rather simple and formula-type plot, concerning an intelligence agent seeking to sabotage an enemy nation's atomic bomb. The characters were decidedly out of the stock bins. Certainly it was no literary gem. Nevertheless, I bought and published it. It was the story "Deadline," which, appearing in our May 1944 issue, was on the stands in April 1944—roughly fourteen months before the Alamagordo test-firing of the first atomic bomb, and fifteen months before Hiroshima.

The Manhattan Project security people were on the spot almost immediately; the story described the arming mechanism of the atomic bomb more accurately than anything published until the Greenglass spy-trial disclosures. It stated that U-235 could be used in a bomb, producing the explosive effect equivalent to 50,000 tons of TNT. That exact figure matched perfectly the performance of the Nagasaki bomb, and slightly exceeded the performance of the Hiroshima bomb. The story contained a description of an atomic-bomb explosion; the one item the author missed was the mushroom cloud effect. That, while visibly spectacular, doesn't cause any damage; the author was interested in the demolition effects of the bomb.

This story was one of the more sensational examples of the values

* From *The Saturday Review*, May 12, 1956. Reprinted by permission.

with which science-fiction is concerned. Published in 1944, by a man who had studied the work of Einstein, Fermi, Hahn, etc., and who was therefore aware that nuclear forces existed and that it was only a matter of time before engineers unlocked them, the story was a prophecy. Had it been saved until 1946, when the explosive products of the theoretical physics of the Twenties and Thirties were common knowledge, it would have possessed none of its prophetic qualities, and could have been judged like any other short story for "plot" or "literary" values. But what folly to judge *prophecy*—and damned accurate prophecy at that—like a fairytale. Of course Hemingway can write a great deal better than Isaac Asimov, one of the top science-fiction authors—but Isaac Asimov is professor of biochemistry at Boston University School of Medicine, and he knows a very great deal more about biochemistry and the trends in modern biological sciences than Hemingway does. It is the total difference in objective which renders irrelevant and fatuous the "literary criticism" of science-fiction by anyone not himself primarily a science-fictioneer.

Science-fiction is written by technically-minded people, about technically-minded people, for the satisfaction of technically-minded people. And these are *different* human people; they're not supermen or inframen.

Let's consider a few examples of the human qualities involved here to get an idea of the points science-fiction tries to put across. There's some highly important research being done now by the Air Force medical department on the problem of survival of the pilot of a jet fighter-plane when he is forced to bail out. How much violence can a human organism stand without coming apart at the seams? How suddenly can a human body be slowed down without coming apart? What happens when human flesh is subjected to a wind of 700 miles per hour? Will a man's eyeballs fall out of his eye-sockets if he is decelerated at 30 Gs?

We're not interested in whether or not a dog's eyes would fall out; dogs don't pilot jet fighters. And it isn't a question of whether a dead man's eyes would fall out; if the pilot is dead there is no further need to worry about saving him. The answer can be determined only by subjecting a living human being to 30 Gs deceleration and seeing whether or not his eyes are torn out.

A Colonel Stapp is in charge of this research; he and his group built a rocket-driven sled-on-rails to test the problem—and Colonel Stapp willingly allowed himself to be strapped immovably onto that roaring contraption to find out whether his eyes could stay in. They did . . . just barely. Stapp's work was advanced . . . and he won his gamble. But how many of us would be willing to make such a gamble? Can you readily conceive of a New York banker accepting a ride on Colonel Stapp's rocket-sled with the express intent of determining whether or not his eyes would be destroyed? So Colonel Stapp is a superman, perhaps? No, he's not—he's a *differentman*. I suspect that Colonel Stapp cannot understand the super-human patience that allows the banker to spend all day, every day, week after week and year after year, in the same office, looking at the same kind of figures about the same kind of stocks without going mad. The Stapp type of personality is no more capable of that mind-destroying, soul-blasting, unending grind of routine than the banker is of that soul-wracking, body-tearing, rocket-driven demon Colonel Stapp lovingly labors over. Stapp is a science-fiction hero—in flesh and blood.

Here's another aspect of science-fiction that classical literary values do not touch on. Where classical values hold that human nature is enduring, unchanging, and uniform, science-fiction holds that it is mutable, complex, and differentiated. David Reisman, of the University of Chicago, in discussing sociology has suggested that there are three basic personality types: the Tradition-Directed man, the Inner-Directed, and the Other-Directed. But there's a fourth type that only *appears* to be Inner-Directed. Let's call it the Universe-Directed type.

The first three types are ruled by opinion; the opinion expressed in traditions, their own inner opinions, or the opinions of others. The Universe-Directed type isn't ruled by opinions—he's dominated by the facts of the Universe.

Perhaps the easier way to express it is to consider a research scientist discussing a machine he is trying to build. "I know that the traditions and authorities say it should work; I know my own convictions say it'll work. I suppose that if I took a poll of opinions of other people it would be held that it will work. But there it is, and it doesn't work." The scientist lives hard against the inflexible, rigid facts of the Universe; opinions don't do him the slightest bit of good. It doesn't matter what his opinion is, or what anybody else's opinion is, has been, or will be. The only thing that will make his device work is the Universe's "opinion."

Now for someone who hasn't appreciated this the reactions we get in dealing with scientists are misleading. The scientist will appear from the viewpoint of someone who considers opinion the dominant force in reality—rigid, cold-blooded, emotionless, and authoritarian—dogmatic. He isn't; the Universe is, and he's acting simply as the messenger of the Universe. Accusing the scientist of being cold-blooded or dogmatic is somewhat like the king who had the messenger beheaded for bringing the news that the battle had been lost. There's no point in holding the messenger responsible; you'll only get your own thinking confused. (You'll also start getting messengers who bring nothing but false reports.)

A *Science-Fiction* story we ran recently illustrates the situation. It was Tom Godwin's story "The Cold Equations"—and the title is significant. The central character is the pilot of an Emergency Dispatch Ship—an EDS—which is, in essence, a sort of space-parachute for making parachute-drops of emergency supplies from a passing interstellar liner to an expedition exploring a new planet. It's a sort of plastic bubble with a rocket motor and a pilot. They use a human pilot simply because any computer capable of the job would be heavier—and hence more expensive—than the human pilot. This particular EDS drop is intended to bring desperately needed medical serums to an exploration crew on the planet below. They had sent a message calling for help; the nearest interstellar cruiser had turned aside from its regular passage, dropped the little EDS bubble, and then gone on its way.

The pilot discovers that he has a stowaway on board—and the stowaway is a twenty-year-old girl. Her brother is on the expedition below; when she heard of the drop while a passenger on the cruiser she stowed away to join him.

She cannot, however. She has to be *thrown out into space.* The EDS is a space parachute; it has a quantity of fuel calculated by the great electronic calculator aboard the cruiser to be just adequate to land the mass of the EDS on the planet. The fuel is *not* adequate to land the unexpected additional mass of the girl. If she stays aboard her added mass will make the EDS fall the last dozen miles.

No matter what is done she must die. She can stay aboard and die in the crash—which means the pilot and the expedition on the planet will also die, because of the loss of the medical supplies. Or she can die alone in cold dark space. So she stays aboard the EDS just long enough to write a couple of short letters—then she has to be thrown out into space. There she dies; the interstellar liner has long gone on its way, and can't get back.

It isn't that the scientist-pilot is cold-blooded or unemotional; the Cold Equations of Motion are. It's a matter of the inexorable facts of gravity, momentum, kinetic energy, and fuel supply, not the pilot's desires or wishes, that determine the case. Not the pilot, but the Equations of Motion determine that at a certain point in time and space the girl's mass must cease to be part of the EDS ship—and it doesn't matter a bit that tradition says the girl must be protected, that the pilot's inner conviction is that she should be, and that the opinions of others hold that she should live.

Don't mistake the messenger for the source of the news; don't mistake this cold, hard ruthlessness as a characteristic of the scientist—it's a characteristic of the Universe. The scientist does sometimes make the human mistake of projecting his own ability to accept that ruthlessness of reality on others. That produces the familiar appearance of the "cold-blooded, unemotional scientist." It's just that, like Colonel Stapp, the true scientist is willing to acknowledge and work with that cold, inexorable system of facts. Since we must know what a living human being can stand, and there is no possible substitute for a living human being, Colonel Stapp rides the rocket-sled.

The modern juvenile delinquent seeks to prove he has courage—that he's brave—and gets into gang fights. He mistakes bravado, and the desperate courage of the cornered animal, for the quiet, conscious courage that can face predicted danger and walk into it knowingly and consciously. But can you imagine the juvenile-delinquent type sitting quietly on that loaded rocket sled while heavy leather and plastic straps bind him absolutely immovably in place, sitting quietly in the knowledge that the question in hand is whether or not he will ever see again? Is such a man as Colonel Stapp unemotional? I think, rather, that he is simply capable of a degree of dedication that we more ordinary people can't quite grasp. The professional research scientist has to understand that when he starts an experiment he must be consciously, knowingly willing to sacrifice his own beliefs, ideas, and deeply held opinions; the answer may not be what he expects. Certainly, Colonel Stapp *expected* to survive in good health—but he faced the fact that he didn't *know* that he would.

The scientist-type, then, is a different (not super-, and not infra-) human type. If a science-fiction author understandingly and accurately characterizes that human type . . . what is his reward from the standard literary critic?

"The characters are inhuman, robot-like automata, lacking normal human motivation," says the critic. Or the author is accused of trying to invent supermen with inhuman motivations. His stories are said to be authoritarian or his characters accused of being dogmatic aristocrats.

It's very difficult to distinguish between an accurate prophet and an authoritarian dictator—but the distinction is very important. The trouble is, each has the characteristic that he tells people around him exactly what they're going to do, and, willy-nilly, like it or not, the people have to do it. That's what *accurate* prophecy means!

There's a human tendency to assume that what the prophet predicts is what he *wants* to have happen. The pilot of the EDS bubble in "The Cold Equations" predicted accurately what *would* happen—but that had no relationship whatever to what he *wanted* to have happen. A mother can tell her child exactly what will happen if he sticks his hand in the fire; that doesn't mean she *wants* it to happen.

People think they want to have someone give them accurate prophecies of tomorrow. That is not what they want; they want inaccurate prophecies—for an accurate prophecy would compel you to go on under an inexorable, inescapable compulsion of preordained and unalterable fate. That's what the concept of accurate prophecy means—and that's why prophecy is so unpopular. What does the term "a regular Jeremiah" mean? It means a prophet whose words are hatefully accurate. Prophetic values have, quite understandably, been given a low rating in human affairs. They can be so unpleasant. But science-fiction's fundamental purpose is to make accurate, loose prophecies of general trends. Like a stock-market analyst, the science-fiction author can't predict any one stock—but he does fairly well on the broad trends. Where the market analyst seeks to predict broad trends of the market, the science-fiction author seeks to predict broad trends in the culture.

Occasionally highly accurate specific hits will be made—as in the case of the atomic bomb. But normally science-fiction does a pretty good job of broad-scale prediction. We have accurately predicted the rise of hypersonic aircraft, the rising use of rocket engines, the introduction of electronic computers, automation, atomic weapons, and atomic power.

Naturally, prophecy being what it is, we can't say how accurate our present predictions are . . . yet. If you're curious you can take a look at the magazines. But if being told what you will be involved in smacks of someone trying to dictate to you—skip science-fiction. It'll irritate you without entertaining or interesting you.

7

In the following selection MacKinley Helm explains "what to look for in pictures." Does he defend his criteria sufficiently? Can you apply them yourself the next time you look at a painting? What kind of readers does the author apparently intend to reach?

WHAT TO LOOK FOR IN PICTURES *

MacKinley Helm

I have said that the Mexican painters are severally interested in the problems of painting, and now I should like to approach some of these problems, but rather from the point of view of the spectator, of appreciation of painting, than from that of the artist himself. I should like to ask what it is that we look for when we look at a picture. I should like to ignore, for the moment, much of the usual critical apparatus, the necessary vocabulary of the specialist, and put a few simple questions.

The first question is merely a repetition of Orozco's challenge: "Do you like it?"

Do you like the picture you are looking at? Especially, do you like

* From MacKinley Helm's *Modern Mexican Painters.* Copyright, 1941, by Harper & Brothers.

it enough to want to go back to it? If you are looking at pictures seriously, and see one you do not like, you are not morally required to treat it as though, being stupid, you had missed its importance. You are not obliged to worry about it; although if you have a naturally catholic taste you are likely to examine your conscience to determine who is at fault, you or the painter.

If you like a picture it is probably because it makes you feel something, arouses your emotions so that you respond to it; because, at the very least, it interests you. There is no reason in the world why you should be persuaded to look at a dull work of art. Dullness is the artist's sin against the Holy Ghost.

But it is possible to feel something when you look at a picture and yet be unable to describe what it is that moves you. Picasso told Christian Zervos that his ambition was to paint a picture in such a way that nobody could tell how it was done, so that nothing but emotion would be given off by it. In the experience of many people emotion is given off first of all by the subject. This is perhaps an elementary form of aesthetic experience, but it is, I think, aesthetically crippling to be snobbish about the subject matter of a painting, like Dr. Barnes of Merion, Pennsylvania, for example, who professes not to remember the subjects of most of the pictures in the vast collection he owns.

For myself, I object to being told, by lady guides who recite misrepresentations of nonrepresentational art in a certain New York gallery, that abstraction is the highest form of art. There is no absolute and universal canon by which a particular art form may be so judged. A man who wants good plain representational painting is entitled to have it. Easel pictures are made for the people who will look at them, like them, and possibly buy them: and I have never met a good painter who paints so entirely for himself that he is content to stack up his canvases in the darkness of his studio storeroom, indifferent to appreciation and sales.

On the other hand, painters, good painters, generally choose subjects not so much because they want to represent them factually in paint, but because in something they see, or have seen and remembered, there are fascinating suggestions of one or another of the essential elements of their special work. They are attracted by the possibilities of projecting, upon canvas or paper, certain lines, forms, relationships and colors which have been observed in, or suggested by, the physical world.

Hence their emotional attitudes toward their subject matter and toward their work, while it is in progress, are likely to be something very different from those of the ultimate spectator, who will not have looked at the world with the painter's professional eye. Still, if the painter has entered emotionally into the treatment of the materials of his art, chances are that then—and probably it is only then—the spectator will feel something; not the painter's emotion, but an emotion nevertheless proper to the aesthetic experience of beholding a form of art; an emotion aroused by lines and forms and their relationships, and by the qualities and harmonies of color. In any case, the emotion is what the spectator is after, and if a picture does not give him an authentic emotion the picture does not exist for him.

Now of the qualities of a picture which you like, which awakens interest and feeling, there is much less of importance to be said than you probably think. If you want to go beyond the simple appreciation of the subject matter of a painting and examine the means through which the artist has reached your emotions, there are only a few things you must look for. No special vocabulary is required in order to talk about the painter's professional means, and probably the less said about them the better. A good work of art, as Renoir said, is in the end inexplicable. But it is the curse of our civilization that we have to talk, we cannot let our emotions alone, and when we are looking at pictures and talking about them the best we can do is try to talk simply and make sense if we can.

Apart from describing the feeling-tones of a picture, such as to note that they are mystical, or romantic, or pessimistic, or gay, most of the things which are to be said about painting from the point of view of the spectator have something to do with lines or forms or composition or color. These are the basic materials of the arts which deal with the things that are tangible and malleable, that can be wrought into forms—the plastic arts of painting and sculpture as compared to literature and music.

In discussing the linear aspect of a work of art it is necessary to distinguish between "line" and "lines." Line is essentially the outline of forms. It is not necessarily something which is drawn; frequently it is merely indicated. Some painters draw their designs (with "lines") and fill them with color. In such a case the work is principally linear. Others, like Rouault, draw unmistakable boundary lines between forms or objects, or, like Renoir, simply differentiate their forms by means of color and light.

In fairly flat painting the outlines of figures are sometimes drawn with dark paint, sometimes even with black ink. In round or sculpturesque painting, "line" is an inherent element of contours which are differentiated not by "lines" but contrasting backgrounds. In other words, the eye does not necessarily demand an actual line of demarcation before it can see where one object leaves off and another begins. Modeling, or merely the modulation of color, may serve to distinguish between forms.

Some painters have used lines as the makers of stained glass use them, to increase the intensity of the vibration of color within the enclosed areas. Cimabue used this device, and Rouault uses it today in exaggerated fashion. However line is employed or indicated, it is of the essence of mature and formal art. Competence in draughtsmanship is a *sine qua non* of the painter's equipment. At the same time, as Dr. Barnes reminds us, "Line gets power from what it does to what is contained between the lines."

The quality of an indicated line depends upon its expressiveness. Manuel Rodriguez Lozano, a Mexican disciple of Picasso, can draw a line from the top of the head to the fingertips, or from the armpit to the toes, in which every part of the body, in its turn, is adequately expressed. The presence of that quality in a continuous line distinguishes great drawing from casual draughtsmanship.

Purity in line-drawing consists in its sure and unfaltering direction, its adequate conveyance of intention. The truth of line does not depend upon its adherence to objective or phenomenal reality. On the contrary, linear distortion is as old as art itself. It is to be found in the art forms of Egypt, the archaic Grecian world and ancient Mexico. True line must obey only the artist's will.

The form of a work of art is the sum of the relationships, or the organization, of the parts of the picture. It is a little confusing, perhaps, that the several parts or objects in a painting are likewise called "forms" by the painters, because then the definition of "form" takes on a question-begging aspect: form is the sum of the forms.

I like John D. Graham's definition of a "form" in his *System and*

Dialectics of Art: a "consequential mode by means of which an artist authoritatively separates a phenomenon from its setting." Painters very often assemble forms taken from a diversity of settings and give them new and sharper significance in a new setting, in new relationships. Much of the piquancy of Surrealist painting lies in the novelty of relationships between familiar forms.

Forms are likely to be thought of as objects with the appearance of solidity, but it is a mistake to confuse pictorial forms with sculptured forms. The painter must be perfectly free to work within the natural two dimensions of his medium. A plastic form ought rather to be thought of simply as a component part of a picture, functioning as an interesting object in itself and harmoniously related to other forms. Variety in interest is largely determined by the contrasting variety of the several forms. Versatility is attributable to a painter who can exhibit, in a sufficient showing of his work, a variety of forms rather than variations in style. A deliberate variation from a painter's natural style is likely to be merely a tour de force.

A painter who is preoccupied with indentical forms may end up with a "formula" which will impede his development. The works of El Greco are relatively poor in subject matter—Saint Francis appears in them at least sixty-six times—but there is infinite variety in his forms. Amongst the Mexican painters there are two or three whose present preoccupations seem to be on the verge of resulting in formulas, but there is no canon for determining just at what moment the forms employed during a given period in a painter's career may be said to have crystallized into a formula. The habitual use of a method of treating forms is a "manner." When a painter has both formula and manner he can be given up for lost.

In considering a plastic composition as a whole, a deliberate painter has probably been concerned with such characteristics of the relationship of forms as proportion, symmetry, and rhythm. Modern painters reject many of the classical canons of proportion and symmetry, of both the several forms and their relationships. In Mexico, for example, there are painters who prefer the usually compressed Maya and Aztec conceptions of human proportions to the seven-heads-to-the-body measurement of the Greeks; just as many painters the world over prefer the sensation of shock generated by asymmetrical designs to the relative restfulness of classical symmetry.

Rhythms occur in repetition (with variety) of similar forms. The Mexican painter Rufino Tamayo introduced architectural columns to repeat the rhythms of his columnar Tehuantepec women. Francisco Dosamantes, in his invariably rhythmical lithographs, manipulates folds of costume or braided hair into musical patterns.

A particularly absorbing problem in composition is that of ordering the forms on a given surface so that the whole space is interestingly filled. I confess to the idiosyncrasy of being preoccupied, at the moment, with the treatment which painters give to the negative areas of their surfaces, the parts of the picture in which, so to speak, nothing much is going on. It should be the object of the painter to make the negative areas come alive. Representational painters are often neglectful of this element of composition, whereas abstract painters are necessarily conscious of the whole of a given surface. Indeed, it is to the abstract painter, Josef Albers, that I owe my present interest in this aspect of painting.

A picture is not successful in which there is a square inch of dull surface. Some of Degas' celebrated behind-the-scenes oils contain woefully dreary background areas. I have spoken of this weakness in Orozco's earlier frescoes, an infirmity which he has not always overcome save by an overcrowding of forms. In watching the development of Siqueiros' sense of mural pattern, and in observing the amazing progress of a young new painter, Guillermo Meza, I have learned—as painters of course know—how negative areas can be made exciting through variation in textures, vibration of color, and the introduction of transparencies and atmospheric play.

There are many beautiful works of art in which color has not been employed, such as drawings and engravings, black-and-white gouaches and frescoes. But when color is used it must have an integral part in the composition, if only, as in some of Gauguin's pictures, an indispensably decorative part. Color is least likely to have the appearance of necessity when it is simply spread over a drawing. It is easy enough to distinguish this technique when you look at the original painting, but its detection is irresistible in a photograph. In the photographic print the structure of such a picture is likely to be suspiciously too good.

In some of Federico Cantu's drawings color is used very slightly for modeling, the forms being hardly modified by it. Raoul Dufy often slashes a patch of color on his paper and draws forms upon it with pen or brush. These techniques are productive of delightful and sometimes even moving effects. They are not intended for finished masterpieces of art. In truly great painting, color is employed for both drawing and modeling. One of the finest examples of drawing with paint is found in Renoir's "Les Confidences" in the collection of Dr. Oscar Reinhart, in which it is impossible to detect any point at which "line" is indicated by actual lines. In Mexico, two figure-painters who excel in this mature form of color painting are Federico Cantu, in his oils, and Jesus Guerrero Galvan.

This kind of painting, in the long run the most satisfying to most people, is difficult to reproduce for the reason that both lightness and brightness of color, two very different qualities, photograph identically, and so do their opposites, depth of color and shadow or obscurity. From the gray values of a photograph you cannot tell which areas in the original are light or bright on the one hand, or deep or dark on the other.

There was a fashionable period in the history of painting when color was applied with little attention to line, or deliberately with none. The Impressionists blurred natural line in atmospheric light. It is difficult to get a good idea of a Monet, for example, from a black and white photograph, because the original is essentially a work of color and light. In Mexico there has been very little Impressionistic painting, but there are painters who handle color beautifully and yet show little interest (and sometimes little capacity) in drawing. Tamayo, one of the most celebrated Mexican colorists, does not always produce solid effects in his water colors because of his relative indifference to drawing, as the photographs plainly show; and until quite lately Maria Izquierdo's works have been valued almost entirely for their rich, varied, and thoroughly Mexican color patterns.

In discussing color it is necessary to distinguish between the objective properties of the dried colors as they appear on canvas or paper and the suggestive effects secured by painters in their use of pigment. The spectator may be satisfied when he has trained himself to look for only three objective properties—value, tone, and intensity. Light and dark and the range between are values; mixtures of color, like blue into green, or blue into yellow are tones; the intensity of color is its purity, its unmixed blueness or redness. These are the terms you will find in the handbooks of the manufacturers of paint, and they are likewise the basic terms of the criticism of art when color is under discussion. Other aspects of color may be introduced into painting by the juxtaposition, contrast and diminution of the several colors. Thus it is correct to speak of the luminosity of color where light is introduced, of low or high key where the general effect is bright, or, on the contrary, obscure. Usually the color patterns are most harmonious when equal values of different colors are used, and when, as in music, the work is executed in a single dominant key. An ascetic palette, in which few colors are used, attains its own beautiful variety when there is an extensive range of the tones and values of the two or three basic colors.

Two effects which painters look for in applied color are quality and texture. These terms are loosely used, but in the speech of painters, which ought to be the spectator's primary source of understanding, each of these terms has two ordinary connotations. When a painting is said to have "quality," in a general sense, it is usually meant that the colors themselves have such qualities as richness, or purity or transparency. But there is also a more technical sense in which painters speak of the quality of a painting or drawing. When Dr. Atl, for example, told me that he had returned to the use of oil paint for the sake of quality he meant that he felt that oil is the best medium for reproducing the qualities of the physical world. He meant that with oils he could produce skies that are more sky-like, trees that are more tree-like and ground that is more earthen.

This use of the term "quality" is confusingly similar to a painter's primary use of the term "texture". Texture in painting is descriptive of surfaces, and perhaps the spectator thinks first of the plastic reproduction of various real or imagined surfaces, as of flesh, or iron, or wood, or fabric. In this sense, a picture is said to be texturally interesting when it contains a variety of textures. But there is also a more abstract use of the term "texture," referring to the look or feel of a painted surface itself, quite apart from any intention to convey a sense of translated textures. The interest which painters feel in surface textures is illustrated in the diversity of technical means employed in modern painting, the use of brushes and knives and fingers and, in extreme form, the pasting of fabrics and papers and threads and the attachment of metallic objects to a painted canvas.

Finally, the spectator looks for unity in every picture, the perfectly harmonious relationship of line, forms and color, organized to endow the work with the crowning excellence of livelihead: not necessarily with physical movement, for stillness may be ultimately more satisfying than motion, but with an interior vitality which suggests that this created thing is instinct with life.

8

Aristotle wrote his *Poetics* over 2000 years ago, but his criteria for early Greek literature are still respected by many critics. How many of the criteria seem to you still applicable to drama and literature of our own times?

POETICS *

ARISTOTLE

. . . Tragedy, then, is an imitation of an action that is serious, complete, and of a certain magnitude; in language embellished with each kind of artistic ornament, the several kinds being found in separate parts of the play; in the form of action, not of narrative; through pity and fear effecting the proper purgation of these emotions. By "language embellished," I mean language into which rhythm, "harmony," and song enter. By "the several kinds in separate parts," I mean, that some parts are rendered through the medium of verse alone, others again with the aid of song.

Now as tragic imitation implies persons acting, it necessarily follows, in the first place, that Scenic equipment will be a part of Tragedy. Next, Song and Diction, for these are the means of imitation. By "Diction" I mean the mere metrical arrangement of the words; as for "Song," it is a term whose full sense is well understood.

Again, Tragedy is the imitation of an action; and an action implies personal agents, who necessarily possess certain qualities both of character and thought. It is these that determine the qualities of actions themselves; these—thought and character—are the two natural causes

The selected passages presented here are from Ingram Bywater's translation, published by the Oxford University Press.

from which actions spring: on these causes, again, all success or failure depends. Hence, the Plot is the imitation of the action—for by Plot I here mean the arrangement of the incidents. By Character I mean that in virtue of which we ascribe certain qualities to the agents. By Thought, that whereby a statement is proved, or a general truth expressed. Every Tragedy, therefore, must have six parts, which parts determine its quality—namely, Plot, Character, Diction, Thought, Scenery, Song. Two of the parts constitute the means of imitation, one the manner, and three the objects of imitation. And these complete the list. These elements have been employed, we may say, by almost all poets; in fact, every play contains Scenic accessories as well as Character, Plot, Diction, Song, and Thought.

But most important of all is the structure of the incidents. For Tragedy is an imitation, not of men, but of an action and of life—of happiness and misery; and happiness and misery consist in action, the end of human life being a mode of action, not a quality. Now the characters of men determine their qualities, but it is by their actions that they are happy or the reverse. Dramatic action, therefore, is not with a view to the representation of character: character comes in as subsidiary to the action. Hence the incidents and the plot are the end of a tragedy: and the end is the chief thing of all. Again, without action there cannot be a tragedy; there may be without character. . . .

These principles being established, let us now discuss the proper structure of the Plot, since this is the first, and also the most important part of Tragedy.

Now, according to our definition, Tragedy is an imitation of an action that is complete and whole, and of a certain magnitude; for there may be a whole that is wanting in magnitude. A whole is that which has beginning, middle, and end. A beginning is that which does not itself follow anything by causal necessity, but after which something naturally is or comes to be. An end, on the contrary, is that which itself naturally follows some other thing, either by necessity, or in the regular course of events, but has nothing following it. A middle is that which follows something as some other thing follows it. A well constructed plot, therefore, must neither begin nor end at haphazard, but conform to the type here described. . . .

Unity of plot does not, as some persons think, consist in the unity of the hero. For infinitely various are the incidents in one man's life, which cannot be reduced to unity; and so, too, there are many actions of one man out of which we cannot make one action. Hence the error, as it appears, of all poets who have composed a Heracleid, a Theseid, or other poems of the kind. They imagine that as Heracles was one man, the story of Heracles ought also to be a unity. . . .

It is, moreover, evident from what has been said, that it is not the function of the poet to relate what has happened, but what may happen—what is possible according to the law of probability or necessity. The poet and the historian differ not by writing in verse or in prose. The work of Herodotus might be put into verse, and it would still be a species of history, with metre no less than without it. The true difference is that one relates what has happened, the other what may happen. Poetry, therefore, is a more philosophical and a higher thing than history: for poetry tends to express the universal, history the particular. The universal tells us how a person of given character will on occasion speak or act, according to the law of probability or necessity; and it is this universality at which Poetry aims in giving expressive names to the characters. The particular is—for example—what Alcibiades did or suffered. . . .

Of all plots and actions the episodic are the worst. I call a plot episodic in which the episodes or acts succeed one another without probable or necessary sequence. Bad poets compose such pieces by their own fault, good poets, to please the players; for, as they write for competing rivals, they draw out the plot beyond its capacity, and are often forced to break the natural continuity. . . .

Plots are either simple or complicated; for such too, in their very nature, are the actions of which the plots are an imitation. An action which is one and continuous in the sense above defined, I call Simple, when the turning point is reached without Reversal of Fortune or Recognition: Complicated, when it is reached with Reversal of Fortune, or Recognition, or both. These last should arise from the internal structure of the plot, so that what follows should be the necessary or probable result of the preceding action. It makes all the difference whether one event is the consequence of another, or merely subsequent to it.

A Reversal of Fortune is, as we have said, a change by which a train of action produces the opposite of the effect intended; and that, according to our rule of probability or necessity. Thus in the *Oedipus*, the messenger, hoping to cheer Oedipus, and to free him from his alarms about his mother, reveals Oedipus' origin, and so produces the opposite effect. . . .

A Recognition, as the name indicates, is a change from ignorance to knowledge, producing love or hate between the persons destined by the poet for good or bad fortune. The best form of recognition is coincident with a reversal of fortune, as in the *Oedipus*. . . .

As the sequel to what has already been said, we must proceed to consider what the poet should aim at, and what he should avoid in constructing his plots; and by what means Tragedy may best fulfil its function.

A perfect tragedy should, as we have seen, be arranged on the simple, not the complicated plan. It should, moreover, imitate actions which excite pity and fear, this being the distinctive mark of tragic imitation. It follows plainly, in the first place, that the change of fortune presented must not be the spectacle of a perfectly good man brought from prosperity to adversity; for this moves neither pity nor fear; it simply shocks us. Nor, again, that of a bad man passing from adversity to prosperity: for nothing can be more alien to the spirit of Tragedy; it possesses no single tragic quality; it neither satisfies the moral sense, nor calls forth pity or fear. Nor, again, should the downfall of the utter villain be exhibited. A plot of this kind would, doubtless, satisfy the moral sense, but it would inspire neither pity nor fear; for pity is aroused by unmerited misfortune, fear by the misfortune of a man like ourselves. Such an event, therefore, will be neither pitiful nor terrible. There remains, then, the character between these two extremes—that of a man who is not eminently good and just, yet whose misfortune is brought about not by vice or depravity, but by some error or frailty. He must be one who is highly renowned and prosperous—a personage like Oedipus, Thyestes, or other illustrious men of such families.

A well constructed plot should, therefore, be single, rather than double as some maintain. The change of fortune should be not from bad to good, but, reversely, from good to bad. It should come about as the result not of vice, but of some great error or frailty, in a character either such as we have described, or better rather than worse. The practice of the stage bears out our view. At first the poets recounted any legends that came in their way. Now, tragedies are found on the story of a few houses—on the fortunes of Alcmaeon, Oedipus, Orestes, Meleager, Thyestes, Telephus, and those others who have done or suffered something terrible. A tragedy, then, to be perfect according to the rules of art should be of this construction. Hence they are in error who censure Euripides just because he follows this principle in his plays, many of which end unhappily. It is, as we have said, the right ending. The best proof is that on the stage and in dramatic competition, such plays, if they are well represented, are most tragic in their effect; and Euripides, faulty as he is in the general management of his subject, yet is felt to be the most tragic of poets. . . .

As in the structure of the plot, so too in the portraiture of character, the poet should always aim either at the necessary or the probable. Thus a person of a given character should speak or act in a given way, by the rule either of necessity or of probability; just as this event should follow that by necessary or probable sequence. It is therefore evident that the unravelling of the plot, no less than the complication, must be brought about by the plot itself, and not by Machinery [1] as in the *Medea*, or in the Return of the Greeks [2] in the *Iliad*. Machinery should be employed only for events external to the drama—either such as are previous to it and outside the sphere of human knowledge, or subsequent to it and which need to be foretold and announced; for to the gods we ascribe the power of seeing all things. Within the action there must be nothing irrational. If the irrational cannot be excluded, it should be outside the scope of the tragedy. Such is the irrational element in the *Oedipus* of Sophocles . . . .

The Chorus too should be regarded as one of the actors; it should be an integral part of the whole, and share in the action, in the manner not of Euripides but of Sophocles. As for the later poets, their choral songs pertain as little to the subject of the piece as to that of any other tragedy. They are, therefore, sung as mere interludes—a practice first begun by Agathon. Yet what difference is there between introducing such choral interludes, and transferring a speech, or even a whole act, from one play to another . . . ?

[1] A machine sent by the Gods, often a chariot.
[2] A goddess appears to stop the soldiers.

9

The Ten Commandments are of course rules for human behavior. With various differences in order, numbering, and phrasing, they have been accepted by both Jews and Christians for many centuries.

To what extent do you think American society in our day accepts these commandments? How many of them are established in our laws?

In the version that follows do you find any defense of any of the commandments? How are they apparently to be numbered in this version, and is this numbering the same as the numbering with which you are familiar?

THE TEN COMMANDMENTS

I am the Lord thy God, which have brought thee out of the land of Egypt, out of the house of bondage. Thou shalt have no other gods before me.

Thou shalt not make unto thee any graven image, or any likeness of any thing that is in the heaven above, or that is in the earth beneath, or that is in the water under the earth. Thou shalt not bow down thyself to them, nor serve them: for I the Lord thy God am a jealous God, visiting the iniquity of the fathers upon the children unto the third and fourth generation of them that hate me.

Thou shalt not take the name of the Lord thy God in vain; for the Lord will not hold him guiltless that taketh his name in vain.

Remember the Sabbath day, to keep it holy. Six days shalt thou labour, and do all thy work: But the seventh day is the sabbath of the Lord thy God: in it thou shalt not do any work, thou, nor thy son, nor thy daughter, thy manservant, nor thy maidservant, nor thy cattle, nor any stranger that is within thy gates.

Honour thy father and thy mother: that thy days may be long upon the land which the Lord thy God giveth thee.

Thou shalt not kill.

Thou shalt not commit adultery.

Thou shalt not steal.

Thou shalt not bear false witness against thy neighbour.

Thou shalt not covet thy neighbour's house, thou shalt not covet thy neighbour's wife, nor his manservant, nor his maidservant, nor his ox, nor his ass, nor any thing that is thy neighbour's.

10

Woodrow Wilson's "Fourteen Points" were his expression of war aims in 1918. He tried to apply them in framing the Treaty of Versailles in 1919, but with very limited success. Some of them, however, are still often quoted as criteria for guiding and judging international relations in our time.

Which of the fourteen points are specific aims of World War I and no longer pertinent?

Which of them are now generally accepted (if any)?

How many of the criteria are debatable?

THE FOURTEEN POINTS

Woodrow Wilson

. . . We entered this war because violations of right had occurred which touched us to the quick and made the life of our own people impossible unless they were corrected and the world secured once for all against their recurrence. What we demand in this war, therefore, is nothing peculiar to ourselves. It is that the world be made fit and safe to live in; and particularly that it be made safe for every peace-loving nation, which, like our own, wishes to live its own life, determine its own institutions, be assured of justice and fair dealing by the other peoples of the world as against force and selfish aggression. All the peoples of the world are in effect partners in this interest, and for our own part we see very clearly that unless justice be done to others it will not be done to us. The programme of the world's peace, therefore, is our programme; and that programme, the only possible programme, as we see it, is this:

I. Open covenants of peace, openly arrived at, after which there shall be no private international understandings of any kind, but diplomacy shall proceed always frankly and in the public view.

II. Absolute freedom of navigation upon the seas, outside territorial waters, alike in peace and in war, except as the seas may be closed in whole or in part by international action for the enforcement of international covenants.

III. The removal, so far as possible, of all economic barriers and the establishment of an equality of trade conditions among all the nations consenting to the peace and associating themselves for its maintenance.

IV. Adequate guarantees given and taken that national armaments will be reduced to the lowest point consistent with domestic safety.

V. A free, open-minded, and absolutely impartial adjustment of all colonial claims, based upon a strict observance of the principle that in determining all such questions of sovereignty the interests of the populations concerned must have equal weight with the equitable claims of the government whose title is to be determined.

VI. The evacuation of all Russian territory and such a settlement of all questions affecting Russia as will secure the best and freest cooperation of the other nations of the world in obtaining for her an unhampered and unembarrassed opportunity for the independent determination of her own political development and national policy and assure her of a sincere welcome into the society of free nations under institutions of her own choosing; and, more than a welcome, assistance also of every kind that she may need and may herself desire. The treatment accorded Russia by her sister nations in the months to come will be the acid test of their goodwill, of their comprehension of her needs as distinguished from their own interests, and of their intelligent and unselfish sympathy.

VII. Belgium, the whole world will agree, must be evacuated and restored, without any attempt to limit the sovereignty which she enjoys in common with all other free nations. No other single act will serve as this will serve to restore confidence among the nations in the laws which they have themselves set and determined for the government of their relations with one another. Without this healing act the whole structure and validity of international law is forever impaired.

VIII. All French territory should be freed and the invaded portions restored, and the wrong done to France by Prussia in 1871 in the matter of Alsace-Lorraine, which has unsettled the peace of the world for nearly fifty years, should be righted, in order that peace may once more be made secure in the interest of all.

IX. A readjustment of the frontiers of Italy should be effected along clearly recognizable lines of nationality.

X. The peoples of Austria-Hungary, whose place among the nations we wish to see safeguarded and assured, should be accorded the freest opportunity of autonomous development.

XI. Rumania, Serbia, and Montenegro should be evacuated; occupied territories restored; Serbia accorded free and secure access to the sea; and the relations of the several Balkan states to one another determined by friendly counsel along historically established lines of allegiance and nationality; and international guarantees of the political and economic independence and territorial integrity of the several Balkan states should be entered into.

XII. The Turkish portions of the present Ottoman Empire should be assured a secure sovereignty, but the other nationalities which are now under Turkish rule should be assured an undoubted security of life and an absolutely unmolested opportunity of autonomous development, and the Dardanelles should be permanently opened as a free passage to the ships and commerce of all nations under international guarantees.

XIII. An independent Polish state should be erected which should include the territories inhabited by indisputably Polish populations, which should be assured a free and secure access to the sea, and whose political and economic independence and territorial integrity should be guaranteed by international government.

XIV. A general association of nations must be formed under specific covenants for the purpose of affording mutual guarantees of political independence and territorial integrity to great and small states alike.

EXERCISES

I. State a restricted problem developing from each of the following unrestricted problems:

1. What, if any, new courses should be included in the liberal arts curriculum?
2. How can parking conditions in this town be improved?
3. What policy should the college adopt regarding intercollegiate football?

4. How do American novelists compare with English novelists?
5. Where should the new playground be located?
6. How much is it worth for a student to get an advanced degree?
7. How good are this year's movies?
8. To what extent, if at all, are American clergymen underpaid?

II. State a problem of policy related to each of the following problems of value:

1. Are farm cooperatives unfairly taxed?
2. Do fraternities have a favorable influence on scholarship?
3. Is political action by labor unions desirable?
4. Are courses in English literature beneficial?
5. How good a job has the basketball coach done?
6. Are tennis and golf good for the health?

III. Restate these problems in such a way that the question is not "begged":

1. How much does marriage increase a man's chances of being promoted?
2. Why are the Germans the most ferocious warriors of the twentieth century?
3. Is the staggering national debt too high?
4. What can we do to improve our shortsighted foreign policy?
5. How can we make the United States a real democracy?
6. Why does the Production Control Officer want to get rid of the most efficient methods we have ever used in this factory?
7. Are we going to permit these communist-inspired textbooks to corrupt the flower of our youth?
8. Why should we continue to take these useless final examinations?
9. Should we appoint this fascistic politician to a judgeship?
10. How can such an inadequate library continue to serve this great university?

IV. Check the following lists of criteria to be used in evaluation. Are they sufficiently specific? Can they be stated more clearly or with more support? Is each criterion (singular) important enough to be listed? Are there other considerations more important?

1. If you want to go into the motel business, the first thing is location. Most oldtimers in the business say the motel should be fairly close to the center of a town so that the guests won't

have to drive very far to eat or find a bit of recreation. But will this and other advantages like sewerage, water, fire protection warrant the high city taxes? And can you get property cheaply enough to be profitable?

Another thing—Is the location on the highway where the motel can be seen from either direction in time for a motorist to slow down?

Finally, can the location be made attractive to the eye? Rolling ground, a few trees, and a stream can help.

2. To prevent accidents to machine operators, we need to ask these questions:

   Are the machine controls in convenient places, easy to use?
   Is the operator exposed to excessive noise, interruptions, or activities that take his mind off his work?
   Does the machine fit the operator's height?
   Is the lighting efficient for working the full work period?
   Are the safety guards adapted to the operator's physiological and psychological makeup?

3. "From the point of view of the whole community the relative merits of private versus public power must be settled on the basis of such objective criteria as efficiency of service, cost per kilowatt-hour, minimum interference with spheres of individual freedom, and over-all efficient utilization of the nation's resources."
4. "The sequence of three airplane crashes in two months in the city of Elizabeth adjacent to Newark Airport—accidents which brought death to 107 plane passengers and crew members and eleven Elizabeth residents—has raised these large questions: *First,* are airports too close to congested areas for safety? *Second,* could the accidents have been avoided if the airport had not been close to a city? *Third,* could airports be relocated away from congested areas?"
5. The University grants these competitive scholarships on the basis of *need, scholastic record, achievements in student activities,* and *attitude.*
6. Aptitude tests used by a company in selecting employees for particular jobs must be judged by these standards:

   Is the test reliable? That is, will it show the same results whenever it is given among a certain number of people with an average range of capabilities?

Is the test valid? That is, will it accurately measure those qualifications we need for a given job?
Is it economical?
Is it reasonably easy to administer?

V. Set up criteria for the evaluation of one of the following. Remember to select essential criteria, to state them clearly and as specifically as necessary, and to explain those that are not self-explanatory.

1. A community swimming pool to accommodate 500 bathers at any given time. (The standards are part of a report to the town council.)
2. A candidate for the state House of Representatives. (The standards are part of a talk to be delivered to the League of Women Voters.)
3. A chair designed primarily for reading. (The standards are part of a paper written for a design course.)
4. A site for a new textile—or some other—plant. (The standards are part of a report to the Chamber of Commerce.)
5. A traffic by-pass. (The standards are part of recommendations sent to the local traffic commission.)
6. An entering freshman. (The standards are a list of "do's" and "don't's" printed in a freshman guide.)

ASSIGNMENTS

I. Write a short restricted definition (200–300 words or less) of one of the following terms for an analysis of a problem:

1. *Propaganda* (as used in the question: Can propaganda fiction be real art?)
2. *Religious* (as used in the question: Should we encourage religious education in our public schools?)
3. *Fair Employment* (as used in the question: Should this state adopt a fair employment law applying to all business?)
4. *Profits* (as used in the question: Should the legislature increase taxes in this state on corporation profits?)
5. *Nontechnical* (as used in the question: Should the College increase the number of nontechnical electives in the__________ curriculum?)

II. List five problems that you think you might effectively investigate in two or three weeks. (Think now of stating the problem and later of defending a judgment on it.) Choose among current, timely problems—those that seem likely to mean most in your own life. Choose problems from which you can learn—from which you can increase useful knowledge at the same time you get real practice in investigating, constructive thinking, and communicating. Here are some examples:

> What policy of admissions should our medical schools adopt?
> What kinds of books should the Postmaster General ban from the mails?
> Who should control atomic research and development?
> How worthwhile is a graduate degree in my field?
> Is World Federalism a reasonable aim?
> Should the college administration adopt an "honors plan" with voluntary class attendance for honor students?
> How much are liberal arts courses worth?
> Should women be subject to the draft?

III. Write an impartial and informative analysis of a problem that you will later study with a view to defending a judgment. (You may address this analysis to an investigating committee.)

CHAPTER 6

Toward Sound Judgments: Using Logic

The Objective Attitude

We refer to scientific thinking as *objective*. That is, it subordinates personal feelings and sentiments; it especially tries to eliminate prejudice—the "pre-judging" of things before the evidence is in. Now in the chemistry laboratory this kind of impersonal attitude is certainly easier to achieve than it is in politics, or in facing any of the problems that involve the wants and faiths of human beings. Yet the ideals of objective thinking are important whenever we seek the most dependable answers to our most significant problems.

First of all, the objective attitude rejects wishful thinking. If you want a balanced answer to the problem, "Do final examinations have genuine educational value?" you cannot permit hatred (or liking) of examinations to influence your thinking. You cannot estimate "educational value" until you try to divorce personal feelings from your thinking.

James Harvey Robinson pointed out the important difference between "real" reasons and "good" reasons:

> We can readily give what seem to us "good" reasons for being a Catholic or a Mason, a Republican or a Democrat . . . But the "real" reasons for our beliefs are concealed from ourselves as well as from others.

As we grow up we simply adopt the ideas presented to us in regard to such matters as religion, family relations, property, business, our country . . . Our "good" reasons ordinarily have no value in promoting honest enlightenment, because, no matter how solemnly they may be marshalled, they are at bottom the result of personal preference or prejudice, and not of an honest desire to seek . . . new knowledge.[1]

None of us can escape prejudice entirely. Faced with a problem, we begin to think of tentative answers, and one of these may seem immediately better than others. That is a good way to begin—with some hypothesis to test and examine. The danger lies in deciding too soon, before the evidence is in and the "real" reasons analyzed. Prejudice closes the door. The best defense against unfounded conclusions is to admit probable prejudice about your favorite hypothesis. Remind yourself: "The best alternative *seems* to be *B*. I like it best. I prefer it. If it will stand up under close scrutiny I'll be happy. But somebody else will likely choose *K*, *M*, or *V*. I want an answer that will stand up against all attacks, so I must examine all the reasons anybody can advance for *K*, *M*, and *V*—all the reasons against *B*. If, then, I can show the inadequacies of every other alternative, if I can eliminate the important arguments against *B*, then *B* is my answer. *B* will hold its own. But if *B* won't meet the test, then I may have to change my mind."

Willingness to change your mind in the light of new information is the key to objective thinking. Some like to call it "scientific thinking." It means: "Learn enough to defend your hypothesis—or seek another."

The term *judgment*, which we use so often in this book, refers to either a process or an end result. The process of judgment includes all the thinking that we do about any problem: the way we decide what issues and criteria are significant; the way we test the reliability of sources and authorities and the consistency and credibility of evidence; and the kind of reasoning we do. Judgment as the end result is a conclusion, or an opinion, reached by this process. A "good judgment" is one based on reliable evidence and valid reasoning.

Remember the Significant Questions

A thorough analysis of the problem should disclose the significant criteria, or issues. If these are phrased as questions, you know what

[1] James Harvey Robinson, *The Mind in the Making*, Harper & Brothers, 1921.

must be answered. You have a plan to follow. The answers must be based upon:

1. Evidence—the facts of direct observation, reports, the opinions of experts
2. Premises—accepted laws or principles, generally known facts, plausible assumptions
3. Inferences—conclusions from reasoning

Your final judgment is the result of all these things: your evaluation of the evidence, your premises, and your subordinate inferences.

Let's see how the questions that express your criteria direct the whole process of arriving at the right judgments. For example:

A main issue: Has the Governor's administration been unsuccessful?

Criteria: How well has it met standards of honesty?
How beneficial are its policies to the people?
How effective is the Governor as an administrator?
How effectively does he get his program accepted?

Evidence, premises, and inferences may lead to these answers:

The Governor's administration has been corrupt.
He has advanced few socially beneficial measures.
He is a comparatively inefficient administrator.
He has failed to get his program accepted.
Therefore the Governor's administration has been altogether unsuccessful.

Of course the answers are seldom so conclusive. Usually they would be expressed in more moderate language:

The Governor is honest himself and no scandals have marred his term; but he has no program that benefits most of the people of the state.
Moreover, in spite of experience and capacity as an administrator, he has failed to get any consistent support in the legislature.
Therefore, measured by accomplishments, this administration does not merit public support.

It is clear, we hope, that these answers to the significant questions are only "opinions" as they stand. Nobody should be expected to take them seriously without very considerable evidence. But at least the answers are pertinent; the opinions all directly concern the issues and criteria.

Fallacies of Ignoring the Issues

Perhaps the most common fallacies are those that result from "ignoring the question," by introducing irrelevant points. They answer no significant question. Usually they divert attention through appeals to emotion and prejudice.

These fallacies were recognized and classified by the ancients under such terms as *argumentum ad hominem* or *ad populum*. In modern times the Institute for Propaganda Analysis gave them such modern names as "Name Calling," "Transfer," "Band Wagon," "Testimonial," and "Plain Folks." The most important to recognize, avoid, and resist are these:

1. *Irrelevant Personal Attack*. Discussion and controversy frequently produce three kinds of personal criticism or attack. Two of these are entirely relevant and proper; the third is not.

First there is the critical judgment about a reporter or witness. Is he honest and truthful? Does he know what he's talking about? Any attack upon the honesty or ability of the witness is relevant if it is related to his testimony.

Second, another kind of criticism may be even more closely related to the central problem. If the Governor wants to be reelected, his record is naturally open to inspection and criticism. An applicant for employment ought to expect close examination of his experience, education, and reputation. Sometimes "the man" is the point of central importance. If he is, then the man himself is a relevant matter for discussion.

But the third kind of personal criticism is not at all relevant. It distracts attention from real issues. This is the *ad hominem*, the attack on a writer or speaker himself rather than on what he says. Suppose, for example, that a magazine article advocates larger appropriations for our national parks. The evidence seems impressive, but you learn that the author has been indicted for misappropriation of funds in Florida. Is the article better or worse because of the indictment—or doesn't it matter? It probably doesn't matter. It is probably irrelevant. If the indictment for misappropriation of funds has something to do with his testimony, then it is pertinent. If not, his "argument" is no better and no worse—it is something to be judged on its merits. Reasoning is what must be judged, not the man who reasons. Moral character in a writer or speaker is not a test of his logic.

Suppose a temperance lecturer has had wide influence in changing the habits of heavy drinkers. Then it is revealed that the lecturer himself is an alcoholic. How does this news affect the contents of his lectures? Does it make alcohol better or worse?

An organization of citizens opposes the "quota system" of a local business school as it applies to Catholics, Jews, and other minorities. During the controversy that ensues it is revealed that the chairman of the citizens' organization has been named by an FBI agent as an active Communist. Does that news make the quota system better, or worse, or neither?

It is important to distinguish the "reporter" or witness, who contributes evidence, from the "advocate" or critic, who defends his judgments with reasons. Sometimes, of course, the advocate is his own witness, reporting as evidence things he has directly observed. As the source of evidence he is properly subject to all the tests of credibility that we reasonably apply to any witness. But as an advocate, critic, or analyst, the only relevant tests are about what he *says*—not what he *is*.

The only way to test reasoning is to look at the reasoning itself.

2. *"Transfer"—Irrelevant Association.* There is an unfortunate human tendency to separate everything into two classes—the good and the bad. Everything associated with the good things then tends to seem good; everything associated with the bad things tends to seem bad. Such associations naturally lead to fallacious conclusions. Atheism is bad; hence an atheist's belief in freedom of worship must be unsound or dangerous.

These irrelevant associations are based on assumptions that seem clearly absurd if we take the trouble to state them:

The Arabs are associated with an international policy in the United Nations. We don't like Arabs, so we don't like that policy. (Assumption: "Everything Arabs do is bad." But don't Arabs eat and sleep, trade, and even adopt many customs similar to ours?)

Patvia's government is vigorously opposed to the enemies of America. Patvia, therefore, deserves our friendship and respect. (Assumption: "Every opponent of the opponents of America deserves our respect." But weren't Napoleon and Stalin, among many others, opponents of the opponents of America? Should we respect them for that?)

3. *"Testimonial"—Irrelevant Use of Authority.* We need specialists and experts to give us advice about things we do not understand ourselves, but that is a different matter from using authorities or "great men" to settle all our problems. Experts are useful to give opinions in their field—not about everything. Einstein was a great scientist, but his views about government were outside his field and so subject to the examination of common men. Washington and Lincoln were great presidents, but they were not "authorities" in any special field. Obviously their opinions do not apply reasonably to NATO or TVA—things they never heard of.

Prejudices and emotional associations get us off the track. They make us forget the significant issues. We all need to reject the temptation to substitute feeling for thought.

The Nature of Inference

Inference is the process of reaching valid conclusions from things we know or assume. It is the application of logic.

An *argument* can state its conclusion first and then supply the reasons supporting it. But *reasoning* must always proceed from what we know to what we conclude or infer. If we already "know" something, no reasoning is necessary to establish it.

For example, we may infer from looking at our thermometer that there will be ice on the lake three miles away: a reading of 18°F (the known fact), together with our general knowledge that water on the lake always freezes at temperatures that low (accepted premise), enables us to draw a conclusion without actually going to the lake to see. This is an inference by *deduction*—the application of a general rule to a specific case. But to arrive at the general premise that water on the lake "always" freezes at certain temperatures, many previous observations were necessary; from many known cases a general conclusion followed—by *induction*. Deduction relies first upon generalizations in our head. Induction places first reliance on observations.

Some questions related to a problem can be answered without any inferences whatever. "Was Factor at the scene of the crime when it occurred?" might be answered by direct evidence: Henty testifies that he saw him there, or Factor himself admits he was there. Most of our significant questions, however, can be answered only by deductive or inductive reasoning, or a combination of both.

Deductions

The laws of logic are the rules of common sense expressed in precise terms. We all make countless deductions and inductions every day whether or not we know the logical labels. We also recognize numerous fallacies in reasoning (usually the other fellow's) even if we don't know their names. But a study of some of the principles of reasoning can sharpen our critical sense. It can make us more alert and careful about accepting or rejecting arguments that we read and hear. It can help us think better ourselves.

A simple deduction may be expressed completely in three sentences, called a *syllogism*:

1. A general rule, called the *major premise*:
   All freshmen at Loomis take Math. 1.
2. A case included under the general rule, called the *minor premise*:
   Perry is a freshman at Loomis.
3. The *conclusion*, which applies the general rule to the case named in the minor premise:
   Perry takes Math. 1.

If we have the premises properly stated and they are true, the conclusion follows inevitably. We don't have to know Perry; we don't have to see him in a Math. 1 class. If *all* freshmen take the course and Perry *is* a freshman, then our conclusion is inescapable.

In everyday discussion we take shortcuts: we don't write or speak in syllogisms. We say "Perry must be taking Math. 1. He's a freshman." We say "Tippett is sure to be elected; the Republican nominee in this city never loses." We say "*The Great Gatsby* must be in the Library of Congress because it has an American copyright." What we do, you see, is leave out one third of the syllogism; one premise we *imply*, assuming that people will see what we mean. This abbreviated syllogism is called an *enthymeme*.

The advantage of understanding the principles of the syllogism is that we can quickly fill in the missing premises, test them, and thus test the whole deduction. We can apply the principles to both our own reasoning and the reasoning of others.

1. *The Categorical Syllogism.* The most common form of syllogism is called *categorical.* The major premise makes an unqualified assertion about all of a class. The formula is this:

All of class A belong to class *B*. (Major premise)
a belongs to class A. (Minor premise)
Therefore *a* belongs to class *B*.

Note that the major premise is not reversible; it does *not* mean that all of class B belong to class A. All dogs are animals, but not all animals are dogs.

Here are the tests to apply to a categorical syllogism:

1. Is the major premise true? Does it make an unqualified assertion about every member of a class?
2. Is the minor premise true? Does it name a specific member of the class covered by the major premise?
3. Does the conclusion apply the generalization stated in the major premise to the case named in the minor premise?
4. Are all the terms unambiguous? Does each term mean the same thing wherever it is used in the syllogism?

Suppose we apply these tests to some everyday inferences expressed in everyday language:

Eddie Prior's father is sure Eddie will earn more money than anybody else in the family because Eddie is the only one to graduate from college.

The unstated premise in this *enthymeme,* or abbreviated syllogism, is that "college graduates earn more than those who never went to college." But that major premise violates Rule 1: it does not include *all* college graduates or *every* college graduate. So, while Eddie may have other qualities that make him superior to his brothers, and other reasons might make the prediction sound, the reason given doesn't hold water. The argument is fallacious.

All books, being human productions, are liable to error.

The unstated premise here, of course, is that "all human productions are liable to error." That seems true enough; everything man does *may* include errors. And certainly books are human productions. The conclusion seems inescapable.

Wilson will make a writer. He has what all great writers have—imagination.

All great writers have imagination, and Wilson has imagination. We have both premises stated in a single sentence. The conclusion, however, does not follow at all from the premises. All great writers may have imagination, but does everybody with imagination become a great writer? The minor premise, you see, places Wilson not in the class of great writers, but in the class of those with imagination.

The Young Americans for Peace must be a Communist Front. They advocate reducing armaments just as the Communists do these days.

This is a fallacy of the same kind. "All Communists advocate reducing armaments" is not the same thing as saying "everybody who advocates reducing armaments is a Communist."

The dictionary defines *engineer* as a *capable manager*. Who, then, is better fitted to become General Manager of this company than Arnold K. Cutty, our most distinguished electrical engineer, member of many engineering societies, a man who has been a practicing engineer for twenty years?

This obviously shifts meanings, a violation of Rule 4. The dictionary definition refers to an entirely different use of the word *engineer* from the meaning in the second sentence.

2. *The Disjunctive Syllogism.* The major premise of a disjunctive syllogism states alternative possibilities, the minor premise accepts or rejects one of them, and the conclusion then rejects or accepts the other:

a. Everybody who works for this company is paid either hourly wages or weekly salary.
b. Dunne is not paid hourly wages.
c. Therefore he must receive a weekly salary.

In everyday discussions the deduction is expressed something like this:

The state administration has to economize. We certainly don't want any higher taxes.

The unstated premise, of course, is that "the state must either economize or raise taxes." If the generalization is true the conclusion logically follows.

Cuthby's failure in life must be due to laziness. He seems bright enough.

The unstated major premise is that "failure in life must be due either to laziness or to stupidity." But of course these are not the only possibilities. Ill health could be one. There are others.

3. *The Hypothetical Syllogism.* The major premise of a hypothetical syllogism begins with an "if" or "when":

a. If prices get too high people stop buying.
b. Prices are too high right now.
c. Therefore people will stop buying.

The major premise here states a conditional generalization, the minor premise satisfies the condition, and the conclusion then makes an *un*conditional assertion. Here are typical enthymemes:

When people lack security at home they don't get along well outside. That's why I think Higby doesn't have security at home.

This is fallacious reasoning. The implied minor premise, "Higby doesn't get along well outside," does not satisfy the condition of the major premise ("when people lack security at home").

Traffic will be light today. If you don't find it heavy by ten in the morning, it is light all day.

The implied minor premise, "traffic is not heavy at ten this morning," fits properly. The truth of the conclusion then depends upon the truth of both premises.

Generalizing from a Sample

Inductive generalizing from a sample is based upon the assumption that a representative part of a class will have the characteristics of the whole class. To judge a barrel of potatoes, for instance, you would hardly look at every potato in the barrel; a few dozen, from various locations in the barrel, ought to give an adequate knowledge of them all. Consumers' testing laboratories do not examine every refrigerator of the Arctic Company's Model K; tests on one of these standardized products would be enough.

A "complete induction," covering every member of a class, is just a matter of counting what we observe. The generalization that "every member of this class is right-handed" would be justified only if every member had been questioned or observed; then it is a statement of fact, not a judgment. But a *reasoned* induction goes beyond the available facts to reach inferences about things not yet observed. So, from experience, we might predict with reasonable probability that "about 65% of this freshman class will graduate," "department store sales will rise in early December," or "the life expectancy of babies born this year is nearly 70 years." All these judgments (they are *not* certainties) are based upon a sample of past experiences. Much of our most useful information consists of inductive generalizations of this kind.

One of the most interesting examples of simple induction is found in public opinion polls. Though these polls haven't always predicted the winner in an election, their percentage of variation from the actual vote is seldom very large. But they were not always so reliable. The old-fashioned "straw vote" was highly inaccurate. What makes the modern "scientific" poll-takers more dependable is the methods they use to get a representative cross-section of the whole public they sample. These experts take a comparatively small sample, only a few thousand out of a total public of millions, but they "weight" this sample to make it representative. They decide first, deductively, what factors are most likely to influence a voter's opinion. For example, in political questions they consider as significant *income, sex, age,* and *party preference.* The sample then contains the same proportion as the whole population of: high, middle, and low incomes; male and female; age 21–35, 36–59, 60 and over; Republicans and Democrats.

So many of our judgments rest upon generalizations from a sample that we need tests to avoid fallacious conclusions:

1. Take a large enough sample. If the class to be sampled is highly homogeneous (like a manufactured product), a small sample is adequate. If the whole class is very heterogeneous (like the people of the United States), a larger sample is needed for reliable conclusions.

2. Don't ignore *negative* instances. Propagandists are accused of "card-stacking"; that is, they may cite only instances that suit their purposes, ignoring all the others. They may, for example, count all

the protests against a law without mentioning or sampling at all the opinions of those who favor it.

3. Put your reliance in "chance" or "the law of averages" by taking a random sample when that is feasible. For instance, every fifth name in the student directory will give a reliable sample of all students. But a sample taken at church would miss all those who don't go to church; one taken at a dance would miss all those who don't dance.

4. If the class is heterogeneous and if random sampling is not feasible, try the weighted sample. You could test the soil in a field by getting samples from different locations. You could test "industrial wages" by getting a proportionate sample of representatives from companies in various parts of the country, manufacturing different products, and employing different numbers of workers.

Typical fallacies of inductive generalizing are shown in the following examples:

The secretary of Wilburn College Class of 1927 sent questionnaires in 1952 to all living members of his class. He received answers from 435 of the 752. His report in the *Alumni News* said: "Nobody in the class of 1927 is unemployed, over 70% own their own homes, their incomes range from $3,900 to $78,000 (before taxes), and most of them live with the first wife they ever married."

The sample appears to be large enough, and it doesn't ignore "negative instances." But this questionnaire does not satisfy Rule 3 or 4 because men with small incomes (or other experiences that make them sensitive about reporting) are less likely to answer and are thus excluded from the sample.

During the past year more than a hundred municipalities have established the City Manager Plan. Its widespread success in a thousand cities that reported to the City Manager League was attested by 100% favorable opinions.

This seems to violate Rule 2 since only favorable opinions might be reported to the League.

Notre Dame shows what a college can gain by means of successful football teams. From a small and little known institution fifty years ago, the university has developed in size, wealth, and academic standing. Other colleges may well look to the experience of Notre Dame.

This generalization seems to ignore all the tests of logical induction. A single college is surely not an adequate sample. All negative instances—colleges that have had football success with little accompanying improvement otherwise—are ignored. No chance selection or weighing of factors such as size, location, academic standing, etc. has been employed.

It has been said that "an ounce of human nature will upset a ton of statistics." Emotionally that is often true; one case we know personally seems more important than a thousand cases reported by others. If the few cases we know intimately are associated with things we love or hate we often generalize with little consideration for logic. We all need to be alert if we don't want this kind of "human nature" to lead us to absurdities.

Analogy

Analogy is inference by comparisons. If two things are alike in significant respects, we may infer that they will be alike in another respect. If the Dantscher family finds Newburg a good suburb in which to live, their friends the Maloneys, who have similar tastes and income, ought to find it a good place too. If it costs $14,000 to build a six-room house of given design in Demont, you might estimate that the same house can be built for about $14,000 in another town where costs of labor and materials are approximately the same.

The one test for literal analogy is whether the things or persons compared resemble each other in the most significant respects.

English people are much like Americans in tradition, habits, and heritage. Hence English experience with compulsory health insurance is a good indication of what we might expect if we adopted the system here.

It would surely be useful to study England's experience with the system thoroughly before we make a decision, But the analogy has numerous weaknesses. Significant differences that might make the effects different here are the very different influences of two world wars upon the health and living standards of the two countries, differences in medical history, different areas that the system would have to cover.

John Exmann of General Steel has had a long and notable experience with the problems of American business that eminently fits him for the Presidency of the United States. Good government is good business. A great executive in business can be a great executive in Washington.

There are, of course, certain important similarities between executive problems in business and those in government, but there are also striking differences. "Getting along with Congress" is a different matter from getting along with subordinates. Bringing public support for administration programs and aiming for "general welfare" rather than profits might be significant differences too.

We expect literal analogies to satisfy the demands of logical validity, but "figurative" analogies have a different use. When we compare the President's cabinet with a baseball team the purpose is not to prove a literal connection but to point up a general principle that men engaged in any common cause need to cooperate. The figurative analogy adds color; it calls certain already accepted premises sharply to mind; but it does not prove anything directly.

Causal Inferences

What caused higher prices? What effect will they have on the volume of business? Cause-and-effect relationships occupy a major share of our attention much of the time.

A cause of a phenomenon is simply "a necessary antecedent." If we say X caused Y, we mean that X had to exist before Y could exist. In the world of reality there is no such thing as *the* cause of anything. There are many causes, or necessary antecedents, for everything that happens. So what we try to find out in thinking about causal relations are answers to questions like these:

1. Is X *a* cause of Y? (That is, did it have an influence on Y? If so, how much?)
2. What caused Y? (That is, which are the most important or most immediate influences in producing Y?)
3. What will be the effects of X?

Causal inference may be either deductive or inductive. A deductive inference about a cause-effect relationship is "theoretical"; it applies general rules or principles and concludes what "must" have happened or what "should" happen. Inductive inference depends upon cases, incidents, examples; it makes causal generalizations from specific details.

Let's see how this works. Suppose automotive engineers develop a new automobile design. They apply principles of mechanics, make applications of established theories to develop this new design. So far they have inferred—deductively—that this new design, based upon established laws, will develop more horsepower than earlier models. After the deductions, the engineers would want some tests—some "controlled" experiments in which the new model could be checked against older models in actual practice. The tests are a means to causal *in*ductions.

Or suppose George Witham argues that fraternities are an aid to good scholarship because they maintain study hours, get regular reports about the work of their members, appoint scholarship chairmen to give guidance, and arrange for upperclassmen to help underclassmen with their studies. By *de*ductive reasoning he infers that fraternities influence scholarship favorably; he applies general premises about good scholastic environment to what he knows about fraternities. But perhaps Jack Wrantham says, "That's nothing but theory; let's look at the record." So Jack compares the scholastic averages of certain fraternity members with the scholastic averages of certain independents, taking care to get two groups that are alike in such factors as IQ, curricula, and outside activities. Whatever difference he finds in scholastic averages, then, he infers *in*ductively must be due to fraternity membership.

Our age seems to put its faith in the inductive method. "Yes," we say, "that sounds all right in theory—but how does it work out in practice?" We want tests, experiments, "a look at the record."

And yet we also want an explanation of inductive results, a theory that will help us answer the question "Why?" If inductive studies show us, for example, that college students who put most time on bridge also get the highest grades, are we to say at once that the time spent at bridge is the cause of the high grades? More likely we would say, "That makes no sense," and search for a deductive explanation. We'd want a "theory" to match the inductive evidence.

We may borrow certain principles of causal induction from John Stuart Mill's laws of scientific investigation. Known as "Mill's Canons," two of them—the Method of Agreement and the Method of Difference—have useful applications in solving everyday problems.

1. *Method of Agreement*. Suppose that every time a certain condition exists you are conscious of another condition which always precedes or accompanies the first. You quite naturally think of a causal

relationship. You are likely to say that the one condition *causes* the other.

Let's say that every time you go out to sea you feel sick; you would probably conclude that the sea trip caused your illness. Or let's say that every time you have studied two hours or more for a quiz you got an A; you would probably conclude the studying earned the grade.

Now Mill's canon of *agreement* warns that there must be one and *only one* antecedent which always precedes the phenomenon if we are to ascribe it as the cause. If two or more antecedents always precede the phenomenon, then we will not know which had the influence. The perfect formula would look like this:

A, B, C, and D are the only antecedents of R (the Result)
A, F, C, and G are the only antecedents of R (another instance)
B, K, C, and L are the only antecedents of R (another instance)

In these three instances, C is the only antecedent which always precedes *R*; hence C must be a necessary antecedent and hence the cause of *R*. It is either "the cause, or an indispensable part of the cause," to use Mill's own words.

Now this method of agreement may be a real help in our reasoning about causes, but it is never a final test. In life there never is a situation in which one, and only one, antecedent always precedes or accompanies an effect. In life there are infinite antecedents of everything that happens. So we must view Mill's method of agreement only as a helpful guide to possibilities—and as a warning.

Psychiatrists studying thousands of cases of alcoholism may discover great differences in wealth, in physical and mental condition, even in quantities of alcohol consumed; but if they find an agreement among the cases in definite neurotic tendencies, they have some basis for assuming that those tendencies are a factor (a "part of a cause") in alcoholism.

If typhoid should break out as an epidemic in your town, the authorities would immediately begin to narrow down the possibilities —a partial application of the method of agreement. They would check the water supply, the milk supplies, and all the places where victims had been. If they should find that the milk and water supplies were entirely different for some of the victims, but that *all* had eaten at a particular restaurant, then the investigation would center upon that restaurant.

So this method of agreement is a useful starting point but never a means of reaching complete certainty. The psychiatrists' use of the method must depend in part upon previous discoveries. The authorities searching for the cause of typhoid are relying also upon medical discoveries of the past; they limit the area of search by this method, but they do not find the certain cause without other methods.

Your use of the method of agreement may be most important in finding fallacies in various inductions. If Jim Carey says, "You know, every time I eat spaghetti I get sick," your knowledge of Mill's canon may suggest certain questions: "Did you eat anything else with the spaghetti? Did you drink any wine? Did you stay up later when you ate spaghetti?" Or look at another inference that might call for application of the method of agreement:

> For a decade we have had our greatest volume of sales in November. General business conditions elsewhere have varied widely; prices and the variety of merchandise differ considerably during different months. The explanation seems to be that there has been a seasonal layoff every summer, and that the men catch up in their purchasing when they are reemployed every fall.

Perhaps this explanation has some sense in it—and we must never overlook even the slightest element of sense; but it is surely important to remember that the month of November is also accompanied by preparations for the Christmas holidays.

2. *Method of Difference*. This second of Mill's Canons says in effect: Here a thing happens and there it doesn't. What's the difference in the two situations? If we find a single point of difference—a single difference among the antecedents—there we have "the cause." Now the perfect formula would look this way:

A, B, C, and D are the only antecedents of R (the Result)
A, B, C, and D occur and we get R
A, B, and D occur and we do not get R

C is here the only point of difference; hence it must be an essential part of the cause.

Actually Mill emphasizes the "one and only one point of difference" as essential to establishing a real cause; however, we cannot apply this method with the hope of getting absolute certainty for a conclusion. The method represents the ideal for every controlled experience in science. In the laboratory, conditions can be kept approximately the same. Elsewhere conditions cannot be controlled to anything like the same degree, but we can do our best to reduce the differences. If educators want to find the effect of closed-circuit television instruction on student progress, they will experiment with two groups of students. They choose the two groups to be as nearly alike as possible: in class, age, curriculum, and scholastic standing. One group will receive the television instruction; the other, or "control" group, will not. All other factors—assignments, discussion sessions, etc.—must be the same for both groups. Finally the two groups will take the same examination. Differences in results may be ascribed to the difference in instruction.

In everyday situations the degree of confidence we can place in our conclusions depends upon how slight the "other differences" are. Suppose Connecticut has capital punishment and Rhode Island does not. We might find the difference in murder rate in these two states and attribute the difference to capital punishment. To have faith in our conclusion, though, we have to consider all other possible differences in the two states: the size of urban population, occupations and living conditions, other laws that might affect crimes of violence, how each state defines murder.

Applying Mill's Canons can keep you from making one of the most common errors in reasoning—establishing a "false cause," more technically known as *post hoc ergo propter hoc*. This error comes about when someone blindly infers that an event preceding or accompanying a phenomenon must be its cause. Perhaps a black cat ran in front of the car just before the car hit the telephone pole. Perhaps Mr. King went to a resort the week before his wife brought divorce action. Is it logical to blame the cat or the resort? Coincidence or precedence doesn't establish cause. The four o'clock plane leaves an hour before the five o'clock plane, but is not the cause of its leaving.

Combination of Reasoning Methods

Seldom is your reasoning all of one kind. You combine causal induction with deduction, and often sampling as well. You use not a single syllogism, but a complex chain of deductions. You seldom generalize from cases or statistics without making some deduction.

Consider the combined reasoning methods in this paragraph:

During World War I the records of 12,492 foreign-born recruits in the American army who took the army intelligence tests showed proportionately lower grades for the more recent immigrants. This seems to show that every wave of immigration up to 1914 brought us people of lower mentality than those who came before.

First, we find a generalization, or simple induction, from a sample of 12,492 foreign-born recruits of World War I; these are used to represent the "waves of immigration" to the United States. (We might question whether the sample is large enough, but especially whether men of army age in 1917–1919 can be used to represent all the immigrants of a century or more.) Secondly, a causal induction is made: recruits of more recent arrival are contrasted with those of earlier arrival, and the time of arrival is inferred to have a causal relationship to their intelligence. There is also a deduction which might be phrased in this syllogism:

1. All those who get low scores in the army intelligence test are of low mentality.
2. Recent immigrants had low scores in these tests.
3. Hence recent immigrants are of low mentality.

(The major premise may be open to some question; perhaps acquaintance with the English language and with Anglo-Saxon customs would affect one's score as much as "mentality.")

Take the reasoning of lawyers and detectives; it consists of more than simple inductions or chains of deductions. So-called circumstantial evidence may add up to highly convincing conclusions under the law:

1. The murder occurred between 9 and 11 p.m. Jones cannot explain where he was during those hours.
2. Jones was seen in the vicinity at 9:15 and again at 11:05.
3. Typewriter experts agree that a threatening note was written on Jones's typewriter.
4. Jones's fingerprints are on what the coroner calls "the murder weapon," a knife that Jones purchased two days earlier.

Many similar pieces of evidence may fit the hypothesis that Jones is guilty. Some will have more significance than others, but no single fact is enough in itself to warrant such a conclusion. There must be a "harmony of the facts"—all known facts fitting properly into place.

The same method works for scientists, who can test their hypotheses by a similar consideration of all the known relevant facts. If *all* the facts fit, then the hypothesis gains credence; if some of them do not fit, then the hypothesis may be discredited.

We often use complex reasoning of this kind in evaluating systems or organizations, laws, or human motives. The process has been likened to the solving of a picture puzzle: the parts fit into place until the shape of the last piece is inevitably determined even if it is missing. The whole explanation must meet these tests:

1. Does the explanation (or conclusion) recognize all the known facts? Or do certain known facts conflict with or contradict the explanation?
2. Are enough significant facts known to warrant this conclusion?
3. Will the conclusion stand without many unproved assumptions? (The simpler the explanation—the less demand it makes on assumption—the more acceptable it will be.)

Avoiding Common Fallacies

A final note on some common faults in reasoning should here be made, even at the risk of repetition elsewhere.

1. *Begging the Question.* The fallacy we call begging the question consists of assuming the truth of a premise that has not been established. Very often the premise is not even expressed—or it is passed over so quickly that it is hardly noticed:

> Shop courses like these are given in over three thousand high schools located in every part of America. Certainly such amazing success is proof of their educational value and good reason for establishing the courses in our own school.

The question begged here is whether the courses *are* successful ("given" is not the same thing as "given with amazing success").

> Opposition to loyalty oaths by all these friends of totalitarian and subversive movements is understandable. It is high time that Americans took steps to eliminate subversives from our schools and our government agencies.

Here apparently two questions are begged: first, *does* the opposition come from "friends of totalitarian and subversive movements"? second, *will* loyalty oaths "eliminate subversives"?

2. *Fallacies of Composition and Division.* The fallacy of composition is assuming that a collective group has the characteristics of its individual members. A football team of great stars is not always a winning team. A dish concocted of a dozen excellent ingredients is not always good to eat.

The fallacy of division is assuming that the individual has the quality of the group or class to which it belongs. For example, "corporation profits rose 23% last year" is no indication whatever that X Corporation's profits rose 23%. Sophomore George Hatchly obviously may have a scholastic average either above or below the "sophomore average." Not every player on the team that wins the World Series is necessarily a great player. Such generalizations as "Irishmen are happy-go-lucky," "Englishmen have no sense of humor," "Americans are optimists," "Italians are hot-headed"—even if they were proved generally true—have so many exceptions that they cannot become useful major premises without great modification.

3. *Overstating Conclusions.* In mathematics and formal logic, the conclusions reached through deduction are expected to be unqualified—that is, "true" beyond doubt. In most of the affairs of life where controversial problems exist, conclusions are probabilities, not unqualified decisions. Though we do our best to keep objective and apply the tests of validity fairly, our inferences can go amiss, our evidence can be misleading. So we must avoid overstating conclusions.

One way to avoid such overstatement is to be very careful in presenting our premises. For example, the major premise, "All applicants who fail the aptitude test will prove failures in their college work," could hardly be proved; but we might say, "All applicants who fail the aptitude test are *poor risks*," and then draw reasonably satisfactory conclusions about applicants A, B, and C. The major premise, "If a man is 30 years old, he will live to be 68," is clearly untenable; but the premise stated like this, "If a man is 30 years old and passes the examination, insurance companies estimate his probable life span as 68," is acceptable.

If you make your premises as accurate as possible, especially not overstated, you will find that deduction becomes potentially more useful as a tool in solving daily problems.

EXERCISES

I. In the following deductions, what premises are unstated or implied? How well do these enthymemes meet the tests? Try to make the enthymemes full-fledged syllogisms.

1. Laws against the use of narcotics are futile. Any law that tries to legislate morality is futile.
2. Our highways are much too crowded with traffic for human safety. That's why large trucks ought to be banned.
3. Unions ought to keep out of politics. Every group should reject the unpatriotic temptation to make political alignments on the basis of selfish interest.
4. Caniffe's attack on Senator Rolfe's vote is pretty silly when you remember that two years ago Caniffe was advocating exactly what Rolfe voted for.
5. This new swimming coach must be a very cultured man. He listens to symphonies hours every evening.
6. Did you read about the Senator's son? The Senator ought to resign. No man should hold public office who can't even manage his own family.
7. I suppose Joe will be a rich man someday. His father owns a good business.
8. I see Tallyho had an undefeated season. They must pay plenty for football players at Tallyho.
9. Curmer is guilty of plagiarism. Eight sentences in this article are verbatim duplicates of sentences from Burtak's book.
10. A nervous man was sitting here in the lobby before us. Look at that pile of Tarryton butts in the ashtray.
11. The postoffice is closed now. It's after six o'clock.
12. The Post House won't be open. It doesn't open till six.
13. I'm convinced that Darhoun is the man for president for the simple reason that South Carolina is against him.
14. Apparently Jack is a Republican. I see the Republicans in Congress voted unanimously against that amendment.
15. The game must be over. All this traffic is heading away from the park.
16. Every successful congressional candidate must campaign hard. That's why Bulkly's chances for election are so good.
17. Brunauer's reputation as a physicist must be grossly undeserved. He's a notorious atheist.

18. Whether good or bad, you have to admit that federal health insurance is socialism. It has been advocated in Socialist platforms for forty years.
19. Putny's divorce is a discredit to the man any way you look at it. It was either his fault or his wife's. If it was his fault then he's immediately discredited. If it was his wife's fault, then he's a sad judge of character—and that's certainly to his discredit.
20. The President couldn't have known about the meeting when he made his decision. News of the meeting didn't appear in the papers till two days later.

II. Analyze and evaluate the following inferences (what is the conclusion? method or methods of reasoning? how valid?):

1. Married women with children of their own are best qualified to teach in our public schools because they have the natural understanding, sympathy, and experience to teach children.
2. Anthropologists present evidence to show that geographic differences of climate and altitude have no influence on language. Individuals of any race or origin, if trained early in life, can learn any language. Peoples in similar geographic environment often speak very different languages; and peoples in very different geographic environments often speak very similar languages.
3. For men, at least, marriage is good for the health. In every age group the death rate of married men is strikingly lower than the death rate of single men, and very much lower than that of divorced men.
4. The JayCees have recently organized in Conicut, Rankton, Branville, and Kent. Davenport is much like these towns in population. It seems reasonable, therefore, that the JayCees could function successfully in Davenport.
5. Industrialism appears to produce racial prejudice. Contrast the United States, where industrialization is most advanced and racial discrimination most prevalent, with European countries like Italy, France, and Norway—all far behind us industrially yet almost totally free of such discrimination.
5. Results of the Zenith Public Opinion poll before and after election:

	Before	*Actual election results*
Case	48%	42%
Rice	42%	31%
Bates	10%	27%

The sampling must have been good, since all candidates finished in the same order in the general election. The same methods used before future elections can be expected to prove equally reliable.

7. Studies made of smokers and non-smokers in a dozen colleges showed that cigarette smokers as a group had considerably lower scholastic averages than non-smokers. Apparently smoking tends to dull the mind.
8. Studies over a period of many years show that families in the lowest third in income have twice as much sickness as families in the middle third. The lack of adequate medical care is, of course, the explanation.
9. Price fixing by manufacturers violates the first principle of our free-enterprise system—man's right to his own property. Once a retailer has bought the manufacturer's product, the product justly belongs to him. Like all other property he owns, he should be entirely free to sell at any price he sees fit.
10. People in the Midwest are more interested in baseball than Easterners. Look at the crowds in Milwaukee and Kansas City.
11. Medical economists point out that of babies born without the aid of doctors and hospitals, twice as many die as among those with proper medical care. Medical care would have saved those lives.
12. Students at Atford High are pretty bad sportsmen. Two of their players were ejected from last week's game for dirty playing.
13. There are ten times as many crimes of violence, measured by arrests, in the "wet" towns and cities of America as there are in all the "dry" towns. These figures are further proof that liquor is a principal cause of crime.
14. Education makes people recognize the superiority of the Republican Party. The lowest-income voters, who have generally less schooling, have since 1936 given substantial majorities to Democratic candidates for President. The highest-income voters, who have the greater education, generally, have given equally substantial majorities to Republican candidates.
15. The mob that last night tried to break up the meeting where Brickton spoke must have been either extreme radicals or sincere believers in American democracy. If they were radicals, they ought to know that their own right to hold meetings depends upon the right given everyone to do the same. If they were sincere believers in American democracy, they should know that the right of free speech and peaceable assembly is essential

American tradition. If free speech is denied to any political group, no matter how repulsive, it can be denied to all.

16. Physical attractiveness in girls generally leads to poor scholarship. Two professors made a classification of 600 girls according to their beauty, then examined their scholastic records. The 54 "beautiful" girls averaged 2.7% below the 192 "fairly attractive," 7.6% below the 111 classified as "plain."
17. The farmer doesn't balance his budget by the month, and couldn't. He buys feed and fertilizer, hires men to plow and cultivate, and waits till harvest time to get back what he has paid out and more. The government is bigger than the farmer, but a government must follow the same system of budgeting. The government has periods of outgo, periods when it can take in more than it pays out. The government shouldn't be asked to balance its budget every year any more than the farmer is asked to balance his every month.

ASSIGNMENT

As your instructor may direct, obtain a piece of writing (magazine article, chapter in a book, editorial, or other reasoned argument) and write a critical evaluation of its reasoning. Your criticism may be positive, negative, or both. Point out examples of *enthymemes, generalizing from a sample, causal inferences, analogies*. Point out any fallacies that you can find. Remember that your writing is itself an example of reasoning.

CHAPTER 7

Toward Sound Judgments: The Evidence

What Is Evidence?

Evidence is important raw material for inference and judgment. It consists of demonstrable fact, reported fact, or opinion of experts that can support premises and generalizations. Some premises, like "All men are mortal," need no supporting evidence because nobody questions their truth. But other premises must be proved. "We need a thorough reassessment of property in Zenith (conclusion) because houses on Harter Street are unfairly assessed (minor premise)." Evidence is needed that assessments on Harter Street are unfair: building costs, assessment figures, descriptive information about the houses. Without constant reference to facts, such judgments are sure to be unreliable.

Sometimes we need evidence to support both major and minor premises:

1. Every member of the Yellow Shirts takes a secret oath to subvert all organized religion.
2. Will Kurdo is a member of the Yellow Shirts.

If these premises are true, the conclusion is inevitable that "Will Kurdo must have taken that secret oath." But such a conclusion does not follow reasonably from mere rumor. Unproved assertions do not establish reliable judgments. Reliable testimony must support both the statement that "every member" does take such an oath and the statement that Will Kurdo belongs to the organization.

Evidence is therefore important in testing your own judgments; it is especially important whenever you want to defend your judgments to others.

Sources of Evidence

Evidence may, of course, consist of *things*: a house, a street, or a dented fender may all lead us to conclusions. Photographs accompanying our writing may approximate the "exhibits" of a courtroom. And evidence about a document or book may consist of direct quotations from it.

But even a photograph needs accompanying statements: when was it taken? where was it taken? who says so? Most of the evidence we can use in writing will be reports *about* the facts:

1. Kurdo attended a meeting of the Yellow Shirts last May 19.
2. Contents of all the desk drawers were strewn on the floor.
3. Bentley attended Coe College three years.
4. Over 22% of these soldiers married within one year of discharge.

Sources of evidence useful in writing include:

Your own experiences and observations
Factual reports from:
  Reading
  Public statements in speeches, forums, lectures
  Interviews or conversations
Opinions of specialists

Tests of Evidence

Evaluating evidence is naturally of first importance in reaching sound judgments. To deserve attention evidence ought to meet certain tests:

1. *Fact Evidence.* Since unsubstantiated opinions from ordinary witnesses have little or no merit as evidence, we demand the relevant facts. We should ask:

a. Is the source (the reporter, author, or agency responsible for the statements) trustworthy? A reputation for exaggeration, prejudice, and careless reporting serves to discredit the source. A reputation for temperate, honest, unbiased reporting lends credence to any report.

b. Are the statements essentially clear and unambiguous?

c. Are the statements of fact verifiable?

d. Are the reported facts consistent—consistent with themselves? with natural laws? with what we know of human nature? with other evidence already fully substantiated?

e. Is the evidence relevant to the question under consideration? For one thing, is it recent enough? A book on the income tax published in 1924 may have been accurate in its time, but how much would it help us in reaching judgments about income taxes today? And finally, do the facts reported actually help answer significant questions?

It is possible to learn a good deal about the reliability of reports from what we call "internal evidence"—the content and style of the reports themselves. Signs of prejudice may appear: loaded words, appeals to prejudice, obvious exaggeration. Important omissions amounting to card-stacking may be noticed. But signs of such one-sided reporting do not make a report totally worthless as evidence. Verifiable statements of fact may be there and worth sifting out. A "bad" report is not necessarily all bad; so don't let your own prejudice about a source lead you to reject evidence that can be checked and made useful.

2. *Opinion Evidence.* For opinion evidence you need somewhat different, more rigid tests:

a. Is this a problem where you need the aid of specialists? Ordinarily, given time and the necessary background, you will prefer to get the facts and do your own thinking. You turn to experts only in limited areas that you can't effectively study for yourself. The opinions of experts alone can never settle broad social problems.

b. Is the specialist providing opinions recognized and approved by colleagues in his field? Do they trust his judgment?

c. Has this specialist limited his opinions to his own field? The great surgeon's opinion of school taxes is not "expert." His *reasoning* on all matters deserves the same critical attention you give to any reasoning.

d. How fully do the experts agree? Wide differences leave the ordinary layman about where he started.

e. Is the specialist disinterested? Since his judgments are more complex than simple observations, prejudice affects the reliability of opinion evidence more than it would affect fact evidence. It all depends upon how much "difference of opinion" can exist. Fingerprint or ballistics experts, however prejudiced, are usually reliable enough because there is so little room for disagreement that false testimony could quickly discredit them. Psychiatric opinion is less certain; hence prejudice is more serious in psychiatric testimony.

You ought to demand objectivity from any authority whose opinion you intend to accept. The naval leader's opinion about naval weapons and tactics would generally be classified as "expert"; but his opinion about the need of increased naval appropriations would hardly be accepted until his reasons were given very close scrutiny. A successful trainer of boxers could give expert opinion evidence about the right cross or left jab; his opinion about the values of boxing to society would be much less "expert."

Recording Evidence for Later Use

It is a rare person who can retain very much relevant information in his head for very long. When you collect evidence bearing on any writing problem, you need some efficient method of recording and storing it. Even your own observations or recollections had better be recorded in note form.

A bound notebook can serve for rough notes that you intend to copy, but the system makes for extra work. You will need notes in a convenient form for shuffling, rearranging, fitting into whatever plan you eventually decide upon. So stiff file cards or half-sheets of heavy typing paper are most satisfactory. Then a single "note"—easily handled and separated from others—can be kept, ready for any eventual use.

But just what is a single note? How much information makes a note? In general, each note should include one item of evidence concerning one issue—no more, no less. A single interview or magazine article might produce ten or twenty separate notes: ten or twenty different items related to ten or twenty different issues.

Classify each note under the appropriate sub-subject or issue. To do that, you may need to keep your list of significant questions with you all the time you read, interview, or investigate your problem. For example:

Problem: Is the motel business a profitable enterprise for young people with modest capital?

5. How much capital is needed?
1. What available locations are best?
    a. State or section?
    b. Which highways?
    c. What local surroundings?
4. What are the prospects for business?
    a. Seasonal?
    b. Days of the week?
    c. Total?
2. What facilities are demanded?
3. What qualifications of management are needed?
6. What are the probable profits?

A single note pertaining to this problem might look like this:

6

What Owners Say

Tourist Court Journal (Aug '51) says avg. earnings of *all* owners about 30% after taxes. "The experts deny this." ". . . oldtimers purse their lips, look dubious, and venture to say" if a man makes 15% before taxes he's doing fine.

"The betting is that the shrewd and experienced motel owners make at least 30 per cent after taxes."

Source: "Money on the Roadside," FORTUNE, Aug., 1951, p. 80.

The symbol "6" in the upper lefthand corner keys the note to issue number 6 in the writer's outline: "What are the probable profits?" The heading, "What Owners Say," is not out of the article quoted;

it is simply the writer's personal comment—to remind him of the nature of this particular note and a possible lead to what he will later write. If you don't want a heading of this kind, you just don't bother with one.

This note is a summary, but it contains direct quotations, *always* carefully enclosed in quotation marks to show what is quoted directly and what is not. The note includes only comments that have some connection with issue number 6—the topic indicated in the upper lefthand corner.

The source is shown, in full, at the bottom of the first page of the note. If the writer has a numbered bibliography, he might save time by putting "27" or "36" at the bottom of the page to show the bibliographical entry from which this evidence is taken. For instance, if No. 36 in your bibliography is "FORTUNE, Money on the Roadside," etc., you might just as well write "No. 36" on the note—and take precautions that you don't mislay that bibliography.

The notes you take ought to be ready for inclusion in your writing. Careful note-taking results in easier writing.

Cases or Statistics?

Fact evidence may concern either individual incidents, situations—*cases*—or aggregates of many cases which we call *statistics*. It is important to understand the advantages you can get from each kind of evidence.

Suppose you wanted to know what happens to honor graduates from college after they get into industry. Do they advance to high positions rapidly, gradually, or not at all? Are they adaptable, cooperative, efficient, "happy"? You might take five or ten high-honor graduates and follow them to Bell Telephone, General Motors, and other large corporations. Or you might take several thousand such graduates from various colleges and try to compile reports of their records in scores of different industries. For five or ten cases you might get highly detailed accounts of their jobs, responsibilities, associations, and difficulties. You would not, however, feel safe in generalizing about "high-honor graduates in industry" because you haven't enough cases for a fair sample.

On the other hand, statistics of thousands of such graduates would permit you to take averages and medians of salary, the percentage who become vice presidents, and a few other matters, and so you could generalize about such things as those. And yet statistics would show you nothing specific about "what an honor student is like" in industry. Both case evidence and statistical evidence have advantages, and both have limitations.

Cases can be very enlightening; they may provide specific information about individuals—hobbies, wife and children, friends, social and religious activities, opinions, and other intimate details that statistics could never touch. And yet individual peculiarities get in the way of generalizations.

Very often the best results come from a combination of the two kinds of evidence. You might use statistics and then try to find a few representative or typical cases to bring the statistics closer to real life.

It is important to remember that statistics are abstractions: they abstract from numerous individual cases only one characteristic at a time. For example, statistics tell us that "3187 families in Zenith have incomes between $3000 and $4000." Here is perhaps a significant piece of evidence and we might infer much from it about these people; but in themselves the statistics tell absolutely nothing except the dollar income range of a certain number of families. We don't know from the figure whether the families are big or small, Republicans or Democrats, intelligent or stupid, happy or unhappy; we don't know their race, religion, occupations, or any of their interests. We don't even know, except by inference, anything at all about their standards of living.

Now of course it is possible to learn more by taking more and more statistics—more abstractions. Whatever we learn from statistics about individuals must come from the deductions we make from the figures. That is why it is so often helpful to get more specific details about at least a few of the individuals that we consider representative.

Interpreting Statistical Data

In a world as complex as ours, statistics are obviously necessary for any adequate general understanding of our civilization. Full understanding of their proper uses and possibilities is something that trained statisticians spend their lives trying to achieve. Yet ordinary citizens must learn enough to read and use them with some discrimination. As we attempt to analyze a statistical statement or table, two questions must be answered:

1. What do they *say?* What facts do they report?
2. What do they *signify?* What useful conclusions follow from them? What can we logically infer from them?

Before we can answer these two basic questions, we need certain tests to apply to statistics as evidence. Of course the general tests for fact evidence apply here, but some further warnings are called for:

1. **Note the statistical unit.** By *unit* we mean *the thing counted.* The statistical unit in population figures is *person,* in illiteracy statistics an *illiterate* person.

We think of statistics as aggregates of facts; however, we cannot have aggregates of facts unless the statistical unit is itself a matter of fact. For example, "48,000 employables in the city of Zenith" means that somebody has counted *employables.* Do you know what that means? Who was counted? Of course somebody had to make a precise definition before the counting started, and since statisticians' judgment was involved, we must place high confidence in them before we accept their figure.

Statistics of "subnormal children" gathered by different agencies might differ widely simply because they defined the unit differently. Ordinary persons have little idea of the meaning of *subnormal,* and hence little idea of the meaning of the statistics. We sometimes may be willing to accept the experts' word for it; nevertheless we ought to be aware that we are not here getting fact evidence, but the opinions of specialists.

On the other hand, statistics of births, deaths, marriages, college enrollments, registered Democrats, car loading, and various other phenomena are factual enough because the statistical units are comparatively unambiguous and we can all understand pretty well just who or what was counted.

2. **Consider the source.** Since compiling statistics is always a somewhat complicated task, we need confidence in the ability and honesty of the reporting agency, whether it is a person or group of persons. We may be especially concerned with the possible prejudice in statistics that originate with propagandists. Generally, we place consider-

able faith in statistics of the Census Bureau, the Bureau of Labor Statistics, and other government agencies that presumably have no axe to grind.

3. **When comparing sets of statistics, generally prefer rates or percentages to gross numbers.** It means little that there are more or less fatal accidents in Denver than in Spokane until you know the populations of the two cities; accident *rates* permit an immediate comparison. Conversely, however, rates can be misleading if the raw figures are very small: "Fifty percent of the freshmen admitted to this college from Windham High School were dropped for poor scholarship" rather misrepresents the facts if only two students from Windham had been admitted.

4. **In examining tabulations of percentages, always ask "percentage *of what*?"** A table showing "Sex of Drivers in Fatal Accidents" reports:

Male	93%
Female	7%

What does this table show? Only that of all drivers in fatal accidents 93% were male. It is in no way a comparison of the driving habits of the sexes. To get that you would need a quite different table at least showing the percentage of male drivers in fatal accidents and the comparable percentage of female drivers in fatal accidents. In other words, of every hundred male drivers, how many are involved in fatal accidents? Of every hundred female drivers, how many are involved in fatal accidents?

Notice how different the results would be in the following instances:

Percentage of persons listed in *Who's Who* with college degrees	Percentage of those with college degrees listed in *Who's Who*
Death rate from accidents at age 30 (percentage of persons at age 30 who die in accidents)	Percentage of all deaths at age 30 caused by accidents

Of course the percentage figures in the lefthand column would be very different from those in the other column. The uses of the statistics would be quite different too. Amazingly fallacious conclusions can result from misreading such percentages.

5. **Be cautious of the word *average*.** Suppose you read this account in a college newspaper:

The *College Gazette* has completed its poll of student character and arrives at some interesting facts. The average student turns out to be 20.2 years old, lives in a town with a population between 10,000 and 25,000, attends the Methodist Church, will vote Republican, expects to marry and have 2.3 children, drives or wants to drive a Buick, intends to go into business, will need an income of $6000 pretty soon and at least $10,167 for a contented life by the time he's thirty-five. This average student thinks history or economics is the best course he's had, math or English the worst. He reads a daily paper about twice a week. He has read 6.8 books since he came to college (not counting texts), and he reads *Time* or *Readers Digest* more or less regularly.

Certainly any intelligent reader understands immediately that no such "average" undergraduate could exist, but the picture is confused somewhat unnecessarily by a confusion of meanings. The very ambiguous term *average* in this story apparently has all three of its common meanings: arithmetic *mean*, as well as *median*, and *mode* (or typical). To arrive at 20.2 years, 2.3 children, $10,167, and 6.8 books, the editors must have added many figures and then divided by the number of answers, thus getting an arithmetic *mean average*. The *median* is the middle point of a scale, as many numbers being below as above; and perhaps the population range of the "average" town in this article is such a median. Most of the other items of information are probably majority votes, or plurality votes—we do not know which. Are a majority Methodists, or is that just the largest single denomination? Did a majority think history or economics best, or just the largest block of votes among a variety of scattered answers? In such a conglomeration of meanings, the word *average* loses all sense. Nobody can be quite sure what the story means. Of course it may be that no reader of such an account cares much anyhow and no harm is done. Even so, it is just as well to recognize what is going on.

Remember first of all that the mean average, arrived at by arithmetic, is always an abstraction. Except by coincidence no such average exists except in the mind. Who can have 2.3 children or own 1.2 cars? And if by chance the figure happens to come out even, it is no less an abstract figure. What a mean average shows is what all the items in the group would be, quantitatively, if they were divided equally. And you can use the mean average only with quantitative data on a scale—never with divisions into Republicans and Democrats, Fraternity and Non-Fraternity.

The *median* average is the middle point in a series. It is useful in showing the "medium" position. (In the group of figures 8, 7, 6, 5, 4, 3, 2, the obvious median is 5.)

The mode, the high point of a statistical curve, represents the largest number of cases. But the word *mode* is not often used, and it is always important to understand whether this kind of average represents a majority or a mere plurality of many almost equally high points.

Sometimes the three kinds of average—mean, median, and typical—arrive coincidentally at the same point. If you took the weights, heights, IQ's, grade averages of all the students in your college class, the three averages would be very nearly the same. But at other times the three might be very far apart. As perhaps an extreme example, suppose you want an "average" of the following eleven incomes:

$7000	$10,000	$11,000	$15,000	$200,000
$7000		$11,000		
$7000				
$7000				
$7000				

The median, middle salary, is $10,000. The largest single group, a mode of almost half the total, gets $7000. But the mean average is $25,636.36.

6. **Neither mean, median, nor typical average is a legitimate basis for a major premise.** "The average IQ at Dently College is 131" tells us nothing about freshman John C. Hafer's IQ, though he attends Dently. "Last year's average corporation profit" provides no information whatever about General Motors' last year's profit.

These tests and checks may suggest nothing but pitfalls in the use of statistics. They may seem to imply that statistics are bad things to use. That is not the point at all. Statistics are certainly here to stay. They can be indispensable aids in defending your judgments. So you must learn to distinguish the true from the false, the sound from the unsound.

Interpreting for Readers

Interpreting facts for readers is something between simple reporting and argument. Interpretation reports and explains what the facts *are*; then it shows what the facts *signify*. The interpretation may be an end in itself for the writer, or of course it may be a necessary element in more complex discussion leading to further conclusions. For instance, the writer's job may be to "report on the accident;" he explains what happened, and he points out why it happened. But such an interpretation may also be part of the defense for a broader judgment—evidence to help demonstrate that new safety equipment is needed, or that the supervisor ought to be fired, or that we need new laws.

Whatever you want to use it for, an interpretation of facts or statements involves two steps:

1. A summary of what is known—to simplify and clarify:
   a. What do witnesses say? If they disagree, exactly what do they disagree about?
   b. What do these statistics say? What relative weights do different figures deserve? Who supplies the statistics?
   c. What did you observe directly? Where? When?
   d. How reliable are the sources and reports?
2. An explanation of inferences—what the facts signify:
   a. What conditions can we infer from the facts?
   b. What causes can we infer?
   c. What trends are suggested? What can we reasonably predict?

1. *Summary and Simplification.* The reason for summarizing evidence is to separate wheat from chaff, the facts we can use from those that do not apply. A news story, a technical report, or the doctor's testimony naturally include some things that are much more important than others. Statistical tables list scores of items that we don't need for our particular problem. The first task of interpretation, then, is to help readers fix their attention on the points of major interest.

Here is a summary-simplification of a group of statistical tables concerning "The Non-Voter":

> These tables show something of the kinds of citizens who vote and the kinds who don't.
>
> Note that in twenty northern states, 75% to 85% of all citizens vote. In six southern states, only 15% to 25% vote. The largest

> percentage of voters is found in the biggest cities, next largest in smaller cities, and lowest percentage in small towns and rural communities.
>
> Perhaps it is surprising that "natives" (citizens with both parents born in this country) are less inclined to vote than "foreigners" (citizens with both parents born elsewhere): 64% of natives vote, 75% of foreigners. But only 34% of all Negroes vote compared with 71% of Caucasians.
>
> The upper quarter in income substantially outvotes the bottom quarter. You will see that income is a more significant factor than education in determining voting habits.
>
> And the older citizens outvote the younger citizens: of those over forty, 75% vote. Of those under forty, 59% vote.

This kind of summary emphasizes the comparisons you want to discuss. It defines terms (such as *natives* and *foreigners* above). The statistical unit in particular may need definition. But there are other means of simplification. For instance, huge numbers—in the billions—are hard to grasp; tiny numbers, like 0.00123, are equally abstract for ordinary readers. It is often possible to translate into everyday terms: "seven men out of twelve," "about $130 for every family in the county," "nearly twenty to an acre."

Death rates and batting averages give so many deaths or hits per thousand: "17 per thousand" is easier to understand for most of us than "1.7%." It is certainly much more convincing to say that "three out of every thousand who would have died in 1930 of this disease are now living" than to say "0.3% who would have died . . ." Figures in a table ought to be precise; but interpretations are often more useful if they eliminate the decimal points and make the kind of comparisons ordinary readers can visualize.

A legitimate part of your interpretive summary is criticism of the source. If no source is named, the report may not be verifiable; if it isn't verifiable, its value is questionable indeed. Accuracy, completeness, consistency—these are matters for the interpreter to consider.

Of course it isn't always desirable to do all your summarizing first, then all your discussion of inferences. Sometimes it is preferable to summarize one set of facts (northern and southern differences, for instance) and interpret the significance of that before turning to another set of facts (such as income difference). If the data demand several distinct divisions, each somewhat complex, this order is generally better.

One function of a good interpretation may be to point out what the evidence does *not* show. Suppose for instance you found this table in a newspaper:

Current Trends (1939–1950)	
Prices	205
Wages	197
Profits	287
Farm income	301

If you are writing about the relation of wages to prices and profits, it might be a service to tell your readers why, without more information, this table is valueless. *What* "prices"? (consumer's? wholesale?) *What* "wages"? (hourly? weekly? annual? for skilled or unskilled workers?) *What* "profits"? (whose? total or average? before or after taxes?) And *what* "farm income"? (net or gross? average farm or total?) You could draw no conclusions whatever from such a table until the terms are all defined, and if you don't know yourself how they are used you cannot define them. Pointing out the inadequacies of reports, whether statistics or not, may then be one contribution of interpretation.

2. *Explaining Inferences.* Summary and simplification are usually means to another end. The facts have value because they point to conclusions. So the most important part of the interpretation may be the inferences you draw and the way you explain them to your readers.

The first question to answer may be *why*? Why are more students studying sociology? Why did the Secretary resign? Why do more automobile accidents in the county occur between 6 and 8 p.m. than during any other period of the day?

Naturally what you are here concerned with are possible causes and influences. A number of different hypotheses may be worth suggesting:

The increased interest in sociology may be due to changes in the program and the staff, differences in the advisory system, or increased recognition of the importance of the study among parents and students. Perhaps all three had some influence.

You evaluate the hypotheses and naturally try to show which of them offer the best explanations. You are careful not to say "cause" when you mean "correlation." If for example you find a greater percentage of people in Vermont over 65 than in Illinois, here is a correlation between place of residence and proportion of older people, but did living in Vermont "cause" people to live longer? Several possible explanations come to mind:

a. A larger proportion of young people may leave Vermont, and so the percentage in the lower age levels is reduced.
b. Older people may like to move to Vermont after retirement.
c. The environment of Vermont may actually be more conducive to longevity.

You may seek other evidence—including more statistics—to help interpret the statistics at hand. Let's say that during the period 1954-1955 the death toll on the State Turnpike has increased by 13%. Expert opinion from the police might be employed as part of your interpretation which seeks to establish causes. You might even get another set of statistics that would tell you how much the horsepower of automobiles had been increased, or how many more trucks had begun to use the Turnpike, or even what the weather had been like during the period in question and other years preceding.

The answers provided by a good interpretation need not be final, and certainly not dogmatic. The differences may be due to various causes and open to various interpretations. A useful interpretation should distinguish between certainties, probabilities, and possibilities. In doubtful situations, it should allow the reader to make up his own mind about matters. In situations of probability and certainty, it should guide without forcing.

One final job the interpreter may do is to find whatever significant relationships, causes, and probabilities there are—and then introduce questions his readers have not previously considered—questions that may lead to a prediction.

Such prediction is a difficult art; you ought to make predictions with considerable restraint. For example, statistics may show that young automobile drivers who have got certificates in safety-driver courses have a lower accident rate than other young drivers. Your interpretation may conclude that the courses were desirable; you infer that the courses had a favorable influence. You might infer further (by deduction or analogy) that making these courses compulsory would reduce automobile accidents among other young drivers, or even older ones. But such a prediction needs to be carefully stated. Perhaps "compulsion" would be less effective than free choice of such a course. Perhaps those who voluntarily chose the course were just naturally more careful than those who didn't choose it. Perhaps, if every high school in America made such a course compulsory, the quality of available teachers and teaching would deteriorate. The probability of success may seem good, but you don't want to claim too much, or fail to point out difficulties that may exist.

Interpretation, then, consists of guidance. In guiding and explaining for your readers, you must make inferences that are consistent with all the information at hand; you must apply reasoning only as far as it can be held "reasonable" in the light of the evidence. If the evidence is statistics, you can make no claims that an ordinarily intelligent reader cannot substantiate for himself in the body of the statistics—or supplementary evidence you have supplied.

READINGS

1

The author of this article states, or implies, judgments that may be open to some dispute. Do you find any statements here that seem unsubstantiated or unwarranted?

It is obvious that the FBI collects highly useful and significant evidence. Must the FBI itself evaluate sources of evidence? To what extent must government officials and courts apply to FBI reports the tests of evidence that have been discussed in this chapter?

If somebody says, "FBI reports show that X belonged to the Communist Party in 1939," is that a statement of fact or of opinion? If opinion, whose opinion? If fact, how fully does it meet the tests for fact evidence?

HOW GOOD IS AN FBI REPORT *

ALAN BARTH

It was a paradox of the mid-nineteen-forties that investigative reports of the Federal Bureau of Investigation—despite the bureau's immense popularity and prestige—were widely discounted, if not dis-

* From *Harper's Magazine*, March, 1954. Reprinted by permission of *Harper's Magazine* and the author.

regarded, by responsible officials of the executive branch of the government. The FBI warned repeatedly of widespread infiltration of the government service by Communists and by Soviet espionage agents. Yet, in many instances, these warnings went unheeded. Among officials the FBI seems to have commanded more adulation than respect.

In the course of his inquest of last November into the Harry Dexter White case, Attorney General Herbert Brownell offered an explanation of this paradox. The previous Administration, he said, had been guilty of "blindness" and of "unwillingness" to face the facts of Communist penetration. If former President Truman alone had been responsible, perhaps this disregard of FBI warnings could be dismissed as political "blindness" or as obtuseness. The responsibility was shared, however, by a variety of unquestionably sober and conscientious members of the Truman Administration.

Harry White himself and a number of other persons who have been accused of espionage served under three successive Secretaries of the Treasury—Henry Morgenthau, Jr., the late Chief Justice Fred M. Vinson, and John Snyder. One of the alleged spies, Harold Glasser, attended the Moscow meeting of the Council of Foreign Ministers—as Senator Jenner took particular pains to point out—in the role of adviser to Secretary of State George C. Marshall two years after the FBI warning about him. At least one of the employees of the Office of Strategic Services accused of espionage, Duncan Lee, retained the full confidence of Major General William Donovan, despite the FBI reports. Nathan Gregory Silvermaster, named by the FBI as a central figure in a spy ring, had been the subject of previous warnings by Military Intelligence and the Civil Service Commission as well as the FBI; yet no less sternly upright a man than the late Judge Robert P. Patterson, then Under Secretary of War (and, like Donovan, a lifelong Republican), reviewed Silvermaster's record and declared:

"I have personally made an examination of the case and have discussed it with Major General G. V. Strong, G-2. I am fully satisfied that the facts do not show anything derogatory to Mr. Silvermaster's character or loyalty to the United States. . . ."

And of course Alger Hiss, about whom the FBI warned in the same report that dealt with Harry White, was retained in a position of trust by Secretary of State James F. Byrnes.

If all these men were blind, then there must have been some common denominator of their blindness. It seems reasonable to look for this common denominator in the nature of the FBI reports on which their judgment was based—on which, indeed, the whole personnel clearance program of the federal government was based. It seems reasonable, indeed, to ask a question that has become in our time almost a form of lese majesty: How good is an FBI report?

An FBI investigative report is one of the most confidential of confidential government documents. Although it amounts to a *laissez-passer* or a *lettre de cachet* for its subject, he is unlikely ever to glimpse it. FBI files become available for public examination only in rare instances—when, for example, someone leaks a portion of their contents, or a Judith Coplon gets hold of a handful of them and is caught with the goods and brought to trial, or when an Attorney General elects to declassify a part of one for the edification of a congressional committee. It is extremely difficult, therefore, for an ordinary citizen to make any independent appraisal of the merits of FBI reports. We have some characterizations of them, however, from authoritative sources.

Arguing against the surrender of FBI reports to a congressional committee in 1941, Robert H. Jackson—at that time Attorney General—said: "Investigative reports include leads and suspicions, and sometimes even the statements of malicious or misinformed people." Mr. Hoover himself gave the following clear account of the limitations of FBI reports at the very outset of his testimony last November before the Senate Internal Security Subcommittee:

"As members of this committee know, the Federal Bureau of Investigation is a service agency. It does not make policy; it does not evaluate; it secures facts upon which determinations can be made by those officials of the United States government who have the responsibility for taking whatever action is indicated.

"We do not inject ourselves into legislative matters. We do not express opinions or draw conclusions in our investigative reports. . . .

"Since we are not an agency for decision as to action, we are legally, morally, and in good conscience obligated to relay all information and facts we secure to the responsible officials and agencies of government."

Refusal to evaluate has been a cornerstone of FBI policy and practice ever since Mr. Hoover became the director of the bureau in 1924.

The restraint does him the greatest credit. It acknowledges a limitation upon police power which is basic to any free society, but which has not always been so plainly understood by members of the legislature. On more than one occasion, Mr. Hoover has resisted congressional efforts to invest him with the authority of a judge.

In 1950, for example, when the House of Representatives passed legislation establishing a National Science Foundation, it provided that no one should receive one of the Foundation's scholarships—which, incidentally, carried with it no access to classified information—unless the FBI certified him to be loyal to the United States. Mr. Hoover promptly pointed out the impropriety of authorizing a police agency to make such a determination. He persuaded the Congress to restrict him to fact-finding and to place the responsibility for evaluation where it belonged.

The refusal to evaluate has operated at the same time, however, to justify the inclusion in FBI reports of a great deal of questionable material.

Mr. Hoover's belief that "since we are not an agency for decision as to action, we are legally obligated to relay all information and facts we secure" has led to the relaying of "information" culled sometimes from knaves and nitwits, sometimes from bigots, sometimes from persons whose own devotion to the United States ought to be suspect, sometimes from men or women with axes to grind or hatchets to bury in the skulls of employees whom they disliked.

In point of fact, FBI reports have sometimes included, in addition to what Mr. Hoover seems disposed to call unproved information, a good deal of material the point and pertinence of which are somewhat obscure.

The FBI was responsible for investigating employees under the federal loyalty program, and the questioning of accused employees in hearings under this program was based on information conveyed in FBI confidential reports. Some exceedingly odd questions were asked. One board member inquired, for instance, if an employee favored or opposed the segregation of blood in Red Cross blood banks; the question arose, he said, out of information given to the board that she had written a letter to the Red Cross about such segregation.

In her careful study, *The Federal Loyalty Security Program,* published by the Cornell University Press last summer, Eleanor Bontecou provides interesting excerpts from transcripts of loyalty board proceedings, which suggest that the FBI was giving the boards some strange stuff. In one hearing, an employee under interrogation, a married man, was confronted with the following assertion: "Information has been received that you expressed to others that you were opposed to the institution of marriage, which is one of the tenets of the Communist party."

And in another hearing, according to Miss Bontecou, an employee was asked to explain this bit of "derogatory information":

> We have a confidential informant who says he visited your house and listened in your apartment for three hours to a recorded opera entitled *The Cradle Will Rock*. He explained that this opera followed along the lines of a downtrodden laboring man and the evils of the capitalist system.

On November 18, 1953, Robert Morris, counsel to the Jenner subcommittee, read into the record information which he said came from "a summary of the loyalty files on [Solomon] Adler." The summary contained information, Mr. Morris said, showing that "a high State Department official" stated that Adler was "intimately connected" with political discussions engaged in by General George C. Marshall in China during 1946–47. And another official, Mr. Morris said, reported that Adler "was critical" of the Chinese Nationalists in that period. What inference is a reader of this report supposed to draw from this "information"?

In the furious Senate debate which took place in March 1953 over the confirmation of Charles E. Bohlen to be Ambassador to Russia, Senator Pat McCarran said on the floor that the security director of the State Department, R. W. Scott McLeod, had found that "he could not clear Mr. Bohlen on the basis of the FBI report," and the Senator charged that Mr. McLeod had been "summarily overridden" by Secretary of State Dulles. The Senate Foreign Relations Committee, assured by Mr. Dulles that "there is no derogatory material whatsoever which questions the loyalty of Mr. Bohlen to the United States, or which suggests that he is not a good security risk," voted 15 to 0 to approve the nomination. Some members of the Senate continued to be troubled, nevertheless, by the "derogatory material" which the report admittedly contained, and kept pressing to find out about it. At last, after prolonged discussion, one member of the Foreign Relations Committee, Senator Guy M. Gillette, gave the Senate the following account of one of the several items of derogatory information about which Secretary Dulles had told the committee in detail:

> One of the derogatory reports—and it was a derogatory report, and Senators may evaluate it, along with members of the Committee on Foreign Relations—concerned a person who said he possessed a sixth sense in addition to the five senses all of us possess. He said that due to his possessing this sixth sense he could look at a man and determine whether or not there was something immoral about him, or something pertaining to moral turpitude in the man's make-up, or some tendency on his part to take action that would not be accepted in good society as moral action. This man said that he looked at Mr. Bohlen and, with this sixth sense of his, he determined that Mr. Bohlen was a man who did have in the back of his mind such a tendency toward immorality as to make him unfit.

Now, if there was much of this sort of stuff in FBI reports, it seems small wonder indeed that responsible administrators tended to discount them. To include in a report the maunderings of mystics may betoken a stern refusal to evaluate; but it does little to clarify the judgment of the man who must eventually do the evaluating. And this becomes especially true when the mystic is identified, as is commonly the case in FBI reports, only by some cabalistic symbol such as A-1 or V-8.

The most illuminating insight into the character of FBI confidential files was afforded by publication of the papers which Judith Coplon was charged with removing from the Department of Justice and attempting to pass on to a Russian agent, Valentin Gubitchev. These lifted documents were introduced in the first trial of Miss Coplon in Washington over the protests of Justice Department spokesmen who argued that publication of them would imperil national security. Federal Judge Albert Reeves, who presided at the trial, ruled, however, that the character of these documents was pertinent to the issue to be tried and must be submitted to the jury.

"If it turns out that the government has come into court exposing itself," he said, in a curiously felicitous phrase, "then it will have to take the peril. If it embarrasses the government to disclose relevant material, then the government ought not to be here."

Truly, the government came into court exposing itself—or at any rate exposing the FBI—in a most embarrassing way. Publication of the files which Miss Coplon had with her revealed that they contained such delectable tidbits of "information" as the statement of an unidentified informant that she had observed her neighbors "moving around the house in a nude state" and that her eleven-year-old boy said he saw one of these neighbors go out on the porch, undressed, to get the morning paper.

These same files supplied the "information" that one of the assistants to the President of the United States had given some help in obtaining a passport for a trip to Mexico to a friend with whose wife, according to an informant, the Presidential aide had once been in love. The files gave officials of the government responsible for evaluation the following "information" concerning Fredric March, a distinguished personality of the theater, who was neither an employee of the government nor an applicant for a government job.

> Confidential Informant ND-305 advised December 25, 1945, that the subject [Fredric March] partook in the entertainment program at a meeting sponsored by the American Society for Russian Relief held at Madison Square Garden, New York City, December 8, 1945. The informant, who was one of about 13,000 attending the meeting, stated that Helen Hayes, a noted actress, and the subject portrayed a Russian schoolteacher and a Soviet soldier, respectively, in a skit, whereby they described the devastation of Russia by the Nazis at the battles of Stalingrad and Leningrad. . . .

When one reflects upon the man-hours of study and research that went into the compilation of this unevaluated goulash of "information and facts"—and the ingenuity and effort expended by the Russians to gain possession of it—one cannot help wondering which was the more bamboozled, the U.S.A. or the U.S.S.R. What kind of fact-finding is this? What basis does it provide for the "determination" which must be made, as Mr. Hoover put it, "by those officials of the United States government who have the responsibility for taking whatever action is indicated?"

We may assume that these are not fair or representative samples of the FBI's work. The stuff removed by Miss Coplon may have been no more than undigested material intended for the bureau's raw files; the stuff made public in the Bohlen debate or read into a Senate subcommittee record by its counsel pretty surely does not constitute the cream of FBI reporting. But these glimpses of FBI reports are the best that are available to us; and even when every reasonable allowance has been made, one is left with the impression that there was a good deal of surplusage in them.

Obliged to discount the reports in part, administrators may well have fallen into a habit of discounting them in their entirety. Made impatient by reading that an employee "was critical" of the Chinese Nationalists or that he had contributed money to the Loyalists in Spain or that he had thought segregated blood banks undemocratic, an administrator might understandably have been less patient than he should have been with an allegation in the same report that the employee was a Communist or a spy. And this is the more possible since such an allegation was commonly attributed to an informant unidentified save by a cryptic numeral.

Although it eschews evaluation of the material it reports, the FBI, Mr. Hoover told the Jenner subcommittee, "of course has a duty to evaluate its sources of information." One specimen of FBI source evaluation was provided by Mr. Hoover at the same hearing. "All information furnished by Miss Bentley which was susceptible to check," he said, "has proved to be correct. She has been subjected to the most searching of cross-examinations; her testimony has been evaluated by juries and reviewed by the courts and has been found to be accurate."

Now, this is by any standard a most generous estimate of Miss Bentley's credibility—and one concerning which a reasonable man might choose to differ with the head of the FBI. Insofar as her testimony has been evaluated by juries—and much of it has not been—it is an overstatement to say that she has been found by these juries to be uniformly accurate. Her most conspicuous success was in the Remington case. She made three charges against Remington: one, that he was a member of the Communist party; two, that he paid Communist party dues to her; and three, that he gave her government material which she was not authorized to receive. In the prosecution of Remington for perjury for his sworn denial of these charges, the government dropped the first count; there was a hung jury in regard to the second count; Remington was convicted in regard to the third.

Elizabeth Bentley went before a grand jury in 1948 and made detailed charges of espionage against thirty employees or former employees of the United States government, Harry White among them. The grand jury did not indict a single one of the thirty. Attorney General Brownell offered the Jenner subcommittee an explanation of this failure: "When he [White] came before the grand jury, of course, as I have made clear, I hope, in my original statement, much of this evidence against him was received by wiretap. Under the rules of the federal courts, you cannot introduce before a grand jury or a federal court in a criminal case evidence obtained by wiretap information." Another explanation might have been that Miss Bentley's testimony in the White case was the rankest hearsay. By her own admission, she had never even met Harry White.

Since Mr. Brownell implies that the wiretaps would prove White's guilt, it is strange that he has permitted the public no glimpse of their content. The Attorney General told the Jenner subcommittee that the FBI report of February 1, 1946, "contains much corroborative evidence which cannot be made public either because it would disclose investigative techniques of the FBI or because it might be harmful to the national interest." But this can scarcely apply to the FBI practice of wiretapping. This particular FBI investigative technique has been unabashedly admitted by Mr. Hoover for some time. And it is hard to see how there could be anything harmful to the national interest in disclosing White's own words as recorded. Others who have read the transcript interpret it very differently from Mr. Brownell.

Although Miss Bentley's testimony about White was mere hearsay, she gave direct evidence that Silvermaster, Mrs. Silvermaster, and William Ludwig Ullman gave her microfilmed classified information to transmit to the Russians. This was espionage committed in time of war—a crime punishable by death as to which there is no statute of limitations. Wiretap corroboration or no wiretap corroboration, the grand jury could have indicted had it believed Miss Bentley. It evidently did not believe her.

Still one more point needs to be borne in mind. To hand down an indictment, a grand jury does not need to be convinced of guilt beyond a reasonable doubt. It needs to be convinced only that there is sufficient evidence against an accused to warrant requiring him to stand trial. Respecting some of the persons accused by Miss Bentley, the government administrators apparently came to the same conclusion as the members of the grand jury. Perhaps there was no greater culpability in the one case than in the other.

Perhaps American officials cannot be expected to accept a policeman's evaluation of the reliability of an anonymous informant. Perhaps American officials are reluctant to turn their backs upon a trusted associate on the mere basis of hearsay in an investigative report. Perhaps the reports made by the FBI, with their fuzzy melange of unevaluated material, compelled discounting. Perhaps the comprehensiveness of their denigration invited doubt. Perhaps, like the boy who cried "Wolf," the FBI had lost in some degree the confidence of its clientele.

Harry White may have been a traitor and a spy. But the simple say-so of a prosecutor and a policeman does not make him so. The same may be said, and ought to be said, of the living individuals summarily accused and condemned by Messrs. Brownell and Hoover. If Lauchlin Currie and Duncan Lee and Harold Glasser and Frank Coe and Solomon Adler and all the others whose names were so easily spilled before the Jenner subcommittee committed crimes, there are courts of law in which they can be tried.

Consider the case of Solomon Adler, a man who has endured the shadow of accusation for nearly a decade. He was among those accused by Miss Bentley, and he was among those inferentially condemned by Hoover and Brownell. Yet the evidence against him had been presented to a grand jury which did not indict him; it had been considered by the Loyalty Board of his department which cleared him; it had been post-audited by the Loyalty Review Board—headed by Seth Richardson, a staunch Republican—which sustained the clearance. And this judgment had been accepted by the Secretary of the Treasury whose responsibility it was to pass upon the fitness of Treasury employees. Adler continued to serve in the Treasury Department until 1950, when he left the government of his own accord. Yet in 1953 he was named in a televised hearing before a Senate Committee, on the authority of an ancient FBI report, as having been a participant in an espionage conspiracy—and this without trial, without a hearing, without even disclosure of the evidence against him.

"Those trained in the law," Mr. Justice Douglas said in an address last spring before the American Law Institute, "know that we need not give up due process of law in order to save ourselves from internal dangers, any more than we need submit prisoners to the rack, or to other forms of torture in order to solve crimes. We have the means and the ability to protect ourselves by fair standards of procedure. There is despair only when we turn to totalitarian techniques to defeat totalitarian forces."

A "police state" may fairly be defined as a state in which individuals can be condemned, without fair standards of procedure, on the mere accusation of police authorities. The term "secret police" may reasonably be applied to a police force which uses secret informers, compiles secret dossiers, and carries on its investigative work in secret without effective restraint by civilian superiors. If these definitions have validity, then the most disturbing inference growing out of the disclosures in the Harry Dexter White case is not that the Truman Administration was indifferent to Soviet espionage in the nineteen-forties, but that the American public has become indifferent to a dangerous extension of police power in the nineteen-fifties.

It should be said in fairness to Mr. Hoover that he has not sought this extension of power. It has been thrust upon him—by unthinking adulators and by an Attorney General who has not scrupled to use the confidential reports of the FBI for partisan political purposes. The very authority to determine guilt or innocence which Mr. Hoover once astutely rejected has now been pressed into his hands.

And this time, strangely, he did not renounce it. It is true that when a member of the Jenner subcommittee asked him to comment on the Attorney General's evaluation of the FBI report of February 1, 1946, he protested that this would be to "violate the very tradition which I have meticulously adhered to over the years, namely that I will refuse to evaluate the contents of any report." But the whole of his preceding prepared statement had been an evaluation.

"Of course," Mr. Brownell told the Jenner subcommittee, "no one could, with any validity, suggest today that there is any doubt that White was in this espionage ring."

The effrontery of this statement should have produced an immediate clamor for the Attorney General's resignation. Why could no one suggest doubt about White's guilt? The only answer seems to be: Because the FBI and the Attorney General had proclaimed him guilty. They identified no new witnesses and presented no new evidence against him. They merely asserted that their case was conclusive. It was, by any criteria of the American past, contemptible to do this in the case of a dead man, without producing proof of the accusation. It was doubly contemptible to do it in the case of a man whom a grand jury had declined to indict. In a single easy sentence, an Attorney General of the United States brushed aside the protection against false accusations afforded by the constitutional stipulation that "No person shall be held to answer for a capital, or otherwise infamous crime, unless on a presentment or indictment of a Grand Jury."

But the disquieting aspect of what occurred lies neither in the recklessness of Mr. Brownell nor in the complaisance of Mr. Hoover; it lies in the apathy of the press and the public. American newspapers, with no more than a few honorable exceptions, accepted Mr. Brownell's condemnation without trial as unprotestingly as *Pravda* and *Izvestia* accepted the Malenkov condemnation of Beria.

In 1924, when he was Attorney General, the late Chief Justice Harlan F. Stone abolished the Division of Investigation which had played an ugly part in the arrest and deportation of aliens under the attorney generalship of A. Mitchell Palmer and established in its place a Bureau of Investigation with J. Edgar Hoover as its director. In doing so, he issued the following statement regarding the Bureau's role:

> There is always the possibility that a secret police may become a menace to free government and free institutions because it carries with it the possibility of abuses of power which are not always quickly apprehended or understood. . . .
>
> The Bureau of Investigation is not concerned with political or other opinions of individuals. It is concerned only with their conduct and then only with such conduct as is forbidden by the laws of the United States. When a police system passes beyond these limits, it is dangerous to the proper administration of justice and to human liberty, which it should be our first concern to cherish. Within them it should rightly be a terror to the wrongdoer.

"There are probably several million reports on individuals in the FBI files," former Attorney General Francis Biddle observed recently. Are they concerned only with "such conduct as is forbidden by the laws of the United States?" If not, they can become, in the hands of a police chief less scrupulous than Mr. Hoover, or in the hands of an ambitious politician, a terrible instrument of oppression.

How good is an FBI report?

Without impugning in any way Mr. Hoover's indubitable patriotism and zeal, or the excellence of his bureau's record in law enforcement, the time is overdue to ask the question. It is imperative to ask it for three reasons: first, because the available evidence would seem to suggest that the value of an FBI report depends upon who is evaluating it; second, because counter-intelligence is too important today to become a political shotgun for those who hunt heretics instead of spies; and third, because a skeptical attitude toward the police is an indispensable attribute of a free people.

2

Marchette Chute is a well-known biographer who has been interested in such great literary figures as William Shakespeare and Ben Jonson. In this article she discusses the temptations and trials of a biographer who comes upon interesting and promising material, but who must test the sources and evaluate the evidence before daring to use it.

What tests of evidence and inference does she apply?

GETTING AT THE TRUTH *

MARCHETTE CHUTE

This is a rather presumptuous title for a biographer to use, since truth is a very large word. In the sense that it means the reality about a human being it is probably impossible for a biographer to achieve. In the sense that it means a reasonable presentation of all the available facts it is more nearly possible, but even this limited goal is harder to reach than it appears to be. A biographer needs to be both humble and cautious when he remembers the nature of the material he is working with, for a historical fact is rather like the flamingo that Alice in Wonderland tried to use as a croquet mallet. As soon as she got its neck nicely straightened out and was ready to hit the ball, it would turn and look at her with a puzzlied expression, and

* From *The Saturday Review,* September 19, 1953. Reprinted by permission.

any biographer knows that what is called a "fact" has a way of doing the same.

Here is a small example. When I was writing my forthcoming biography, *Ben Jonson of Westminster,* I wanted to give a paragraph or two to Sir Philip Sidney, who had a great influence on Jonson. No one thinks of Sidney without thinking of chivalry, and to underline the point I intended to use a story that Sir Fulke Greville told of him. Sidney died of gangrene, from a musket shot that shattered his thigh, and Greville says that Sidney failed to put on his leg armor while preparing for battle because the marshal of the camp was not wearing leg armor and Sidney was unwilling to do anything that would give him a special advantage.

The story is so characteristic both of Sidney himself and of the misplaced high-mindedness of late Renaissance chivalry that I wanted to use it, and since Sir Fulke Greville was one of Sidney's closest friends the information seemed to be reliable enough. But it is always well to check each piece of information as thoroughly as possible and so I consulted another account of Sidney written by a contemporary, this time a doctor who knew the family fairly well. The doctor, Thomas Moffet, mentioned the episode but he said that Sidney left off his leg armor because he was in a hurry.

The information was beginning to twist in my hand and could no longer be trusted. So I consulted still another contemporary who had mentioned the episode, to see which of the two he agreed with. This was Sir John Smythe, a military expert who brought out his book a few years after Sidney's death. Sir John was an old-fashioned conservative who advocated the use of heavy armor even on horseback, and he deplored the current craze for leaving off leg protection, "the imitating of which . . . cost that noble and worthy gentleman Sir Philip Sidney his life."

So here I was with three entirely different reasons why Sidney left off his leg armor, all advanced by careful writers who were contemporaries of his. The flamingo had a legitimate reason for looking around with a puzzled expression.

The only thing to do in a case like this is to examine the point of view of the three men who are supplying the conflicting evidence. Sir Fulke Greville was trying to prove a thesis: that his beloved friend had an extremely chivalric nature. Sir John Smythe also was trying to prove a thesis: that the advocates of light arming followed a theory that could lead to disaster. Only the doctor, Thomas Moffet, was not trying to prove a thesis. He was not using his own explanation to reinforce some point he wanted to make. He did not want anything except to set down on paper what he believed to be the facts; and since we do not have Sidney's own explanation of why he did not put on leg armor, the chances are that Dr. Moffet is the safest man to trust.

For Moffet was without desire. Nothing can so quickly blur and distort the facts as desire—the wish to use the facts for some purpose of your own—and nothing can so surely destroy the truth. As soon as the witness wants to prove something he is no longer impartial and his evidence is no longer to be trusted.

The only safe way to study contemporary testimony is to bear constantly in mind this possibility of prejudice and to put almost as much attention on the writer himself as on what he has written. For instance, Sir Anthony Weldon's description of the Court of King James is lively enough and often used as source material; but a note from the publisher admits that the pamphlet was issued as a warning to anyone who wished to "side with this bloody house" of Stuart. The publisher, at any rate, did not consider Weldon an impartial witness. At about the same time Arthur Wilson published his history of Great Britain, which contained an irresistibly vivid account of the agonized death of the Countess of Somerset. Wilson sounds reasonably impartial; but his patron was the Earl of Essex, who had good reason to hate that particular countess, and there is evidence that he invented the whole scene to gratify his patron.

Sometimes a writer will contradict what he has already written, and in that case the only thing to do is to investigate what has changed his point of view. For instance, in 1608 Captain John Smith issued a description of his capture by Powhatan, and he made it clear that the Indian chief had treated him with unwavering courtesy and hospitality. In 1624 the story was repeated in Smith's "General History of Virginia," but the writer's circumstances had changed. Smith needed money, "having a prince's mind imprisoned in a poor man's purse," and he wanted the book to be profitable. Powhatan's daughter, the princess Pocahontas, had recently been in the news, for her visit to England had aroused a great deal of interest among the sort of people that Smith hoped would buy his book. So Smith supplied a new version of the story, in which the once-hospitable Powhatan would have permitted the hero's brains to be dashed out if Pocahontas had not saved his life. It was the second story that achieved fame, and of course it may have been true. But it is impossible to trust it because the desire of the writer is so obviously involved; as Smith said in his prospectus, he needed money and hoped that the book would give "satisfaction."

It might seem that there was an easy way for a biographer to avoid the use of this kind of prejudiced testimony. All he has to do is to construct his biography from evidence that cannot be tampered with—from parish records, legal documents, bills, accounts, court records, and so on. Out of these solid gray blocks of impersonal evidence it should surely be possible to construct a road that will lead straight to the truth and that will never bend itself to the misleading curve of personal desire.

This might be so if the only problem involved were the reliability of the material. But there is another kind of desire that is much more subtle, much more pervasive, and much more dangerous than the occasional distortions of fact that contemporary writers may have permitted themselves to make; and this kind of desire can destroy the truth of a biography even if every individual fact in it is as solid and as uncompromising as rock. Even if the road is built of the best and most reliable materials it can still curve away from the truth because of this other desire that threatens it: the desire of the biographer himself.

A biographer is not a court record or a legal document. He is a human being, writing about another human being, and his own temperament, his own point of view, and his own frame of reference are unconsciously imposed upon the man he is writing about. Even if the biographer is free from Captain Smith's temptation—the need for making money—and wants to write nothing but the literal truth, he is still handicapped by the fact that there is no such thing as a completely objective human being.

An illustration of what can happen if the point of view is sufficiently strong is the curious conclusion that the nineteenth-century biographers reached about William Shakespeare. Shakespeare joined a company of London actors in 1594, was listed as an actor in 1598 and 1603, and was still listed as one of the "men actors" in the company in 1609. Shortly before he joined this company Shakespeare dedicated two narrative poems to the Earl of Southampton, and several years after Shakespeare died his collected plays were dedicated to the Earl of Pembroke. This was his only relationship with either of the two noblemen, and there is nothing to connect him with them during the fifteen years in which he belonged to the same acting company and during which he wrote nearly all his plays.

But here the desire of the biographers entered in. They had been reared in the strict code of nineteenth-century gentility and they accepted two ideas without question. One was that there are few things more important than an English lord; the other was that there are few things less important than a mere actor. They already knew the undeniable fact that Shakespeare was one of the greatest men who ever lived; and while they could not go quite so far as to claim him as an actual member of the nobility, it was clear to them that he must have been the treasured friend of both the Earl of Southampton and the Earl of Pembroke and that he must have written his plays either while basking in their exalted company or while he was roaming the green countryside by the waters of the river Avon. (It is another basic conviction of the English gentleman that there is nothing so inspiring as nature.) The notion that Shakespeare had spent all these years as the working member of a company of London actors was so abhorrent that it was never seriously considered. It could not be so; therefore it was not.

These biographers did their work well. When New South Wales built its beautiful memorial library to Shakespeare, it was the coat of arms of the Earl of Southampton that alternated with that of royalty in dignified splendor over the bookshelves. Shakespeare had been recreated in the image of desire, and desire will always ignore whatever is not relevant to its purpose. Because the English gentlemen did not like Shakespeare's background it was explained away as though it had never existed, and Shakespeare ceased to be an actor because so lowly a trade was not suited to so great a man.

All this is not to say that a biography should be lacking in a point of view. If it does not have a point of view it will be nothing more than a kind of expanded article for an encyclopedia—a string of facts arranged in chronological order with no claim to being a real biography at all. A biography must have a point of view and it must have a frame of reference. But it should be a point of view and a frame of reference implicit in the material itself and not imposed upon it.

It might seem that the ideal biographical system, if it could be achieved, would be to go through the years of research without feeling any kind of emotion. The biographer would be a kind of fact-finding machine and then suddenly, after his years of research, a kind of total vision would fall upon him and he would transcribe it in his best and most persuasive English for a waiting public. But research is fortunately not done by machinery, nor are visions likely to descend in that helpful manner. They are the product not only of many facts but also of much thinking, and it is only when the biographer begins to get emotional in his thinking that he ought to beware.

It is easy enough to make good resolutions in advance, but a biographer cannot altogether control his sense of excitement when the climax of his years of research draws near and he begins to see the pieces fall into place. Almost without his volition, A, B, and D fit together and start to form a pattern, and it is almost impossible for the biographer not to start searching for C. Something turns up that looks remarkably like C, and with a little trimming of the edges and the ignoring of one very slight discrepancy it will fill the place allotted for C magnificently.

It is at this point that the biographer ought to take a deep breath and sit on his hands until he has had time to calm down. He has no real, fundamental reason to believe that his discovery is C, except for the fact that he wants it to be. He is like a man looking for a missing piece in a difficult jigsaw puzzle, who has found one so nearly the right shape that he cannot resist the desire to jam it into place.

If the biographer had refused to be tempted by his supposed discovery of C and had gone on with his research, he might have found not only the connecting, illuminating fact he needed but much more besides. He is not going to look for it now. Desire has blocked the way. And by so much his biography will fall short of what might have been the truth.

It would not be accurate to say that a biographer should be wholly lacking in desire. Curiosity is a form of desire. So is the final wish to get the material down on paper in a form that will be fair to the reader's interest and worthy of the subject. But a subconscious desire to push the facts around is one of the most dangerous things a biographer can encounter, and all the more dangerous because it is so difficult to know when he is encountering it.

The reason Alice had so much trouble with her flamingo is that the average flamingo does not wish to be used as a croquet mallet. It has other purposes in view. The same thing is true of a fact, which can be just as self-willed as a flamingo and has its own kind of stubborn integrity. To try to force a series of facts into a previously desired arrangement is a form of misuse to which no self-respecting fact will willingly submit itself. The best and only way to treat it is to leave it alone and be willing to follow where it leads, rather than to press your own wishes upon it.

To put the whole thing into a single sentence: you will never succeed in getting at the truth if you think you know, ahead of time, what the truth ought to be.

3

The following letters to the editors of *Life* magazine are answers to a story that purported to show a sensational secret "behind the damnation of Stalin." Documented evidence presented by *Life* had indicated that Stalin had once been a Czarist police informer against his comrades of the Communist Party. The three letters that follow are from professional scholars. The first two attack the evidence. The third, defending the evidence, is by the man who wrote the commentary accompanying the *Life* article.

WAS STALIN A CZARIST SPY? *

A

Sirs:

You have performed an important service by publishing the article by Orlov and the document commented on by Levine dealing with Stalin's past, so that they can be subjected to further verification.

All of us who have done research in this field have come across

* These are three letters dealing with a magazine article and commentary that appeared in *Life*, April 23, 1956, in which Stalin's early "betrayal" of the revolutionary cause to Czarist police is the subject. The letters appeared in the "Letters to the Editors" column of *Life*, May 14, 1956, and are reprinted by permission of the authors. See Assignment I at end of chapter.

references to Stalin's relations with the czarist police. In *Three Who Made a Revolution* I wrote, "There are so many such accusations against him . . . that it is important to note that men who worked with Stalin should have thought him capable of framing up his comrades. . . . Lenin and Trotsky, too, made bitter enemies. . . . Yet in all the polemical literature against them, there is a notable absence of charges such as these."

In 1952 I was consulted by an official of the State Department, expert on Russia, concerning a document which seems to be the one you have now published. We came to the conclusion that the charge was plausible but difficult to prove, and that the results of publication at that time were incalculable. Now that Mr. Levine plans to put it into a book, there are several points to check:

(1) The repetition of the pseudonym Stalin, Djugashvili's first recorded use of that name is on Jan. 12, 1913.

(2) Trotsky's authority is invoked on Stalin's arrest and release in 1906. Actually Trotsky was murdered before he could finish his book, and the chronological appendix was completed by Charles Malamuth.

(3) If the raid occurred on April 15, Russian calendar, as Mr. Levine's newspaper story indicates, Stalin could not have been in it, since he was in Stockholm.

If the Levine document requires further checking, the Orlov article carries complete conviction. I got to know Mr. Orlov at the end of 1953. In one of our early talks he told me of an agent named "Marc" (whose last name he had not been able to learn) who had been close to Trotsky's son Sedov. Several years later those following his clues turned up the agent Marc Zborowsky, whose testimony before a senatorial committee confirmed in the smallest details Mr. Orlov's prior account. Since 1953 I have known that Orlov carried with him one more secret not yet published and because of which he feared for his life. All he would tell me then were some details linking it to the Tukhachevsky purge. I am sure his story will stand up under any check to which it can be submitted. Whether it is sufficient to explain the great difficulties that Khrushchev and his lieutenants are having with Stalin's ghost is something I cannot treat within the compass of a letter.

Bertram D. Wolfe

Brooklyn Heights, N. Y.

B

Sirs:

A careful consideration, in the light of known facts and documents, makes me doubt the assertions made by Mr. Orlov and Mr. Levine that Stalin was a czarist police agent.

According to Mr. Orlov, Stalin was active as a spy in 1912–13 and reported to Vissarionov, Vice-Director of the Police Department.

Sergei Vissarionov was interrogated after the revolution of 1917 by a special investigation commission. Vissarionov was most cooperative, giving names of secret agents and many other details. Asked whether leaders of revolutionary parties had worked under his direct guidance, he replied that there had been only one, Roman Malinovsky. He did not mention Stalin, although there would have been no reason for him to conceal any connection of Stalin with the Okhrana.

Vissarionov's superior, Stepan Beletsky, director of the police department, also discussed the activities of the police department and made no mention of Stalin.

In 1917, when Russian newspapers were reporting the revelations of the former czarist police officials, Stalin would have had good reason to flee had he been involved, but he continued to live and work in Petrograd as a member of the Bolshevik Central Committee. After 1917 the archives of the czarist police were the subject of study by a number of people. Had Stalin been a czarist police agent, then his behavior during that period would appear incomprehensible.

Mr. Orlov says that the czarist police never kept Stalin in jail for long periods and argues that this circumstance supports the theory that Stalin was an Okhrana agent. But Stalin actually spent long periods in jail and in exile: almost four years in all from 1902 to 1913.

I do not doubt the accuracy of Mr. Orlov's report of what he learned from his cousin Zinovy Katsnelson, but this was only hearsay. Orlov himself has not seen the file in question. Perhaps Zinovy himself, aware of, or even involved in Marshal Tukhachevsky's plot to "liquidate" Stalin (if there was such a plot), gave his cousin in Paris the story that was to be spread after his fall if the conspiracy were successful. Under Stalinism this would have been good strategy.

There is no doubt of Mr. Levine's expertness in Russian affairs, but careful analysis leads me to the conclusion that the document of the

Russian police department which he presents cannot be accepted as genuine, and that it was fabricated, probably after the last war, somewhere in the Far East.

The letter, purportedly written by an official of the police department, refers to Stalin as "Djugashvili-Stalin," or simply "Stalin." This is surprising, for the Russian police department used only legal names, never aliases, although it might have referred to "Djugashvili (alias Stalin)."

In the letter the city of St. Petersburg is referred to as "Petersburg." The use of this colloquial form of St. Petersburg would have been highly irregular in an official document or letter, although the abbreviation SPB would have been permissible.

And where was the document during the years from 1913 to 1947? If it is genuine, it must have been smuggled out of Russia sometime between 1918 and 1921, for after 1921 all Siberian Okhrana archives were in Bolshevik hands. The Japanese or Germans would have been willing to pay exorbitantly for such a document. But it remained unknown to them.

I have no doubt that Stalin was capable of committing the worst of political and criminal deeds, but the facts do not confirm the specific accusations made by Mr. Orlov and Mr. Levine.

David Dallin

New York, N. Y.

C

Sirs:

Disputed points in my *Life* article, including the problem of dates, are treated in detail in my book *Stalin's Great Secret*, to be published May 25, but here is a brief explanation of the major issues: (1) The alias of "Stalin" was well known to the Okhrana at the time the letter was written. There are notes signed "Stalin" dated two years before the letter, and for 15 months "Stalin" had been signing articles in *Pravda*. (2) I have consulted many Okhrana documents in my work, and there is no set style for referring to prisoners by name. Sometimes the proper name is used, sometimes the alias, sometimes both. (3) The Okhrana letter was an informal exchange between two officials, and the informal reference to "Petersburg" is thoroughly in keeping with this fact. (4) Although I did not see the document until 1947, my associate Mr. Makaroff saw a photostat as early as 1934 and began negotiations at that time. There was hardly any international interest in Stalin before 1930.

Isaac Don Levine

Waldorf, Md.

The next two selections illustrate the specialized use of statistics—to correct common misinterpretations or misconceptions. See if you can state in a paragraph, after reading each article, what the misconceptions are and to what extent they should be changed in the light of this information.

4.

WHO OWNS BUSINESS? *

When the Brookings Institution recently announced that there are approximately 6,500,000 stockholders in the U. S., the news was hailed as evidence of the widespread ownership of American industry. The *Wall Street Journal* was pleased that "One in Every 16 Adults Owns Stocks." The New York *Daily News* gloated that the report "seems certain to encourage believers in U. S. capitalism and spread further gloom and hatred for our economic system among Reds and Pinks." Well, the more gloom among the Reds and Pinks the better, but some of the capitalist cheering is a bit premature. What the report actually portrays is not so much a capitalist achievement as a capitalist opportunity.

The Brookings report, *Share Ownership in the United States*, is a competent and long overdue analysis of a highly amorphous segment of the population, based on interviews with 15,000 people and voluminous data procured from securities exchanges and nearly 3,000 corporations. Many of the findings, to be sure, merely corroborate previous assumptions: viz., that stock ownership tends to increase with such things as age, income, and educational level. But among the welter of statistics were a few that should explode some popular myths. We note, for example, that the ladies have yet to establish a

* From *Fortune*, September, 1952. Reprinted by permission.

matriarchy in the financial marts; men still outnumber women shareholders slightly (3,260,000 to 3,230,000) and, what's more, own some 30 per cent more shares (1.8 billion shares *vs.* 1.3 billion).

The report also torpedoes the pious claim that today's stockholders are, in the words of the president of the New York Curb Exchange, "buying more with an idea to investment." Not so; only 22 per cent of all stockholders say that they buy primarily for investment. Twenty per cent acquire stock through gifts or inheritances, 10 per cent because their brokers, bankers, or attorneys tell them to (for numerous purposes including, of course, investment), and others for a variety of lesser reasons. The biggest number, however (28 per cent), continue to buy stocks for capital appreciation—and not as a protection against inflation either. Only 1 per cent of all stockholders say they buy stocks as an inflationary hedge. Most others who seek capital gains are apparently motivated by the gambling instinct and view the market as a sort of legalized horse parlor.

Now findings such as these may have disappointed the New York Stock Exchange, which paid $90,000 for the survey. But what really bothered us, and we hope also G. Keith Funston, president of the N.Y.S.E., were those figures on the distribution of ownership. It is hardly a testament to securities salesmanship that fewer than 5 per cent of the individuals and 10 per cent of the families in the U. S. own stock today. Four times that number of families invest in "E" bonds (a patriotic but highly uncertain investment in terms of future dollar value), five times as many have savings accounts, and *eight* times as many own life insurance (see table below). With only 6.4 per cent of the adult, voting population owning stocks, it is hardly surprising that, as a group, stockholders are abysmally pressureless and forever being sat upon.

There is, moreover, little cause for rejoicing because 75 per cent of all stockholders are people earning less than $10,000 a year, and nearly a third earn less than $5,000. These figures may superficially suggest that Main Street and Wall Street have already merged, but that is hardly the case. People earning less than $5,000 may account for a third of the total number of stockholders, but they also comprise 57 per cent of the total adult population. And less than 3½ per cent of this sizable political majority has any direct interest in corporate ownership and profits today.

FAVORITE AMERICAN INVESTMENTS

Type of investment	*Per cent of total family units with one or more owners*	*Estimated number of family units with one or more owners*
Life insurance (including G.I.)	82.3	41,160,000
Savings accounts	52.8	26,390,000
U.S. Series "E" bonds	41.8	20,940,000
Annuities and pensions (excluding social security)	20.9	10,470,000
Publicly owned stocks	9.5	4,750,000
Other government bonds	5.5	2,760,000
Privately held stocks	4.6	2,300,000
Real-estate mortgages and bonds *	2.7	1,370,000
Corporate bonds	1.3	640,000
One or more of nine forms of investments	90.7	45,330,000

What is most shocking, perhaps, is the apparent lack of appetite for stocks among the men who run U. S. business. According to the Brookings report, only 45 per cent of the "administrative executives" in the country own corporate stocks. This is admittedly a better showing than for any other group—only one in four professional people is a stockholder, one in fifteen farmers, and one in 200 unskilled workers—but it is hardly a reassuring statement of management's confidence in its own ability to turn a profit.

Some observers profess to see a healthy trend in stock acquisitions in recent years. Some 6 per cent of all stockholders, for example, entered the market during 1951. When you consider, however, that the population has been growing 2 per cent annually since World War II, that the age level is advancing, and that one of the longest bull markets in history is still in progress, the number of converts last year can scarcely be considered spectacular.

If there is any solace or inspiration to be derived from the Brookings report, it is that such a tremendous job remains to be done. A huge market remains untouched; millions of potential capitalists have billions of dollars of untapped savings to invest in industry's further growth.

* Outright ownership of real estate is, of course, a form of investment, but is not included in the tabulation above.

Source: Share Ownership in the United States, the Brookings Institution.

That many of these potential capitalists *can* be sold—by patient indoctrination and resort to such selling instruments as payroll-deduction plans and mutual-investment funds—seems beyond dispute. Employees, for example, are a virtually untouched market. Only the utilities have made any significant attempt to sell stock to employees, and it is noteworthy that nearly 16 per cent of their employees are shareholders whereas only 1.4 per cent of the employees of manufacturing concerns are also part owners in the business.

The fact that more than two million people with incomes of $5,000 or less are stockholders is not, in itself, particularly impressive, but it is convincing proof that a low income is not an insurmountable barrier to stock ownership. Securities men now have at hand authoritative figures on just who owns American industry and who does not. The latter figures are the more important ones.

5

FICTION AND FACT ABOUT AGING WORKERS *

PERRIN STRYKER

Sweeping statements about old age and retirement have become so common that experts as well as laymen are now likely to accept them as true. Here four of the most repeated and most questionable contentions are analyzed:

Claim: The aging worker is needed not only for defense production but for raising national income and standard of living.

Correction: Among those who make this claim is Harvard's eminent economist, Sumner Slichter, who estimates that some 1,500,000 able workers have been forced to retire, and that, if allowed to work, they could increase the national product by $5 billion. However, a recent analysis by a Federal Security Agency statistician, Jacob Fisher, shows that by the end of last year about 23 per cent of those sixty-five and over (nearly three million) were in the working force, and if employment in this group were to return to wartime peaks (52 per cent of the men, 10 per cent of the women), the net addition might total only 600,000 workers. . . . Fisher puts the aged-labor reserve in proper perspective by noting that it is equal to about 1 per cent of the present labor force. Even assuming that all these men and women were as productive as the average worker—which they would not be—the equivalent of their maximum output could be achieved by an increase of less than a half-hour in the present work week.

A STATISTICAL PRIMER ON THE AGED

This chart illustrates some basic facts about the older men and women in the U.S. population:

- Between 1900 and 1950 the *number* of people sixty-five and over quadrupled to a total of more than 12 million.
- In the same period the *proportion* of the population included in this aged group doubled (to more than 8 per cent).
- The proportion of men sixty-five and over who are actually in the labor force had fallen from 63 per cent in 1900 to about 42 per cent (1950 total: 2,400,000).
- The proportion of women in the same group has remained close to 8 per cent for over fifty years (1950 total: 500,000).
- Of the 9,400,000 aged people not in the working force in 1950, three million were physically disabled and 5,800,000 were unavailable for work for other reasons, e.g., keeping house, caring for sick spouse, unwilling to work or try a different job, skills obsolete etc.
- The 1950 net reserve of aged workers is estimated at some 600,000, or just about 1 per cent of the total labor force.
- Women, who have a longer life expectancy than men, are fast becoming the nation's major old-age problem: in 1950 women sixty-five and over outnumbered the old men by nearly a million, and by 1875 (see bar at extreme right) they are expected to total over 12 million, which is nearly twice their preesnt total. By then they will outnumber aged men almost three to two.

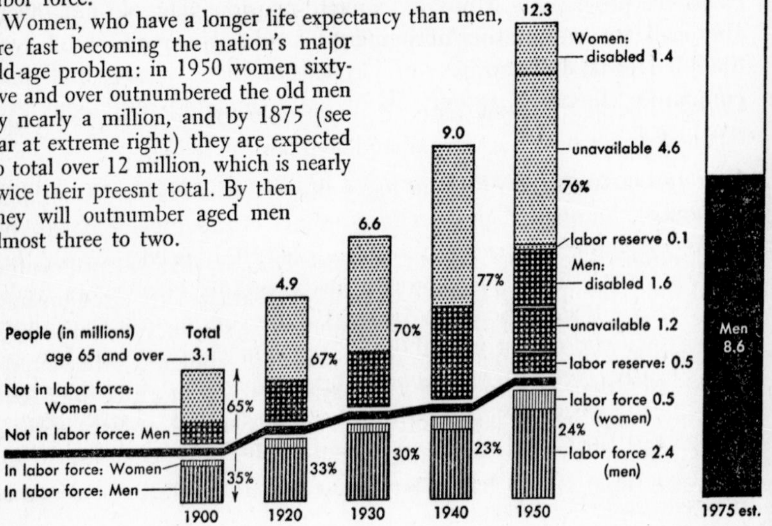

Claim: Aging workers want to stay on the job.

Correction: This contention is at best a half-truth. While some old employees do want to continue, many others do not. At Socony-Vacuum Oil Co., which has a generous pension plan calling for compulsory retirement at sixty-five, the average retirement age has been sixty-three. On the other hand, surveys of retired workers receiving government OASI pensions (some 2,400,000 now) show that their average retirement age is sixty-nine, and one sampling indicated that only about 5 per cent voluntarily left their jobs. But in the latest OASI survey of 22,000 such beneficiaries, nearly three-fourths said they were unable to work. Moreover, nearly half of the men and two-thirds of the women who were willing to work wanted only part-time or occasional jobs.

Claim: Company pension plans are chiefly responsible for forcing older workers to retire.

Correction: This statement is not even a half-truth. There are now 16,000 industrial pension plans that cover some 10 million workers, or approximately a sixth of the regular labor force. Only about 400,000 workers have retired under these plans. On the other hand, 86 per cent of all paid workers are covered by government pension plans (OASI, Railroad Retirement, federal, state, and local-government employee programs). Moreover, private pension plans do not invariably call for compulsory retirement. A recent survey (by Edwin Shields Hewitt & Associates) of 496 pension plans of large and small companies showed that only about half stipulated retirement at a fixed age.

Claim: The economy cannot support in idleness the growing number of aged.

Correction: The short answer to this claim is that no one knows what the economy will be able to support. Statistics are cited on both sides of the argument. Most often quoted is the fact that the aged population is increasing. Even more pertinent—but less often cited—is the fact that whereas in 1900 nearly two out of three men over sixty-five were in the labor force, now only two out of five are—and the economy seems to be doing all right.

It is estimated that by 1975 the cost of $100-a-month pensions for all those sixty-five and over might run over $25 billion a year. But it can be argued that even if the pension load proves to be much bigger than this, the economy still might well be able to bear it. The U. S. birth rate has declined over the years, and in relation to the working group (ages eighteen to sixty-four), the proportional growth of the aged population has been more than offset by the proportional shrinkage of the young dependents. At the same time, both per capita income and productivity have gone up despite (1) a drastically shortened work week, and (2) a rising proportion of older people who retire. In view of these long-term trends there is no very convincing evidence that support of the aged will be an insuperable economic problem.

6

In various fields—business, science, education—statistics of the past and present are commonly employed in making decisions for the future. Peter F. Drucker's article here illustrates this type of projection or extrapolation.

Analyze the author's evidence. Consider his organization, methods, and interpretations. How clear? How logical? How objective?

AMERICA'S NEXT TWENTY YEARS *

PETER F. DRUCKER

The most important economic event of 1954 went almost unreported in the newspapers. It was the announcement that four million sixty thousand babies had been born in this country during the past year—the largest baby crop ever. Yet 1954 should have brought a record low in births rather than a record high. For the young women who reached marriageable age, married, and had their first child during 1954 were born, for the most part, in the dark Depression years of 1933 and 1934, when the birth rate ran 30 or 40 per cent below the present figures. The number of marriages last year was smaller than

* This is the first in a series of statistical projections made by Peter F. Drucker for *Harper's Magazine*. It was presented as Part 1, "The Coming Labor Shortage," in the March, 1955, issue. Reprinted by permission of Harper & Brothers and the author.

usual, but the total married population had more than the usual number of children.

Between now and 1975, that is, the number of young people reaching marriageable age will tend to increase. Since romance is reliably constant, this means an appreciable increase in the rate of family-formation and in the number of births to be expected each year. Eight or ten years from now the birth figure should take another mighty leap upward as the children born in the years of the "baby boom" since 1942 begin to reach maturity and form families of their own.

What now appears to be true, therefore, is that the low birth rate of the Depression decade was a freak. The higher birth rate which reasserted itself in the early forties now appears to be "normal" rate at which the American people reproduce themselves. Only ten years ago the Census Bureau, misled by the Depression birth rate, predicted that the American population would become static within a few years and start to decline soon thereafter. It was this interpretation which underlay most of the talk about a "mature economy" that played such an important role in American public policy during the thirties and early forties. But now we can say with some certainty that nothing short of a tremendous catastrophe—that is, an atomic war—could possibly stop or even slow down the growth of the American population for the next twenty years.

The reason we can be so certain, of course, is that in reckoning the adult population for the next two decades we do not have to predict; we know. *The major events that determine the future have already happened—irrevocably*. Everybody who will reach marriageable age during the next eighteen or twenty years has by now been born. Everyone who will join the work force within the next eighteen or twenty years has by now been born. And so, obviously, has everyone who will retire. The economic population of the next twenty years—its numbers, its age and sex distribution—is not just predictable today; *it is already in being.*

This article will examine some of the implications arising from the single stupendous fact of 1954's birth rate. As in any prophecy, there will presumably be some boners—but with a difference. In order to keep them to as few as possible, we will severely limit our forecasting to those future happenings that are already under way. There will be no need for crystal-gazing. We will find plenty to occupy us in what we *know* about America's next twenty years from events that have already occurred.

We start with a paradox: there are going to be more people, and hence more jobs, but not more people to fill the jobs. It is more than possible, in fact, that a continuing feature of the next two decades will be a labor shortage—and that the basic problem of the period will not be unemployment but inflation. Let's look at some of the figures which show why this is true.

The total population of the United States, now at 162,000,000, can be expected to top 190,000,000 by 1965 and 220,000,000 by 1975. These are conservative assumptions. They make full allowance for a continuing drop in the birth rate in the one major sector of the populace where it is still high, and still dropping: the Negro. They allow for several years of birth rates as low as those of the thirties. They hardly take into account at all the fact that ten years hence the number of young people old enough to start their own families will be very much larger than it is at present. And they do not make allowances for any growth in the size of the families. If the three-child family again becomes the norm, of course, as against the present average of two-and-a-half, the growth of population will be much faster.

The *rate* of population growth which the figures anticipate is no larger than our rate of growth for the past fifty years, including the thirties. It is the rate of population growth which has prevailed in this country virtually since colonial days, and which has brought about the steady doubling of the American people every half century. But the *total* number of new Americans this rate will add to our population is now exceptionally large. It took forty years—from 1910 to 1950—for America to grow forty million people. Now it should take only twenty years.

At the same time that the total population will grow very rapidly, however, the *working population* will grow very slowly, if at all. With total population increasing by thirty million, the number between twenty and sixty-five years of age (the bulk of our working population) will go up at the most by seven million. In the group from twenty-five to forty-five—the one from which every employment manager in the country prefers to choose—there will actually be a shrinkage of two million. On the other hand, there will be six million more people over sixty-five, and at least sixteen million more under twenty, than there are today.

From 1965 on, in the second decade ahead, total population and working population should be in better balance. Beginning in the early sixties, the large baby crops of the forties will reach maturity. Population of working age will thus increase by twelve million or so during the second decade. And assuming that there is a slight drop rather than an increase in the birth rate of the families these grown-up children form, the subsequent increase in total population and in working population will stand in the same ratio (five to two) in which they stand today.

But the size of the working population is not entirely determined by the number of people of working age. An important factor is the number who are not available for work because they are in school.

If the 1954 birth rate was the year's most important economic event, the second most important was the announcement that the number of full-time and part-time college students had increased by 10 per cent, to an all-time high of two-and-a-half million. The increase in the birth rate was contrary to all expectations; the increase in the number of college students was nothing short of miraculous. Not only did an abnormally low number of young people reach college age during the past year (the delayed result of the lean thirties) but the veterans studying under the GI Bill have all but disappeared. Five or six years ago, three-quarters of the male students in many undergraduate colleges were GIs; today the figure is down to 10 or 15 per cent, most of them in the older classes. Yet the 1954 jump was in the *freshman* class, which contains almost no GIs and was drawn from the smallest college manpower reservoir of the recent past or the foreseeable future.

It had long been clear that the early fifties would show whether there had been any real change in the educational habits of the country, or whether the GI Bill (and the attempt of many young veterans to make up for lost time) had just created a temporary "bulge" in college enrollment. A drop of one-third during these years would still have supported the conclusion that going to college was rapidly becoming the normal thing to do. That there has been an increase rather than drop is thus overwhelming proof that—far from being a freak—the jump in college enrollment is another new "normal." The college enrollment figures now show exactly the same trend that high-school enrollment showed after World War I, when a high-school education first became "normal" throughout the country.

Twenty years from now, at least nine and perhaps as many as twelve million young people can be expected to attend colleges and universities. Therefore, even though they are of working age, they will not be available for full-time work. Such a projection is again a conservative one; twelve million college students will still be less than half the young Americans of college or university age. Yet within a similar period—from the early twenties to the early forties—the number of young people in high school increased from a little under 20 to close to 90 per cent.

Such a substantial gain in college enrollment would come none too soon. For our problem is not the breeding of an "intellectual proletariat" for whom there will be no jobs, but a greater need for trained and educated man- and woman-power than the country can possibly supply. Indeed, as we will see in a subsequent article, the technological revolution of "Automation," already under way, primarily requires a tremendous increase in the number of trained and educated people. And it is already true today that the short supply of such people is *the major limiting factor* on the rapid growth of our economy and of our principal industries. We need not worry, therefore, about our ability to absorb these millions of college-trained people; we have to worry principally about increasing their number and quality fast enough.

The explosive growth of college enrollment will create problems which lie well beyond the scope of these articles. It certainly raises the most serious questions of educational policy, curriculum, and educational standards. It makes me wonder whether the colleges, especially the independent liberal-arts colleges, really know what they are doing in their fund-raising and other campaigns. If I were a college president I would not—as so many seem to be doing—lower educational standards in the belief that this is the way to draw more students. I would try instead to raise standards, so as to make my college known for the quality of its education and the toughness of its academic requirements. There will be students aplenty.

What concerns us here, however, is merely the impact of this development on the size of the working population. We can expect that there will be only four million more men and women available for work in 1965 than there are today—that is, an increase of seven million of working age minus an increase of three million in college attendance. And, of the twelve million who will be reaching working age between 1965 and 1975, five may go to college rather than straight to work, leaving a net increase for the second decade of only seven million.

Finally, the size of the working population must also be adjusted for time at work. There can be little doubt that total hours worked will continue to decline as a result of longer vacations, more holidays, and a shorter work-week. The American people have made it thoroughly clear that they have decided to take, in the form of greater leisure, a big slice of any increase in productivity.

The statements in the box at the top of the next page * define a trend exactly opposite to that which dominated the twenties and thirties. Then, partly as a result of the drop in the birth rate and partly because of the cutting off of immigration, the population of working age tended to grow faster than the total population. It is the exact opposite, in other words, of the basic assumptions that underlay Keynesian economics; and the basic problem of economic policy in the two decades ahead should therefore not be unemployment but inflation.

The supply of people to do the work, and of hours to do it in, will in fact be so short as to make any prolonged period of large-scale national unemployment highly improbable. This does not mean that we shall have no depression, or even that a depression is unlikely (though the constant new demands created by a rapidly growing population can be expected to act as a substantial cushion). It also does not mean that there may be no serious and chronic unemployment in any one industry, as there is today in the Pennsylvania anthracite fields. But though depressions—even serious ones—may well happen, depression unemployment of the kind that characterized the thirties is unlikely.

Lest this be considered incongruous, if not silly—for we have come to consider the two words "depression" and "unemployment" as interchangeable—let me refer only to Soviet Russia, where for the

* Information supplied at the end of this article.

past thirty years there have been violent and extreme economic fluctuations without unemployment; and where, though for entirely different reasons, there has been a labor shortage much like the one we are about to experience. What form such a depression-without-unemployment might take may be suggested by our experience from 1946 to 1949, when the three-quarters of the working population who were not unionized (and were therefore not protected against inflationary price increases) suffered a cut in their real purchasing power fully comparable to the impact of a severe and prolonged depression. Even with high employment, inflation could have the same kind of destructive effect over the next twenty years.

Now, there is only one effective way to control long-range inflationary pressures, and that is increased productivity. Certainly it is the only way to convert inflation from a serious threat of economic and social disruption into an opportunity for economic and social advance. As one of several consequences of the population revolution, therefore, *increased productivity* will be the paramount need of the American economy in the decades ahead.

Mr. Ralph J. Cordiner, the president of General Electric, announced last December that by 1965 his company will have to produce and sell twice the volume of goods it turned out in 1954 with only 11 per cent more people on its payroll. Adjusted for the expected decrease in working hours, this means that ten years hence General Electric must be able to produce twice as much for every hour its employees work.

This is a sharper increase in both production and productivity than the over-all economy will have to show, for the electrical industry is growing a good deal faster than the national average. But even for an industry that grows only as fast as the nation at large, the increase ahead will have to be tremendous. A company that intends to maintain its competitive position in its own industry will have to be able, ten years from now, to produce two-fifths more than it does today without much, if any, increase in its hours worked. Twenty years hence it will have to be able to turn out twice as much with only one-tenth more hours of work.

Put it in another way. Today every American at work supports himself (or herself) and one-and-a-half other people besides. Twenty years from now every American at work should produce enough to support, at today's standard of living, himself and three-and-a-half other people. And he will have to do this in fewer working hours.

This assumes, moreover, that the standard of living will only go up at the same rate it has been advancing for the past twenty-five years, half of which were years of depression and war. To achieve this—hardly an ambitious goal—productivity will, however, have to increase 40 per cent in the next ten years; it will have to be almost doubled in the next twenty years.

Despite all the emphasis we have given to productivity in recent years, we really know very little about it—and we certainly do not know how to measure it. But even if we take the most optimistic of the various guesses about the rise in productivity in the past few years—a guess that puts the net annual increase above 3 per cent—we are going to have to step up the rate considerably to make possible increased growth.

The first requirement is capital. We may not know much, but we do know that an increase in capital investment and an increase in productivity are tied together, and that the higher the capital per worker the higher the productivity—and, incidentally, the wages and salaries paid.

We are at present spending forty billion dollars a year on capital investment. A good many economists consider even this tremendous sum to be too low; they feel that we have not yet made adequate allowance for the inflation of the forties, and they point to the fact that a good many businesses (especially the small ones) still base their provision for future new equipment on the deflated prices that prevailed in the thirties. These economists feel that in three major areas of the national economy we have an over-age plant which needs more capital investment than it gets: in housing, in transportation, and above all in education. They feel, too, that in many industries the machinery is rapidly wearing out and that American equipment, far from being modern, might well—in important respects—be on the verge of obsolescence.

But let us assume that forty billion dollars in capital investment are adequate for the needs of the 1955 economy. We would then need sixty-five billion dollars a year in 1965 and at least one hundred billion dollars twenty years from now. To obtain such gigantic sums would not be easy under the best of circumstances. To make matters worse, as a later article in this series will point out, the large investment trusts and pension funds are currently emerging as the country's only real "capitalists"; and this development by no means encourages the supply of that kind of capital.

But there is another and more important question: can the nation afford investment at such a rate? Today eleven cents out of every dollar produced in this country is put back into capital for the future. To obtain an adequate amount in 1975, however, we would have to put back fifteen cents out of every dollar. Eleven cents is already high—higher than we have ever ploughed back except in wartime. Fifteen cents may be wholly impossible, except under such stringent government control of interest rates or installment buying as would be considered unbearable—and rightly so.

We must, if this is the case, find ways to obtain more productivity for our investment dollar than we do today. If capital investment is to be kept at or below 10 per cent of national product, we must learn by 1965 to get as much additional productivity out of fifty-five billion dollars per year as we now would get out of sixty-five—as much, in 1975, out of seventy billions as we now would get out of a hundred. We must, in other words, increase the productivity of capital itself by one-sixth during the next decade and by one-third during the next twenty years.

This is not a new problem, to be sure. Economic progress might even be defined as the process of continually obtaining more productivity for less money. The means to achieve this is *innovation.* Without constant innovation, that is, all the capital invested in this country since 1750 might have been barely enough to permit the present population to live at a 1750 scale of living; the entire improvement in living standards since then is the result of innovation. Innovation has been the real "frontier" of the Western world these past two centuries. And what now distinguishes an "underdeveloped country"—and *keeps* it "underdeveloped"—is not so much a shortage of capital as it is shortage of innovation.

To the layman—and the typical businessman—"innovation" means "research" or "engineering," new products or new productive processes. These are indeed important aspects of innovation; and the fourfold increase (from one billion dollars in 1950 to four billion dollars in 1954) in the sums spent by American business on research and engineering for new products and new processes is therefore a highly encouraging sign. We already know that the next twenty years will bring about major changes in manufacturing, amounting to a technological revolution. And we also know that in a major industry like housing we badly need both radically new products and much more efficient production. But it is a serious mistake to think of innovation exclusively as technological innovation. The most important area of innovation—and the most productive one—may well be the opposite of technological.

During the past ten or fifteen years, the innovations that have had a major impact on the American economy were nearly all non-technological, were nearly all innovations in something else than product or process. First among them certainly stands the tremendous changes in distribution methods. Hardly less important, especially in its impact on productivity, has been the development of new concepts of business organization. There have been tremendous innovations in plant, store, and office architecture; similarly in respect to the management of worker and work, whether industrial engineering, human relations, or personnel management. Finally there is the emergence of new basic management tools, especially measurements and controls like budgets, cost accounting, production scheduling, and inventory controls.

Among the major innovations of the past ten or fifteen years, only one can even remotely be called an innovation in product or productive process. That is the development of systematic and organized methods of materials handling. Otherwise, in their aggregate, the basically non-technological innovations have had a greater impact on the American economy, and have contributed more to the increase in productivity in this country, than all technological innovations of the past ten or fifteen years. In the long view of history, it is for social inventions—and not technical ones—that Americans may be best remembered.

During the period ahead, in any event, the greatest need for innovation seems more likely to lie in the social than in the technological area. Indeed, the technological revolution itself, as another article in this series will show, will be totally unproductive unless it is accompanied by major innovations in the non-technological field. Among them, above all, is again innovation in marketing. Equally badly needed are innovations in methods, tools, and measurements for doing the managerial job in the modern enterprise, large or small; for the development of competence, skill, and imagination among managers (still considered a luxury by many companies) is probably the greatest necessity any business, let alone the economy, faces. Finally, the need is for effective innovation in the management of workers and in the organization of work; despite the progress in this area, it may well be the most backward sphere, and the one with the greatest potential for increased productivity.

Compared to electronics, rocket engines, or synthetic chemistry, these are unglamorous subjects. They are rarely discussed except by professional managers, and not as often as they should be, even so. Yet our success at innovating in these four areas may very well decide

Here, in summary, is the basic population structure within which the American economy will function during the next twenty years:

There will be a population increase of one-fifth ***in the next ten years.***

But total population of working age will increase only by one-tenth.

Population actually available for work will increase only by 6 per cent.

And total hours worked by the whole economy in the course of one year *may not increase at all.*

And in the next twenty years, total population will increase by at least two-fifths.

Populatiton of working age, however, will increase by less than one-third.

Labor force will go up by one-fifth, and total hours worked by 10 per cent.

And even more intensive employment, on a larger scale, of older people who are willing and able to work—however desirable in itself—would not materially affect these conclusions.

whether the population revolution, which has already taken place, will be an opportunity for further growth and strength, or whether it will prove a strain, a burden, and perhaps even a threat to social and economic stability.

7

The battle has long raged over who make the more successful graduates—those who get high grades or those who are "big men on campus." This chapter from the book *They Went to College* draws upon statistics to shed light on the controversy.

Do you agree with the authors' interpretations? Are any other conclusions possible from the same statistics?

PHI BETA KAPPA AND BIG MAN ON CAMPUS *

ERNEST HAVEMANN AND PATRICIA SALTER WEST

There are two completely opposite theories about how to get the most out of a college career. Educators, and most parents, like to hold up the Phi Beta Kappa as the good example: if you study hard you are sure to go to heaven, and incidentally have the happiest and most profitable life enroute. But a good many students have the notion that grades are mostly nonsense; they figure that an A in philosophy sells no insurance policies, and that the way to get ahead in life is to be a campus leader and make a lot of friends. Thus the Phi Beta Kappa, a bookish fellow, and the Big Man on Campus, a hail fellow well met, are generally considered to be two antithetical types.

Actually they are not so far apart as commonly thought. The all-A students, by and large, are not so unsociable and retiring as pictured. Indeed they are more likely than anyone else to be the campus leaders. Among our group of graduates it turns out that 29 percent of the A students held at least two campus offices, as opposed to 22 percent of the B students and only 16 percent of the C and D students. The better a student's grades, in other words, the more likely he is to "get around" on the campus. And, conversely, the students who accumulate a long list of extra-curricular activities and

* From Havemann and West, *They Went to College*, Harcourt, Brace and Company. Copyright, 1952, by *Time*, Inc. Reprinted by permission of Time, Inc.

offices are more likely to be the better students than the poorer ones. The Phi Beta Kappa usually has a lot of interests, of which grades are only one.

The question remains, however: Are A's the key to a career, or are they just a waste of effort? Grades certainly seem to bear a direct relation to the types of jobs the graduates hold after college. The A students tend to wind up in the professions. Fewer B students are found in the professions, and more of them in business. Among C and D students, the professional men are fewest of all and the businessmen the most numerous.

Another part of the answer is contained in these figures: at the time of the survey 50 percent of the male A students were making $5,000 a year or more, compared with 41 percent of the C and D students. To carry the income bracket a step higher, 27 per cent of the A students were making $7,500 a year or more, compared with 21 percent of the C and D students. In general, therefore, the best students were doing better financially than the poorest students—but hardly enough better to inspire anyone to burn the midnight oil for a Phi Beta Kappa key, or to strike terror to the heart of the student who is just hanging on by the skin of his teeth.

But these salary figures do not tell the full story. Included among the professions, which the A students enter in such notable numbers, are teaching and the clergy—the lowest paid of all U. S. professional fields. In fact 38 percent of all the A graduates were in the low-paid professions, in contrast to only 23 percent of the C and D graduates. Thus in substantial numbers, the better students have chosen a life work which almost never provides entree to the highest income brackets. To get the full picture of how grades affect earnings, we shall have to divide the graduates into occupational groups.

In every occupational field, it develops, the A graduates have the best earnings record. Their advantage is most pronounced in the learned (and low-paid) professions. Despite the difficulty of attaining a high salary in this field, a total of 31 percent of the A graduates has managed to hit the $5,000 mark, compared with only 16 percent of the C and D students. In the high-paid professions, mostly law, medicine, and dentistry, they also have a clear advantage. Even in government jobs, they reach the top more frequently.

In the field of business, however, the advantage of the A student, while still fairly clear-cut, is much more tenuous. The A graduates have done only slightly better than the B graduates, and the B students only slightly better than the C and D students. For all practical purposes, and thinking only of income, the man who plans to enter the business world can well argue that grades mean nothing at all. The college diploma has a great financial value in business as well as in other fields. But a degree *summa cum laude* is not much more valuable than a degree that was in jeopardy until the last examination grade was in. It appears that in all truth an A in philosophy does not sell many insurance policies—or make a man a much better factory foreman, file clerk, junior executive, merchant, or manufacturer.

This matter of grades is one thing that seems to affect the earnings of women in much the same way that it affects the earnings of men. . . . There are not so many women graduates as men to begin with, and many of the women are housewives and therefore out of the job market. Of the women who work, most are concentrated in the teaching field, as has been noted, and very few have entered the high-paid professions. Moreover, as is inevitable in a survey of this kind, we do not know the college grades of all the working women. The upshot is that, while the sample of A, B, and C and D students in the learned professions is adequate, we have only 70 cases of businesswomen who made A grades, only 25 cases of A women in law, medicine, or dentistry, and only 20 cases of C and D women in the high-paid professions. . . .

. . . In the field of the learned professions, where the total sample involves 1,136 women, earnings rise in direct proportion to grades. In the high-paid professions and in government, although the small sampling produces some freaks, we are entitled to assume that the same pattern exists. In business, on the other hand, one is immediately struck by the remarkably similar records of the A women and the women who made C's and D's. We can probably take for granted that, just as for men, grades make a difference in a woman's financial success in every field except business. And it should be pointed out again here that of all the factors in this section of the book that affect the earnings of men, this is the only one that seems to matter for the women.

At the point where we left off discussing the men graduates, to whom we must now return after noting this single exception to the general rule that women have no place in this part of the book, we had just discovered that grades play a much smaller role in business success than in any other field. If grades do not, then perhaps extra-curricular activities do? Perhaps there is something to the theory of being a campus leader and making a lot of friends?

We throw out the first fact, and with it a large dash of cold water. For the most prominent men on the campus, those who participated in four or more extra-curricular activities, the median income is $4,345. For those who never participated in any extra-curricular activities at all, the median is $5,248! Try to find any justification for the winning-friends-and-influencing-people theory in those figures!

Actually, however, the medians are a little unfair. They seem to indicate that extra-curricular activities are a handicap to later-life earning ability, and such is not really the case. It so happens that the older graduates, who as we have seen make the most money, went to school at a time when extra-curricular activities were less popular than now. It also happens that the graduates in law, medicine, dentistry, engineering, and similar fields of great specialization, who also have a good earnings record, are not so prominent in campus affairs as other students. (Most of these courses are pretty strenuous; possibly the students do not have much time for anything but study.) If we rule out the matters of age and of occupational field, it turns out that there are practically no differences at all in the earnings of graduates who avoided extra-curricular activities completely or who engaged in one, two, three, or a dozen. Not even the matter of leadership, as measured by the number of campus offices held, seems to have the slightest effect.

These figures hold for the business field, where grades do not seem to matter very much, as well as for other fields where grades seem to make a fairly substantial difference. To cite just one piece of evidence, without going into all the statistical ramifications: among the officers of at least two campus organizations, 19 percent have had to settle for the routine rank-and-file jobs in business, either as white collar or manual workers. For the men who held one campus office, the proportion is 17 percent—and for those who never held a campus office the proportion is 19 percent. It may be that business is more a matter of whom you know than what you know—but obviously you do not meet them through campus activities. Nor does leadership or lack of it in college necessarily imply leadership in the business world.

We started out the chapter by noting that good grades and campus activities are not necessarily incompatible, that indeed they often tend to go together. And in recognition of this fact we have in previous parts of the book divided the students into four groups rather than two: we have spoken of the Greasy Grinds, who make A's but seldom engage in any campus activities outside the library; the All-Around Students, who make A's and at the same time run the clubs and are the life of the party at the dances; the Big Men on Campus, whom we have identified as the students who concentrate on extra-curricular activities while just skinning by on grades; and the Students Who Just Sat There—that is, the men and women who did not make good grades but did not set the campus afire either. Perhaps we should use these categories, rather than the matter of grades alone or extra-curricular activities alone, as a guide to earnings in later life. Certainly this is done in the college yearbooks—where almost invariably an All-Around man is chosen the most likely to succeed.

Dividing the men into these four groups, we get the following pattern of median earnings:

Greasy Grinds	$5,141
All-Around Students	4,775
Big Men on Campus	4,648
Those Who Just Sat There	4,300

When you think about it, the figures are rather strange. The Greasy Grind, often considered by his classmates as hopelessly impractical, sits right on top in the very practical matter of post-graduate finances. The All-Around Student, the cynosure and envy of all eyes, does not surpass everybody else nearly so often as the yearbooks predict. The Big Men on Campus, who probably consider themselves the most practical and down-to-earth of all, come in third in a four-horse race. The Students Who Just Sat There come in last, but their showing is by no means disreputable and entitles them to feel, in retrospect, that the effort of making better grades and going out for more activities would simply not have been worth the trouble.

But again the figures are rather distorted, this time chiefly by the fact that many of the specialists, who usually wind up making high salaries, are too busy or are disinclined to bother with extra-curricular activities. (The Greasy Grind nowadays, as a matter of fact, is less often a long-haired poet than a very pragmatic fellow with a slide rule in his pocket.) If we divide the graduates into the A.B.'s and the specialists, we can probably get a fairer picture. Suppose we make this separation, and then inquire how many of the graduates were earning $5,000 a year or more at the time of the study. Among the graduates of the humanities or other "general" courses, the proportions work out to 39 percent of the Greasy Grinds, 39 percent of the All-Around Students, 40 percent of the Big Men on Campus, and 35 percent of the Men Who Just Sat There. For the specialists, the proportions are 54 percent of the Grinds, 59 percent of the All-Arounders, 57 percent of the BMOC's, and 48 percent of the Sitters.

From this point of view, the differences between the Grinds, the All-Arounders, and the BMOC's are negligible. The Students Who Just Sat There, on the other hand, are at a disadvantage, but only a very slight one. Perhaps the most surprising message of all about the figures in this chapter is that the parents, friends, and fiancee of the Student Who Is Just Sitting There, barely hanging on from one examination to the next, and meanwhile winning no popularity contests, need not worry so much as they usually do. Even though his college record may be undistinguished in every respect, he is not necessarily doomed.

EXERCISES

Choose any of the following groups of tables. Write an interpretation using any data relevant to your purpose.

GROUP I:

CAUSES OF DEATH

(Policyholders, Equitable Life Insurance Company of Iowa)

	1927	*1937*	*1947*
Respiratory diseases	21.4%	12.6%	6.9%
Cancer	8.3	13.4	15.1
Heart & circulatory system	33.9	39.9	57.7
Accident	12.7	10.2	7.0
Suicide	4.3	5.3	2.3
All other	19.4	18.6	11.0

1955

	All Ages	Under 40	40–59	60 and over
Heart & circulatory system	60.3%	13.7%	53.7%	64.8%
Cancer	17.5	15.1	21.0	16.6
Accidents	4.9	40.4	7.1	2.2
Influenza & pneumonia	1.9	2.3	.8	2.2
Suicide	1.8	5.8	4.7	.8
Diseases of kidneys	1.7	2.8	1.4	1.7
Tuberculosis	.4	.4	.5	.4
All other	11.5	19.5	10.8	11.3
	100.0%	100.0%	100.0%	100.0%

GROUP II:

COMBAT INCENTIVES NAMED BY OFFICER AND ENLISTED VETERANS OF WORLD WAR II

Percentage of Incentives Named by Enlisted Men

(QUESTION: "Generally, from your combat experience, what was most important to you in making you want to keep going and do as well as you could?")

Incentives	*Percentage*
Ending the task	39
Solidarity with group	14
Sense of duty and self-respect	9
Thoughts of home and loved ones	10
Self-preservation	6
Idealistic reasons	5
Vindictiveness	2
Leadership and discipline	1
Miscellaneous	14

Percentage of Incentives Named by Officers

(QUESTION: "When the going is tough for your men, what do you think are the incentives which keep them fighting?")

Incentives	*Percentage*
Ending the task	14
Solidarity with group	15
Sense of duty and self-respect	15
Thoughts of home and loved ones	3
Self-preservation	9
Idealistic reasons	2
Vindictiveness	12
Leadership and discipline	19
Miscellaneous	11

GROUP III:

Table I

DISTRIBUTION OF AGE GROUPS IN THE U.S. POPULATION
(U. S. Bureau of Labor Statistics)

AGE:	*0–4*	*5–10*	*20–29*	*30–44*	*45–65*	*65 and over*
1900	12.1%	32.3%	18.3%	19.5%	13.7%	4.1%
1920	11.0	29.8	17.4	21.0	16.1	4.7
1950	7.2	23.3	16.6	22.7	21.8	8.5

Table 2

PERCENTAGE OF U.S. MALE POPULATION IN VARIOUS AGE GROUPS WHO ARE GAINFULLY EMPLOYED
(U. S. Bureau of Labor Statistics)

AGE:	*10–15*	*16–64*	*65 and over*
1900	26.1%	92.2%	68.4%
1920	16.8	93.3	60.2
1950	0.1	95.4	41.0

ASSIGNMENTS

I. Write an evaluation (500–1000 words) of conflicting evidence in the following materials: "The Sensational Secret behind Damnation of Stalin," *Life*, April 23, 1956; (2) letters to Editors of *Life* included in Readings selection No. 3 of this chapter; (3) Dallin's review of Levine's *Stalin's Great Secret, New York Times Book Review,* Nov. 11, 1956; (4) Levine's answer, *New York Times Book Review,* Nov. 18, 1956; (5) Levine's article in *Saturday Review,* Sept. 22, 1956; (6) review by Gregory Aronson in *The New Leader,* Aug. 20, 1956; (7) Levine's reply in *The New Leader,* Oct. 1, 1956. Use whatever additional sources of information you may find.

II. Find your own raw materials and from them write an interpretation for a specific audience. Though we have here concentrated on interpretation of statistics as evidence, remember that there are verbal matters which also call for explanation: poems, scientific papers, legal documents, etc. Your instructor may want you to try several types of interpretation—papers of varying length.

CHAPTER 8

Defending a Judgment

Judgments Need Defense

However sure you may feel about your own conclusions, other people are likely to differ. If you expect your ideas to have influence you will need to show why they deserve it. You may need to present reasons adequate to convince the skeptical, uninformed, or positively antagonistic. And you may also need to contribute a sounder basis of belief—pertinent new evidence, logical analysis—for those who already agree with you.

Expository defense of a judgment differs decidedly from contentious argument or propaganda in the emphasis it gives to evidence and reason. It need not be lacking in persuasive effect; it certainly recognizes related human interests; it quite naturally uses methods to hold attention. But unlike the propaganda that seeks quick converts regardless of the means, this kind of writing actually encourages critical thinking. Beliefs founded on reliable information and valid inference are more stable than those based on emotion.

Expository defense of this kind has wide application. It is used, as we have seen, in evaluating books, plays, pictures, symphonies, architecture, and jazz. It presents critical judgments of sailboats, refrigerators, motors, and highways. It supports opinions about laws and customs, institutions, and men. It may or may not recommend a particular course of action.

It varies widely, too, in scope and method. A scientist may defend his new hypothesis to other scientists. A technical report may propose specific equipment for a plant. A dissertation in psychology, linguistics, or history may defend a thesis for specialists in its field. All these are formal, thorough, and fully documented; they face the closest scrutiny of informed and critical readers. Much less formal and usually shorter are book reviews, magazine articles, consumer's reports, letters and memoranda about all kinds of problems; these never pretend to give the last word on a subject, yet they do show respect for facts and logic.

This kind of writing is very different from the personal essay of feelings and attitudes. Here the author's "opinion" is of little consequence unless it is backed up with factual reports, analysis and definition, interpretations of evidence, reasoned answers to the issues. Substantiation gives meaning and weight to opinions.

State Your Purpose

To defend a judgment implies a central judgment worth defending. All the subordinate, supporting judgments about sources and evidence, issues and criteria, ought to point to one final conclusion. You should express that final conclusion in terms you are ready and able to defend. Here are some rules that can help you do so:

1. **Make the form fit your purpose.** Is your conclusion a judgment of fact or probability, a judgment of value, or a judgment of policy?

Examples:
a. A high correlation exists between smoking and cancer (judgment of probability)
b. Smoking is dangerous (judgment of value)
c. Young people should not learn to smoke (judgment of policy)
d. Recent engineering graduates have more employment opportunities than graduates of other curricula (judgment of fact)
e. Engineering offers better employment opportunities than other fields (judgment of value)
f. Young men with mathematical aptitude should study engineering (judgment of policy)

2. **Don't overstate your conclusion.** As we have said all along, your judgment need not express an extreme position—all right or all

wrong, all good or all bad. And be sure that the evidence available will support the judgment you express.

Overstated	*Moderately Stated*
This movie is wonderful.	In spite of an over-simple theme, this movie has suspense and character interest.
Football is the greatest developer of courage, stamina, and sportsmanship.	Football has important values for those who play it.
Congress should eliminate all economic aid to foreign countries. (Can you go that far with the available evidence?)	Congress should look seriously to reducing if not entirely eliminating economic aid to foreign countries.

The available evidence, the time and space you have to use, and your readers' interests are all limiting factors. For example, you could hardly prove that "*The Belltown Gazette* is the best edited weekly in America" because you have seen only a few of the weeklies that exist; but perhaps you could support the conclusion that it is "the best edited weekly in a hundred-mile radius." Again, a 500-word letter to the local editor cannot possibly prove that "the Governor should not be reelected"; it might successfully show that "the Governor's tax measures are unfair to local citizens," or "the Governor has made bad appointments," or "the Governor can't get along with the legislature."

3. **Don't beg the question in stating your conclusion.** We have mentioned this error before; that is, using terms indicating bias or assuming the truth of points you still must prove:

Biased Statement	*Impartial Statement*
Congress should repeal the discredited Labor Relations Act. (You must prove that it is *discredited.*)	Congress should repeal the Labor Relations Act. (This tells what is to be proved.)
This overpriced, overadvertised set is a poor buy. (You must prove that it is *overpriced* and *overadvertised.*)	This set is overpriced and overadvertised. (Or—this set is a poor buy. Either would be a legitimate statement of what needs to be proved.)

Preliminary Planning

The amount of planning necessary to defend a judgment successfully naturally varies with the subject, readers, and form. A one-page memorandum on selection of typewriter paper can likely be planned in a few minutes; a report on selecting a site for a new plant may require days or weeks of careful preparation. What we say here about thorough planning may be modified to fit the needs of various situations.

1. *Analysis of Readers.* The better you understand your readers, the more likely you are to say things effectively to them. This cannot be stressed too much. Here are some things it is useful to find out about your readers:

a. Attitude toward your problem: How will they respond to your conclusion? Will they be antagonistic, favorable, skeptical, or neutral?
b. Interest and knowledge: How closely does the problem touch their lives? What preconceptions or prejudices are they likely to have about it? How much do they know about it?
c. General background: What do they read—and how much? What is their general or special education?

If you know your readers intimately it is not difficult to answer these questions. If not, you will have to infer the answers from things you do know about them. If they all belong to the bricklayers' union, or the Methodist Church, or 4-H Clubs, you at least know some interests they all have in common. If you are writing for a periodical, you can infer much about the readers from the paper or magazine they read.

2. *Answering Issues.* An important preliminary step is to decide upon your main reasons for reaching the conclusion you have reached. That means simple answers to each issue and criterion that seems important to you. The answers ought to add up—if they themselves are established—to your final conclusion about the whole problem. Yet these answers to issues need not all point the same way. Now is the time to decide what you can answer, honestly and with adequate reason, about each one. For example:

Problem: Which fountain pen is most satisfactory for undergraduate use?	*Conclusion:* The Partridge Pen is generally most satisfactory for undergraduate use.
Criteria:	*Judgments:*
Which pen has the best point?	The Partridge offers the widest selection of good points.
Which pen is most convenient to fill?	The Partridge is about as convenient to fill as others.
Which pen is most reliable?	The Partridge seems less likely to get out of order.
Which pen is most durable?	No other pen seems likely to outlast the Partridge.
Which is most attractive?	Though not the most attractive, it is not ugly.
Which is most economical?	It costs slightly more, but its durability makes it fairly economical.

Now look at your conclusion and your judgments. Be sure you have the evidence to give the proper support. If you don't your judgments will have to be modified, perhaps even reversed or dropped, and others substituted for them.

3. *Answers to Counter-arguments.* If the problem is controversial, or if your conclusion is likely to meet considerable resistance, it is a good idea to prepare now to answer the points that may be brought against your judgments. List such points in one column, a summary of your answers in an opposite column, like this:

For subsidized athletes	*My answers*
1. Athletic success advertises a college. . . . Look at Notre Dame.	1. Athletic victories advertise the wrong things. . . . Look at Chicago, Harvard, California Tech. Athletic advertising does not attract the best students or teachers; nor does it raise endowments. (Compare schools.)
2. The athlete who earns money for the college deserves a share.	2. According to this premise the athlete who loses money for the college (track, crew, golf) should be forced to pay to compete.

For subsidized athletes	*My answers*
3. If talent in chemistry, music, or mathematics deserves scholarship recognition, so does skill in athletics.	3. College scholarships properly encourage the development of talents in directions for which the college exists: science, technology, humanities, arts.
4. Many boys can go to college who could not otherwise go.	4. These boys are no more deserving of help—often much less so—than boys without athletic ability . . . Let them compete for scholarships with all others, on the basis of fitness for college work.

4. *Selecting Notes.* First, reject issues that now appear of little importance. Reject points and evidence that seem trivial or unsubstantial, and especially evidence that seems either inconsistent or of doubtful reliability. Next, select points and evidence that seem especially suited for the readers you hope to convince. If your readers will have more respect for Fieldwood the chemist than for Bradman the banker, then Fieldwood probably becomes a better witness for you than Bradman when both have reported the same facts.

For the time being, you may simply put notes together that go to support a single conclusion.

5. *Effective Order.* Not all expository defense will follow the same order or plan. Two main directions, quite opposite ones, suggest themselves: the *climax order* begins with an introduction to the problem—with questions; it proceeds to evidence, discussion of alternatives, inferences; it ends with the final judgment or general conclusion. In contrast, the *anti-climax order* begins with your final judgment; it proceeds then to the reasons and evidence supporting that judgment. Of course it is also possible to make certain combinations of the two general orders: you may, for example, begin with questions yet use anti-climax order for various sections of the composition.

An outline for anti-climax order would look like this:

The Borough of Elton should appropriate $50,000 for improvement of the municipal airport (general conclusion)

1. The community needs improved airport facilities because—

   1. In winter months the runways are unsafe for transport planes (examples, evidence)
   2. Discontinuance of passenger service is a serious inconvenience to many people (examples, evidence)
   3. The community suffers considerable financial loss (testimony, evidence)
2. The proposed appropriation will substantially improve the airport (testimony of experts)
3. The city can afford this appropriation (evidence about financial condition of the city, sources of new income, etc.)

An outline for climax order would look like this:

Should the Borough of Elton appropriate $50,000 for improvement of the municipal airport? (statement of the problem)
1. Does the community need improved airport facilities?
   1. Consider conditions during winter months (examples, evidence)
   2. How many passengers are inconvenienced? (evidence)
   3. Does the community suffer much financial loss? (evidence)
2. Will this appropriation substantially improve the airport (testimony of experts)
3. Is it financially feasible? (testimony, evidence)

CONCLUSION: The Borough should therefore make this appropriation.

Both climax and anti-climax orders have advantages—for different situations and purposes. The climax order is closer to the order of constructive thinking: the question comes first, then the weighing of alternatives, finally the logical inference from all the facts and premises. So the climax order seems more naturally fitted to encourage an inquiring, unprejudiced consideration of the whole problem. It encourages comparisons and thoughtful evaluation of evidence and arguments.

Climax order may also seem more likely to get the fair attention of readers who might respond unfavorably to an immediate expression of opinions. So climax order has much to recommend it for expository defense.

But anti-climax order has advantages also. It often seems easier to follow: first the judgment or "answer," then all the reasons and evidence to support the judgment. It may also seem much easier to write, since it seems human nature to want to express opinions as soon as possible. Anti-climax order, interestingly enough, is the order required in the reports of technical specialists. Executives interested in such reports sometimes want the recommendation at the beginning of a report; so the order is something like this:

Object and Scope of the Report
Conclusions and Recommendations
Discussion and Data

You must decide which order is more likely to satisfy your writing situation and the effect you want to produce.

Writing to be Read

To make writing convincing you must hold the reader's attention. You must find ways to create suspense, escape dullness, and stimulate curiosity. Primarily you must make readers feel the importance of your subject and the significance of your judgments to them.

1. *How to Begin.* Of course the introduction has to be interesting to its readers, but there are many kinds of readers and many different ways of creating interest.

If you are writing a formal report or research paper, your readers may be assumed to have a general interest in your subject ahead of time. The reader may have asked for the report; or he finds your paper in a publication limited to subjects that have considerable value or interest to him. Your introduction then is most effective when it states the problem as objectively and economically as possible. Your reasons for investigating, the scope of your study, and questions you want to answer: these are the matters that belong in such an introduction.

The debate-like opening—"It is my purpose to prove the following points"—is not very often advisable. Even formal writing can adopt a style less cumbersome than the lawyer's brief. In the practical reports of business, however, it is often customary to place "Conclusions and Recommendations" right after the introductory "Object and Scope."

If readers have less certain interest in the problem ahead of time, the introduction needs to provide special incentives for reading. Some possibilities are:

a. Narrative or anecdote—evidence or example that shows in concrete ways a need, a promise, or a condition deserving attention

b. Statistics—surprising figures showing the importance of the problem
c. Quotation—striking statement or statements to demonstrate existence of a controversy, or to summarize

2. *Concreteness.* It is hard to hold attention with abstractions. Even if readers agree with all your generalizations, they lose interest fast unless you bring the discussion down to realities.

Concrete language refers to specific persons, places, things. Its use constitutes one of the most efficient methods of writing interestingly. It makes sense impressions with word pictures, and it is especially called for when your readers are unschooled or nonintellectual. Some minds are trained to do abstract thinking in mathematics or philosophy or about the complex social and economic problems of our time. Most readers are somewhere in between: they can follow abstract reasoning for short periods, but lose all interest and understanding unless they find examples, instances, *facts* to bring the discussion "down to earth."

Abstract words do undoubtedly have emotional values—and thus interest-getting values. *Patriotism, loyalty, success, democracy,* and *dictatorship* are all highly abstract and all have strong emotional connotations. But effective writing cannot rely upon such terms. They may serve a purpose, but they do not hold attention long. A writer makes *patriotism* mean something to his readers for his purposes only if he illustrates it with concrete examples.

In short, to be *specific* is the first step in making writing clear and vivid. "Omaha and Des Moines" is more interesting than "two cities in the Midwest." "Five members of the White Sox" is more interesting than "some big league ball players."

3. *Familiarity.* Familiarity is another essential factor in achieving concreteness. "Plum Street" is more concrete to the man who lives there than to those who never saw it. "Selling short," "tail sawyer," "buffing wheel," and "tuyeres" are vivid enough to those who use the terms every day; to others, even if clearly defined, the terms are still abstractions.

To *localize* your examples to suit reader experience, to find things that move and live, to make the timely reference—all help make writing vivid for readers.

The following example represents concreteness in a highly colloquial style; it illustrates equally well how a writer connects his subject to reader interests:

Taxes

We all hate to pay taxes. After the interest on the mortgage, and the plumber's bill, and having the roof fixed, along comes the tax bill, higher than last year. The tax-eaters are never satisfied.

That's not the worst of it. You pay a lot of taxes that don't hurt as much but cost more than you think. There are sales taxes, and amusement taxes, and gasoline taxes, and tobacco taxes. There are high prices because the tariff keeps you from having a chance to buy cheap goods from other countries. Business is taxed going and coming; the tax is added to the price of everything, and you have to pay. Pretty bad. And what do you get for it? Just a chance, people say, to help support a lot of grafters and bureaucrats.

You'd be surprised, though, if you ever tried to figure out what you do get. Two hundred years ago there weren't any paved roads. Most city streets were either mud or dust. No street lights. The watchman with lantern and rattle walked around at night in fear of his life. No public schools. No sewers. No running water. No libraries. No parks. If your ancestors wanted any of these things they paid for them personally.

Do you realize what it would cost you to send your children to private schools? Or to have a private well and pump, with a private sewer system? The reason we have these public services in our towns and cities is that we can get them for less money by paying taxes than we can by buying them privately. As Justice Holmes once pointed out, taxes are not a burden but a luxury. In paying taxes you have the privilege of buying necessary services at reduced prices. In most places we could save money by doubling our taxes and getting twice as many free services as we get now.

—David Cushman Coyle, *Uncommon Sense*

4. *Suspense.* One of the most fundamental elements in holding attention is suspense—the art of keeping readers expectant. As soon as a reader says, "Well, I guess I have it all now," you have lost him. You must keep him looking ahead if you want to hold him.

Other things being equal, climax order naturally provides more susense because it postpones stating the final judgment. If you can make readers genuinely curious about the problem, analyze the situation with apparent impartiality, and avoid very much generalizing, most readers will want to know where it all leads and just how you will state your final judgment. But you must be careful to preserve "drift." You must give readers confidence that you are going *somewhere*; by frequent questions, a clear interpretation of evidence as you present it, and constant reminders that here are facts and ideas leading to necessary answers, you can give your writing direction and still introduce suspense. Just be sure your readers can sense a definite progress towards an important conclusion.

The anti-climax order is by nature somewhat discouraging to the development of suspense. The "answer" to the problem comes first—or early. Suspense thereafter depends upon the reader's curiosity about the reasons you can advance to support the conclusion. If you can indicate that reasons and evidence are unusual or surprising, you still provide suspense.

5. *Implication.* Implication in writing is saying less than you mean in ways that suggest inferences and judgments. It is possible, of course, to make the whole defense of a judgment implicative: you can array evidence and expository analysis in such a way that your final judgment inevitably follows; you may not even need to state it. More commonly, however, implication is simply an incidental device to avoid dullness by giving the reader something to do for himself.

Everybody is familiar enough with one type of implication—the so-called rhetorical question. Instead of asserting, "This is a gross injustice!" the writer demands, "Is this justice?" The reader knows the answer intended. Only the most naive writers answer their own rhetorical questions: "Is this justice? It certainly is not." An explicit answer destroys the whole force of the question.

Two warnings are necessary about rhetorical questions: Don't use too many of them. And don't introduce questions that could be answered more than one way. A whole paragraph of rhetorical questions is like a page of exclamation points. The strain on reader attention is too great; the result is monotony. And questions that don't point to one inescapable answer are not "rhetorical" at all: if they demand explanation they may be useful for your purpose, but not as implication.

Narrative, descriptive, and expository analysis frequently serve the purpose of defending a judgment even better than explicit argument. You could, for example, describe a national park in such a way that readers will say "this is a valuable public asset" without your telling them so. You could tell your experiences with a boat so vividly that your readers want such a boat; the directive "buy one for yourself" might even weaken the effect.

One special kind of implication is what we call *irony*, which consists of saying something quite different from—if not the exact opposite of—what we mean. It is a common device for ridiculing practices or systems, even persons, that one wants to attack. If it succeeds at all it is because readers "get the point." For instance:

> It is a happy coincidence this fall that so many of our undergraduates who came all the way from the Atlantic seaboard to study ceramics, industrial education, and music appreciation at the University are also good football players. It only goes to show that a solid academic reputation can win lots of games too. The cynics, of course, point out that 92 per cent of our enrollment come from high schools within the state, while 84 per cent of our football squad come from other states. It may seem unusual that our reputation in certain courses should be more appealing in distant places to scholars who also happen to be football players, but it's nice to have it that way. Everybody, including the coaching staff, must be surprised and delighted.

To have to explain irony is as unsatisfactory as to have to explain a joke; a joke explained is no longer a joke. Irony may be exciting to readers who get the point; it is only confusing to those who don't get it. That is the main reason why irony is dangerous to employ. Some readers, unfortunately, take what you're saying seriously. One solution, of course, is to end your ironical passages with a clear label: "But to be serious . . . ," you say—and in that way inform all readers that you were only fooling.

Elements of Support

The elements useful in supporting a judgment and convincing readers are varied. You may choose from numerous possible means:

Definition and explanation
Facts for evidence
Opinion from authority
Interpretation of facts
Deductive reasoning
Inductive reasoning

Example
Hypothetical illustration
Analogy

1. *Definition and Explanation.* It is surprising how many beliefs that men hold are the result of misunderstandings. Strong antagonism to such things as "progressive education," "social security," "public power," and "health insurance" have sometimes been greatly reduced by simple explanations of what those terms mean in a particular discussion. Definition can often reduce opposition by clearing up mistaken ideas of what words mean.

We commonly think of definition and other kinds of explanation as the function of an introduction, not part of the actual process of substantiating judgments. But a clear exposition of a machine, an organization, a means of doing something may do nearly the entire job of opening men's minds. Prejudice founded on ignorance can be effectively eliminated by removing areas of ignorance.

2. *Fact Evidence.* Facts, of course, are nowhere more useful than in providing essential evidence to support judgments. The facts you found to reach your own conclusions may be exactly those that will convince your readers. More often, however, you will not want or need everything you have assembled. Readers will seldom give you unlimited attention for very long; "all" the evidence available may be neither interesting nor essential to satisfy reader demands. You must make an intelligent selection.

Fact evidence, we have seen, may include both cases and statistics. Evidence about specific events or conditions can be concrete and vivid. Figures cover a wider range and lead to more general conclusions, but are more abstract. A combination of statistics and specific details of representative cases can often furnish the most convincing evidence:

This survey disclosed that the mean average cost for a year at college was $1456, but more than half of the undergraduates in this area (57% of them) spent less than that. The median for this group was actually only $1325, and a substantial number (24%) got along for less than a thousand dollars—usually by working for room and board and earning enough at odd jobs to take care of various other expenses.

Harvey Clennan is representative of the *median group*. Last year Harvey kept accurate books and knows precisely what he spent between September 11 when he came to the campus and June 5 when he left for a summer job. His total expenditures were $1354.27. He had a scholarship paying part of this tuition. An uncle bought him a suit and topcoat and paid his fare home for Christmas. All other costs figure out this way:

Balance for tuition and fees	$200.00
Room	180.00
Board	468.00
Books and supplies	110.55
Dues (clubs, etc.)	80.00
Clothes	119.50
Laundry, cleaning	69.10
Incidentals	127.12

Harvey lives in a dormitory, belongs to several campus organizations, dresses about as well as most of his associates, takes a girl to three *big dances* a year, and has all the equipment he needs for scholastic assignments. Of course, he has no car, he takes no trips out of town, and he never has a really expensive weekend. He has to live frugally. But as you can see, it isn't so bad. Harvey is a somewhat better than average student (B−). He says: "College is fine. I get along all right. I'm having a wonderful time here."

This profile of "Harvey Clennan" adds some meaning to the statistical averages, medians, and percentages. Harvey is reality. He shows a reader something of what living on an "average" budget is like. Without a Harvey to represent reality, statistics often carry little meaning. They have to be abstract; Harvey is specific.

Both statistics and specific cases provide possible evidence. If 46% of all juvenile delinquents in the city come from South Hills, two or three detailed accounts of representative South Hills delinquents can give the abstract figures concreteness. But any evidence—statistical or case, fact or opinion—is effective only when readers can believe it. The reputation of the source and the possibility of verification are important to any critical readers. Reliability is the first requisite.

3. *Opinion Evidence.* Not every opinion from men with prestige deserves consideration, but no opinion can merit attention in itself unless the man who expresses it merits recognition as an authority on that point. Opinion evidence is useful only when we have extraordinary confidence in its source.

Whenever you have a choice, therefore, you ought to select for use in writing those sources, authorities, or specialists who are likely to have most prestige with your readers. That doesn't necessarily mean the "biggest names." A man known to your readers as an expert window-washer may be a better source for opinion about the best detergents for washing windows than Senator Witham or the Archbishop of Canterbury. The test is: "What standing does this authority have with my readers for this subject?" Your readers may never have heard of him before; yet if his position commands respect for the point at issue, the authority may very well be the right one.

If opinions of authorities conflict, as they sometimes do, the conflicting sides ought to have adequate representation. You cannot ignore all evidence that goes contrary to your own conclusion. Choose the most representative authorities—as many as time and space permit. Then you may offer critical comments about them, comparing the reliability of one with another. A writer's comments about his authorities may run something like this:

The Federal Trade Commission reports, generally considered objective and carefully reasoned, have important information on this subject . . .

Unfortunately the engineers disagree about the best way to get the water. There are differing estimates of costs for laying pipe lines to Graybrun and to Hoffman. Because of Mr. Hutson's wider experience and the accurate estimates he made last year for the Bowman Reservoir, we consider his figures the most reliable of the three submitted. He has carefully explained these figures in his report. Those are the figures we are using here.

Eight different bankers and manufacturers were called before the committee for testimony, but we have no reason to consider their broad generalizations either expert or objective. What they said conflicts directly with what the economist Henry Foschild says. Foschild has no connection with any single enterprise that would influence his opinion. His analysis was essentially correct in 1946, 1949, 1952, and 1956. We think his views deserve close attention now.

Since every writer wants fair and favorable attention given to what he says, it is important to avoid the use of names that arouse needless antagonism. If you know that your readers either dislike or distrust a source—reporter, newspaper, expert, or agency—it is the part of wisdom to find another source of evidence if you can.

4. *Effective Reasoning.* Even if time permitted (and it never does) it would never be practicable to try to establish every premise on which an important conclusion rests. What premises, then, do you need to support?

First, quite naturally, you must support all the premises that your readers are sure to question. If they are likely to doubt that "government employees never work very hard," the assertion has no value as a premise—at least until you have produced considerable evidence to back it up. Every premise must not only be true—your reader must see that it is true.

Secondly, even if your readers will accept certain premises uncritically, you may need to support them if you know they are under attack by others. You are trying to help your readers understand as well as believe, and you want them to stay convinced. So if it is fairly certain that someday your readers will encounter evidence and objections that throw doubt on basic assumptions in your reasoning, it is well to prepare them now for such encounters.

On the other hand, premises that are well-founded and generally accepted can stand on their own feet; in fact, time devoted to proving the obvious is worse than wasted—it results in dullness.

Generalizations from a sample need enough evidence—a large enough sample—to meet the tests of adequate induction. A handful of instances carefully selected to eliminate all that don't point your way can never provide adequate expository defense. You need to avoid superficial and poorly founded generalizations; you ought to expose them in the arguments of others.

Analogies are of two kinds: figurative and literal. Literal analogy compares things actually alike; it has logical substance in proportion to the proved similiarities—in Route 26 and Route 34; in one college with another; one nation with another nation. Figurative analogy proves nothing by itself; it is essentially a device for clarifying other kinds of reasoning and making them interesting. For instance, you might compare a grocer's business with the federal government simply to enforce the premise, "Any enterprise that has more liabilities than assets is in a precarious condition." The grocer's business is not literally like the federal government's, but the analogy serves as a reminder of the widespread truth of the premise.

Example or illustration may be useful either to explain a meaning or to support a judgment. A few illustrations are less than evidence because they are insufficient of themselves to establish premises or answer issues. But like figurative analogy they serve to emphasize and sharpen truths already more than half accepted:

As children we believed everything told us—until experience or conflicting statements forced us to doubt. I remember overhearing a neighbor say, when I was about seven, "Of course musicians are all insane," and I believed that implicitly for several years because nobody thought to tell me otherwise. Eventually I met a musician who did not seem the least insane, and after a little struggle I gave up the notion. But I'm sure the idea would be firmly fixed in my head today unless later experience had destroyed it.

The first sentence of that paragraph will hardly be questioned, but it doesn't force itself on our attention. The personal example gives the generalization concreteness and force.

When you want to show cause-and-effect relationships—how a law reduced hunting accidents, what effect teaching by television has on learning—you do well to combine inductive with deductive reasoning. Evidence from tests and experiments provides convincing support for many conclusions, but the question "Why?" must be answered by applying general law or theory to the case. Example:

Results of the placement test show its validity for predicting success in college. There is high correlation between score in this test and general academic average. For instance, the top quartile in this test has a general college average of 84.2 for freshman and sophomore years, and only 2% of this group fell below 70. The lowest quartile in this test had an average of 68.1 for the first two years, only 4% had averages over 80, and 20.3% were dismissed from college for unsatisfactory scholarship.

Since the placement test consists mainly of vocabulary, the question arises, "Why should a large vocabulary have any connection with mathematics, science, and the technical courses?" The answer seems to be that those most capable of learning any subject are those who also have verbal sense. Probably high intelligence leads to better vocabulary and better reading. Lower intelligence creates difficulties in these areas as well as most others, and so vocabulary proves a sign of intelligence. In other words, vocabulary may not itself be a major factor in learning, but vocabulary will be a sign of probable ability to learn—in mathematics and all the other subjects in college.

Conciliation

You can expect fair and undivided attention from readers only when you show respect for their intelligence and preconceptions. The need for tact is particularly apparent when your readers are somewhat suspicious or hostile to the conclusions you want them to understand. Fighting your readers is the worst way possible to get agreement, or understanding.

The difficulties in the way of reaching some audiences are well stated in this analysis by Louis J. Halle, Jr.:

> Most of us are open to persuasion only within narrow limits. We have made up our minds on the basic issues with which life confronts us. We have done our accepting and rejecting and have emerged from the process with convictions that we are prepared to defend against the world. You should not expect us to give up these convictions easily, because our sanity depends on them. They represent for each of us the order he has brought out of chaos. I am delighted with books that confirm and reinforce me in my convictions and will listen endlessly to the speeches of any man who does the same, but I cannot tolerate your attack because it threatens me with a return to the original chaos. The more persuasive your argument, the greater my alarm and indignation, until at last I bar my door against you . . .*

Perhaps this view of human prejudice seems exaggerated to you, and of course it doesn't mean that you can never change a man's mind—especially about current problems that do not involve his basic philosophies. But it does point to the difficulties when you encounter genuine antagonism to your ideas. It also suggests the absurdity of trying to alter your reader's whole attitude toward life in a single piece of writing. It suggests the importance of limiting your aims for particular readers.

You could not hope, for example, to show lifelong socialists the absurdity of socialism in a few thousand words. You could not expect to induce a Republican congressman to register as a Democrat. You could not convince a lawyer, a sociologist, or an osteopath that his profession is a menace to society even if you could get him to read a whole book packed with what seems to you overwhelming proof.

* Louis J. Halle, Jr., "Raw Materials of Persuasion," *Saturday Review,* March 11, 1950.

The lesson is this: First, limit your conclusions to matters you can probably support effectively. Secondly, concede, or at least disregard for the time, points that your readers will not surrender under any circumstances. Concentrate on issues that are vital and necessary, but never insist that your readers change their fundamental beliefs when those beliefs do not seriously interfere with the judgments you want them to accept. The purpose of expository defense of a judgment is not to reform mankind or change human nature.

Take a possible situation. The water system in your town is owned by a private corporation but you have studied the town's needs and the water supply and have reached the conclusion that the town ought to own the system and extend it. Some people in town call this "socialism," and almost everybody in town is firmly convinced that "socialism" is bad. Do you have to defend socialism? Of course not. To get into a dispute over the merits of "socialism" would divert attention from the local problem, and it would take at least a generation to make "socialists" out of the town's citizens, even if you wish to devote your life to that purpose. You might as well concede the evils of socialism (unless, of course, that concession would conflict with your honest beliefs); at least it would be easy to show that many of the firmest believers in capitalism and private enterprise have found publicly owned water systems a desirable means of encouraging and expanding private business.

In general, the way to conciliation—which means winning the friendly attention of an audience—is through recognizing some of your reader's important interests, and if possible, using them as important bases in your defense. Here are some examples:

(The writer knows his readers are, for the most part, members of fraternities and therefore probably strongly favorable to the fraternity system. He wants to advocate housing all freshmen and sophomores in dormitories—something that would affect the existing fraternity system. He writes:)

The fraternity is an established institution here. Nobody proposes abolishing fraternities. Nobody wants to do anything to interfere with the truly constructive contributions that fraternities make. The problem is how we can extend these contributions beyond the fraternity houses themselves. We have to find a way to do that without endangering fraternity social or economic stability. How can this be done?

(This writer wants to show that a tax measure proposed by Democrats in the legislature is a good thing. Readers in his town are overwhelmingly Republican. He writes:)

In the last session of the legislature Republicans introduced a tax measure that seemed wise and sound, but Democrats opposed it. The measure lost. "Politics," we all said, and I think we were right. Now I hope Republicans won't be guilty of similar tactics. What is good for the state is good for the state, and there's every reason why Republicans ought to be broader-minded than their opponents. Republicans, we can say then, "put the public interest ahead of mere politics."

The connotations of words have much to do with conciliation. Some words suggest "bad" things and some words suggest "good" things. Often the choice of a word can make or break an expository defense. The wrong word can change the whole effect of a paragraph—even a whole piece of writing. You have a choice, for example, of words to use in describing a college course: is it "dull"? or "prosaic"? or "factual"? or "objective"? or "informative"? or "devoid of essential interpretations"? All those terms might apply to the same course, and even the same general agreement about what it was like, but the choice of term could influence the attitude of the reader. Which term most accurately, and with the least emotional connotation, would tell what the course was like?

A *euphemism* is a softer, more agreeable, less unpleasant word than its synonym. *Liquidation* is a euphemism for *murder, assassination,* or *execution. Retarded* is sometimes a euphemism for *moronic,* and *moronic* itself was perhaps originally a euphemism for *half-witted.* Euphemisms are important in conciliation. In fact euphemisms may be important in the whole process of getting objective attention of readers on important problems. Whenever you think a particular word may arouse intense feelings, you need a synonym or euphemism if you want the thoughtful and unprejudiced attention of your readers.

Refutation

Because defending a judgment may imply controversy and hence resistance or attack, a part of such defense is often negative; that is, a part of the job consists of answering arguments that stand in the way. Your conclusion is not so acceptable that everybody agrees.

Often arguments against it have already appeared. So what you do to answer such attacks is very important.

Strictly defined, refutation means answering opposing "reasons why." It is the destruction of judgments that stand in the way. It includes attacks on any or all of the elements that may be used to support a judgment. It may direct attention to weaknesses in:

1. The credibility of sources, witnesses, authorities
2. The evidence
3. Generalizations from a sample
4. Basic premises or deductions
5. Analogies
6. Causal inferences

It may emphasize the inadequacies or inconsistencies of a whole opposing case. It may point out fallacies of irrelevancy—ignoring the issues.

For effective expository defense all the elements—facts, descriptions, testimony, and explanations—must bear directly on the problem and the writer's judgment concerning that problem. You cannot afford to ignore evidence that "points the other way" for two important reasons. First, readers may recognize the omissions and lose confidence in your fairness. Second, your readers may encounter the missing evidence later and fail to see its inadequacies. Whenever intelligent minds are likely to view evidence or judgments as significant, you ought to give such things your attention. It is advisable to report the most impressive evidence and arguments that do not agree with your conclusions so that you can put them in their proper perspective.

An effective pattern for handling refutation is something like this:

1. The supporters of Plan A have advanced considerable defense for it . . . (A concise summary of the arguments then follows.)

2. Some of these points deserve our respect. (Concession of matters that can be conceded without serious loss, or of matters that are irrefutable. The purpose of concessions is to remove from the field of controversy everything that is undebatable or unessential to proving the conclusion. The more common ground that everybody can agree about, the smaller the area of discussion.)

3. On the other hand, some of this discussion needs closer scrutiny . . . (A restrained analysis providing essential refutation of the arguments.)

Refutation naturally consists mainly of applying the tests for evaluating evidence and sound thinking, but you must never forget the attitudes of your reader in working out your deductive counter-defense.

Endings

Perhaps you think of the ending as a summary of points. Occasionally, if the discussion has been long and complex, such a summary is very much needed. The summary does have the positive value of pushing the most important ideas into the foreground of attention, and the negative value of relegating less important or conflicting ideas into the background. But a really good summary is never a mere listing of points—"This discussion has therefore proved the following: First . . . Second . . . ." A good summary ought to give fresh expression, new emphasis, to what has been said before. It must seem to add something that makes it worth reading even by one who clearly remembers everything said before. Here is the summary conclusion of *The House that Hitler Built,* written by Stephen H. Roberts in 1937:

> That is what makes the German position so tragic. The nation has been duped in the sense that it has been launched along a road that can only lead to disaster. The nation may be reborn, it may be a *new Germany*, but, unless it learns the habit of political and economic collaboration in international matters, it is a nation confronted by ultimate ruin. That is the infinite tragedy of it all, for the Germans of the last two decades have had more than their share of suffering, and the middle-aged and the old so sincerely want peace in the land for the rest of their time.

Besides the summary for an ending, what other possibilities do you have? Of course it depends largely on the kind of judgment you want to support. A judgment of truth or value is different from a judgment of policy or action. You have the same methods to choose from that you had for an introduction: quotation, narrative—even restatement of the problem if you want to rely upon implication to bring your readers to the decision in mind. But the judgment of action—recommending something for readers to *do*—demands, usually, another kind of ending.

If your judgment directs your readers to do something, the ending had better direct all attention towards that goal. A summary of "reasons why" may or may not be useful just before the ending; the final emphasis should be on *what to do*. Sometimes this requires a rather complete set of directions: here is the way to organize a Little League; this is next step in getting a zoning code; these are the methods of preparing to meet an air attack. The earlier discussion has shown *why* the action is desirable and feasible; the ending must put the emphasis on *how*.

A final word—your ending, or what commonly goes by the name *conclusion*, need not always be very long, and it certainly need not read like a formal debate. The whole idea is to end in a way that leaves your reader with the impression in his mind that you intended to put there.

READINGS

A

Critical Evaluation

Defending a judgment of value has traditionally gone by the name of *criticism*, though that term is more often applied to evaluations of music, art, literature, and drama. As a "critic," whether your subject is art, men, or machines, you try to point out both merits and defects, advantages and disadvantages.

The subjects of critical evaluation are widely varied: "How efficient is this washing machine?" "How good a buy is the Hudson Wasp?" "How competent has John Phillips been as City Engineer?" "How convincing an actress is Helen Hayes?" "How effective is the Farm Price Support Act?" The subjects go beyond questions of fact or probability; they stop short of questions of policy.

Critical evaluation must naturally apply the right standards or criteria. Your first task as a critic, then, is to decide which criteria are most important to your readers—and why. Chapter 5 provides considerable discussion of this selection of the right criteria. Even the right selection, however, may not be enough: you may need to convince your readers that some of the criteria you name are as important as you say they are. If, for example, you insist that a winter coat should be made of "pure virgin wool" woven into a pattern of so many woofs and warps per square inch, you owe your readers an explanation: what are the characteristics of pure virgin wool? what do the terms mean? and what evidence supports your judgment that such a coat is superior to one made of some other materials? Often you will need to prove, with adequate evidence, that your criteria of value are justified.

A critical evaluation is far more than a well-expressed opinion—or many opinions. Every opinion, unless you are sure your readers already understand and accept it fully, deserves evidence and explanation to support it. If you say a swimming pool meant to accommodate 500 bathers at one time should be able to change its water completely every four hours, you ought to explain *why*.

Good critical evaluation includes new information for its readers, reasons to support its judgments, and especially evidence. The supporting evidence about a book may include various summaries, quotations, and specific references. Evidence about the value of a machine may include specifications, results of tests, specific records.

In the actual writing, two general patterns are available. You may present the criteria first, defending those that need it, and then apply them one by one with the essential evidence, ending with your concluding judgment about the whole subject; or you may state your broad conclusion first, then state and defend each criterion, one by one, and apply it. The first pattern is, of course, that of climax order, the second anti-climax. Usually the climax order is better adapted to the objective, balanced spirit of critical evaluation. Here is an example in outline:

1. General purpose. (Room 202 Dobbs Building is to be evaluated by the Department of Grounds and Buildings as a classroom. A program of new building and reconstruction is under way.)
2. Accepted criteria for judging classrooms. (Safety, comfort, seating capacity, lighting, instructional facilities, etc. Some of the criteria may be stated as definite "specifications" with evidence from instructors, students, and architects to defend them. Others may appear as broad questions: "How good are acoustics?" "How satisfactory is the ventilation?")
3. Application of criteria, one at a time, with supporting evidence. ("The color of walls and ceiling is important for efficient work. The walls of 202 Dobbs are a light tan, which experts consider less restful than a soft green but comparatively satisfactory . . .")
4. Final judgment. ("In spite of its age, rather uneven heat in the

coldest winter days, and limited blackboards, 202 Dobbs will accommodate most classes of 20 to 35 satisfactorily . . .")

You might apply these criteria in evaluating your own critical evaluations:

1. Have I considered the knowledge and interests of my readers and written accordingly?
2. Have I stated every criterion that is important to my readers?
3. Have I defended my selection of criteria wherever it is necessary?
4. Have I recognized the different weights of different criteria, making it clear why some are more important than others?
5. Have I made pertinent comparisons between my subject and other things in the same class?
6. Have I presented enough facts (and expert opinions) to support my judgment for each criterion?
7. Does my statement of final judgment follow clearly from the analysis and evidence?

Here are three critical evaluations: of a product ("Motaloy"), of a process (fluoridation), and of literary works (Cooper's novels).

How fairly, thoroughly, and effectively do the critics defend their judgments?

1

MOTALOY: CLAIMS *vs.* TESTS *

"A complete . . . ring and valve job while you drive! . . . Good for the life of your engine! Stops costly oil burning! Increases gas mileage! Raises compression!"

Thus runs some of the advertising for *Motaloy*—a product which comes in a small cardboard package in the form of four metal pills, each a little larger than a tablet of aspirin. The price is $6.

As a rule, CU [Consumers Union] does not attempt to keep tabs on the short-cut items, gimmicks, additives, pepper-uppers, and what not that are advertised, particularly to automobile owners, in such vast variety. The claims of many of these products are so general as to defy analysis. But the claims for Motaloy are, at least, refreshingly specific; they can be checked. It seemed to CU's engineers that if

* From *Consumer Reports,* March 1954. Reprinted by permission.

Motaloy could deliver for $6 even a reasonable facsimile of a ring-and-valve job—which would cost at least $100 at a garage—consumers ought to welcome it with open arms. And if not—since even $6 still has some value these days—consumers ought to know.

So CU's shoppers went out and bought some. CU's engineers read with interest the techniques and the theory of the automotive wonder drug as contained in the accompanying literature. And an automotive consulting laboratory employed by CU set out to see what it could do.

The operational theory of *Motaloy*, it seems, is quite simple. You open the cardboard package, drop the set of four tabs into the gas tank, and drive off. Soon, according to *Motaloy's* brochure, things begin to happen to your car's worn, sluggish engine:

"*Motaloy* will give increased compression, better pick-up, reduced oil consumption, better gas mileage, smoother performance, and will reduce hard carbon deposits. Piston slap will be deadened or eliminated. . . . Gives improved performance with regular (cheaper) gasoline."

The brochure illuminates these claims with the cold, hard light of science:

"The tabs are activated as the vehicle is being driven. The friction of the tabs in the fuel tank and the sloshing of the fuel begins a chemical process as *Motaloy* passes through to the combustion chambers and cylinders where the flash fire and intense heat creates a reaction dissolving hard carbon. Then, a metallic plating is deposited on the surfaces of the pistons, cylinder walls, rings and valves and is gradually worked into any pores, as well as pitted or scratched spots. This is an anti-friction plating which provides a smoother, more powerful and quieter engine."

It all sounds perfectly reasonable to the non-technical reader. Indeed, thousands of consumers have apparently responded to the *Motaloy* advertisements, and hopefully dropped the little metal pellets into thousands of gas tanks. This new phenomenon in the additive field was also greeted with guarded enthusiasm by such publications as *Business Week* and *The Wall Street Journal*. There was a quite different reaction at the headquarters of the National Better Business Bureau, which issued a report casting serious doubt on *Motaloy's* claims. The National Better Business Bureau pointedly suggested that all media which carry advertising have a responsibility to protect the public from claims which the manufacturer cannot back up with conclusive proof. Nevertheless, advertisements for

Motaloy have continued to appear, and the public has presumably kept on buying.

CU's interest in *Motaloy* dates back to last August, when there were indications that the product might establish a more-or-less permanent place in the American market. It was decided to test *Motaloy* by actual field tests on worn engines in order to determine what improvements, if any, would result from its use.

For its tests, CU picked three Chevrolet engines of 1952 vintage which had accumulated, respectively, 45,000, 92,000, and 110,000 miles in taxicab service. All were road tested in the same 1953 Chevrolet sedan, over the same route, under similar conditions. The worn engines were operated with no special preparation or repair work except for a tune-up job on their carburetors and ignition systems. Each engine powered the test car over an 8000-mile route without the benefit of *Motaloy,* and then two of the three ran up another 8000 miles over the same route, with *Motaloy* in the gasoline tank. (The test on the engine with 110,000 miles on it had to be discontinued about half-way during the 8000-mile *Motaloy* run; the engine had deteriorated to such a degree that further testing with it was impossible.) A new set of *Motaloy* #1 tabs (recommended for cars making eight miles or more per gallon of gas) was used with each engine; these tabs were weighed before and after use. Engine compression was measured and acceleration tests were performed before and after each 8000-mile run. A record of gasoline and oil consumption was kept throughout the tests, and measurements were made of gasoline consumption at constant speed over a test course.

After testing *Motaloy* over a three-month period, CU is forced to the regretful conclusion that it can't tell its readers how to save $100 or more by spending $6. In fact, if the claims made for *Motaloy* were recited in the true-or-false technique of the quiz shows, CU's consultants would be forced in all honesty, on the basis of the tests made, to give the following answers:

"*Motaloy* improves acceleration." ***False.*** The time required to accelerate the test car from 10 to 60 miles per hour increased as steadily during the 8000-mile run with *Motaloy,* as in the previous 8000-miles without it. On one engine, for example, acceleration time was 31.6 seconds as received, 34.6 seconds after 8000 miles without *Motaloy,* and 41.4 seconds after 8000 miles with Motaloy in the gas tank.

"*Motaloy* gives you better gas mileage." ***False.*** Both on the basis of total mileage, and on gasoline consumption during constant-speed, measured-mile tests, gas consumption became poorer as the engines accumulated wear. During the constant-speed tests over a measured mile, gas mileage fell off on the average of 1.5 miles per gallon after 8000 miles with *Motaloy* in the tank.

"*Motaloy* reduces oil consumption." ***False.*** Throughout the tests, oil consumption increased in all three engines as they accumulated wear, with or without *Motaloy*.

"*Motaloy* improves engine compression." ***False.*** Engine compression declined constantly as the three engines accumulated mileage; the decline was least on the engine with the lowest previous mileage and greatest on the engine with the most mileage. In no case did the loss of compression seem to be slowed by the use of *Motaloy*.

"*Motaloy* dissolves the carbon deposits in the engine." ***False,*** if the claim means that *Motaloy* dissolves all carbon deposits. Although the performance figures indicated clearly that *Motaloy* had not performed a "ring and valve job" as claimed for it, the test engines were torn down and checked visually. The finding was that all contained heavy deposits of carbon; certainly whether or not *Motaloy* dissolved any carbon, there was still plenty left in the engines.

"*Motaloy* puts an anti-friction metallic plating on cylinder walls, pistons, rings, and valves." On this point, no categorical answer can be made. Of the three sets of *Motaloy* tabs used in the three engines, one set of four lost no weight during the 8000-mile run, one was one milligram lighter at the end of the run, and one was two milligrams lighter. There are about 28,000 milligrams in one ounce; one milligram is about .00004 ounce. Examination of the engine showed no metal plating. But whether or not any loss in weight of *Motaloy* distributed itself in a neat layer over the pistons, cylinder walls, rings and valves, is beside the point; there was no evidence in CU's tests that it did anything for the engine's performance.

"Good for the life of your engine." ***True.*** If you put a set of four *Motaloy* tabs in your gas tank, they'll probably still be there when the car reaches the scrap heap.

2

FLUORIDATION *

In September 1952, CU [Consumers Union] presented a summary of scientific studies bearing on the question of adding fluorides to

* Reprinted by permission from *Consumer Reports,* June 1954.

community water supplies to prevent tooth decay. As of May 1, 1954, 937 communities throughout the United States had approved the controlled fluoridation of their water supplies. Thirty-five communities had rejected proposals to fluoridate the water supply.

In many communities, fluoridation is a controversial public health measure, and in some it has become a political issue. As Dr. Leslie M. Fitzgerald, President of the American Dental Association, has said: "When a health measure becomes a political issue, heat takes precedence over light and the only losers are the small children of the community . . ."

In the view of Dr. Fitzgerald and other leaders of medicine and dentistry, fluoridation is a health measure of proved effectiveness and safety. This is also the official view of all the leading health and scientific organizations in this country. There remain, however, a few scientists, and many consumers, who, without questioning the effectiveness of fluoridation in preventing tooth decay, are concerned about its potential or actual toxic effects.

Tooth decay is an almost universal disorder affecting persons of all ages, with little regard for race or economic status. Because dental defects are not corrected as rapidly as they occur, the defects increase and accumulate each year. The dimensions of the dental decay problem were dramatically brought to light by the physical examinations of the first two million selective service candidates in 1941, when almost 10% had to be rejected for military service because of poor dental status alone.

Much research on the control of dental caries has been reported in recent years. The findings show that scrupulous attention to toothbrushing immediately after meals is perhaps the most important single prophylactic measure that the individual can apply to prevent dental decay. Proper and prompt brushing serves to remove food deposits from the teeth before bacteria have a chance to break them down into the acids which cause decay. Unfortunately, the practice of brushing the teeth immediately after meals is hard to inculcate. Reduction of sugar and other carbohydrate materials in the diet will also help prevent decay, since such materials serve as nutrients for the bacteria that produce the acid of dental decay. A third important individual prophylactic measure is systematic care by a dentist.

There is no doubt that if children could be persuaded to brush their teeth properly three times a day after meals, if they avoided sweets and soft drinks, and if they could obtain competent dental care consistently, dental health in America would be raised substantially from its deplorable state of today. But these are counsels of perfection, observed only by a tiny minority of the population.

In 1951, the American Dental Association announced that "Of all the preventive methods in use . . . fluoridation . . . offers the greatest help for preventing caries. . . ." This opinion was based on a very large amount of scientific data gathered from carefully controlled experiments involving many thousands of persons. The individuals in the tests were under more-or-less continuous study since 1945 in various communities in Michigan, Illinois, New York, and Texas. Studies of communities with naturally occurring fluorides in the water supply started in 1935. All of the controlled experiments and studies of the effects of artificially and naturally fluoridated water supply on the teeth of children and adults point up the following facts:

1. In practically all parts of the U. S., fluoride occurs as a "trace element" present in minute amounts in the water and in many foods. The concentration in the water ranges from a mere trace to 15 or more parts of fluoride per million parts of water. More than three million persons in the United States live in areas where the drinking water naturally contains one part per million or more of fluorides.

2. If the drinking water used throughout childhood contains approximately one part per million of fluoride, the dental decay rate will be about 60% lower than if the drinking water is very low in fluoride content. This childhood protection is carried over into adult life to an appreciable degree. One part per million is regarded as an optimum concentration in northern communities; in southern (warmer) communities, where more water is drunk, a somewhat lower concentration is preferred. The protective effect of a water supply containing about one part of fluoride per million parts of water has been confirmed repeatedly, and is considered to be one of the outstanding public health discoveries of this century.

3. Studies, made principally in the Midwest, indicate that water which naturally contains more than 1½ parts per million of fluoride causes "dental fluorosis"—mottling—when drunk during the years of tooth development. The extent of the mottling is in direct propor-

tion to the amount of fluoride in the water. But the mild fluorosis which may occur with concentrations of about 2 parts per million of fluoride is associated with a glistening enamel, and is not unsightly. At the 1 p.p.m. level, no mottling occurs.

The issue today is not whether fluoride is effective, or whether it will cause mottled teeth. The question is whether fluorides added to water supplies may not cause either obvious or subtle toxic effects on the organs of children and adults, and particularly of elderly persons.

One of the best studies of the effects of fluoridation on both the teeth and the internal organs was conducted in the neighboring cities of Newburgh and Kingston, New York. Since May 1945, the concentration of fluoride in the water supply of Newburgh has been maintained at a level between 1 and 1.2 parts per million. Kingston's water supply was unfluoridated; it contained about the same low concentration of fluoride as Newburgh's did before 1945. Kingston was the control city. All grade-school children were examined annually in both cities from 1945 through 1950. In 1951 and 1952, every second child in each city was examined. The most recent analysis of the examinations, completed in 1953, showed that the rate of dental decay among the six-to-twelve-year-old children who drank Newburgh's fluoridated water supply was about 50% lower than among children of the same age in Kingston.

In summing up some of the medical aspects of studies in the cities of Newburgh and Kingston, Dr. David B. Ast, Director of the Bureau of Dental Health in the New York State Department of Health, points out that examinations have been particularly scrupulous with respect to potential or actual toxic effects of fluoride on children. The medical examinations included a general physical examination, blood and urine analyses, and X rays of bones of the hands, forearms and legs. Smaller groups of children also had eye and ear examinations. According to Dr. Ast, there was ". . . no significant deviation in any of the factors studied in the group of Newburgh children age 3 through 14, as compared with the control group in Kingston. The literature on fluorine toxicology indicates that the first evidence of chronic deleterious effects of ingested fluorides is found in the teeth and bones. During the thousands of dental examinations made annually in Newburgh, not a single case of disfiguring mottled enamel was found.

"Bone changes, if they were to occur, would be expected to manifest themselves during the years of most rapid growth and development. About 2000 X rays of growing children are taken annually in Newburgh and Kingston. All films are read by Dr. John Caffey, Professor of Clinical Pediatrics, College of Physicians and Surgeons, Columbia University, without knowledge of the clinical records or the city from which the children come. After more than six years of fluoride experience in Newburgh, Dr. Caffey reports no significant differences in bone density in the groups of children studied in both cities."

In 1952, the Illinois State Department of Health issued a comprehensive bulletin on "Mortality in Fluoride and Non-Fluoride Areas." In this report, vital statistics for areas using waters ranging in fluoride concentrations from .8 to 2 parts per million were compared with those for areas using fluoride-deficient water. The report states:

"Mortality statistics show that there is no significant difference in the general death rates between areas where fluoride is present and those where it is absent. Similarly, there is no significant difference in the risk of death from specific diseases such as heart, cancer, nephritis and diabetes. This is borne out by the experience in Illinois when we compare mortality for certain cities, some of which have had an appreciable natural fluoride content in their water supply for many years."

A similar analysis has been made of the proportionate mortality from cancer, diabetes, cardiovascular-renal disease, and acute and chronic nephritis in Newburgh as against Kingston during the period 1944 to 1951. In no case is it possible to show a correlation between ingested fluoride in Newburgh and deaths from the above causes.

Another reassuring report has come from the Southbury State Training School at Southbury, Conn., where water fluoridation has been going on since 1945. This school has a population of 1500 inmates at various age levels. Reporting on the medical findings in the middle-aged and elderly inmates after seven years of fluoride experience, the medical superintendent stated:

"We have seen absolutely no evidence of any deleterious effect on these patients. Our studies have included frequent X rays of the skeleton on a large number of these people; urinary studies; blood counts and smear examinations and occasional studies of liver function. There has been no significant change in our mortality rates here during this period, and we have found nothing in our autopsies' analyses which could in any way be tied in with fluoridation. Our studies have also included many of the above examinations on a large number of our employees who are in this age bracket."

An argument frequently heard in opposition to the fluoridation of water supplies is that "fluorides are poisonous"; that some rat poisons contain fluorine compounds; and that some individuals have died of fluoride poisoning. There is no doubt that excessive amounts of fluoride are poisonous, but this is true of a great many substances taken into or applied to the body, including such simple and commonly used medications as aspirin, bicarbonate of soda, and penicillin. But when the amount is limited, all of these materials are not only safe but very useful. Chlorine, used to make water safe to drink, was notorious in 1918 as a poison war gas. But in the amounts used in water purification it hurts no one, and it is of immeasurable benefit to the general welfare. The amounts of fluoride useful for the prevention of tooth decay are considered by the overwhelming majority of those who have studied the matter as well below the toxic level.

The Commission on Chronic Illness (an independent national agency founded for the purpose of studying problems of chronic disease and disability by the American Hospital Association, the American Medical Association, the American Public Health Association, and the American Public Welfare Association) did not feel that it could recommend fluoridation of public water supplies without first taking cognizance of the possibility of detrimental effects. At the request of the Board of Directors of the Commission, a committee of distinguished scientists reviewed and evaluated the available evidence to decide whether at this time a positive position could be taken with regard to this hypothetical danger. The committee was under the chairmanship of Dr. Kenneth F. Maxcy, Professor of Epidemiology, Johns Hopkins University School of Hygiene and Public Health, Baltimore. The other members were Dr. Edward J. Stieglitz, outstanding geriatrician of Washington, D. C., and Dr. Nathan Shock, Chief of the Section on Gerontology, National Institutes of Health, Public Health Service. This committee reports as follows (April 1954):

"The question posed by the minority of scientists is whether fluorides added to drinking water in quantities insufficient to cause mottled enamel [i.e., to a level of approximately 1 p.p.m.] have, by cumulation in tissues, any physiological effects which may be detrimental to adults and to the chronically ill. . . .

"In our judgment there has been a sufficient number of observations on human subjects, with support of animal experiments, to establish the pattern of metabolism. Up to a daily intake of 4 or 5 mg. or more [drinking about 4 to 5 quarts of water, containing 1 part per million of fluoride, each day] fluorides absorbed are almost completely eliminated in the urine and sweat. Any residual is stored in the skeletal system, teeth and bones. Little, if any, remains in the soft tissues, liver, spleen, kidneys, etc. As the level of intake is lowered, stored fluorides tend to be partially eliminated. At high levels of fluoride intake (8 p.p.m. or more) changes occur in bones which may become evident by X ray (bone fluorosis). However, storage of fluorides in the skeletal structure in the amounts considered here results in no functional disadvantage. In other words, the body possesses two potent protective mechanisms: 1) rapid excretion in the urine; 2) storage in the skeleton. . . .

". . . In the United States, more than a million people, served by 453 different water supplies have, for generations, used drinking water with a natural fluoride content from 1.5 to 8.0 p.p.m. No definite evidence has been forthcoming that continued consumption of such water is in any way harmful to health. There have been no reports of evidence of changes in bone structure when the water supply contained less than 5 p.p.m.

"In a radiologic survey of 114 persons who had lived for at least 15 years at Bartlett, Texas, where the water supply contained 8 p.p.m., 12% of those examined showed minimal X-ray evidence of increased density of the bones but in no case was there any deformity or interference with function. Medical examinations, which included urinalysis and blood counts, revealed no indication that the residents of Bartlett were less healthy than those of nearby Cameron, where the water contained only 0.3 p.p.m. Reports of bone fluorosis in studies conducted in Italy, India, South Africa and Argentina indicate similar relationships to the use of high fluoride-bearing waters.

"It is to be emphasized that the proponents of fluoridation of water recognize that excessive ingestion of fluorides is undesirable. . . .

They stress the necessity of keeping the fluoride content of drinking water below the level of that which causes mottled enamel, the most sensitive indication of an excess.

"It is the contention of the minority that epidemiological studies or analysis of vital statistics cannot be relied upon to determine whether the condition of sick persons, such as those afflicted with chronic illness, particularly kidney ailments, would or would not be worsened by the ingestion of fluoridated water. Although the data are limited, experiments recently carried out at the National Institute of Dental Research on somewhat more than 50 cases who have evidence of damaged kidney function and who use drinking water containing 1 p.p.m. of fluoride . . . indicate that the excretion pattern of fluorides in these patients with damaged kidneys is similar to that reported by McClure * for healthy young men. . . . Generally speaking, consideration of the primary factors in the causation of such illnesses far overshadows any minor or secondary effects which, in the light of present knowledge, could be assumed from ingestion of trace amounts of fluoride in drinking water."

Extensive research into the toxicology of fluorine compounds has revealed no definite evidence that the continued consumption of drinking water containing fluorides at a level of about 1 p.p.m. is in any way harmful to the health of adults or those suffering from chronic illnesses. While the evidence does not absolutely exclude this possibility, if a risk exists at all it is so insignificant that it has not been revealed in many years of investigation. The Commission, therefore, urges American communities to adopt water fluoridation as a positive step in the prevention of dental caries.

It has been said by some that fluorides cause or accelerate the growth of cancer. This statement stems from the wide publicity given to an experiment in mouse cancer, conducted by a biochemist at the University of Texas. However, a report in the Texas Dental Journal for September 1951 showed that while the biochemist was intentionally feeding less than ½ part per million of fluorine, he was unintentionally giving an additional 42 p.p.m. fluorine in the dog chow which formed the exclusive diet of the mice. Moreover, it was noted that the mice used in the experiment came from a special

* McClure, F. J. and Kinser, C. A., "Fluoride Domestic Waters and Systemic Effects." *Public Health Reports,* Vol. 59, p. 1575, 1944.

strain, highly inbred for susceptibility to mammary tumors, and 96% to 100% of the mice in this strain eventually succumb to mammary tumors regardless of the diet or the water.

The Council on Dental Health of the American Dental Association points out:

"Additional information on this subject is provided in the records of bureaus of vital statistics in various states. The statistics indicate that cancer rates are lower in states where there are many fluoride endemic areas than in states where the waters are fluoride free. There is no reason to believe, however, that these lower cancer rates are due to the presence of fluorides in drinking water."

The possibility that there may be other significant sources of fluoride than the water supply has been considered. Fruits and vegetables may be contaminated with fluoride-containing insecticides. The Federal Food & Drug Administration is at present setting a limit on such residues compatible with the presence of 1 p.p.m. in drinking water.

Another argument is that fluoridation is best accomplished by having the dentist apply the chemical to a child's teeth directly—that this saves money inasmuch as children drink only a tiny share of the water supply, and that this method leaves any parent who disagrees with fluoridation free to refuse to have it done.

Until fluoridation of the water supplies is available in a given community, individual application is the only way children can receive effective fluoride prophylaxis. It should be observed, however, that local application of fluoride by a dentist is a difficult, tedious and expensive method of prophylaxis. Furthermore, it appears to be less effective than the small daily allowance of fluoride administered by way of the drinking water.

It is also stated that addition of measured amounts of fluoride to table salt, milk, bread or other foodstuffs by the individual or family is preferable to fluoridation of the entire community's water supply. The consumption of salt and foods varies considerably among people. However, the intake of water is less variable than any other single item in human nutrition. The water supply of a community is constantly subject to control by health authorities and does not require action on the part of individuals.

A number of law suits have been instituted in various parts of the country to enjoin communities from proceeding with water fluoridation. The principal arguments used by the complainants dealt with interference with municipal police power, violation of the Federal Food & Drug Act, and invasion of the Constitutional rights of citizens by subjecting them to "mass medication" against their will. In all of the cases which have been pressed to judgment, the courts have upheld the right of municipalities to fluoridate their water supplies.

So far as interference with Constitutional rights is concerned, there have been ample precedents in which it was decided that the First Amendment to the Constitution of the United States does not give to a special group the right to interfere unreasonably with the right of a communiy as a whole to enjoy what it determines is beneficial for its well-being. Thus, vaccination and chlorination of the water supply are universally practiced, though both have been objected to on religious grounds.

In February and March 1952, a Congressional Committee known as the Select Committee to Investigate the Use of Chemicals in Foods and Cosmetics (also known as the Delaney Committee) heard testimony from a number of witnesses on the question of water fluoridation.

A major point in the Committee's report was that a few scientists had questioned the physiological effects of fluoride on the aged and chronically ill. At the same time, the Committee stated: "Such highly qualified and reputable organizations as the American Medical Association, the National Research Council, the American Public Health Association, the American Dental Association, and the Association of State and Territorial Health Officers have endorsed the program of fluoridating the public drinking-water supply. The United States Public Health Service has issued an unqualified endorsement of the program."

The National Research Council is an agency of Congress appointed specifically to advise the Federal government on matters of scientific research. Likewise, the United States Public Health Service is the official Federal agency charged with the responsibility for establishing health standards for the people of this country.

It should also be mentioned that the Congress, acting as the administrative agency for the District of Columbia, approved water fluoridation, and the District is now using fluoridated water.

The succinct summary of Dr. Ast, Director of the Bureau of

Dental Health of New York State Department of Health, is worth quoting:

"Almost invariably each new milestone in public health practice has met with vigorous opposition. . . . Thus, such universally accepted practices as vaccination, water chlorination and pasteurization of milk were fought when first initiated, and even today one occasionally hears of some opposition. If the arguments used today against water fluoridation were compared with those used about 50 years ago against water chlorination, a very decided similarity would be noted. Scientific journals and lay periodicals carried the water chlorination arguments pro and con, often with more emotion than reason. Some communities had to resort to court action before chlorinating their water supplies. But today, it is well known that water purification and milk pasteurization are largely responsible for the decrease in typhoid fever. This disease, which accounted for 32 deaths per 100,000 population in 1900, has dropped to the vanishing point in 1951. Likewise, vaccination against smallpox, which was fought bitterly in the press and in the courts, has now become a routine practice. As a result, smallpox is virtually non-existent in New York State. . . .

"Because of the very nature of scientific investigation, it is impossible to answer with certainty all questions on any scientific problem. If the application of scientific knowledge were to be delayed until every fine point was settled, there would be no progress. Water fluoridation has had more thorough investigation over a longer period of time before it was applied than most public health procedures. Continued study will without question be pursued. However, present information should be applied for the benefit of the present generation of children who otherwise would suffer unnecessary dental disease."

3

FENIMORE COOPER'S LITERARY OFFENSES *

MARK TWAIN

The Pathfinder and *The Deerslayer* stand at the head of Cooper's novels as artistic creations. There are others of his works which contain

* From Mark Twain's *In Defense of Harriet Shelley, and Other Essays.*

parts as perfect as are to be found in these, and scenes even more thrilling. Not one can be compared with either of them as a finished whole.

The defects in both of these tales are comparatively slight. They were pure works of art.

—Prof. Lounsbury

The five tales reveal an extraordinary fullness of invention. . . . One of the very greatest characters in fiction, Natty Bumppo. . . . The craft of the woodsman, the tricks of the trapper, all the delicate art of the forest, were familiar to Cooper from his youth up.

—Prof. Brander Matthews

Cooper is the greatest artist in the domain of romantic fiction yet produced by America.

—Wilkie Collins

It seems to me that it was far from right for the Professor of English Literature in Yale, the Professor of English Literature in Columbia, and Wilkie Collins to deliver opinions on Cooper's literature without having read some of it. It would have been much more decorous to keep silent and let persons talk who have read Cooper.

Cooper's art has some defects. In one place in *Deerslayer*, and in the restricted space of two-thirds of a page, Cooper has scored 114 offenses against literary art out of a possible 115. It breaks the record.

There are nineteen rules governing literary art in the domain of romantic fiction—some say twenty-two. In *Deerslayer*, Cooper violated eighteen of them. These eighteen require:

1. That a tale shall accomplish something and arrive somewhere. But the *Deerslayer* tale accomplishes nothing and arrives in the air.

2. They require that the episodes of a tale shall be necessary parts of the tale, and shall help to develop it. But as the *Deerslayer* tale is not a tale, and accomplishes nothing and arrives nowhere, the episodes have no rightful place in the work, since there was nothing for them to develop.

3. They require that the personages in a tale shall be alive, except in the case of corpses, and that always the reader shall be able to tell the corpses from the others. But this detail has often been overlooked in the *Deerslayer* tale.

4. They require that the personages in a tale, both dead and alive,

shall exhibit a sufficient excuse for being there. But this detail also has been overlooked in the *Deerslayer* tale.

5. They require that when the personages of a tale deal in conversation, the talk shall sound like human talk, and be talk such as human beings would be likely to talk in the given circumstances, and have a discoverable meaning, also a discoverable purpose, and a show of relevancy, and remain in the neighborhood of the subject in hand, and be interesting to the reader, and help out the tale, and stop when the people cannot think of anything more to say. But this requirement has been ignored from the beginning of the *Deerslayer* tale to the end of it.

6. They require that when the author describes the character of a personage in his tale, the conduct and conversation of that personage shall justify said description. But this law gets little or no attention in the *Deerslayer* tale, as Natty Bumppo's case will amply prove.

7. They require that when a personage talks like an illustrated, gilt-edged, tree-calf, hand-tooled, seven-dollar Friendship's Offering in the beginning of a paragraph, he shall not talk like a negro minstrel in the end of it. But this rule is flung down and danced upon in the *Deerslayer* tale.

8. They require that crass stupidities shall not be played upon the reader as "the craft of the woodsman, the delicate art of the forest," by either the author or the people in the tale. But this rule is persistently violated in the *Deerslayer* tale.

9. They require that the personages of a tale shall confine themselves to possibilities and let miracles alone; or, if they venture a miracle, the author must so plausibly set it forth as to make it look possible and reasonable. But these rules are not respected in the *Deerslayer* tale.

10. They require that the author shall make the reader feel a deep interest in the personages of his tale and in their fate; and that he shall make the reader love the good people in the tale and hate the bad ones. But the reader of the *Deerslayer* tale dislikes the good people in it, is indifferent to the others, and wishes they would all get drowned together.

11. They require that the characters in a tale shall be so clearly defined that the reader can tell beforehand what each will do in a given emergency. But in the *Deerslayer* this rule is vacated.

In addition to these large rules there are some little ones. These require that the author shall:

12. Say what he is proposing to say, not merely come near it.
13. Use the right word, not its second cousin.
14. Eschew surplusage.
15. Not omit necessary details.
16. Avoid slovenliness of form.
17. Use good grammar.
18. Employ a simple and straightforward style.

Even these seven are coldly and persistently violated in the *Deerslayer* tale.

Cooper's gift in the way of invention was not a rich endowment; but such as it was he liked to work it; he was pleased with the effects, and indeed he did some quite sweet things with it. In his little box of stage-properties he kept six or eight cunning devices, tricks, artifices for his savages and woodsmen to deceive and circumvent each other with, and he was never so happy as when he was working these innocent things and seeing them go. A favorite one was to make a moccasined person tread in the tracks of the moccasined enemy, and thus hide his own trail. Cooper wore out barrels and barrels of moccasins in working that trick. Another stage-property that he pulled out of his box pretty frequently was his broken twig. He prized his broken twig above all the rest of his effects, and worked it the hardest. It is a restful chapter in any book of his when somebody doesn't step on a dry twig and alarm all the reds and whites for two hundred yards around. Every time a Cooper person is in peril, and absolute silence is worth four dollars a minute, he is sure to step on a dry twig. There may be a hundred handier things to step on, but that wouldn't satisfy Cooper. Cooper requires him to turn out and find a dry twig; and if he can't do it, go and borrow one. In fact, the Leatherstocking series ought to have been called the Broken Twig Series.

I am sorry there is not room to put in a few dozen instances of the delicate art of the forest, as practised by Natty Bumppo and some of the other Cooperian experts. Perhaps we may venture two or three samples. Cooper was a sailor—a naval officer; yet he gravely tells us how a vessel, driving toward a lee shore in a gale, is steered for a particular spot by her skipper because he knows of an *undertow* there which will hold her back against the gale and save her. For just pure woodcraft, or sailorcraft, or whatever it is, isn't that neat? For several years Cooper was daily in the society of artillery, and he ought to have noticed that when a cannon-ball strikes the ground it either buries itself or skips a hundred feet or so; skips again a hundred feet or so—and so on, till finally it gets tired and rolls. Now in one place he loses some "females"—as he always calls women—in the edge of a wood near a plain at night in a fog, on purpose to give Bumppo a chance to show off the delicate art of the forest before the reader. These mislaid people are hunting for a fort. They hear a cannon-blast, and a cannon-ball presently comes rolling into the wood and stops at their feet. To the females this suggests nothing. The case is very different with the admirable Bumppo. I wish I may never know peace again if he doesn't strike out promptly and *follow the track* of that cannon-ball across the plain through the dense fog and find the fort. Isn't it a daisy? If Cooper had any real knowledge of Nature's way of doing things, he had a most delicate art in concealing the fact. For instance: one of his acute Indian experts, Chingachgook (pronounced Chicago, I think), has lost the trail of a person he is tracking through the forest. Apparently that trail is hopelessly lost. Neither you nor I could ever have guessed out the way to find it. It was very different with Chicago. Chicago was not stumped for long. He turned a running stream out of its course and there in the slush in its old bed, were that person's moccasin tracks. The current did not wash them away, as it would have done in all other like cases —no, even the eternal laws of Nature have to vacate when Cooper wants to put up a delicate job of woodcraft on the reader.

We must be a little wary when Brander Matthews tells us that Cooper's books "reveal an extraordinary fullness of invention." As a rule, I am quite willing to accept Brander Matthews' literary judgments and applaud his lucid and graceful phrasing of them; but that particular statement needs to be taken with a few tons of salt. Bless your heart, Cooper hasn't any more invention than a horse; and I don't mean a high-class horse, either; I mean a clotheshorse. It would be very difficult to find a really clever "situation" in Cooper's books, and still more difficult to find one of any kind which he has failed to render absurd by his handling of it. Look at the episodes of "the caves"; and at the celebrated scuffle between Maqua and those others on the tableland a few days later; and at Hurry Harry's queer water-transit from the castle to the ark; and at Deerslayer's half-hour with his first corpse; and at the quarrel between Hurry Harry and Deerslayer later; and at—but choose for yourself; you can't go amiss.

If Cooper had been an observer his inventive faculty would have worked better; not more interestingly, but more rationally, more plausibly. Cooper's proudest creations in the way of "situations" suffer noticeably from the absence of the observer's protecting gift. Cooper's eye was splendidly inaccurate. Cooper seldom saw anything correctly. He saw nearly all things as through a glass eye, darkly. Of course a man who cannot see the commonest little everyday matters accurately is working at a disadvantage when he is constructing a "situation." In the *Deerslayer* tale Cooper has a stream which is fifty feet wide where it flows out of a lake; it presently narrows to twenty as it meanders along for no given reason, and yet when a stream acts like that it ought to be required to explain itself. Fourteen pages later the width of the brook's outlet from the lake has suddenly shrunk thirty feet, and become "the narrowest part of the stream." This shrinkage is not accounted for. The stream has bends in it, a sure indication that it has alluvial banks and cuts them; yet these bends are only thirty and fifty feet long. If Cooper had been a nice and punctilious observer he would have noticed that the bends were oftener nine hundred feet long than short of it.

Cooper made the exit of that stream fifty feet wide, in the first place, for no particular reason; in the second place, he narrowed it to less than twenty to accommodate some Indians. He bends a "sapling" to the form of an arch over this narrow passage, and conceals six Indians in its foliage. They are "laying" for a settler's scow or ark which is coming up the stream on its way to the lake; it is being hauled against the stiff current by a rope whose stationary end is anchored in the lake; its rate of progress cannot be more than a mile an hour. Cooper describes the ark, but pretty obscurely. In the matter of dimensions "it was little more than a modern canal-boat." Let us guess, then, that it was about one hundred and forty feet long. It was of "greater breadth than common." Let us guess, then, that it was about sixteen feet wide. This leviathan had been prowling down bends which were but a third as long as itself, and scraping between banks where it had only two feet of space to spare on each side. We cannot too much admire this miracle. A low-roofed log dwelling occupies "two-thirds of the ark's length"—a dwelling ninety feet long and sixteen feet wide, let us say—a kind of vestibule train. The dwelling has two rooms—each forty-five feet long and sixteen feet wide, let us guess. One of them is the bedroom of the Hutter girls, Judith and Hetty; the other is the parlor in the daytime, at night it is papa's bedchamber. The ark is arriving at the stream's exit now, whose width has been reduced to less than twenty feet to accommodate the Indians—say to eighteen. There is a foot to spare on each side of the boat. Did the Indians notice that there was going to be a tight squeeze there? Did they notice that they could make money by climbing down out of that arched sapling and just stepping aboard when the ark scraped by? No, other Indians would have noticed these things, but Cooper's Indians never notice anything. Cooper thinks they are marvelous creatures for noticing, but he was almost always in error about his Indians. There was seldom a sane one among them.

The ark is one hundred and forty feet long; the dwelling is ninety feet long. The idea of the Indians is to drop softly and secretly from the arched sapling to the dwelling as the ark creeps along under it at the rate of a mile an hour, and butcher the family. It will take the ark a minute and a half to pass under. It will take the ninety-foot dwelling a minute to pass under. Now, then, what did the six Indians do? It would take you thirty years to guess, and even then you would have to give it up, I believe. Therefore, I will tell you what the Indians did. Their chief, a person of quite extraordinary intellect for a Cooper Indian, warily watched the canal-boat as it squeezed along under him, and when he had got his calculations fined down to exactly the right shade, as he judged, he let go and dropped. And missed the house! That is actually what he did. He missed the house, and landed in the stern of the scow. It was not much of a fall, yet it knocked him silly. He lay there unconscious. If the house had been ninety-seven feet long he would have made the trip. The fault was Cooper's, not his. The error lay in the construction of the house. Cooper was no architect.

There still remained in the roost five Indians. The boat has passed under and is now out of their reach. Let me explain what the five did —you would not be able to reason it out for yourself. No. 1 jumped for the boat, but fell in the water astern of it. Then No. 2 jumped for the boat, but fell in the water still farther astern of it. Then No. 3 jumped for the boat, and fell a good way astern of it. Then No. 4 jumped for the boat, and fell in the water away astern. Then even No. 5 made a jump for the boat—for he was a Cooper Indian. In the matter of intellect, the difference between a Cooper Indian and the Indian that stands in front of the cigar-shop is not spacious. The scow episode is really a sublime burst of invention; but it does not thrill, because the inaccuracy of the details throws a sort of air of fictitiousness and general improbability over it. This comes of Cooper's inadequacy as an observer.

The reader will find some examples of Cooper's high talent for inaccurate observation in the account of the shooting-match in *The Pathfinder*.

> A common wrought nail was driven lightly into the target, its head having been first touched with paint.

The color of the paint is not stated—an important omission, but Cooper deals freely in important omissions. No, after all, it was not an important omission; for this nail-head is *a hundred yards* from the marksmen, and could not be seen by them at that distance, no matter what its color might be. How far can the best eyes see a common house-fly? A hundred yards? It is quite impossible. Very well; eyes that cannot see a house-fly that is a hundred yards away cannot see an ordinary nail-head at that distance, for the size of the two objects is the same. It takes a keen eye to see a fly or a nail-head at fifty yards, one hundred and fifty feet. Can the reader do it?

The nail was lightly driven, its head painted, and game called. Then the Cooper miracles began. The bullet of the first marksman chipped an edge of the nail-head; the next man's bullet drove the nail a little way into the target—and removed all the paint. Haven't the miracles gone far enough now? Not to suit Cooper; for the purpose of this whole scheme is to show off his prodigy, Deerslayer-Hawkeye-Long-Rifle-Leatherstocking-Pathfinder-Bumppo before the ladies.

> "Be all ready to clench it, boys!" cried out Pathfinder, stepping into his friend's tracks the instant they were vacant. "Never mind a new nail; I can see that, though the paint is gone, and what I can see I can hit at a hundred yards, though it were only a mosquito's eye. Be ready to clench!"

The rifle cracked, the bullet sped its way, and the head of the nail was buried in the wood, covered by the piece of flattened lead.

There, you see, is a man who could hunt flies with a rifle, and command a ducal salary in a Wild West show to-day if we had him back with us.

The recorded feat is certainly surprising just as it stands; but it is not surprising enough for Cooper. Cooper adds a touch. He has made Pathfinder do this miracle with another man's rifle; and not only that, but Pathfinder did not have even the advantage of loading it himself. He had everything against him, and yet he made that impossible shot; and not only made it, but did it with absolute confidence, saying, "Be ready to clench." Now a person like that would have undertaken that same feat with a brickbat, and with Cooper to help he would have achieved it, too.

Pathfinder showed off handsomely that day before the ladies. His very first feat was a thing which no Wild West show can touch. He was standing with the group of marksmen, observing—a hundred yards from the target, mind; one Jasper raised his rifle and drove the center of the bull's-eye. Then the Quartermaster fired. The target exhibited no result this time. There was a laugh. "It's a dead miss," said Major Lundie. Pathfinder waited an impressive moment or two; then said, in that calm, indifferent, know-it-all way of his, "No, Major, he has covered Jasper's bullet, as will be seen if any one will take the trouble to examine the target."

Wasn't it remarkable? How *could* he see that little pellet fly through the air and enter that distant bullet-hole? Yet that is what he did; for nothing is impossible to a Cooper person. Did any of those people have any deep-seated doubts about this thing? No; for that would imply sanity, and these were all Cooper people.

The respect for Pathfinder's skill and for his *quickness and accuracy of sight* [the italics are mine] was so profound and general, that the instant he made this declaration the spectators began to distrust their own opinions, and a dozen rushed to the target in order to ascertain the fact. There, sure enough, it was found that the Quartermaster's bullet had gone through the hole made by Jasper's, and that, too, so accurately as to require a minute examination to be certain of the circumstance, which, however, was soon clearly established by discovering one bullet over the other in the stump against which the target was placed.

They made a "minute" examination; but never mind, how could they know that there were two bullets in that hole without digging the latest one out? for neither probe nor eyesight could prove the presence of any more than one bullet. Did they dig? No; as we shall see. It is the Pathfinder's turn now; he steps out before the ladies, takes aim, and fires.

But alas! here is a disappointment; an incredible, an unimaginable disappointment—for the target's aspect is unchanged; there is nothing there but that same old bullet-hole!

"If one dared to hint at such a thing," cried Major Duncan, "I should say that the Pathfinder has also missed the target!"

As nobody had missed it yet, the "also" was not necessary; but never mind about that, for the Pathfinder is going to speak.

"No, no, Major," said he, confidently, "that would be a risky declaration. I didn't load the piece, and can't say what was in it; but if it was lead, you will find the bullet driving down those of the Quartermaster and Jasper, else is not my name Pathfinder."

A shout from the target announced the truth of this assertion.

Is the miracle sufficient as it stands? Not for Cooper. The Pathfinder speaks again, as he "now slowly advances toward the stage occupied by the females":

"That's not all, boys, that's not all; if you find the target touched at all, I'll own to a miss. The Quartermaster cut the wood, but you'll find no wood cut by that last messenger."

The miracle is at last complete. He knew—doubtless saw—at the distance of a hundred yards—that his bullet had passed into the hole *without fraying the edges*. There were now three bullets in that one hole—three bullets embedded processionally in the body of the stump back of the target. Everybody knew this—somehow or other—and yet nobody had dug any of them out to make sure. Cooper is not a close observer, but he is interesting. He is certainly always that, no matter what happens. And he is more interesting when he is not noticing what he is about than when he is. This is a considerable merit.

The conversations in the Cooper books have a curious sound in our modern ears. To believe that such talk really ever came out of people's mouths would be to believe that there was a time when time was of no value to a person who thought he had something to say; when it was the custom to spread a two-minute remark out to ten; when a man's mouth was a rolling-mill, and busied itself all day long in turning four-foot pigs of thought into thirty-foot bars of conversational railroad iron by attenuation; when subjects were seldom faithfully stuck to, but the talk wandered all around and arrived nowhere; when conversations consisted mainly of irrelevancies, with here and there a relevancy, a relevancy with an embarrassed look, as not being able to explain how it got there.

Cooper was certainly not a master in the construction of dialogue. Inaccurate observation defeated him here as it defeated him in so many other enterprises of his. He even failed to notice that the man who talks corrupt English six days in the week must and will talk it on the seventh, and can't help himself. In the *Deerslayer* story he lets Deerslayer talk the showiest kind of book-talk sometimes, and at other times the basest of base dialects. For instance, when some one asks him if he has a sweetheart, and if so, where she abides, this is his majestic answer:

"She's in the forest—hanging from the boughs of the trees, in a soft rain—in the dew on the open grass—the clouds that float about in the blue heaven—the birds that sing in the woods—the sweet springs where I slake my thirst—and in all the other glorious gifts that come from God's Providence!"

And he preceded that, a little before with this:

"It consarns me as all things that touches a fri'nd consarns a fri'nd."

And this another of his remarks:

"If I was Injun born, now, I might tell of this, or carry in the scalp and boast of the expl'ite afore the whole tribe; or if my inimy had only been a bear"—[and so on].

We cannot imagine such a thing as a veteran Scotch Commander-in-Chief comporting himself in the field like a windy melodramatic actor, but Cooper could. On one occasion Alice and Cora were being chased by the French through a fog in the neighborhood of their father's fort:

"*Point de quartier aux coquins!*" cried an eager pursuer, who seemed to direct the operations of the enemy.

"Stand firm and be ready, my gallant 60ths!" suddenly exclaimed a voice above them; "wait to see the enemy; fire low, and sweep the glacis."

"Father! father!" exclaimed a piercing cry from out the mist; "it is I! Alice! thy own Elsie! spare, O! save your daughters!"

"Hold!" shouted the former speaker, in the awful tones of parental agony, the sound reaching even to the woods, and rolling back in solemn echo. "Tis she! God has restored me my children! Throw open the sally-ports; to the field, 60ths, to the field! pull not a trigger, lest ye kill my lambs! Drive off these dogs of France with your steel!"

Cooper's word-sense was singularly dull. When a person has a poor ear for music he will flat and sharp right along without knowing it. He keeps near the tune, but it is *not* the tune. When a person has a poor ear for words, the result is a literary flatting and sharping; you perceive what he is intending to say, but you also perceive that he doesn't *say* it. This is Cooper. He was not a word-musician. His ear was satisfied with the *approximate* word. I will furnish some circumstantial evidence in support of this charge. My instances are gathered from half a dozen pages of the tale called *Deerslayer*. He uses "verbal" for "oral"; "precision" for "facility"; "phenomena" for "marvels"; "necessary" for "predetermined'; "unsophisticated" for "primitive"; "preparation" for "expectancy"; "rebuked" for "subdued"; "dependent on" for "resulting from"; "fact" for "condition"; "fact" for "conjecture"; "precaution" for "caution"; "explain" for "determine"; "mortified" for "disappointed"; "meretricious" for "factitious"; "materially" for "considerably"; "decreasing" for "deepening"; "increasing" for "disappearing"; "embedded" for "enclosed"; "treacherous" for "hostile"; "stood" for "stooped"; "softened" for "replaced"; "rejoined" for "remarked"; "situation" for "condition"; "different" for "differing"; "insensible" for "unsentient"; "brevity" for "celerity"; "distrusted" for "suspicious"; "mental imbecility" for "imbecility"; "eyes" for "sight"; "counteracting" for "opposing"; "funeral obsequies" for "obsequies."

There have been daring people in the world who claimed that Cooper could write English, but they are all dead now—all dead but Lounsbury. I don't remember that Lounsbury makes the claim in so many words, still he makes it, for he says that *Deerslayer* is a "pure work of art." Pure, in that connection, means faultless—faultless in all details—and language is a detail. If Mr. Lounsbury had only compared Cooper's English with the English which he writes himself—but it is plain that he didn't; and so it is likely that he imagines until this day that Cooper's is as clean and compact as his own. Now I feel sure, deep down in my heart, that Cooper wrote about the poorest English that exists in our language, and that the English of *Deerslayer* is the very worst that even Cooper ever wrote.

I may be mistaken, but it does seem to me that *Deerslayer* is not a work of art in any sense; it does seem to me that it is destitute of every detail that goes to the making of a work of art; in truth, it seems to me that *Deerslayer* is just simply a literary *delirium tremens*.

A work of art? It has no invention; it has no order, system, sequence, or result; it has no life-likeness, no thrill, no stir, no seeming of reality; its characters are confusedly drawn, and by their acts and words they prove that they are not the sort of people the author claims that they are; its humor is pathetic; its pathos is funny; its conversations are—oh! indescribable; its love scenes odious; its English a crime against the language.

Counting these out, what is left is Art. I think we must all admit that.

B

The Review

The *review* is a specialized type of evaluative writing that combines news and criticism. Subjects include plays and movies, TV and radio programs, operas and ballets; but more commonly the review is associated with books. Book reviews concern not only "literary" books, poetry and fiction, but works on geology, history, psychology, astronomy, government, religion, war, and almost everything else. Practice in writing book reviews provides good training in careful and critical reading, selection of evidence for a purpose, and organization.

The book review has two main jobs to do: First, it gives readers pertinent news. A new book has been published. What's it about? Who wrote it? What's it like? The news about the book may cover many different areas. Second, the review makes a judgment about the value of the book, and of course a good review really defends that judgment. Our newspapers, magazines, and specialized journals include book reviews of all kinds that give their readers information and opinion about new publications.

Not all book reviews published do the two jobs equally well. Some are mere synopses; they tell something of what the book is about but offer no interpretation or criticism. Other reviews provide little news but much detailed criticism. Still others are personal essays or specialized articles.

The kind of review we discuss here as a type of writing worth trying combines factual reporting (including the informative summary) with critical evaluation. Of course the process varies according to your purpose, readers, the space allotted, and the kind of book. But here is a general plan to use for practice:

1. **Give the most interesting news.** This naturally includes information about the nature of the book. It may also include facts about author, publisher, and events leading to the publication. For example:

A classification of the book: "*Brave New World* is not so much science fiction as futuristic satire . . ."

Summary of the author's problem or subject: "The muddle of intellectual strife in modern Paris is a difficult thing to depict fictionally, but *The Mandarins* makes the attempt . . ."

A quotation giving the feel of the book: " 'Nobody dies,' the front-line soldiers in *A Walk in the Sun* assure each other . . ."

About the author's previous work for comparison: "As in *Never Come Morning* and *The Man with the Golden Arm* Nelson Algren once more leads us into the nightmarish life of the underdog in our society. This time it's *A Walk on the Wild Side* . . ."

Comparison with works of other authors: "Anyone who has read Flaubert's *Madame Bovary* and Tolstoy's *Anna Karenina* will want to re-read them after finishing Herman Wouk's *Marjorie Morningstar* . . ."

Information about the author's background: "The late Harry Soderman was one of the leading modern criminologists: organizer and long-time director of Sweden's National Institute of Technical Police . . ."

2. **Include an informative summary of the book.** Usually this requires attention to the most important elements of the book as the author emphasized them. (Remember: an "informative" summary tells what the book *says*, not merely what it's "about.") In reviewing fiction you should ordinarily give some analysis of leading charac-

ters and setting, as well as the direction of the story—but without "the ending."

3. **Include critical judgments, with your support.** Remember that few books (and few elements of books) are all good or all bad; your judgments ought to be balanced. In this respect, comparison with other books is usually desirable, often necessary.

Of course your reasons and evidence supporting your opinions are what give the review substance. Most of the evidence will be "internal"—that is, in the book itself: situations, organizational methods, topics, quotations, characters.

No writing of a book review can be better than the reading that preceded it. You have to read with a purpose, to answer these questions:

What was the author trying to do?
How well has he done it?
Was it worth doing?

Take notes, perhaps under various headings: THEME, ORGANIZATION, SETTING, CHARACTERS, PLOT, etc. You cannot be sure what you need until you have finished the book and had time to think it over. Then you have your notes to refresh your memory of details. Don't neglect prefaces and introductions; they usually give the key to an author's intent.

In the three book reviews that follow, how much news and how much criticism does each include?

Analyze the reviewer's organization: How does he begin? Does the review have an effective plan?

How much support does the reviewer offer for his judgments?

4

REVIEW OF THE GRAPES OF WRATH *

PETER MONRO JACK

The Grapes of Wrath. By John Steinbeck. 610 pp. New York: The Viking Press. $2.75.

* From *The New York Times,* Apr. 16, 1939. Reprinted by permission.

There are a few novelists writing as well as Steinbeck and perhaps a very few who write better; but it is most interesting to note how very much alike they are all writing. Hemingway, Caldwell, Faulkner, Dos Passos in the novel, and MacLeish in poetry are those whom we easily think of in their similarity of theme and style. Each is writing stories and scenarios of America with a curious and sudden intensity, almost as if they had never seen or understood it before. They are looking at it again with revolutionary eyes. Stirred like every other man in the street with news of foreign persecution, they turn to their own land to find seeds of the same destructive hatred. Their themes of pity and anger, their styles of sentimental elegy and scarifying denunciation may come to seem representative of our time. MacLeish's "Land of the Free," for instance, going directly to the matter with poetry and pictures—the matter being that the land is no longer free, having been mortgaged, bought and finally bankrupted by a succession of anonymous companies, banks, politicians and courts; or, for the present instance, Steinbeck's "The Grapes of Wrath," as pitiful and angry a novel ever to be written about America.

It is a very long novel, the longest that Steinback has written, and yet it reads as if it had been composed in a flash, ripped off the typewriter and delivered to the public as an ultimatum. It is a long and thoughtful novel as one thinks about it. It is a short and vivid scene as one feels it.

The opening scene is in Oklahoma, where a change in the land is taking place that no one understands, neither the single families who have pioneered it nor the great owners who have bought it over with their banks and lawyers. As plainly as it can be put, Mr. Steinbeck puts it. A man wants to build a wall, a house, a dam, and inside that a certain security to raise a family that will continue his work. But there is no security for a single family. The cotton crops have sucked out the roots of the land and the dust has overlaid it. The men from the Bank or the Company, sitting in their closed cars, try to explain to the squatting farmers what they scarcely understand themselves: that the tenants whose grandfathers settled the land have no longer the title to it; that a tractor does more work than a single family of men, women and children put together; that their land is to be mechanically plowed under, with special instructions that their hand-built houses are to be razed to the ground.

The most interesting figure of this Oklahoma family is the son who has just been released from jail. He is on his way home from prison, hitch-hiking across the State in his new cheap prison suit, picking up a preacher who had baptized him when young, and arriving to find the family setting out for California. The Bank had come "to tractorin' off the place." The house had been knocked over by the tractor making straight furrows for the cotton. The Joad family had read handbills promising work for thousands in California, orange picking.

The journey across is done in superb style, one marvelous short story after another, and all melting into this long novel of the great trek. The grandfather dies on the way, and then the grandmother. The son Noah stops at a river and decides to stay there. Tom and his brother take turns driving the truck, easing her over the mountains, grinding her valves, scraping the plugs: they are the mechanics. The sister, Rosasharn christened for Rose of Sharon, expects to have her baby. Her husband disappears, aims to better himself in his own selfish way. The Joad family meet people coming and going, going to California from the Western States with hope and the orange handbills and a $75 jalopy; people coming from California embittered and broke, speaking darkly of deputies, double-crossing, 20 cents an hour and labor trouble.

Californians are not going to like this angry novel. The Joad family drive over the mountains, through the desert, the great valley, through Tehacapi in the morning glow—"Al jammed on the brake and stopped in the middle of the road. * * * The vineyards, the orchards, the great flat valley, green and beautiful, the trees set in rows, and the farm houses."

The beauty and fertility of California conceal human fear, hatred and violence. "Scairt" is a Western farmer's word for the inhabitants, frightened of the influx of workers eager for jobs, and when they are frightened they become vicious and cruel. This part of the story reads like the news from Nazi Germany. Families from Oklahoma are known as "Okies." While they work they live in what might as well be called concentration camps. Only a few hundred are given jobs out of the thousands who traveled West in response to the handbills. Their pay is cut from 30 cents an hour to 25, to 20. If any one objects he is a Red, an agitator, a trouble-maker who had better get out of the country. Deputy sheriffs are around with guns, legally shooting or clubbing any one from the rest of the union who questions the law of California. The Joad family finds only one place of order and decency in this country of fear and violence, in a government camp, and it is a pleasure to follow the family as they take a shower bath and go to the Saturday night dances. But even here the deputy sheriffs, hired by the banks who run the Farmers Association, are poking in their guns, on the pretext of inciting to riot and the necessity of protective custody. The Joad family moves on through California, hunted by anonymous guns while they are picking peaches for 2½ cents a box, hoping only for a little land free of guns and dust on which they might settle and work as they were accustomed to. The promised grapes of California have turned into grapes of wrath that might come to fruition at any moment.

How true this may be no reviewer can say. One may very easily point out that a similar message has been read by the writers mentioned above, and that Mr. Steinbeck has done the same thing before. It is easy to add that the novel comes to no conclusion, that the preacher is killed because he is a strikebreaker, that Tom disappears as a fugitive from California justice, that the novel ends on a minor and sentimental note; that the story stops after 600 pages merely because a story has to stop somewhere. All this is true enough but the real truth is that Steinbeck has written a novel from the depths of his heart with a sincerity seldom equaled. It may be an exaggeration, but it is the exaggeration of an honest and splendid writer.

5

REVIEW OF *THE GROWTH OF THE AMERICAN REPUBLIC* *

William MacDonald

The Growth of the American Republic, by Samuel Eliot Morison and Henry Steele Commager. 956 pp. With maps. New York: Oxford University Press.

No one who has read Professor Morison's two-volume "Oxford History of the United States" need be deterred from reading this

* From *The New York Times*, Dec. 21, 1930. Reprinted by permission.

new book by fear of getting only a warmed-over version of the earlier one, for while the present work has grown out of a call for a revision of the "Oxford History" and a reduction of its bulk to a single volume, the two books are in fact quite different. For one thing, the beginning of the story has been carried back from 1783 to 1760, thereby bringing into the narrative the immediate origins of the American Revolution and the events of the Revolutionary War. This, with a considerable expansion of what in the earlier work concerned the period since the Civil War, suffices to fill fifteen additional chapters, while a good many other passages have been rewritten in condensed or enlarged form.

Exactly how much of the book is to be credited to Professor Commager and how much to Professor Morison, the latter, who alone subscribes the preface, thinks that the reader would probably not be interested to know, but he at least suggests that Professor Commager is responsible for a good deal in both method and substance. Professor Commager, he tells us, is "a Middle Westerner of the post-war generation, with Southern affiliations," while he himself is "a New England historian approaching middle age, with Oxonian and Pacific Coast affiliations." The product, as far as this book is concerned, "represents the work of two men whose paths crossed only very recently and the fusion of two points of view."

Both of these points of view are blended in this really notable book by Professors Morison and Commager. The New England and Oxford savor which one detected in the "Oxford History" is hardly at all apparent, and the aggressive dissent of the West has been held in check. There is an admirable account of the Revolution, a clear description of the process of forming the national government, abundant but not undue material about Western growth, a sound exposition of the development of American foreign policy, a sensible treatment of the economic and political life of the old South, and all that the average person needs to remember about the Civil War and the dreary wastes of reconstruction. For the period since the Civil War and reconstruction the distinguishing feature is the emphasis upon economic development in general, labor and immigration, agriculture and the movements of political and social reform that centered in Roosevelt. The story ends with the eve of the World War—a self-imposed restriction which might well have been overstepped to the extent at least of recounting the events of the war. There is no better book for whoever wants a well-balanced view of the growth of the American Republic.

6

REVIEW OF *THE HORSE SOLDIERS* *

EARL SCHENCK MIERS

The Horse Soldiers, by Harold Sinclair, 336 pp. Harper $3.95.

Few documents can be more unreliable upon occasion than the sentimental memoirs of old soldiers. For sheer audacity and imagination, perhaps no exploit during the Civil War excelled the cavalry raid under Ben Grierson. Across six hundred miles of Mississippi in those spring months when the Vicksburg campaign started to boil, fierce-bearded Ben and his horsemen cut three different railroad lines, destroyed sixty miles of telegraph, and thus isolated the state capital on the north, south, and west. Yet in later years Henry Clayton Forbes, who had ridden with Grierson, recalled the raid as "essentially a game of strategy and speed . . . a strenuous game, rather than a bloody one, intensely exciting, but not necessarily very dangerous."

Harold Sinclair knows better. In "The Horse Soldiers" he employs the sensitivity of a competent novelist to reconstruct in full human detail this astonishing episode. And a rousing story he makes of it, not abusing the historical essentials, but infusing them with an imaginative depth denied the literary historian.

A critical sport during the next few years likely will be to compare all Civil War novels to MacKinlay Kantor's "Andersonville," and an unfair game it should prove. Kantor had one problem and Sinclair another. His objective in "The Horse Soldiers" is to fashion a tale of high adventure concerned with men who believe they are riding into an inevitable doom, and who through luck and skill, courage and tenacity succeed in making a seemingly impossible escape. A splendid novel of suspense results, and also an absorbing study of the soul-searing bedevilments that the responsibility of command brings to a man.

* From *The Saturday Review,* Feb. 18, 1956. Reprinted by permission.

For Colonel Jack Marlowe the war began when a period of his own life had ended with the death of his wife. Marlowe therefore went to war for much the same reason that leads a man to emigrate to a new country—he needed a fresh start in life. Quickly he learned that the Bible of the Union Army, Hardee's "Tactics," was of scant usefulness to him. In the cavalry, each situation created its own rules of war.

Nor was there anything in Hardee's "Tactics" to tell an officer how to deal with the sickening futility that command produces. How did you decide which company to sacrifice for the good of the brigade? When fatigue dulled your mind and brittle temper warped your judgment, what then? Stranded in the middle of an enemy-infested country, with one chance in a hundred of getting out, how did you make the right guess?

In terms such as these Sinclair gives Marlowe flesh and spirit, conscience and magnificence. The colonel is no hero to himself; few men in war ever are. He is simply caught in a trap from which, with God's good help, he must escape. Yet the will to command rises in Marlowe; in the true sense, at thirty-six, he becomes the tough-fibered Old Man the brigade needs to muddle through, paying his own price for that accomplishment.

Around Marlowe are all the others swept through this same human gristmill. For one, there is Colonel Blaney, a stalwart commander to equal Grant except that history forgets more heroes than it remembers. Another is Surgeon Keller, believing medicine was a craft to practice wherever the need existed and encountering a conflict between professional ethics and military regulations that could have shattered Marlowe and himself.

In the end Marlowe and his ragged, dirty, foul-smelling boys reach Baton Rouge and the safety of the spit-and-polish Union command operating there. By then they had become a legend of gigantic proportions—to the history books rather than to themselves.

"The Horse Soldiers" is nothing at all like "Andersonville." In its own right, however, this vigorous, compact, intensely human novel by Harold Sinclair deserves a place in the first rank of recent American historical fiction. In its own right it sheds a telling wisdom onto those motives that lead men to suffer and bleed, to fight and die.

The two selections that follow deal with reading problems. State in a sentence the main question, in another sentence the author's broad judgment. Does the author use climax or anti-climax order? Evaluate the evidence and reasoning. Do you find examples of definition? classification? irony?

Write down objections you have to any of the judgments in these pieces. How well could you support these objections?

7

SO YOU THINK YOU CAN READ? *

SELWYN JAMES

Not so long ago, a worried young salesman walked into a suite of offices on New York's Fifth Avenue. "Is this where they'll teach me how to read?" he asked the receptionist. "I've got to learn right away —my promotion depends on it!"

The young man was dead serious. And he had come to the right place—New York's Reading Laboratory, which teaches anyone from backward children to sharp-minded executives how to read fast and better. Basic research at the 400-odd such clinics all over the U. S. reveals this startling fact: three out of five Americans are woefully inefficient readers, who jog across the printed page at a horse-and-buggy rate—a mere 250 words a minute, or hardly faster than they talk.

Most of us are using only about 20 per cent of our capacity to read swiftly and intelligently. We are rather like hunt-and-peck typists who use only two fingers instead of one. It's no wonder William Benton, former U. S. Senator, calls us a nation of "reading cripples."

Today, however, the latest scientific instruction can help almost everybody—housewives, businessmen, college students and youngsters—to double or even triple their reading speeds, as well as to absorb more of what they read. Why should *you* bother, you ask? Because reading, one of the most vital skills you ever learn, directly influences the size of your income, the pleasures you enjoy, and often the degree of your social success.

* From *Coronet*, April 1953. Copyright 1953 by Esquire, Inc. Reprinted by permission.

The plodding, half-interested reader is frequently the victim of old-fashioned teaching methods. For instance, many Americans were schooled in the obsolete "oral technique," which stressed pronunciation and reading a single word at a time. Visual defects, most of them correctable once they are detected, account for a great number of other slow readers.

Take the anxious salesman in New York. Tested by the Reading Laboratory, he scored a whopping 145 on his I.Q. exam—yet he could read no better than an average 10-year-old schoolboy. What was his trouble? Tests showed that his eyes often failed to act as a team, due to a conflict between the right and left sides of his brain. Sometimes he saw letters in reverse, and had a tendency to read backwards.

Though this hindrance slowed his reading, he had progressed as a salesman because the job called for more talking than reading. Now he was up for a junior executive position, which would require him to wade through sales reports every day. Could his eyes be trained to do their work properly?

After 14 hour-and-a-half lessons at the laboratory, he was sprinting along at over 600 words a minute—better than three times as fast as before. Moreover, he had learned to skim at an even quicker rate, getting the gist of what he was reading by picking out key words and phrases. His promotion went through promptly.

Nothing wrong with *your* eyes? Probably not. But no matter how well you read, you can teach your eyes to move faster and see more. Consider what happens when you read a line of print. Your eyes, each controlled by six delicate muscles, make a series of stops or "fixation pauses" as they move across the page. What is important is the number of words your eyes cover in a single pause, for it is during these hesitations that the visual impression is transmitted to your brain and interpreted.

If you utilize your total eye span, you will see more words at once and get their meaning more rapidly. The slowest reader (150 words or less a minute) stops at almost every word, quickly tires because he overworks his eyes, and remembers little of what he has read. The average reader (250 words a minute) makes three or four brief pauses a line. And the exceptionally fast reader (700 words a minute and up) will grasp an entire line of type or even short paragraphs at one glance. He is unlikely to complain of eyestrain or fatigue because his eyes, sweeping rhythmically down the page, will make fewer stops and starts.

More effective reading thus means taking bigger visual bites of the printed page—training yourself to see and digest phrases or complete sentences, rather than single words. This is called reading by "thought-units," which are ideas conveyed by groups of words. In the long run it's the easiest way to read, just as assembling a jigsaw puzzle composed of ten big pieces is easier than assembling one of thirty small pieces.

At reading clinics, scientific devices quickly reveal your reading faults and help you to correct them. One diagnostic instrument records on a strip of movie film, the width of your eye span, the number of pauses your eyes make per line, how long they rest at each stop, as well as how many times you allow your eyes to swing back to clarify the meaning of the words.

A Flashmeter, which is derived from the simple slide projector, is used to help you widen your eye span. It throws up on a screen numbers, words and phrases, at speeds ranging from one second to 1/100th of a second. After only a few hours' practice, a trainee begins to recognize seven-digit numbers and whole sentences at a glance.

When you sit down to read a book, the clinic provides you with a Reading Accelerator—a pacing instrument with an opaque shutter which lowers over the page like a curtain as you read. Set at specific rates of speed, the accelerator not only tells you how fast you're reading, but sharpens your concentration and prods you into reading still more rapidly. Because the shutter quickly covers up each line as you read, it also prevents backtracking, a common habit among sluggish readers.

Well-equipped reading laboratories have produced such amazing results that today, dozens of big corporations are enrolling key personnel in classes. Surveys at Harvard, Chicago and Ohio University clinics show that the top-level executive spends from 15 to 20 hours a week poring over industry reports, correspondence and trade journals. But at such firms as Motorola, Inc., Chicago Title & Trust Co. and U. S. Steel Export Co., desks are cleared of essential reading matter in less than half the time.

Recently, the New York Mutual Life Insurance Company put 50

employees through reading school, and later announced that time saved on paper work had boosted the output of these people by an astonishing 25 per cent. Several company presidents are themselves graduates of reading clinics.

One Chicago businessman, habitually loaded down with necessary reading, went back to school when his wife and children complained he was neglecting them. "I used to come home with a bulging briefcase every evening," he says. "Today my family can't remember what a briefcase looks like!"

A Cleveland market researcher was able to sign up three additional clients after taking a faster-reading course, and a freelance reader for a publishing house doubled her output—and her income—within a matter of weeks.

A young engineer is perhaps the best example of how reading skill can be developed through study and training. When this man registered at the Laboratory and was tested, it was found he could already read at 500 words per minute—twice the average speed.

He explained that he had been training himself at home for three years. Each week he read several magazines from cover to cover as quickly as he could, timed himself, computed the word count for each magazine and maintained a chart showing his progress. By this method he had reached his present speed. Now he needed expert assistance to attain the added speed he felt was required for advancement in his work.

The Laboratory put him through an intensive course, at the end of which he reached the phenomenal speed of 1,000 to 1,800 words a minute of highly factual material. Rigorous comprehension tests showed this to be a practical speed for him.

With the help of his new skill, he won a graduate scholarship at a university which further prepared him for success.

However, business people are not the only ones to benefit. Some reading labs are used by housewives who want to keep up with the flow of best sellers and magazines, and to stay abreast of their husbands in day-to-day newspaper reading. Disturbed children who have blocks against reading are helped, too.

Prof. Paul Witty of Northwestern University tells of a highschool student named Bill, a dawdler at reading, who was ready to abandon plans for a college education. Bill's ability to *learn* was good enough, but his reading handicap prevented him from keeping up with studies.

Tests revealed that his understanding of what he read was also adequate, but he just couldn't cover more than 150 words a minute.

A training program spread over two semesters raised his rate to 375 words a minute. Too, he suddenly found school assignments easier and study periods a good deal less fatiguing. His improvement at reading was soon reflected in higher grades and a renewed self-assurance about his future.

Of course, not everyone is able to attend a reading laboratory, but it is possible to increase reading efficiency by applying the same principles on your own. It is largely a matter of eye-training exercises and ending bad reading habits.

A home-training schedule should consist of a 30-minute daily session in a room away from distracting noises and interruptions. To begin with, you should find out if you are moving your lips as you read, pronouncing words or even actually whispering them. Dr. Stella Center, who until 1950 was with the New York University Reading Institute, advises: "Touch your lips as you read to see if you are vocalizing."

Next, avoid word-by-word reading; train your eyes to grasp whole phrases at a glance. "Try to respond to ideas rather than words," recommends Professor Witty. "When a friend tells you something, you respond to the ideas he presents, not to the words he says. Do the same when you read."

You can act as your own reading accelerator by constantly forcing yourself to read a little faster than you are used to. You will be surprised at how quickly your eyes will adjust. Remember, though, that comprehension is as important as speed. Don't let yourself look back, but when you have finished the material, you can reread to find out whether you have missed anything essential. Better still, get a member of your family to ask questions based on what you have read.

Your speed will vary according to the type of reading matter you select. To skim through a newspaper, practice moving your eyes almost vertically down the narrow columns, catching the key phrases that contain the meat of the story. Naturally, technical reading will slow you down. For example, you can't expect to zip through a scientific textbook as you would a mystery novel. But by increasing your reading rate of easy material to, say, 500 words a minute, your technical rate will speed up proportionately to 300 or 400 words a minute.

With regular practice sessions totaling 20 hours, four to six weeks is sufficient to boost your current reading speed 100 words per minute. And don't forget, faster reading means easier more enjoyable reading. . . .

8

EDUCATION BY BOOKS *

MARK VAN DOREN

Let us assume that an institution was founded today for the sole purpose of requiring its members to read certain books. These members were called students, for the instruction was something like that in a school or college; and there were a few exacting elders on hand who, after announcing their authority, began to teach.

The teaching in this institution, like the studying, was at the same time simple and difficult. It consisted in the first place, as I have said, in requiring the students to read certain books. It consisted next in requiring that an intelligible account be rendered of the contents of each book. And it consisted last of all in requiring that the readers be able, in the course of discussing a given book, to prove that their memory of all previous books was accurate and complete.

It was as simple as that, and as difficult. The books were the acknowledged masterpieces of the last three thousand years—masterpieces of poetry, of history, of philosophy, of fiction, of theology, of natural science, of political and economic theory. There were two hundred or so of them, and none of them was read in an abridged edition. Neither was any of them approached through a digest or a commentary, or through a biography of the author which told how many wives he had and what the biographer believed to be the modern significance of his mind. No, these books which the teachers had selected for the students to read—Homer, the Bible, Herodotus, Thucydides, Aeschylus, Sophocles, Euripides, Aristophanes, Plato, Aristotle, Cicero, Lucretius, Vergil, Horace, Ovid, Plutarch, Lucian, Marcus Aurelius, Plotinus, St. Augustine, the Volsunga Saga, the Song of Roland, Thomas Aquinas, Dante, Petrarch, Chaucer, Leonardo da Vinci, Machiavelli, Erasmus, More, Rabelais, Montaigne, Cervantes, Bacon, Shakespeare, Galileo, Grotius, Hobbes, Descartes,

* From *The Nation*, December 6, 1933. Reprinted by permission.

Leibnitz, Corneille, Racine, Moliere, Milton, Spinoza, Locke, Newton, Swift, Voltaire, Fielding, Hume, Rousseau, Adam Smith, Kant, Gibbon, Bentham, Goethe, Malthus, Hegel, Schopenhauer, Balzac, Mill, Darwin, Dickens, Thackeray, Marx, Tolstoy, Dostoevski, Pasteur, Ibsen, Nietzsche, Freud, Proust, Einstein—these authors, or rather the principal works of these authors, were read naked and entire; and understood.

A few students—some say a good many—had got into the institution by mistake. They complained about the lack of freedom to read what they pleased; some of these books, they insisted, were not suited to their personalities, and they had supposed that what one went to college for was to develop one's personality. Precisely, answered the head preceptor, closing the door behind them with the most obvious and reckless relief. Others proved to be helpless once they were face to face with an author's original sentences; they had been brought up on outlines, introductions, histories of literature and thought, and collections of excerpts, and so had long ago lost whatever ability to read they had been born with. Still others had expected to learn a trade or a profession. Then there was a final group of pedantic youngsters who snorted at the reading list because it was not contemporary. They wanted as swift an introduction as possible to the civilization about them. To the reply that this was that, they were very scornful as they scurried off to become freshmen in some up-to-date college where field trips to factories alternated in the weekly schedule with lectures on large and immediate subjects.

These gone, the others settled down to the task that had been so arbitrarily assigned them. At regular intervals they met in small groups with two or more teachers who questioned them closely concerning the contents of the required, the inevitable book. If they revealed by their answers that they had read it badly, they were forced to read it again. There was no going forward until Aristotle's conception of the individual, or Grotius's theory of natural law, or the unity of King Lear was clearly stated. No excursions were made into the culture of the Greeks or the domestic life of the Middle Ages; merely the books themselves were read, discussed, and understood. And so on for four years.

At the end of which time a generation of students were set loose upon a world with many of whose aspects they were not at the moment prepared to cope. The only thing, indeed, to be said in their favor was that they were educated. They were equipped, that is, with so much understanding of what the best human brains had done in three thousand years that they realized without difficulty how few contemporary brains—naturally—were of the best. They were so competent in the recognition of theory that they felt strangely at home in a world most of whose citizens lived by theories without knowing it. They were able to reduce a kind of order out of the childish chaos which they slowly recognized contemporary literature to be. They missed a great many ideas and distinctions which they knew had been fruitful in past centuries, and some of them set about considering the possibility of restoring these to an intellectually impoverished world. Whether they succeeded is not yet known. But it can be said of them that in their own minds they continued to be reasonably secure. For never would there be written a book which they could not understand simply by reading it from the first word to the last. They might not save the world. They might not change it. But they would comprehend it.

The following articles advance unusual, unpopular, or paradoxical conclusions. What means do the authors use to defend their judgments?

Can you find examples of factual reporting, definition, analysis of an organization, or other basic elements discussed in the early chapters of this book?

How fully do you agree with the author's conclusions? If you disagree, how would you support your own judgments?

9

LET'S NOT GET OUT THE VOTE *

ROBERT E. COULSON

Three years ago anyone who failed to vote had to face the combined scorn of both political parties, the schoolteachers, boy scouts,

* From *Harper's Magazine*, November, 1955. Reprinted by permission of the author.

war veterans, chambers of commerce, and leagues of women voters. Last year bar associations, girl scouts, tavern keepers, President Eisenhower, radio and TV stations, and junior chambers of commerce joined the crusade. There is every prospect that in future elections, nonvoters will face jail sentences or fines, or be called to testify before investigating committees.

Before this happens, someone should come to their defense. Nonvoters are often more intelligent, more fair-minded, and just as loyal as voters. The right not to vote is as basic as the right to. If voting is made a duty, it ceases to be a privilege.

Let's look at the voting behavior of Mr. and Mrs. Whipcord and Mrs. Whipcord's brother Harold, on the day of the local school-board election. Mrs. Whipcord says, "I have studied the candidates and have made up my mind. I will vote for Jones." Mr. Whipcord says, "I know nothing about the candidates or the issues. I will stay home, and allow the election to be decided by the votes of those who have made a study and formed an opinion." Harold says, "I don't know anything about the candidates or the problems, but by golly, I'm going to vote. It's my duty. I'll pick the fellows with the shortest names."

If there is a bad citizen among these three, which one is it? Whose procedure is least likely to bring good government to the school district?

Non-voting, multiplied by the thousands, is said to mean voter apathy, and this is supposed to be a sin. Have we lost our sacred American right to be apathetic? Suppose Mr. Whipcord studied the candidates carefully and concluded that Candidate Jones was a boob and Candidate Smith was a thief. Is it un-American to refuse to choose between them? Or suppose he is satisfied that Jones and Smith are equally qualified, equally able, and that the school's problems are in good hands no matter which man wins. He is not apathetic; he is satisfied. Why should he be forced to choose between candidates on some esoteric basis?

The notion that "getting out the vote" makes for better election results is neither non-partisan, patriotic, nor logical. It is a device to favor the machines of both parties. It handicaps independent candidates, unfairly burdens the party in power, makes elections more expensive to conduct, greatly slows the tallying, and—worst of all—places the emphasis on the ritual of voting rather than the thought behind the vote.

If you fill in all the blank spaces on the ballot, the political machines will steal three-fourths of your vote. Let's see how this works, in a typical primary election.

Here are seven offices to be filled by nomination, with two or three candidates for each office. Citizen Stringfellow is interested in seeing Jones win for Auditor. He has no information about the candidates for Attorney General, Treasurer, Superintendent of Schools, or the others. He votes for Jones and then looks on down the list. He has been persuaded that it is his duty to vote for *somebody* for each office. So for six of the seven offices, he marks an X opposite the name best known to him, or the name on top, or the name suggested by his committeeman. These are machine candidates, and Citizen Stringfellow has given away six-sevenths of his vote.

After him, comes Citizen Stalwart, who knows the candidates for two of the seven offices. He also fills in all the blanks, letting the machine steal five-sevenths of his vote. One of his blind votes cancels out the intelligent vote cast by Citizen Stringfellow. At this rate, during a day's balloting, the candidates backed by the strongest machines with the biggest publicity budgets will win, even though not a single voter had an intelligent preference for them.

Is this what Thomas Jefferson had in mind?

"Getting out the vote" is always partisan. A calm and dignified effort benefits the party in power. An excited or hysterical effort benefits the party out of power. The Republicans were very happy to use the pressure of "neutral" groups in the 1952 elections. But they had better learn that this is a two-edged sword. Next time, the girl scouts, veterans' groups, radio stations, newspapers, and community funds may be out needling the Republicans with propaganda.

"Vote this time or your vote may be gone forever." "This may be your last chance." "Vote now or never." Anyone who is led to the polls by such arguments is going to vote against whoever brought us to the edge of this crevasse. As the pressure on the public increases, the party out of power is most likely to benefit in direct proportion to it.

All public-opinion surveys show that a certain proportion of the electorate has no opinion about many vital issues, does not know who is running for office, and does not care. A gentle campaign to bring a submissive one-third of the apathetic sheep to the polls gets out a voting majority for the candidates who have had the greatest amount of publicity—who usually belong to the party in power. A rip-snorting effort to get out all the ignoramuses tends to turn them into the rebel column, and thus benefits the outs.

In either event, the girl scouts should wash their hands of it. The job of getting out the vote in a partisan effort which belongs to the professionals.

The silliest idea of all is the notion that it is un-American or unpatriotic not to vote. "A plague on both your houses" is a fair American attitude—all too often a logical one. Stupidity does not become wisdom by being multiplied.

In every election not more than one-third of the people care very much how it comes out. A certain percentage may have some sort of belief or opinion without feeling very strongly about it; another percentage may have studied the matter a little without forming an opinion; another percentage may not even have studied it; and so on, until we come to the people who are not even aware that an election is being held. The more we urge these people to clutter up the polling place, the more delay there is in voting, the more the cost of ballots and clerks, and the slower the returns.

If Candidate Jones would normally have won by 3,000 votes to 1,000, and we corral 10,000 more people into the polling places, won't Candidate Jones still win, by 8,000 to 6,000? Mathematically the last-minute coin flippers may make the election look close, but what patriotic purpose is accomplished?

And if the coin-flippers should happen to defeat the will of the informed majority, the cause of good government would emphatically not have been served.

Our city had a referendum recently in which the people voted for a tax increase to build an incinerator and against a tax increase to operate it. Every one of your communities has probably known referendums where the voters approved the bonds for a school but disapproved the sites, or voted for the site and against the bonds. All those voters who marked in opposite directions on the same afternoon were unwisely pressured into voting.

You have also seen primary elections where the boob with the catchy name ran away from the able man whose publicity was colorless. You have seen final elections where the straight party voters and the blank fillers smothered any discriminating choices which the thoughtful voters had made. You may have noticed with distress some of the undignified didos, cruel epithets, pompous verbosities, and Shakespearean gestures with which even good men become burdened early in their campaigns. All of these are caused in large measure by "get out the vote" efforts which emphasize putting a cross in half the squares.

Instead of urging people to vote, we ought to be urging them to study and form opinions. If thought and inspection of the candidates do not create a real desire to vote, then the citizen should be encouraged to stay at home on election day. A low vote is part of the public record and itself a significant voter reaction which ought to be preserved. Maybe neither of the candidates was worth voting for.

Certainly the right to vote is important and should not be curtailed. A fool who is willing to walk all the way to the polling place should be given every freedom to record every stupid impulse he feels, for these will tend to cancel each other out. But no one should pretend that marking X in a square is any proof of patriotism or even intelligence. It is not your duty to vote, but, if you choose to, then it should be your duty to be intelligent about it.

10

THE USEFULNESS OF USELESS KNOWLEDGE *

ABRAHAM FLEXNER

Is it not a curious fact that in a world steeped in irrational hatreds which threaten civilization itself, men and women—old and young—detach themselves wholly or partly from the angry current of daily life to devote themselves to the cultivation of beauty, to the extension of knowledge, to the cure of disease, to the amelioration of suffering, just as though fanatics were not simultaneously engaged in spreading pain, ugliness, and suffering? The world has always

* From *Harper's Magazine*, October, 1939. Reprinted by permission of the author.

been a sorry and confused sort of place—yet poets and artists and scientists have ignored the factors that would, if attended to, paralyze them. From a practical point of view, intellectual and spiritual life is, on the surface, a useless form of activity, in which men indulge because they procure for themselves greater satisfactions than are otherwise obtainable. In this paper I shall concern myself with the question of the extent to which the pursuit of these useless satisfactions proves unexpectedly the source from which undreamed-of utility is derived.

We hear it said with tiresome iteration that ours is a materialistic age, the main concern of which should be the wider distribution of material goods and worldly opportunities. The justified outcry of those who through no fault of their own are deprived of opportunity and a fair share of worldly goods therefore diverts an increasing number of students from the studies which their fathers pursued to the equally important and no less urgent study of social, economic, and governmental problems. I have no quarrel with this tendency. The world in which we live is the only world about which our senses can testify. Unless it is made a better world, a fairer world, millions will continue to go to their graves silent, saddened, and embittered. I have myself spent many years pleading that our schools should become more acutely aware of the world in which their pupils and students are destined to pass their lives. Now I sometimes wonder whether that current has not become too strong and whether there would be sufficient opportunity for a full life if the world were emptied of some of the useless things that give it spiritual significance; in other words, whether our conception of what is useful may not have become too narrow to be adequate to the roaming and capricious possibilties of the human spirit.

We may look at this question from two points of view: the scientific and the humanistic or spiritual. Let us take the scientific first. I recall a conversation which I had some years ago with Mr. George Eastman on the subject of use. Mr. Eastman, a wise and gentle farseeing man, gifted with taste in music and art, had been saying to me that he meant to devote his vast fortune to the promotion of education in useful subjects. I ventured to ask him whom he regarded as the most useful worker in science in the world. He replied instantaneously: "Marconi." I surprised him by saying, "Whatever pleasure we derive from the radio or however wireless and the radio may have added to human life, Marconi's share was practically negligible."

I shall not forget his astonishment on this occasion. He asked me to explain. I replied to him somewhat as follows:

"Mr. Eastman, Marconi was inevitable. The real credit for everything that has been done in the field of wireless belongs, as far as such fundamental credit can be definitely assigned to anyone, to Professor Clerk Maxwell, who in 1865 carried out certain abstruse and remote calculations in the field of magnetism and electricity. Maxwell reproduced his abstract equations in a treatise published in 1873. At the next meeting of the British Association Professor H. J. S. Smith of Oxford declared that 'no mathematician can turn over the pages of these volumes without realizing that they contain a theory which has already added largely to the methods and resources of pure mathematics.' Other discoveries supplemented Maxwell's theoretical work during the next fifteen years. Finally in 1887 and 1888 the scientific problem still remaining—the detection and demonstration of the electromagnetic waves which are the carriers of wireless signals—was solved by Heinrich Hertz, a worker in Helmholtz's laboratory in Berlin. Neither Maxwell nor Hertz had any concern about the utility of their work; no such thought ever entered their minds. They had no practical objective. The inventor in the legal sense was of course Marconi, but what did Marconi invent? Merely the last technical detail, mainly the now obsolete receiving device called coherer, almost universally discarded."

Hertz and Maxwell could invent nothing, but it was their useless theoretical work which was seized upon by a clever technician and which has created new means for communication, utility, and amusement by which men whose merits are relatively slight have obtained fame and earned millions. Who were the useful men? Not Marconi, but Clerk Maxwell and Heinrich Hertz. Hertz and Maxwell were geniuses without thought of use. Marconi was a clever inventor with no thought but use.

The mention of Hertz's name recalled to Mr. Eastman the Hertzian waves, and I suggested that he might ask the physicists of the University of Rochester precisely what Hertz and Maxwell had done; but one thing I said he could be sure of, namely, that they had done their work without thought of use and that throughout the whole history of science most of the really great discoveries which had ultimately proved to be beneficial to mankind had been made by men and women who were driven not by the desire to be useful but merely the desire to satisfy their curiosity.

"Curiosity?" asked Mr. Eastman.

"Yes," I replied, "curiosity, which may or may not eventuate in something useful, is probably the outstanding characteristic of modern thinking. It is not new. It goes back to Galileo, Bacon, and to Sir Isaac Newton, and it must be absolutely unhampered. Institutions of learning should be devoted to the cultivation of curiosity and the less they are deflected by considerations of immediacy of application, the more likely they are to contribute not only to human welfare but to the equally important satisfaction of intellectual interest which may indeed be said to have become the ruling passion of intellectual life in modern times."

II

What is true of Heinrich Hertz working quietly and unnoticed in a corner of Helmholtz's laboratory in the later years of the nineteenth century may be said of scientists and mathematicians the world over for several centuries past. We live in a world that would be helpless without electricity. Called upon to mention a discovery of the most immediate and far-reaching practical use we might well agree upon electricity. But who made the fundamental discoveries out of which the entire electrical development of more than one hundred years has come?

The answer is interesting. Michael Faraday's father was a blacksmith; Michael himself was apprenticed to a bookbinder. In 1812, when he was already twenty-one years of age, a friend took him to the Royal Institution where he heard Sir Humphrey Davy deliver four lectures on chemical subjects. He kept notes and sent a copy of them to Davy. The very next year, 1813, he became an assistant in Davy's laboratory, working on chemical problems. Two years later he accompanied Davy on a trip to the Continent. In 1825, when he was thirty-four years of age, he became Director of the Laboratory of the Royal Institution where he spent fifty-four years of his life.

Faraday's interest soon shifted from chemistry to electricity and magnetism, to which he devoted the rest of his active life. Important but puzzling work in this field had been previously accomplished by Oersted, Ampere, and Wollaston. Faraday cleared away the difficulties which they had left unsolved and by 1841 had succeeded in the task of induction of the electric current. Four years later a second and equally brilliant epoch in his career opened when he discovered the effect of magnetism on polarized light. His earlier discoveries have led to the infinite number of practical applications by means of which electricity has lightened the burdens and increased the opportunities of modern life. His later discoveries have thus far been less prolific of practical results. What difference did this make to Faraday? Not the least. At no period of his unmatched career was he interested in utility. He was absorbed in disentangling the riddles of the universe, at first chemical riddles, in later periods, physical riddles. As far as he cared, the question of utility was never raised. Any suspicion of utility would have restricted his restless curiosity. In the end, utility resulted, but it was never a criterion to which his ceaseless experimentation could be subjected.

In the atmosphere which envelopes the world to-day it is perhaps timely to emphasize the fact that the part played by science in making war more destructive and more horrible was an unconscious and unintended by-product of scientific activity. Lord Rayleigh, president of the British Association for the Advancement of Science, in a recent address points out in detail how the folly of man, not the intention of the scientists, is responsible for the destructive use of the agents employed in modern warfare. The innocent study of the chemistry of carbon compounds, which has led to infinite beneficial results, showed that the action of nitric acid on substances like benzene, glycerine, cellulose, etc., resulted not only in the beneficent aniline dye industry but in the creation of nitro-glycerine, which has uses good and bad. Somewhat later Alfred Nobel, turning to the same subject, showed that by mixing nitro-glycerine with other substances, solid explosives which could be safely handled could be produced—among others, dynamite. It is to dynamite that we owe our progress in mining, in the making of such railroad tunnels as those which now pierce the Alps and other mountain ranges; but of course dynamite has been abused by politicians and soldiers. Scientists are, however, no more to blame than they are to blame for an earthquake or a flood. The same thing can be said of poison gas. Pliny was killed by breathing sulphur dioxide in the eruption of Vesuvius almost two thousand years ago. Chlorine was not isolated by scientists for warlike purposes, and the same is true of mustard gas. These substances could be limited to beneficent use, but when the airplane was perfected, men whose hearts were poisoned and whose brains were addled perceived that the airplane, an innocent invention, the result of long disinterested and scientific effort, could be made an instrument of destruction, of which no one had ever dreamed and at which no one had ever deliberately aimed.

In the domain of higher mathematics almost innumerable instances can be cited. For example, the most abstruse mathematical work of the eighteenth and nineteenth centuries was the "Non-Euclidian Geometry." Its inventor, Gauss, though recognized by his contemporaries as a distinguished mathematician, did not dare to publish his work on "Non-Euclidian Geometry" for a quarter of a century. As a matter of fact, the theory of relatively itself with all its infinite practical bearings would have been utterly impossible without the work which Gauss did at Göttingen.

Again, what is known now as "group theory" was an abstract and inapplicable mathematical theory. It was developed by men who were curious and whose curiosity and puttering led them into strange paths; but "group theory" is to-day the basis of the quantum theory of spectroscopy, which is in daily use by people who have no idea as to how it came about.

The whole calculus of probability was discovered by mathematicians whose real interest was the rationalization of gambling. It has failed of the practical purpose at which they aimed, but it has furnished a scientific basis for all types of insurance, and vast stretches of nineteenth century physics are based upon it.

From a recent number of *Science* I quote the following:

> The stature of Professor Albert Einstein's genius reached new heights when it was disclosed that the learned mathematical physicist developed mathematics fifteen years ago which are now helping to solve the mysteries of the amazing fluidity of helium near the absolute zero of the temperature scale. Before the symposium on intermolecular action of the American Chemical Society Professor F. London, of the University of Paris, now visiting professor at Duke University, credited Professor Ein-

stein with the concept of an "ideal" gas which appeared in papers published in 1924 and 1925.

The Einstein 1925 reports were not about relativity theory, but discussed problems seemingly without any practical significance at the time. They described the degeneracy of an "ideal" gas near the lower limits of the scale of temperature. Because all gases were known to be condensed to liquids at the temperatures in question, scientists rather overlooked the Einstein work of fifteen years ago.

However, the recently discovered behavior of liquid helium has brought the side-tracked Einstein concept to new usefulness. Most liquids increase in viscosity, become stickier and flow less easily, when they become colder. The phrase "colder than molasses in January" is the layman's concept of viscosity and a correct one.

Liquid helium, however, is a baffling exception. At the temperature known as the "delta" point, only 2.19 degrees above absolute zero, liquid helium flows better than it does at higher temperatures and, as a matter of fact, the liquid helium is about as nebulous as a gas. Added puzzles in its strange behavior include its enormous ability to conduct heat. At the delta point it is about 500 times as effective in this respect as copper at room temperature. Liquid helium, with these and other anomalies, has posed a major mystery for physicists and chemists.

Professor London stated that the interpretation of the behavior of liquid helium can best be explained by considering it as a Bose-Einstein "ideal" gas, by using the mathematics worked out in 1924–25, and by taking over also some of the concepts of the electrical conduction of metals. By simple analogy, the amazing fluidity of liquid helium can be partially explained by picturing the fluidity as something akin to the wandering of electrons in metals to explain electrical conduction.

Let us look in another direction. In the domain of medicine and public health the science of bacteriology has played for half a century the leading role. What is its story? Following the Franco-Prussian War of 1870, the German Government founded the great University of Strasbourg. Its first professor of anatomy was Wilhelm von Waldeyer, subsequently professor of anatomy in Berlin. In his *Reminiscences* he relates that among the students who went with him to Strasbourg during his first semester there was a small, inconspicuous, self-contained youngster of seventeen by name Paul Ehrlich. The usual course in anatomy then consisted of dissection and microscopic examination of tissues. Ehrlich paid little or no attention to dissection, but, as Waldeyer remarks in his *Reminiscences*:

I noticed quite early that Ehrlich would work long hours at his desk, completely absorbed in microscopic observation. Moreover, his desk gradually became covered with colored spots of every description. As I saw him sitting at work one day, I went up to him and asked what he was doing with all his rainbow array of colors on his table. Thereupon this young student in his first semester supposedly pursuing the regular course in anatomy looked up at me and blandly remarked, "*Ich probiere.*" This might be freely translated, "I am trying" or "I am just fooling." I replied to him, "Very well. Go on with your fooling." Soon I saw that without any teaching or direction whatsoever on my part I possessed in Ehrlich a student of unusual quality.

Waldeyer wisely left him alone. Ehrlich made his way precariously through the medical curriculum and ultimately procured his degree mainly because it was obvious to his teachers that he had no intention of ever putting his medical degree to practical use. He went subsequently to Breslau where he worked under Professor Cohnheim, the teacher of our own Dr. Welch, founder and maker of the Johns Hopkins Medical School. I do not suppose that the idea of use ever crossed Ehrlich's mind. He was interested. He was curious; he kept on fooling. Of course his fooling was guided by a deep instinct, but it was a purely scientific, not an utilitarian motivation. What resulted? Koch and his associates established a new science, the science of bacteriology. Ehrlich's experiments were now applied by a fellow student, Weigert, to staining bacteria and thereby assisting in their differentiation. Ehrlich himself developed the staining of the blood film with the dyes on which our modern knowledge of the morphology of the blood corpuscles, red and white, is based. Not a day passes but that in thousands of hospitals the world over Ehrlich's technic is employed in the examination of the blood. Thus the apparently aimless fooling in Waldeyer's dissecting room in Strasbourg has become a main factor in the daily practice of medicine.

I shall give one example from industry, one selected at random; for there are scores besides. Professor Berl, of the Carnegie Institute of Technology (Pittsburgh), writes as follows:

The founder of the modern rayon industry was the French Count Chardonnet. It is known that he used a solution of nitro cotton in ether-alcohol, and that he pressed this viscous solution through capillaries into water which served to coagulate the cellulose nitrate filament. After the coagulation, this filament entered the air and was wound up on bobbins. One day Chardonnet inspected his French factory at Besançon. By an accident the water which should coagulate the cellulose nitrate filament was stopped. The workmen found that the spinning operation went much better without water than with water. This was the birthday of the very important process of dry spinning, which is actually carried out on the greatest scale.

III

I am not for a moment suggesting that everything that goes on in laboratories will ultimately turn to some unexpected practical use or that an ultimate practical use is its actual justification. Much more am I pleading for the abolition of the word "use," and for the freeing of the human spirit. To be sure, we shall thus free some harmless cranks. To be sure, we shall thus waste some precious dollars. But what is infinitely more important is that we shall be striking the shackles off the human mind and setting it free for the adventures which in our own day have, on the one hand, taken Hale and Rutherford and Einstein and their peers millions upon millions of miles into the uttermost realms of space and, on the other, loosed the boundless energy imprisoned in the atom. What Rutherford and others like Bohr and Millikan have done out of sheer curiosity in the effort to understand the construction of the atom has released forces which may transform human life; but this ultimate and unforeseen and unpredictable practical result is not offered as a justification for Rutherford or Einstein or Millikan or Bohr or any of their peers. Let them alone. No educational administrator can possibly direct the channels in which these or other men shall work. The waste, I admit again, looks prodigious. It is not really so. All the waste that could be summed up in developing the science of bacteriology is as nothing compared to the advantages which have accrued from the discoveries of Pasteur, Koch, Ehrlich, Theobald Smith, and scores of others—advantages that could never have accrued if the idea of possible use had permeated their minds. These great artists—for such are scientists and bacteriologists—disseminated the spirit which prevailed in laboratories in which they were simply following the line of their own natural curiosity.

I am not criticizing institutions like schools of engineering or law in which the usefulness motive necessarily predominates. Not infrequently the tables are turned, and practical difficulties encountered in industry or in laboratories stimulate theoretical inquiries which may or may not solve the problems by which they were suggested, but may also open up new vistas, useless at the moment, but pregnant with future achievements, practical and theoretical.

With the rapid accumulation of "useless" or theoretic knowledge a situation has been created in which it has become increasingly possible to attack practical problems in a scientific spirit. Not only inventors, but "pure" scientists have indulged in this sport. I have mentioned Marconi, an inventor, who, while a benefactor to the human race, as a matter of fact merely "picked other men's brains." Edison belongs to the same category. Pasteur was different. He was a great scientist; but he was not averse to attacking practical problems—such as the condition of French grapevines or the problems of beer-brewing—and not only solving the immediate difficulty, but also wresting from the practical problem some far-reaching theoretic conclusion, "useless" at the moment, but likely in some unforeseen manner to be "useful" later. Ehrlich, fundamentally speculative in his curiosity, turned fiercely upon the problem of syphilis and doggedly pursued it until a solution of immediate practical use—the discovery of salvarsan—was found. The discoveries of insulin by Banting for use in diabetes and of liver extract by Minot and Whipple for use in pernicious anemia belong in the same category: both were made by thoroughly scientific men, who realized that much "useless" knowledge had been piled up by men unconcerned with its practical bearings, but that the time was now ripe to raise practical questions in a scientific manner.

Thus it becomes obvious that one must be wary in attributing scientific discovery wholly to any one person. Almost every discovery has a long and precarious history. Someone finds a bit here, another a bit there. A third step succeeds later and thus onward till a genius pieces the bits together and makes the decisive contribution. Science, like the Mississippi, begins in a tiny rivulet in the distant forest. Gradually other streams swell its volume. And the roaring river that bursts the dikes is formed from countless sources.

I cannot deal with this aspect exhaustively, but I may in passing say this: over a period of one or two hundred years the contributions of professional schools to their respective activities will probably be found to lie, not so much in the training of men who may to-morrow become practical engineers or practical lawyers or practical doctors, but rather in the fact that even in the pursuit of strictly practical aims an enormous amount of apparently useless activity goes on. Out of this useless activity there come discoveries which may well prove of infinitely more importance to the human mind and to the human spirit than the accomplishment of the useful ends for which the schools were founded.

The considerations upon which I have touched emphasize—if emphasis were needed—the overwhelming importance of spiritual and intellectual freedom. I have spoken of experimental science; I have spoken of mathematics; but what I say is equally true of music and art and of every other expression of the untrammeled human spirit. The mere fact that they bring satisfaction to an individual soul bent upon its own purification and elevation is all the justification that they need. And in justifying these without any reference whatsoever, implied or actual, to usefulness we justify colleges, universities, and institutes of research. An institution which sets free successive generations of human souls is amply justified whether or not this graduate or that makes a so-called useful contribution to human knowledge. A poem, a symphony, a painting, a mathematical truth, a new scientific fact, all bear in themselves all the justification that universities, colleges, and institutes of research need or require.

The subject which I am discussing has at this moment a peculiar poignancy. In certain large areas—Germany and Italy especially—the effort is now being made to clamp down the freedom of the human spirit. Universities have been so reorganized that they have become tools of those who believe in a special political, economic, or racial creed. Now and then a thoughtless individual in one of the few democracies left in this world will even question the fundamental importance of absolutely untrammeled academic freedom. The real enemy of the human race is not the fearless and irresponsible thinker, be he right or wrong. The real enemy is the man who tries to mold the human spirit so that it will not dare to spread its wings, as its wings were once spread in Italy and Germany, as well as in Great Britain and the United States.

This is not a new idea. It was the idea which animated von Humboldt when, in the hour of Germany's conquest by Napoleon, he conceived and founded the University of Berlin. It is the idea which animated President Gilman in the founding of the Johns Hopkins University, after which every university in this country has sought in greater or less degree to remake itself. It is the idea to which every individual who values his immortal soul will be true whatever the personal consequences to himself. Justification of spiritual freedom goes, however, much farther than originality whether in the realm of science or humanism, for it implies tolerance throughout the range of human dissimilarities. In the face of the history of the human race, what can be more silly or ridiculous than likes or dislikes founded upon race or religion? Does humanity want symphonies and paintings and profound scientific truth, or does it want Christian symphonies, Christian paintings, Christian science, or Jewish symphonies, Jewish paintings, Jewish science, or Mohammedan or Egyptian or Japanese or Chinese or American or German or Russian or Communist or Conservative contributions to and expressions of the infinite richness of the human soul?

IV

Among the most striking and immediate consequences of foreign intolerance I may, I think, fairly cite the rapid development of the Institute for Advanced Study, established by Mr. Louis Bamberger and his sister, Mrs. Felix Fuld, at Princeton, New Jersey. The founding of the Institute was suggested in 1930. It was located at Princeton partly because of the founders' attachment to the State of New Jersey, but, in so far as my judgment was concerned, because Princeton had a small graduate school of high quality with which the most intimate cooperation was feasible. To Princeton University the Institute owes a debt that can never be fully appreciated. The work of the Institute with a considerable portion of its personnel began in 1933. On its faculty are eminent American scholars—Veblen, Alexander, and Morse, among the mathematicians; Meritt, Lowe, and Miss Goldman among the humanists; Stewart, Riefler, Warren, Earle, and Mitrany among the publicists and economists. And to these should be added scholars and scientists of equal caliber already assembled in Princeton University, Princeton's library, and its laboratories. But the Institute for Advanced Study is indebted to Hitler for Einstein, Weyl, and von Neumann in mathematics; for Herzfeld and Panofsky in the field of humanistic studies, and for a host of younger men who during the past six years have come under the influence of this distinguished group and are already adding to the strength of American scholarship in every section of the land.

The Institute is, from the standpoint of organization, the simplest and least formal thing imaginable. It consists of three schools—a School of Mathematics, a School of Humanistic Studies, a School of Economics and Politics. Each school is made up of a permanent group of professors and an annually changing group of members. Each school manages its own affairs as it pleases; within each group each individual disposes of his time and energy as he pleases. The members who already have come from twenty-two foreign countries and thirty-nine institutions of higher learning in the United States are admitted, if deemed worthy, by the several groups. They enjoy precisely the same freedom as the professors. They may work with this or that professor, as they severally arrange; they may work alone, consulting from time to time anyone likely to be helpful. No routine is followed; no lines are drawn between professors, members, or visitors. Princeton students and professors and Institute members and professors mingle so freely as to be indistinguishable. Learning as such is cultivated. The results to the individual and to society are left to take care of themselves. No faculty meetings are held; no committees exist. Thus men with ideas enjoy conditions favorable to reflection and to conference. A mathematician may cultivate mathematics without distraction; so may a humanist in his field, an economist or a student of politics in his. Administration has been minimized in extent and importance. Men without ideas, without power of concentration on ideas, would not be at home in the Institute.

I can perhaps make this point clearer by citing briefly a few illustrations. A stipend was awarded to enable a Harvard professor to come to Princeton: he wrote asking,

"What are my duties?"

I replied: "You have no duties—only opportunities."

An able young mathematician, having spent a year at Princeton, came to bid me good-by. As he was about to leave, he remarked:

"Perhaps you would like to know what this year has meant to me."

"Yes," I answered.

"Mathematics," he rejoined, "is developing rapidly; the current literature is extensive. It is now over ten years since I took my Ph.D. degree. For a while I could keep up with my subject; but latterly that has become increasingly difficult and uncertain. Now, after a year here, the blinds are raised; the room is light; the windows are open. I have in my head two papers that I shall shortly write."

"How long will this last?" I asked.

"Five years, perhaps ten."

"Then what?"

"I shall come back."

A third example is of recent occurrence. A professor in a large Western university arrived in Princeton at the end of last December. He had in mind to resume some work with Professor Morey (at Princeton University). But Morey suggested that he might find it worth while to see Panofsky and Swarzenski (at the Institute). Now he is busy with all three.

"I shall stay," he added, "until next October."

"You shall find it hot in midsummer," I said.

"I shall be too busy and too happy to notice it."

Thus freedom brings not stagnation, but rather the danger of overwork. The wife of an English member recently asked:

"Does everyone work until two o'clock in the morning?"

The Institute has had thus far no building. At this moment the mathematicians are guests of the Princeton mathematicians in Fine Hall; some of the humanists are guests of the Princeton humanists in McCormick Hall; others work in rooms scattered through the town. The economists now occupy a suite at the Princeton Inn. My own quarters are located in an office building on Nassau Street, where I work among shopkeepers, dentists, lawyers, chiropractors, and groups of Princeton scholars conducting a local government survey and a study of population. Bricks and mortar are thus quite inessential, as President Gilman proved in Baltimore sixty-odd years ago. Nevertheless, we miss informal contact with one another and are about to remedy this defect by the erection of a building provided by the founders, to be called Fuld Hall. But formality shall go no farther. The Institute must remain small; and it will hold fast to the conviction that The Institute Group desires leisure, security, freedom from organization and routine, and, finally, informal contacts with the scholars of Princeton University and others who from time to time can be lured to Princeton from distant places. Among these Niels Bohr has come from Copenhagen, von Laue from Berlin, Levi Civita from Rome, André Weil from Strasbourg, Dirac and G. H. Hardy from Cambridge, Pauli from Zurich, Lemaitre from Louvain, Wade-Gery from Oxford, and Americans from Harvard, Yale, Columbia, Cornell, Johns Hopkins, Chicago, California, and other centers of light and learning.

We make ourselves no promises, but we cherish the hope that the unobstructed pursuit of useless knowledge will prove to have consequences in the future as in the past. Not for a moment, however, do we defend the Institute on that ground. It exists as a paradise for scholars who, like poets and musicians, have won the right to do as they please and who accomplish most when enabled to do so.

11

In other readings we will get to see writers using refutation as a means to reaching a judgment, but nowhere will we see it any more directly employed than in this letter to the Editor of *The New York Times*:

CONTROLLING FLOODS *

To the Editor of *The New York Times*:

The letter of Frank Steiner in The Times on Jan. 12, concerning the causes and cures of floods cannot be allowed to go unanswered.

Although his facts are essentially correct, the conclusions and inferences he draws from them are most certainly not. His conclusions are not only wrong, they are dangerous.

In order to understand why Mr. Steiner is wrong, it is first necessary to distinguish between "flash" floods and the more general, widespread floods, such as occurred in California.

Flash floods occur when large quantities of rain fall on a relatively small area in a short time. If most of this runs over the ground surface and finds its way to stream beds quickly, large streamflows build up rapidly. Flood waters rise with astounding rapidity and recede almost as rapidly when the rain stops.

The other type of flood is caused in a number of ways, among them

* A letter to the Editor of *The New York Times*, appearing Jan. 26, 1956.

the manner in which the California floods developed. Such a flood may develop when major storms drop large quantities of rain over large areas over a period of time measured in days or weeks. In this case, the capacity of the soil to hold water is exceeded.

If more rain falls, it cannot percolate into the ground, it can only flow over the surface into stream channels. This, of course, is true no matter what the condition of the soil surface.

Maintaining a forest cover is an excellent way of maintaining high infiltration rates. But other natural vegetative coverings (as opposed to crops, which are cultivated) are nearly as effective as forests in maintaining high infiltration rates, as long as the cover is complete. It is also true that even cutover areas, if logging is done properly, recover high infiltration rates in a very few years.

Thus, maintaining a good vegetative cover will reduce the likelihood of damaging flash floods. It will reduce the peak flows of such floods as compared with similar areas with the vegetative cover nonexistent or in poor condition. But the significance of cover diminishes as the size of a rainstorm increases.

Thus it is quite fallacious and dangerous to rely on vegetation management to remove the threat from damaging floods. Although vegetation management is an essential part of any program of flood control, it is imperative such management be supplemented by man-made structures where the values protected warrant the expense of such structures.

It may be a long time before we are able to control the weather sufficiently to prevent flood-producing rains. Until that time comes, it is incumbent upon us to maintain an objective view of the causes and cures of floods and not to be misled by panaceas.

William E. Reifsnyder,
Assistant Professor of Forest Meteorology,
Yale University.
New Haven, Conn., Jan. 14, 1956.

The three selections that follow reach decisions about broad questions of policy—all concerning political behavior.

What instances do you find where authors summarize opposing opinions and then refute them?

How much specific evidence do you find?

What important premises does each author emphasize as the basis for his inferences?

What kind of readers do these authors apparently want to reach?

12

THE INDISPENSABLE OPPOSITION *

WALTER LIPPMANN

Were they pressed hard enough, most men would probably confess that political freedom—that is to say, the right to speak freely and to act in opposition—is a noble ideal rather than a practical necessity. As the case for freedom is generally put to-day, the argument lends itself to this feeling. It is made to appear that, whereas each man claims his freedom as a matter of right, the freedom he accords to other men is a matter of toleration. Thus, the defense of freedom of opinion tends to rest not on its substantial, beneficial, and indispensable consequences, but on a somewhat eccentric, a rather vaguely benevolent, attachment to an abstraction.

It is all very well to say with Voltaire, "I wholly disapprove of what you say, but will defend to the death your right to say it," but as a matter of fact most men will not defend to the death the rights of other men: if they disapprove sufficiently what other men say, they will somehow suppress those men if they can.

So, if this is the best that can be said for liberty of opinion, that a man must tolerate his opponents because everyone has a "right" to say what he pleases, then we shall find that liberty of opinion is a luxury, safe only in pleasant times when men can be tolerant because they are not deeply and vitally concerned.

Yet actually, as a matter of historic fact, there is a much stronger foundation for the great constitutional right of freedom of speech, and as a matter of practical human experience there is a much more compelling reason for cultivating the habits of free men. We take, it seems to me, a naïvely self-righteous view when we argue as if the right of our opponents to speak were something that we protect

* From *The Atlantic Monthly*, August, 1939. Reprinted by permission of the author.

because we are magnanimous, noble, and unselfish. The compelling reason why, if liberty of opinion did not exist, we should have to invent it, why it will eventually have to be restored in all civilized countries where it is now suppressed, is that we must protect the right of our opponents to speak because we must hear what they have to say.

We miss the whole point when we imagine that we tolerate the freedom of our political opponents as we tolerate a howling baby next door, as we put up with the blasts from our neighbor's radio because we are too peaceable to heave a brick through the window. If this were all there is to freedom of opinion, that we are too good-natured or too timid to do anything about our opponents and our critics except to let them talk, it would be difficult to say whether we are tolerant because we are magnanimous or because we are lazy, because we have strong principles or because we lack serious convictions, whether we have the hospitality of an inquiring mind or the indifference of an empty mind. And so, if we truly wish to understand why freedom is necessary in a civilized society, we must begin by realizing that, because freedom of discussion improves our own opinions, the liberties of other men are our own vital necessity.

We are much closer to the essence of the matter, not when we quote Voltaire, but when we go to the doctor and pay him to ask us the most embarrassing questions and to prescribe the most disagreeable diet. When we pay the doctor to exercise complete freedom of speech about the cause and cure of our stomachache, we do not look upon ourselves as tolerant and magnanimous, and worthy to be admired by ourselves. We have enough common sense to know that if we threaten to put the doctor in jail because we do not like the diagnosis and the prescription it will be unpleasant for the doctor, to be sure, but equally unpleasant for our own stomachache. That is why even the most ferocious dictator would rather be treated by a doctor who was free to think and speak the truth than by his own Minister of Propaganda. For there is a point, the point at which things really matter, where the freedom of others is no longer a question of their right but of our own need.

The point at which we recognize this need is much higher in some men than in others. The totalitarian rulers think they do not need the freedom of an opposition: they exile, imprison, or shoot their opponents. We have concluded on the basis of practical experience, which goes back to Magna Carta and beyond, that we need the opposition. We pay the opposition salaries out of the public treasury.

In so far as the usual apology for freedom of speech ignores this experience, it becomes abstract and eccentric rather than concrete and human. The emphasis is generally put on the right to speak, as if all that mattered were that the doctor should be free to go out into the park and explain to the vacant air why I have a stomachache. Surely that is a miserable caricature of the great civic right which men have bled and died for. What really matters is that the doctor should tell *me* what ails me, that I should listen to him; that if I do not like what he says I should be free to call in another doctor; and that then the first doctor should have to listen to the second doctor; and that out of all the speaking and listening, the give-and-take of opinions, the truth should be arrived at.

This is the creative principle of freedom of speech, not that it is a system for the tolerating of error, but that it is a system for finding the truth. It may not produce the truth, or the whole truth all the time, or often, or in some cases ever. But if the truth can be found, there is no other system which will normally and habitually find so much truth. Until we have thoroughly understood this principle, we shall not know why we must value our liberty, or how we can protect and develop it.

II

Let us apply this principle to the system of public speech in a totalitarian state. We may, without any serious falsification, picture a condition of affairs in which the mass of the people are being addressed through one broadcasting system by one man and his chosen subordinates. The orators speak. The audience listens but cannot and dare not speak back. It is a system of one-way communication; the opinions of the rulers are broadcast outwardly to the mass of the people. But nothing comes back to the rulers from the people except the cheers; nothing returns in the way of knowledge of forgotten facts, hidden feelings, neglected truths, and practical suggestions.

But even a dictator cannot govern by his own one-way inspiration alone. In practice, therefore, the totalitarian rulers get back the reports of the secret police and of their party henchmen down among the crowd. If these reports are competent, the rulers may manage to remain in touch with public sentiment. Yet that is not enough to know what the audience feels. The rulers have also to make great decisions that have enormous consequences, and here their system provides virtually no help from the give-and-take of opinion in the nation. So they must either rely on their own intuition, which cannot be permanently and continually inspired, or, if they are intelligent despots, encourage their trusted advisers and their technicians to speak and debate freely in their presence.

On the walls of the houses of Italian peasants one may see inscribed in large letters the legend, "Mussolini is always right." But if that legend is taken seriously by Italian ambassadors, by the General Staff, and by the Ministry of Finance, then all one can say is heaven help Mussolini, heaven help Italy, and the new Emperor of Ethiopia.

For at some point, even in a totalitarian state, it is indispensable that there should exist the freedom of opinion which causes opposing opinions to be debated. As time goes on, that is less and less easy under a despotism; critical discussion disappears as the internal opposition is liquidated in favor of men who think and feel alike. That is why the early successes of despots, of Napoleon I and of Napoleon III, have usually been followed by an irreparable mistake. For in listening only to his yes men—the others being in exile or in concentration camps, or terrified—the despot shuts himself off from the truth that no man can dispense with.

We know all this well enough when we contemplate the dictatorships. But when we try to picture our own system, by way of contrast, what picture do we have in our minds? It is, is it not, that anyone may stand up on his own soapbox and say anything he pleases, like the individuals in Kipling's poem who sit each in his separate star and draw the Thing as they see it for the God of Things as they are. Kipling, perhaps, could do this, since he was a poet. But the ordinary mortal isolated on his separate star will have an hallucination, and a citizenry declaiming from separate soapboxes will poison the air with hot and nonsensical confusion.

If the democratic alternative to the totalitarian one-way broadcasts is a row of separate soapboxes, then I submit that the alternative is unworkable, is unreasonable, and is humanly unattractive. It is above all a false alternative. It is not true that liberty has developed among civilized men when anyone is free to set up a soapbox, is free to hire a hall where he may expound his opinions to those who are willing to listen. On the contrary, freedom of speech is established to achieve its essential purpose only when different opinions are expounded in the same hall to the same audience.

For, while the right to talk may be the beginning of freedom, the necessity of listening is what makes the right important. Even in Russia and Germany a man may still stand in an open field and speak his mind. What matters is not the utterance of opinions. What matters is the confrontation of opinions in debate. No man can care profoundly that every fool should say what he likes. Nothing has been accomplished if the wisest man proclaims his wisdom in the middle of the Sahara Desert. This is the shadow. We have the substance of liberty when the fool is compelled to listen to the wise man and learn; when the wise man is compelled to take account of the fool, and to instruct him; when the wise man can increase his wisdom by hearing the judgment of his peers.

That is why civilized men must cherish liberty—as a means of promoting the discovery of truth. So we must not fix our whole attention on the right of anyone to hire his own hall, to rent his own broadcasting station, to distribute his own pamphlets. These rights are incidental; and though they must be preserved, they can be preserved only by regarding them as incidental, as auxiliary to the substance of liberty that must be cherished and cultivated.

Freedom of speech is best conceived, therefore, by having in mind the picture of a place like the American Congress, an assembly where opposing views are represented, where ideas are not merely uttered but debated, or the British Parliament, where men who are free to speak are also compelled to answer. We may picture the true condition of freedom as existing in a place like a court of law, where witnesses testify and are cross-examined, where the lawyer argues against the opposing lawyer before the same judge and in the presence of one jury. We may picture freedom as existing in a forum where the speaker must respond to questions; in a gathering of scientists where the data, the hypothesis, and the conclusion are submitted to men competent to judge them; in a reputable newspaper which not only will publish the opinions of those who disagree but will reëxamine its own opinion in the light of what they say.

Thus the essence of freedom of opinion is not in mere toleration as such, but in the debate which toleration provides: it is not in the venting of opinion, but in the confrontation of opinion. That this is the practical substance can readily be understood when we remember how differently we feel and act about the censorship and regulation of opinion purveyed by different media of communication. We find then that, in so far as the medium makes difficult the confrontation of opinion in debate, we are driven towards censorship and regulation.

There is, for example, the whispering campaign, the circulation of anonymous rumors by men who cannot be compelled to prove what they say. They put the utmost strain on our tolerance, and there are few who do not rejoice when the anonymous slanderer is caught, exposed, and punished. At a higher level there is the moving picture, a most powerful medium for conveying ideas, but a medium which does not permit debate. A moving picture cannot be answered effectively by another moving picture; in all free countries there is some censorship of the movies, and there would be more if the producers did not recognize their limitations by avoiding political controversy. There is then the radio. Here debate is difficult: it is not easy to make sure that the speaker is being answered in the presence of the same audience. Inevitably, there is some regulation of the radio.

When we reach the newspaper press, the opportunity for debate is so considerable that discontent cannot grow to the point where under normal conditions there is any disposition to regulate the press. But when newspapers abuse their power by injuring people who have no means of replying, a disposition to regulate the press appears. When we arrive at Congress we find that, because the membership of the House is so large, full debate is impracticable. So there are restrictive rules. On the other hand, in the Senate, where the conditions of full debate exist, there is almost absolute freedom of speech.

This shows us that the preservation and development of freedom of opinion are not only a matter of adhering to abstract legal rights, but also, and very urgently, a matter of organizing and arranging sufficient debate. Once we have a firm hold on the central principle, there are many practical conclusions to be drawn. We then realize that the defense of freedom of opinion consists primarily in perfecting the opportunity for an adequate give-and-take of opinion; it consists also in regulating the freedom of those revolutionists who cannot or will not permit or maintain debate when it does not suit their purposes.

We must insist that free oratory is only the beginning of free speech; it is not the end, but a means to an end. The end is to find the truth. The practical justification of civil liberty is not that self-expression is one of the rights of man. It is that the examination of opinion is one of the necessities of man. For experience tells us that it is only when freedom of opinion becomes the compulsion to debate that the seed which our fathers planted has produced its fruit. When that is understood, freedom will be cherished not because it is a vent for our opinions but because it is the surest method of correcting them.

The unexamined life, said Socrates, is unfit to be lived by man. This is the virtue of liberty, and the ground on which we may best justify our belief in it, that it tolerates error in order to serve the truth. When men are brought face to face with their opponents, forced to listen and learn and mend their ideas, they cease to be children and savages and begin to live like civilized men. Then only is freedom a reality, when men may voice their opinions because they must examine their opinions.

III

The only reason for dwelling on all this is that if we are to preserve democracy we must understand its principles. And the principle which distinguishes it from all other forms of government is that in a democracy the opposition not only is tolerated as constitutional but must be maintained because it is in fact indispensable.

The democratic system cannot be operated without effective opposition. For, in making the great experiment of governing people by consent rather than by coercion, it is not sufficient that the party in power should have a majority. It is just as necessary that the party in power should never outrage the minority. That means that it must listen to the minority and be moved by the criticisms of the minority. That means that its measures must take account of the minority's objections, and that in administering measures it must remember that the minority may become the majority.

The opposition is indispensable. A good statesman, like any other sensible human being, always learns more from his opponents than from his fervent supporters. For his supporters will push him to disaster unless his opponents show him where the dangers are. So if he is wise he will often pray to be delivered from his friends, because they will ruin him. But, though it hurts, he ought also to pray never to be left without opponents; for they keep him on the path of reason and good sense.

The national unity of a free people depends upon a sufficiently even balance of political power to make it impracticable for the administration to be arbitrary and for the opposition to be revolutionary and irreconcilable. Where that balance no longer exists, democracy perishes. For unless all the citizens of a state are forced by circumstances to compromise, unless they feel that they can affect policy but that no one can wholly dominate it, unless by habit and necessity they have to give and take, freedom cannot be maintained.

13

UNWRITTEN RULES OF AMERICAN POLITICS *

JOHN FISCHER

The basic argument for a third party always remains the same. It is a persuasive argument, especially for well-meaning people who have not had much first-hand experience in politics. It runs something like this:

"Both of the traditional American parties are outrageous frauds. Neither the Republicans nor the Democrats have any fundamental principles or ideology. They do not even have a program. In every campaign the platforms of both parties are simply collections of noble generalities, muffled in the vaguest possible language; and in each case the two platforms are very nearly identical.

"Obviously, then, both parties are merely machines for grabbing power and distributing favors. In their lust for office they are quite

* From *Harper's Magazine*, November, 1948. Reprinted by permission.

willing to make a deal with anybody who can deliver a sizable block of votes. As a result, each party has become an outlandish cluster of local machines and special interest groups which have nothing in common except a lecherous craving for the public trough.

"This kind of political system"—so the argument runs—"is clearly meaningless. A man of high principles can never hope to accomplish anything through the old parties, because they are not interested in principle. Moreover, the whole arrangement is so illogical that it affronts every intelligent citizen. Consequently, it is the duty of every liberal to work for a tidier and more sensible political system.

"We ought to separate the sheep from the goats—to herd all the progressives on one side of the fence and all the conservatives on the other. Then politics really will have some meaning; we will know who the enemy is and where he stands; every campaign can be fought over clearly-defined issues. The Europeans, who are more sophisticated politically than we simple Americans, discovered this long ago, and in each of their countries they have arranged a neat political spectrum running from Left to Right.

"As a first step toward such a logical scheme of politics, we need to organize a progressive party with a precise ideology and a clearly formulated program." (Nowadays the implication usually is that such a program must be more or less Marxist, whether in the Communist or Social Democratic tradition.) "Such a party will rally together the labor movement, the farmers, and the white-collar liberals—and then it should have little trouble in defeating the reactionary business men who have long held such strategic positions in our old-fashioned political system." . . .

It sounds so plausible—at least on the surface—that it is hard to see why the idea has never made much headway. Indeed, many veteran third party enthusiasts have been able to account for their failure only by assuming a perverse and rock-headed stupidity among the American electorate. This, in turn, sometimes leads to a secret conviction that the dopes don't know what is good for them—and that what this country needs is a Strong Leader or a small, tough party of the enlightened, which can herd the ignorant masses up the road to Utopia whether they like it or not.

There is, however, one other possible explanation for the chronic failure of the third-party argument: maybe there is something wrong with the idea itself. Maybe it never gets to first base, not because the American voter is a hopeless dullard, but simply because he rejects instinctively a notion which doesn't make sense in terms of his own experience.

It can be argued, indeed, that a third party movement usually is an attempt to transplant a European concept of politics into an American setting—and that it fails because our own political tradition is more vigorous, more deeply rooted, and far better suited to our own peculiar needs. Such attempts often serve a useful purpose, as we shall see; but it is not the purpose which the evangels of the new party have in mind. Their whole endeavor, in fact, springs out of a profound misunderstanding of the way in which the American political system works.

Moreover, it seems to me that a careful look will show that our native scheme of politics is a more complex and subtle conception than the crude blacks and whites of the European ideological parties. And finally there is considerable evidence that our own system—in spite of certain dangerous weaknesses—has on the whole worked out more successfully than the European.

II

Perhaps it is the very subtlety of the American political tradition which is responsible for the almost universal misunderstanding of it abroad. Every practicing American politician grasps its principles by instinct; if he does not, he soon retires into some less demanding profession. Moreover, the overwhelming majority of citizens have a sound working knowledge of the system, which they apply every day of their lives—though many of them might have a hard time putting that knowledge into words. There are almost no foreigners, however (except perhaps D. W. Brogan), who really understand the underlying theory. Even the editors of the London *Economist*—probably the most brilliant and well-informed group of journalists practicing anywhere today—display their bewilderment week after week. To them, and to virtually all other European observers, our whole political scene looks arbitrary, irrational, and dangerous.

Another reason for this misunderstanding lies in the fact that surprisingly little has been written about the rules of American politics during our generation. The newspapers, textbooks, and learned journals are running over with discussions of tactics and mechanics—but no one, so far as I know, has bothered to trace out the basic tradition for a good many years.

In fact, the most useful discussion of this tradition which I have come across is the work of John C. Calhoun, published nearly a century ago. Today of course he is an almost forgotten figure, and many people take it for granted that his views were discredited for good by the Civil War. I know of only one writer—Peter F. Drucker of Bennington College—who has paid much attention to him in recent years. It was he who described Calhoun's ideas as "a major if not the only key to the understanding of what is specifically and uniquely American in our political system"; and I am indebted to Dr. Drucker for much of the case set forth here.

Calhoun summed up his political thought in what he called the Doctrine of the Concurrent Majority. He saw the United States as a nation of tremendous and frightening diversity—a collection of many different climates, races, cultures, religions, and economic patterns. He saw the constant tension among all these special interests, and he realized that the central problem of American politics was to find some way of holding these conflicting groups together.

It could not be done by force; no one group was strong enough to impose its will on all the others. The goal could be achieved only by compromise—and no real compromise could be possible if any threat of coercion lurked behind the door. Therefore, Calhoun reasoned, every vital decision in American life would have to be adopted by a "concurrent majority"—by which he meant, in effect, a unanimous agreement of all interested parties. No decision which affected the interests of the slaveholders, he argued, should be taken without their consent; and by implication he would have given a similar veto to every other special interest, whether it be labor, management, the Catholic Church, old-age pensioners, the silver miners, or the corn-growers of the Middle West.

Under the goad of the slavery issue, Calhoun was driven to state his doctrine in an extreme and unworkable form. If every sectional interest had been given the explicit legal veto power which he called for, the government obviously would have been paralyzed. . . . It is the very essence of the idea of "concurrent majority" that it cannot be made legal and official. It can operate effectively only as an informal, highly elastic, and generally accepted understanding. Perhaps the best example is the Quaker church meeting, where decisions are not reached by formal vote at all, but rather by a give-and-take discussion which continues until "the sense of the meeting" jells and is accepted by everybody present.

Moreover, government by concurrent majority can exist only when no one power is strong enough to dominate completely, *and then only when all of the contending interest groups recognize and abide by certain rules of the game.*

These rules are the fundamental bond of unity in American political life. They can be summed up as a habit of extraordinary toleration, plus "equality" in the peculiar American meaning of that term which cannot be translated into any other language, even into the English of Great Britain. Under these rules every group tacitly binds itself to tolerate the interests and opinions of every other group. It must not try to impose its views on others, nor can it press its own special interest to the point where they seriously endanger the interests of other groups or of the nation as a whole.

Furthermore, each group must exercise its implied veto with responsibility and discretion; and in times of great emergency it must forsake its veto right altogether. It dare not be intransigent or doctrinaire. It must make every conceivable effort to compromise, relying on its veto only as a last resort. For if any player wields this weapon recklessly, the game will break up—or all the other players will turn on him in anger, suspend the rules for the time being, and maul those very interests he is trying so desperately hard to protect. That was what happened in 1860, when the followers of Calhoun carried his doctrine to an unbearable extreme. Much the same thing, on a less violent scale, happened to American business interests in 1933 and to the labor unions in 1947.

This is the somewhat elusive sense, it seems to me, in which Calhoun's theory has been adopted by the American people. But elusive and subtle as it may be, it remains the basic rule of the game of politics in this country—and in this country alone. Nothing comparable exists in any other nation, although the British, in a different way, have applied their own rules of responsibility and self-restraint.

It is a rule which operates unofficially and entirely outside the Constitution—but it has given us a method by which all the official and Constitutional organs of government can be made to work. It also provides a means of selecting leaders on all levels of our political life, for hammering out policies, and for organizing and managing the conquest of political power.

III

The way in which this tradition works in practice can be observed most easily in Congress. Anyone who has ever tried to push through a piece of legislation quickly discovers that the basic units of organization on Capitol Hill are not the parties, but the so-called blocs, which are familiar to everyone who reads a newspaper. There are dozens of them—the farm bloc, the silver bloc, the friends of labor, the business group, the Midwestern isolationists, the public power bloc—and they all cut across party lines.

They are loosely organized and pretty blurred at the edges, so that every Congressman belongs at different times to several different blocs. Each of them represents a special interest group. Each of them ordinarily works hand-in-hand with that group's Washington lobby. In passing, it might be noted that these lobbies are by no means the cancerous growth which is sometimes pictured in civics textbooks. They have become an indispensable part of the political machine—the accepted channel through which American citizens make their wishes known and play their day-to-day role in the process of government. Nor is their influence measured solely by the size of the bankrolls and propaganda apparatus which they have at their disposal. Some of the smallest and poorest lobbies are often more effective than their well-heeled rivals. For example, Russell Smith, the one-man lobby of the Farmers Union, was largely responsible for conceiving and nursing through Congress the Employment Act of 1946, one of the most far-reaching measures adopted since the war.

Now it is an unwritten but firm rule of Congress that no important bloc shall ever be voted down—under normal circumstances—on any matter which touches its own vital interests. Each of them, in other words, has a tacit right of veto on legislation in which it is primarily concerned. The ultimate expression of this right is the institution—uniquely American—of the filibuster in the Senate. Recently it has acquired a bad name among liberals because the Southern conservatives have used it ruthlessly to fight off civil rights legislation and protect white supremacy. Not so long ago, however, the filibuster was the stoutest weapon of such men as Norris and the LaFollettes in defending many a progressive cause. . . .

Naturally no bloc wants to exercise its veto power except when it is absolutely forced to—for this is a negative power, and one which is always subject to retaliation. Positive power to influence legislation, on the other hand, can be gained only by conciliation, compromise, and endless horse-trading.

The farm bloc, for instance, normally needs no outside aid to halt the passage of a hostile bill. As a last resort, three or four strong-lunged statesmen from the corn belt can always filibuster it to death in the Senate. If the bloc wants to put through a measure to support agricultural prices, however, it can succeed only by enlisting the help of other powerful special interest groups. Consequently, it must always be careful not to antagonize any potential ally by a reckless use of the veto; and it must be willing to pay for such help by throwing its support from time to time behind legislation sought by the labor bloc, the National Association of Manufacturers, or the school-teachers' lobby.

The classic alliance of this sort was formed in the early days of the New Deal, when most of the Roosevelt legislation was shoved onto the statute books by a temporary coalition of the farm bloc and urban labor, occasionally reinforced by such minor allies as the public power group and spokesmen for the northern Negroes. Mr. Roosevelt's political genius rested largely on his ability to put together a program which would offer something to each of these groups without fatally antagonizing any of them, and then to time the presentation of each bill so that he would always retain enough bargaining power to line up a Congressional majority. It was also necessary for him to avoid the veto of the business group, which viewed much of this legislation as a barbarous assault upon its privileges; and for this purpose he employed another traditional technique, which we shall examine a little later.

This process of trading blocs of votes is generally known as log-rolling, and frequently it is deplored by the more innocent type of reformer. Such pious disapproval has no effect whatever on any practicing politician. He knows that log-rolling is a sensible and reasonably fair device, and that without it Congress could scarcely operate at all.

In fact, Congress gradually has developed a formal apparatus—the committee system—which is designed to make the log-rolling process as smooth and efficient as possible. There is no parallel system anywhere; the committees of Parliament and of the Continental legislative bodies work in an entirely different way.

Obviously the main business of Congress—the hammering out of a series of compromises between many special interest groups—cannot be conducted satisfactorily on the floor of the House or Senate. The meetings there are too large and far too public for such delicate negotiations. Moreover, every speech delivered on the floor must be aimed primarily at the voters back home, and not at the other members in the chamber. Therefore, Congress—especially the House—does nearly all its work in the closed sessions of its various committees, simply because the committee room is the only place where it is possible to arrange a compromise acceptable to all major interests affected.

For this reason, it is a matter of considerable importance to get a bill before the proper committee. Each committee serves as a forum for a particular cluster of special interests, and the assignment of a bill to a specific committee often decides which interests shall be recognized officially as affected by the measure and therefore entitled to a hand in its drafting. "Who is to have standing before the committee" is the technical term, and it is this decision that frequently decides the fate of the legislation.

IV

Calhoun's principles of the concurrent majority and of sectional compromise operate just as powerfully, though sometimes less obviously, in every other American political institution. Our cabinet, for example, is the only one in the world where members are charged by law with the representation of special interests—labor, agriculture, commerce, and so on. In other countries, each agency of government is at least presumed to act for the nation as a whole; here most agencies are expected to behave as servants for one interest or another. The Veterans' Administration, to cite the most familiar case, is frankly intended to look out for Our Boys; the Maritime Commission is the spokesman for the shipping industry; the National Labor Relations Board, as originally established under the Wagner Act, was explicity intended to build up the bargaining power of the unions.

Even within a single department, separate agencies are sometimes set up to represent conflicting interests. Thus in the Department of Agriculture under the New Deal the old Triple-A became primarily an instrument of the large-scale commercial farmers, as represented by their lobby, the Farm Bureau Federation; while the Farm Security Administration went to bat for the tenants, the farm laborers, and the little subsistence farmers, as represented by the Farmers Union.

This is one reason why federal agencies often struggle so bitterly against each other, and why the position of the administration as a whole on any question can be determined only after a long period of inter-bureau squabbling and compromise. Anyone who was in Washington during the war will remember how these goings-on always confused and alarmed our British allies.

Calhoun's laws also govern the selection of virtually every candidate for public office. The mystery of "eligibility" which has eluded most foreign observers simply means that a candidate must not be unacceptable to any important special interest group—a negative rather than a positive qualification. A case of this process at work was the selection of Mr. Truman as the Democrats' Vice Presidential candidate in 1944. As Edward J. Flynn, the Boss of the Bronx, has pointed out in his memoirs, Truman was the one man "who would hurt . . . least" as Roosevelt's running mate. Many stronger men were disqualified, Flynn explained, by the tacit veto of one sectional interest or another. Wallace was unacceptable to the business men and to many local party machines. Byrnes was distasteful to the Catholics, the Negroes, and organized labor. Rayburn came from the wrong part of the country. Truman, however, came from a border state, his labor record was good, he had not antagonized the conservatives, and—as Flynn put it—"he had never made any 'racial' remarks. He just dropped into the slot."

The same kind of considerations govern the selection of candidates right down to the county, city, and precinct levels. Flynn, one of the most successful political operators of our time, explained in some detail the complicated job of making up a ticket in his own domain. Each of the main population groups in the Bronx—Italians,

Jews, and Irish Catholics—must be properly represented on the list of nominees, and so must each of the main geographical divisions. The result is a ticket which sounds like the roster of the Brooklyn Dodgers: Loreto, Delagi, Lyman, Joseph, Lyons, and Foley.

Comparable traditions govern the internal political life of the American Legion, the Federation of Women's Clubs, university student bodies, labor unions, Rotary Clubs, and the thousands of other quasi-political institutions which are so characteristic of our society and which give us such a rich fabric of spontaneous local government.

The stronghold of Calhoun's doctrine, however, is the American party—the wonder and despair of foreigners who cannot fit it into any of their concepts of political life.

The purpose of European parties is, of course, to divide men of different ideologies into coherent and disciplined organizations. The historic role of the American party, on the other hand, is not to divide but to unite. That task was imposed by simple necessity. If a division into ideological parties had been attempted, in addition to all the other centrifugal forces in this country, it very probably would have proved impossible to hold the nation together. The Founding Fathers understood this thoroughly; hence Washington's warning against "factions."

Indeed, on the one occasion when we did develop two ideological parties, squarely opposing each other on an issue of principle, the result was civil war. Fortunately, that was our last large-scale experiment with a third party formed on an ideological basis—for in its early days that is just what the Republican party was.

Its radical wing, led by such men as Thaddeus Stevens, Seward, and Chase, made a determined and skillful effort to substitute principles for interests as the foundations of American political life. Even within their own party, however, they were opposed by such practical politicians as Lincoln and Johnson—men who distrusted fanaticism in any form—and by the end of the Reconstruction period the experiment had been abandoned. American politics then swung back into its normal path and has never veered far away from it since. Although Calhoun's cause was defeated, his political theory came through the Civil War stronger than ever.

The result is that the American party has no permanent program and no fixed aim, except to win elections. Its one purpose is to unite the largest possible number of divergent interest groups in the pursuit of power. Its unity is one of compromise, not of dogma. It must—if it hopes to succeed—appeal to considerable numbers on both the left and the right, to rich and to poor, Protestant and Catholic, farmer and industrial worker, native and foreign born.

It must be ready to bid for the support of any group that can deliver a sizable chunk of votes, accepting that group's program with whatever modifications may be necessary to reconcile the other members of the party. If sun worship, or Existentialism, or the nationalization of industry should ever attract any significant following in this country, you can be sure that both parties would soon whip up a plank designed to win it over.

This ability to absorb new ideas (along with the enthusiasts behind them) and to mold them into a shape acceptable to the party's standpatters is, perhaps, the chief measure of vitality in the party's leadership. Such ideas almost never germinate within the party itself. They are stolen—very often from third parties.

Indeed, the historic function of third parties has been to sprout new issues, nurse them along until they have gathered a body of supporters worth stealing, and then to turn them over (often reluctantly) to the major parties. A glance at the old platforms of the Populists, the Bull Moosers, and the Socialists will show what an astonishingly high percentage of their once-radical notions have been purloined by both Republicans and Democrats—and enacted into law. Thus the income tax, child-labor laws, minimum wages, regulation of railroads and utilities, and old-age pensions have all become a part of the American Way of Life. . . .

While each major party always must stand alert to grab a promising new issue, it also must be careful never to scare off any of the big, established interest groups. For as soon as it alienates any one of them, it finds itself in a state of crisis.

For sixteen years the Republicans lost much of their standing as a truly national party because they had made themselves unacceptable to labor. Similarly, the Democrats during the middle stage of the New Deal incurred the wrath of the business interests. Ever since Mr. Truman was plumped into the White House, the Democratic leadership has struggled desperately—though rather ineptly—to regain the confidence of business men without at the same time driving organized labor out of the ranks. It probably would be safe to predict that if the Republican party is to regain a long period of health, it must . . . make an equally vigorous effort to win back the confidence of labor. For the permanent veto of any major element in American society means political death—as the ghosts of the Federalists and Whigs can testify.

V

The weaknesses of the American political system are obvious—much more obvious, in fact, than its virtues. These weaknesses have been so sharply criticized for the past hundred years, by a procession of able analysts ranging from Walter Bagehot to Thomas K. Finletter, that it is hardly necessary to mention them here. It is enough to note that most of the criticism has been aimed at two major flaws.

First, it is apparent that the doctrine of the concurrent majority is a negative one—a principle of inaction. A strong government, capable of rapid and decisive action, is difficult to achieve under a system which forbids it to do anything until virtually everybody acquiesces. In times of crisis, a dangerously long period of debate and compromise usually is necessary before any administration can carry out the drastic measures needed. The depression of the early thirties, the crisis in foreign policy which ended only with Pearl Harbor, the equally great crisis of the Marshall program a few months ago all illustrate this recurring problem.

This same characteristic of our system gives undue weight to the small but well-organized pressure group—especially when it is fighting against something. Hence a few power companies were able to block for twenty years the sensible use of the Muscle Shoals dam which eventually became the nucleus of TVA, and—in alliance with the railroads, rail unions, and Eastern port interests—they are still holding up the development of the St. Lawrence Waterway . . . .

The negative character of our political rules also makes it uncommonly difficult for us to choose a President. Many of our outstanding political operatives—notably those who serve in the Senate—are virtually barred from a Presidential nomination because they are forced to get on record on too many issues. Inevitably they offend some important interest group, and therefore become "unavailable." Governors, who can keep their mouths shut on most national issues, have a much better chance to reach the White House. Moreover, the very qualities of caution and inoffensiveness which make a good candidate—Harding and Coolidge come most readily to mind—are likely to make a bad President.

An even more serious flaw in our scheme of politics is the difficulty in finding anybody to speak for the country as a whole. Calhoun would have argued that the national interest is merely the sum of all the various special interests, and therefore needs no spokesmen of its own—but in this case he clearly was wrong.

In practice, we tend to settle sectional and class conflicts at the expense of the nation as a whole—with results painful to all of us. The labor troubles in the spring of 1946, for instance, could be settled only on a basis acceptable to both labor and management: that is, on the basis of higher wages plus higher prices. The upshot was an inflationary spiral . . . Countless other instances, from soil erosion to the rash of billboards along our highways, bear witness to the American tendency to neglect matters which are "only" of national interest, and therefore are left without a recognized sponsor.

Over the generations we have developed a series of practices and institutions which partly remedy these weaknesses, although we are still far from a complete cure. One such development has been the gradual strengthening of the Presidency as against Congress. As the only man elected by all the people, the President inevitably has had to take over many of the policy-making and leadership functions which the Founding Fathers originally assigned to the legislators. This meant, of course, that he could no longer behave merely as an obedient executor of the will of Congress, but was forced into increasingly frequent conflicts with Capitol Hill.

Today we have come to recognize that this conflict is one of the most important obligations of the Presidency. No really strong executive tries to avoid it—he accepts it as an essential part of his job. If he simply tries to placate the pressure groups which speak through Congress, history writes him down as a failure. For it is his duty to enlist the support of many minorities for measures rooted in the national interest, reaching beyond their own immediate concern—and, if necessary, to stand up against the ravening minorities for the interest of the whole.

In recent times this particular part of the President's job has been made easier by the growth of the Theory of Temporary Emergencies. All of us—or nearly all—have come around to admitting that in time of emergency special interest groups must forgo their right to veto. As a result, the President often is tempted to scare up an emergency to secure legislation which could not be passed under any other pretext. Thus, most of the New Deal bills were introduced as "temporary emergency measures," although they were clearly intended to be permanent from the very first; for in no other way could Mr. Roosevelt avoid the veto of the business interests.

Again, in 1939 the threat of war enabled the President to push through much legislation which would have been impossible under normal circumstances. And Mr. Truman recently found it necessary to present the Greco-Turkish situation under the guise of a world crisis, in order to get authority and funds to carry out a rather small, routine police operation.

VI

Because we have been so preoccupied with trying to patch up the flaws in our system, we have often overlooked its unique elements of strength. The chief of these is its ability to minimize conflict—not by suppressing the conflicting forces, but by absorbing and utilizing them. The result is a society which is both free and reasonably stable—a government which is as strong and effective as most dictatorships, but which can still adapt itself to social change.

The way in which the American political organism tames down the extremists of both the left and right is always fascinating to watch. Either party normally is willing to embrace any group or movement which can deliver votes—but in return it requires these groups to adjust their programs to fit the traditions, beliefs, and prejudices of the majority of the people. The fanatics, the implacable radicals cannot hope to get to first base in American politics until they abandon their fanaticism and learn the habits of conciliation. As a consequence, it is almost impossible for political movements here to become entirely irresponsible and to draw strength from the kind of demagogic obstruction which has nurtured both Communist and Fascist movements abroad.

The same process which gentles down the extremists also prods along the political laggards. As long as it is in a state of health, each

American party has a conservative and a liberal wing. Sometimes one is dominant, sometimes the other . . . .

The strength of this tug is indicated by the fact that the major New Deal reforms have now been almost universally accepted. A mere ten years ago, the leading Republicans, plus many conservative Democrats, were hell-bent on wiping out social security, TVA, SEC, minimum-wage laws, rural electrification, and all the other dread innovations of the New Deal. Today no Presidential aspirant would dare suggest the repeal of a single one of them. In this country there simply is no place for a hard core of irreconcilable reactionaries, comparable to those political groups in France which have never yet accepted the reforms of the French Revolution.

This American tendency to push extremists of both the left and right toward a middle position has enabled us, so far, to escape class warfare. This is no small achievement for any political system; for class warfare cannot be tolerated by a modern industrial society. If it seriously threatens, it is bound to be suppressed by some form of totalitarianism, as it has been in Germany, Spain, Italy, Russia, and most of Eastern Europe.

In fact, suppression might be termed the normal method of settling conflicts in continental Europe, where parties traditionally have been drawn up along ideological battle lines. Every political campaign becomes a religious crusade; each party is fanatically convinced that it and it alone has truth by the tail; each party is certain that its opponents not only are wrong, but wicked. If the sacred ideology is to be established beyond challenge, no heresy can be tolerated. Therefore it becomes a duty not only to defeat the enemy at the polls, but to wipe him out. Any suggestion of compromise must be rejected as treason and betrayal of the true faith. The party must be disciplined like an army, and if it cannot win by other means it must be ready to take up arms in deadly fact.

Politics thus becomes merely a prelude to civil war—and all too often the prelude is short. In Italy the Partisan brigades are drilling today on the same parade grounds where Mussolini's Blackshirts once trained for their march on Rome. And in France both Communists and DeGaullists are reported to be squirreling away Bren guns against the day when each expects to "save the Republic" from the other.

Under this kind of political system the best that can be hoped for is a prolonged deadlock between parties which are too numerous and weak to exterminate one another. The classic example is prewar France, where six revolutions or near-revolutions broke out within a century, where cabinets fell every weekend, and no government could ever become strong enough to govern effectively. The more usual outcome is a complete victory for one ideology or another, after a brief period of electioneering, turmoil, and fighting in the streets; then comes the liquidation of the defeated.

Because this sort of ideological politics is so foreign to our native tradition, neither Socialists, Communists, nor Fascists have ever been accepted as normal parties. So long as that tradition retains its very considerable vitality, it seems to me unlikely that any third party founded on an ideological basis can take root. The notion of a ruthless and unlimited class struggle, the concept of a master race, a Fascist elite, or a proletariat which is entitled to impose its will on all others—these are ideas which are incompatible with the main current of American political life. The uncompromising ideologist, of whatever faith, appears in our eyes peculiarly "un-American," simply because he cannot recognize the rule of the concurrent majority, nor can he accept the rules of mutual toleration which are necessary to make it work. Unless he forsakes his ideology, he cannot even understand that basic principle of American politics which was perhaps best expressed by Judge Learned Hand: "The spirit of liberty is the spirit which is not too sure that it is right."

14

CAN WE AFFORD TO KEEP OPEN MINDS? *

BERTRAND RUSSELL

When I was in Russia in 1920 I made friends with a man of a very rare species. He was an officer in the Red Army, but was an aristocrat and had been an officer in the Imperial Guards. I said something critical of the new regime for its denial of intellectual freedom. "You English," he replied, "can permit outward freedom be-

* From *The New York Times Magazine*, June 1, 1950. Reprinted by permission of the author.

cause your souls are in strait-jackets. We Russians have free souls and therefore need external discipline."

This Russian officer felt that if you thought freely about everything you would become hopelessly chaotic. Is it not necessary to have fixed points about which to build the system of one's conduct and one's belief?

Should I be Communist or anti-Communist? Should I be orthodox or liberal in ideology? Should I think that science opens the gateway to paradise or that it is inspired by the devil and leads to hell? It is scarcely possible to live a consistent and fruitful life unless one has already come to a decision on such issues.

It may be said that a mind perpetually open will be perpetually vacant. It is none the less clear that it would be disastrous for the mind to be in no degree open. I wish to discuss what compromise ought to be arrived at between these two opposites.

Let us begin with a parable. There were once upon a time two motorists, each of whom had to find an obscure village on a dark winter evening. The village could be approached only by small winding roads, and the map was confusing. One of the motorists had an open mind; at every fork in the road he studied the map, but found it puzzling, so he waited till someone came by. He took this person's advice tentatively, but the next person he met said the opposite. So, with great difficulty in the narrow lane, he turned around and went back to the fork. After innumerable zigzags he was compelled to sleep in the inadequate shelter of a haystack. So much for the open mind.

The other motorist, who was a believer in vigorous action, studied the map carefully, chose his road, and then kept on as nearly in a straight line as the road would let him. In spite of the darkness and of sudden turns and twists, he drove fast to show his will power. But alas! poor fellow, he did not know that the road ended abruptly at the top of a cliff. He drove straight over the edge and was drowned. So much for resoluteness.

It is obvious that an open mind is a good thing within certain limits, but not outside them. However sure you may feel that you are on the right road, if you see a large notice saying: "Stop! Precipice Ahead," you will be well advised to change your mind. But if you keep an open mind all the time, you will never get anywhere.

The questions about which you should have an open mind depend upon your age and your occupation. It is no use perpetually reconsidering the decisions that have determined the framework of your life. A young man, let us say, is in doubt as to whether he shall become a doctor or a lawyer, and until the moment when a decision becomes necessary he does well to weigh the pros and cons carefully. But when he has decided, no purpose whatever is served by asking himself once a day, or once a month, or once a year, whether the opposite decision would not have been wiser. Even this, however, cannot be said absolutely. He might be a lawyer in a country that became totalitarian, and he might find that, if he remained in the profession, he would have to help in securing the condemnation of innocent men. In that case he might decide to throw up his profession.

But such cases are extreme. You cannot expect, say, the Archbishop of Canterbury, the Grand Mufti, and the Dalai Lama, if they met by accident on a ship, to be completely receptive to each other's theology, since no one of the three could carry on his work if he allowed one of the others to convert him. On the other hand, if you were a university professor whose subject was comparative religion, it would be your duty to see the good and bad in each impartially, and to divest yourself as far as possible of the bias derived from your upbringing. In that case, however, you would have to close your mind against arguments to the effect that the study of comparative religions is dangerously subversive.

It is clear that for every man at every moment there is a degree of open-mindedness, and a direction of open-mindedness, which is desirable; more than this, or less than this, leads to bad results. A completely open mind is either a disease or a pretense; a completely closed mind is a useless assemblage of indefensible prejudices.

As a general rule, it is good to be open-minded about whatever does not affect adversely the broad pattern of your life. For this reason, the young should have a larger area of uncertainty than the old or middle-aged. When you have not yet chosen your profession or your wife, the region of profitable inward debate is much more extensive than it becomes when your choice is made. But you still need an open mind about technical questions in your profession.

Suppose, like the doctor in Shaw's "Philanderer," you think you have discovered a new disease, and some other doctor shows that you were mistaken; you should admit the fact, however painful it may be to your self-esteem. Suppose Lysenko were to produce irrefutable experimental evidence of the inheritance of acquired characters; Mendelians would be to blame if they refused to recognize his results. Suppose the leader of your political party turns out to be criminally corrupt; you will show less than the right degree of open-mindedness if you refuse to give due weight to the evidence.

I think it may be laid down that one should never refuse to admit definitely ascertained facts, however awkward they may be. But the scope of this principle is not nearly so wide as it seems to be. Awkward facts are denied by dishonest propagandists, and the plain man does not know whom to believe. How much time can a plain man be expected to spend trying to find out who is right when the facts are in dispute? Obviously not much. The newspapers ought to help him, but often they do not, especially as he probably reads only those with whose bias he agrees. Political passions make party issues of matters which ought to be uncontroversial. In the Presidential election of 1800 it was a party question whether there were still mammoths in America. Was Trotsky killed by agents of the Soviet Government? Communists say no; everybody else says yes. What is the plain man to do in such circumstances? His only choice is between party prejudice and skepticism, since he cannot devote years to ascertaining the facts.

But this is too absolute. How about democracy? you may object—and, I think, with justice. We are faced with large and difficult issues, and if we believe in democracy we think that, in their main lines, they should be decided by busy men and women with little knowledge and little time for political thinking. I myself hold this view, but it would not be difficult to make a plausible case against it.

In a democracy, if party government is established, about 90 per cent of the population are unshakable adherents of this party or that. It is the remaining 10 per cent who decide which party shall be in power. This 10 per cent, therefore, really govern the country. Since they change their party from time to time, they may be supposed to be more open-minded about a small number of questions. There are many things about which the parties in one country agree, while those in another country agree in an opposite opinion. Do we desire the larger degree of open-mindedness that would extend to matters in which there are national differences of opinion?

The question is so difficult and complex, and my own feelings are so divided, that I do not see how to discuss it except in the form of a debate. I shall bring forward Mr. A as the advocate of openmindedness, and Mr. B as the champion of vigorous group-cooperation. I sympathize with the sentiments of both, except when they think each other completely mistaken. I will call first on Mr. A.

Mr. A. I don't see how there can be two sides to this question. Here we are, all quarreling, all getting ready to exterminate each other, for what? To uphold by force what cannot be upheld by reason. If only everybody would recognize that politics is a very complicated affair, and that there is no such certainty about it as there is about the multiplication table, all our troubles would be at an end. If great nations were mentally adult, instead of saying to each other, "I'm right and you are wrong, and if you don't admit it I shall kill you," they would say, "This is a difficult problem, and on the whole I think there is a slight balance of probability on my side, but I quite admit that you *may* be right." If nations behaved in this way, we could all be happy.

Mr. B. My dear fellow, you must have been living in the moon. Of course, all would be well if we were all angels. That is not the problem. The problem is what to do with people who very obviously are not angels. If you found a burglar in your house, and you had the means to deal with him, would you say: "I am aware that there have been many disputes as to the way in which property should be distributed, and it may be that you have less and I have more than would result from an equitable division. As to that, I have an open mind, so I shall let you go with your booty." If you said this, the burglar would be the first to conclude that you were mad. And that is just the sort of situation with which we are faced.

Mr. A. I don't think you are being quite fair to our enemies. Absurd as it may seem to you, they would maintain that it is we who are the burglars. Proudhon said: "Property is theft." Communists believe this, or profess to believe it. And so, when they invade a capitalist country and oust the owners of property, they can justify themselves by saying that they are depriving a set of robbers of their ill-gotten gains. I am not saying that I agree with them, but I am saying that we ought to keep an open mind on such a difficult question as the rights of property.

Mr. B. Open mind! There is a time for thought and a time for action. When you are designing a ship, it is the time for thought; but when the ship is sinking in a storm it is too late for delicate hydostatic calculations. Our ship of state is in a storm, and it is time for the order "all hands to the pumps."

Mr. A. You can prove anything by metaphors, but your ship in a storm can be turned against you, since information by radio may enable the captain to get out of the storm. Perhaps there is information available which would enable our ship of state to get into calmer waters, and perhaps the hysterical excitement that you seem to recommend will close people's minds against this information. I don't say this is so, I only say it may be.

Mr. B. My dear sir, you make me sick. If you were a man and not a worm, you would be up and doing, not sitting still thinking up frivolous nonsense. Good day to you.

Mr. A. (to himself). Well I daresay he's right.

And so Mr. A preserves an open mind to the last. Presently they drop a hydrogen bomb on him, and as he is about to disintegrate he murmurs once more, for the last time, the words by which he has guided his life: "Well, I daresay they're right." Mr. B. is equally exterminated, but his last words are: "We'll get even with the swines yet."

Is either right? And is either wrong?

If you preserve an open mind all the time and about everything, you will accomplish nothing, and it is hard to see why the world should accord board and lodging to so useless a person. But if you close your mind too soon or too absolutely, you may persist in a course that ends in avoidable disaster. The right course, whether for an individual or for a nation, is first to think carefully, with a completely open mind, and then, having come to a decision, not to reconsider it, unless some very important new fact changes the situation. I cannot respect a man who, on the great issues of his time, shirks the responsibility of a decision, and is content to repeat endlessly: "Well, on the other hand . . . but on the other . . ." In such an attitude on an issue that is vital to everybody there is something that savors of cowardice. Men who take this attitude are like those who incur Dante's contempt for being neither for God nor for his enemies.

Nevertheless, there remains always a field for open-mindedness. One should still make an effort to get facts straight. How many people in Russia are condemned to forced labor? Various estimates have been made, and if one has decided against Russia there is a temptation to adopt the largest estimate, even if the evidence is inadequate, while a fellow-traveler will automatically adopt the smallest estimate. And worse than this: there must still be a *possibility* of fundamental change of direction. Russia may some day become more liberal and more conciliatory, and if that happened it would be a misfortune if the West persisted in an attitude which had ceased to be reasonable. Communists, for the most part, are singularly incapable of this type of open-mindedness; when they are not, it is all to the good, as anybody may see by reading "The God That Failed," in which six ex-Communists give the reasons for their loss of faith.

This brings us up sharply against the real issue. When there is a clash between two groups of fanatics everybody will admit that the fanaticism of the opposite party is regrettable, but neither side will condemn its own. I think this was a mistake then, and is a mistake now. A good cause can be upheld without fanaticism, and when it invokes the aid of fanaticism it becomes less good. In the late war the Japanese were certainly more fanatical than the Americans, but that did not save them from defeat; on the contrary, by leading them to embark on war it was the direct cause of their defeat. It is easy, without any fanaticism, to see that life in America is happier than life in Russia or in pre-war Japan. If we, on our side, had been as fanatical as the Japanese and the Nazis, the war would not have been won a day sooner; in fact, victory would probably have come later than it did. The more we substitute fanaticism for a rational appraisal of evils to be combated, the more we sacrifice the moral advantages which are our greatest assets.

I conclude that there is a degree of open-mindedness which is disastrously paralyzing at any time, and that at moments of acute crisis there has to be less willingness to reconsider fundamental decisions than at other times. But mankind is so prone to prejudice, party bias, collective hysteria, and unthinking acceptance of propaganda, that there is almost always and almost everywhere too little of the open mind, not too much. While, therefore, truth compels me to acknowledge the theoretical limitations of the open mind, in practice I should find it almost always wise to advocate it, since the utmost advocacy is not likely to produce enough of it, and since its absence is one of the chief reasons for the appalling dangers by which, in our age, the human race is beset.

C

The Research Paper

To scholars and scientists *research* means intensive, critical investigation leading to new knowledge. A "research paper" in learned circles therefore contributes something original in its field. Of course its scope is limited: it is less than a book or dissertation. But to be worth the time of the experts it has to be thorough and original; its evidence must be verifiable; its conclusions must be fully supported.

The so-called research papers that students in English courses are asked to write have less ambitious aims. These papers will not very likely startle the experts. Rather they teach students something about the method and attitude necessary to write well for informed, critical, and even skeptical readers.

This assignment gets the student acquainted with the library and some of its resources. It teaches something of reading and taking notes *for a purpose*. It teaches the elements of "documentation"—that is, footnoting and other devices for carefully labeling the sources of evidence. Finally, it gives the student an opportunity to apply many things he has learned about reporting facts, analyzing, and reasoning—all to produce a coherent, original defense of his own judgment.

So the assignment to "write a research paper" is quite a challenge. It says, "Here, put to constructive use what you've learned about finding evidence, defining, analyzing, reasoning. Let's see you write something *all your own* that would stand up pretty well under the skeptical gaze of readers who know the field you're writing about."

Of course this research paper is not a string of quotations or summaries from things you've read or heard. That's a way to show you've read widely, perhaps, but it does nothing for readers.

Again, this research paper is not dependent upon a single source. If one of your sources "has everything" you want to say, then you have no reason for writing a research paper.

Chapter 5, 6, 7, and 8 of this book can all contribute to writing a good research paper. If you understand your purpose and the kind of readers you have to satisfy, it isn't necessary to repeat here all the requirements of analyzing a problem and defending a judgment.

The one element of the research paper that does need special attention is *documentation*. The research paper is expected to cite the exact source (with enough detail to enable the reader to check everything for himself) of any information or evidence that has signficance. The conventional means of documentation are:

1. Within the text itself
2. In footnotes
3. In end notes

The simplest method, when it doesn't interrupt the reader in a hurry to get along with your discussion, is to name the source of a quotation or statement right in the text:

The Fourth Amendment to the Constitution reads:

(The "Constitution" has no copyright. It is available in many publications. A footnote citing a particular publisher, etc. would be unnecessary.)

In the College Catalog the course Art 74 is described as follows:

(The "College Catalog" is the source. If we know the college we know where to look. A footnote here would serve no useful purpose.)

Even when you use footnotes, if the *name* of your witness or source is important or interesting, *put it in the text.* An important quotation from George Washington or Adolf Hitler should name him first, regardless of footnote.

The general principle here is: Never *make* a reader go to footnotes except for supplementary information that isn't necessary to understand your main discussion.

When do you use footnotes? Generally for these reasons:

1. You quote directly—use the exact words of an author—and must give the precise source for possible verification.

2. You use facts, expert testimony, or statistics—not necessarily as actual quotations—and must tell your reader exactly where you got them.
3. You present some hypothesis, interpretation or argument that you got from somebody else. If it isn't original, tell your readers where you got it.

But don't use footnotes—and don't name the "source"—for matters of general knowledge. You don't document a statement that "water doesn't run uphill" or "President Eisenhower was victor over Adlai Stevenson in 1956."

One troublesome problem may be: "What do I quote—and how much?" If most or all your material, except your judgments and what you do with the material, comes from reading, how much do you quote and how much do you summarize or paraphrase?

Generally, use direct quotations only for some clear purpose:

1. To show exactly what an expert or authority actually said.
2. To support your case with a reasoned argument by somebody else.
3. To set up an argument or view that you want to criticize or attack.
4. To present phrases or statements that are points of issue (such as provisions in a contract or law).
5. Just for emphasis, to take advantage of some original and striking expressions—better said than you can say them yourself.

Most students use too many quotations. They are useful—often necessary. But don't quote anything you don't need; be sure you get more when you quote than you would get from summary or paraphrase.

The advantages of *conventional* footnotes (or endnotes) is that educated readers are familiar with the conventions, know what the common abbreviations mean, and can get what they're after with a minimum of confusion.

You indicate the existence of a footnote by an arabic numeral [1] or an asterisk * which directs the reader to the bottom of the page or the end of chapter or whole composition. Put that symbol at a key position, after a word, statement, or quotation that might lead a critical reader to ask questions:

a. Lloyd Paul Stryker [2] insists . . . (*who* is Stryker? the footnote says who he is.)
b. Lloyd Paul Stryker, well-known trial lawyer, has said [2] . . . (*where* did he say this? the footnote tells exactly where.)
c. In a period of ten weeks more than 2300 cases came to the attention of physicians.[3] (*what* is the source of this report? the footnote tells the exact source.)

The footnotes themselves include the essential information about sources that enable any reader to look them up for himself if he doubts your word or wants to learn more.

Reference to quotations or other details from a book:

4 Frederick Barry, *The Scientific Habit of Thought,* Columbia University Press, 1927, pp. 141–2

Reference to an article in a magazine or journal:

5 Joyce Cary, "Political and Personal Morality," *The Saturday Review,* December 31, 1955

Reference to newspaper pieces:

6 "TVA's Letter on Dixon-Yates Deal" (letters to editor), *Knoxville News-Sentinel,* Aug. 11, 1954, p. 18, col. 3–5

Reference to the source named immediately above:

7 *Ibid.*

Reference to book or "work" named in an earlier footnote:

8 Barry, *op. cit.,* p. 230

Reference to article named in earlier footnote:

9 Cary, *loc. cit.*

Reference to sources you haven't seen at first hand, named by sources you name:

10 Theodor Mommsen, *History of Rome,* vol. ii, p. 43 (Dickson's translation, edition of 1873)—quoted *by* Gerald W. Johnson in *Incredible Tale,* Harper & Brothers, 1950, pp. 273–4

Here are common abbreviations appropriate in footnotes that you may want to use yourself. You will need to know what they mean to understand footnotes in what you read:

c., ca. (Latin *circa,* meaning "about"—used to show an approximate date: *c.* 1250)

cf. ("Compare"—now generally replaced by "see": *cf.* Chambers, or see Chambers . . .)

ch., chap. (chapter, chapters)
col. (column, columns)
et al. (and others)
f., ff. (and following page, and following pages)
n.d. (no date)
p., pp. (page, pages)
sic (inserted in brackets within a quotation, means "*thus*—this is the exact quotation, no error of mine!")
vol., vols. (volume, volumes)

Bibliographies have various purposes, but the most useful of them are more than lists of "works consulted." Your bibliography can suggest further study of your subject by including not only the works you have used in the paper, but other books and articles that cover certain areas much more thoroughly than you do. The minimum bibliography lists everything that has proved useful to you, directly or indirectly. A better bibliography will list other sources for the diligent reader who wishes to investigate more thoroughly.

Entries in the bibliography are the same as items in footnotes except that a bibliography is alphabetized—by author first, by title of periodical *article* if no author is given, and by title of *periodical* if neither author nor article is named:

Barry, Frederick (last name first in bibliography)
"Caretaker Board," *Fortune*, September 1952
Cartool Journal (item on waste) November 1956, p. 1246

The final question is: "Why footnotes? Why not end notes—or, better yet, a numbered bibliography that eliminates all the *ibid.*'s and *op. cit.*'s?" These end-note, numbered-bibliography methods are becoming more popular and much can be said for them. The main factor in reaching a decision ought to be: "Which method is most useful to my readers?" Footnotes are certainly more convenient to a reader *who reads them*. End notes (and especially the numbered bibliography) are most convenient for the writer—no question about that whatever. So, if you think most of your readers will be happy with an end-note system, that's the best system for you. If not, stay with footnotes.

For practice, footnoting is best. You learn all you will need to know about end notes by learning how to footnote. You also learn how to use—and how to read—footnote symbols when the need arises.

"The Southern Dilemma," which follows, illustrates the trained historian's method of presenting the results of his research. It is part of the book *The Age of Jackson.*

THE SOUTHERN DILEMMA *

ARTHUR M. SCHLESINGER, JR.

John C. Calhoun was facing a major decision. As he rode north from Pendleton in the Indian summer of 1837, his lips compressed, his face drawn with concentration, his manner absent and taciturn, he weighed his future course with infinite exactness. Before him lay the special session of Congress and the battle over the independent treasury. On his decision—on every decision till the insoluble question was solved—might tremble the future of the South.

1

Calhoun was no longer merely the aspiring politician who had feuded with Jackson in 1830. Personal ambition was now increasingly submerged in a cold monomania for South Carolina and slavery. Many, like Harriet Martineau, found they could no longer communicate with him. He felt so deeply that he rarely heard argument, so passionately that he never forgot his responsibility. "There is no relaxation with him," cried his devoted friend Dixon H. Lewis of Alabama (who weighed three hundred and fifty pounds, and spoke with feeling). "On the contrary, when I seek relaxation in him, he screws me only the higher in some sort of excitement." He appeared to subsist in an unimaginable intellectual solitude, his mind committed to his interminable obligation, focusing forever on a single shining point, which for him was the center of the universe. He was becoming "the cast-iron man," as Miss Martineau saw him, "who looks as if he had never been born, and never could be extinguished." [1]

* From *The Age of Jackson* by Arthur M. Schlesinger, Jr., by permission of Little, Brown & Company.

[1] Lewis to R. K. Cralle, March 20, 1840, F. W. Moore, ed., "Calhoun by His Political Friends." *Publications of the Southern History Association,* VII, 355. Harriet Martineau, *Retrospect,* I, 243-244.

But he became a startling figure when he rose to speak in the Senate, eyes burning like live coals in his pale face, hair bristling and erect, skin loose over his prominent bones, words pouring out in an abrupt, condensed, closely reasoned flow. His voice was metallic and harsh, his gestures monotonous, and his ventriloquist's tones came from nowhere and sounded equally in all corners of the chamber. Yet the commanding eye, the grim earnestness of manner, the utter integrity of sentiment held the galleries in anxious attention. Standing in the narrow aisle of the Senate, bracing himself on the desks beside him, he averaged perhaps one hundred and eighty words a minute of terse and unconquerable argument.[2]

His was the supreme intelligence among the statesmen of the day. Where Clay relied on a richness and audacity of feeling, Webster on certain massiveness of rhetoric, Benton on the sheer weight of facts, and all indulged in orgies of shameless verbiage, Calhoun's speeches were stripped bare, arguing the facts with an iron logic drawn to the highest pitch of tension. Nourished on Aristotle, Machiavelli, and Burke, he possessed an uncanny ability to cut through to the substance of problems.[3] His processes of thought were intricate, merciless, and unsentimental in a day when none of these qualities was in demand.

More than any of the others, he understood that he was living in one of the critical periods of history. It was, for him, a revolutionary age—"a period of transition, which must always necessarily be one of uncertainty, confusion, error, and wild and fierce fanaticism"—and he looked with anxiety on what was plainly a "great approaching change in the political and social condition of the country." "Modern society," he exclaimed, almost with horror, "seems to be rushing to some new and untried condition." The "great question" of the future would be that of "the distribution of wealth—a question least explored, and the most important of any in the whole range of political economy." [4]

[2] For sketches of Calhoun in action, see *New York Evening Post,* February 19, 1838; *Boston Post,* December 16, 1833; Millburn, *Ten Years of Preacher-Life,* 152–153; Willis, *Hurry-Graphs or Sketches of Scenery, Celebrities and Society,* 180–181; Ingersoll, *Historical Sketch,* II, 258.

[3] Meigs, *Calhoun,* II, 100; Calhoun to A. D. Wallace, December 17, 1840, Calhoun, *Correspondence,* J. F. Jameson, ed., 468–469.

[4] Calhoun, "A Disquisition on Government," *Works,* I, 90; Calhoun to J. H. Hammond, February 18, 1837, *Correspondence,* 367; Calhoun in the Senate, January 13, 1834, *Register of Debates,* 23 Congress 1 Session, 218.

The emerging outlines of industrial society filled him with foreboding. The new economy, he felt, was enriching a small group of capitalists at the expense of the great mass of the people. The "tendency of Capital to destroy and absorb the property of society and produce a collision between itself and operatives" was a source of deep alarm. "In the North you are running into anarchy," he told Albert Brisbane. ". . . The capitalist owns the instruments of labor, and he seeks to draw out of labor all of the profits, leaving the laborer to shift for himself in age and disease. This can only engender antagonism; the result will be hostility and conflict, ending in civil war, and the North may fall into a state of social dissolution." Both the growing power of the capitalists and the growing frustration of the masses seemed to threaten the fabric of society.[5]

And the consequences for the South? The business party placed a premium on conservatism and stability; yet no group was more concerned to expand the power of the central government and whittle away the rights of the states. If, as Calhoun believed, the union of bank and state would "inevitably draw all the powers of the system into the vortex of the general government," what safe guards would remain for the South? [6] And a second danger lay in the inescapable economic clash between Northern finance and Southern cotton. As Francis W. Pickens candidly stated the hard facts which underwrote Calhoun's logic, the South must decide "whether cotton shall control exchanges and importations, or whether the banks and the stock interest shall do it . . . Break down the swindling of bankers, . . . and cotton will do the exchanges of the commercial world." [7]

On the other hand, the party which opposed the business class contained in itself ominous threats to Southern security. Equalitarian and radical, thriving on agitation and forever fomenting new projects of reform, it must prove an ever-flowing fount of libertarian dogma.

[5] Memorandum of a conversation with Calhoun, December 4, 1831, Calhoun, *Correspondence,* 305; Redelia Brisbane, *Albert Brisbane: a Mental Biography,* 222.

[6] Calhoun to R. H. Goodwyn, *et al.,* September 1, 1838, *Niles' Register,* September 29, 1838.

[7] Pickens to J. H. Hammond, July 13, 1837, R. C. McGrane, *Panic of 1837,* 159. See also Calhoun to J. E. Calhoun, September 7, 1837, *Correspondence,* 377; Calhoun in the Senate, October 3, 1837, *Register of Debates,* 25 Congress 1 Session 475–476; Calhoun to Calvin Graves, *et al.,* September 6, 1838, *Washington Globe,* October 13, 1838.

Yet, for all its excesses, it was primarily interested in limiting the power of the business community, and in so doing it was employing the State-rights doctrine so vital to the South.

The Southern dilemma was this: which was the greater menace to the plantation system—radical democracy or finance capital? Should the ruling class of the South ally itself to the upper class of the North, and thus to broad construction, capitalism, and conservatism, or to the lower classes of the North, and thus to State rights, agrarianism, and reform? Should the South join the Whigs in their fight against radicalism, or should it join the Democrats in their fight against business rule?

2

Many Southerners had already made their choice. Thomas Cooper voiced a profound planting conviction when he observed, in 1830, that universal suffrage was the root of political evil. Political power must fall thereby "into the hands of the operatives, mechanics, and labouring classes, the men of no property." The consequence? "We say, without hesitation, the wealth of the wealthy is in danger." [8] This was clearly no sectional problem, and Cooper himself by 1837 was turning to Nicholas Biddle, the very embodiment of finance capital, as the best hope for the South.

George McDuffie similarly managed to be a champion both of nullification and the United States Bank. In 1834 he declared that "the wealth and intelligence of the northern and middle States" provided the South its best security against abolitionism as it would emerge from "unbalanced democracy." [9] Northern Whigs responded to such sentiments with feeling. We shall "appeal to our brethren of the south for their generous cooperation," said one group rather explicitly, "and promise them that those who believe that the possession of property is an evidence of merit, will be the last to interfere with the rights of property of any kind." [10] The Southern support for White in 1836 showed the strength of the belief in an alliance with Northern conservatism. In Virginia even strict State-rights men backed the

[8] [Thomas Cooper], "Agrarian and Education Systems," *Southern Review*, (August, 1830), VI, 29–30, 31.

[9] McDuffie's inaugural address as Governor of South Carolina, *Washington Globe*, December 25, 1834.

[10] Report of the Committee of Fifty, *Plaindealer*, May 13, 1837.

Whig ticket, and John Tyler, who had cast the single vote against the force bill in nullification days, now stood as Whig candidate for Vice-President.[11]

Yet Calhoun knew that the business community would in the end exact a price for its protection, and the price would be Southern acquiescence in the American System and broad construction. Could the South afford to pay it? Calhoun was skeptical. If the South surrendered its economic and constitutional bastions, it would exist only on the sufferance of the North.

And the alternative? In 1836 Calhoun could not bring himself to support the Democrats any more than the Whigs. But the panic of 1837 transformed the situation. If Van Buren remained faithful to the hard-money policy, he must come out for the divorce of bank and state. Should not the South seize this opportunity to strengthen its economic position, fortify its constitutional bulwarks and check Northern capitalism, even at the cost of giving more power to Northern radicals?

John Taylor had already endorsed the alliance with radicalism as the best strategy against finance capital. "The question is," he had written, "whether the landed interest . . . had not better unite with the other popular interests, to strangle in its cradle any infant visibly resembling this terrible giant." [12] In the end, Calhoun could not but see the struggle in Jeffersonian terms, between landed capital and business capital—not, as the Southern Whigs saw it, in Federalist terms, between property, whether in land or business, and the propertyless. His decision showed how profoundly he inherited the Jeffersonian tradition.

Van Buren's message sealed his intention. "We have now a fair opportunity to break the last of our commercial Shackles," Calhoun declared with delight.[13] With a sense of vast relief, now restored to a position "much more congenial to my feelings," he broke his partnership with the Whigs, throwing his influence to what he had called not many months before the "more filthy" portion of the Democratic

[11] H. H. Simms, *Rise of the Whigs in Virginia, 1824–1840,* 67–81; O. P. Chitwood, *John Tyler: Champion of the Old South,* 115, 155.

[12] John Taylor, *Inquiry,* 551–552; see also *Tyranny Unmasked,* 197–199.

[13] Calhoun to J. E. Calhoun, September 7, 1837, Calhoun, *Correspondence,* 377. See also Calhoun to J. Bauskett, *et al.,* November 3, 1837, *Niles' Register,* December 2, 1837.

party, "under Benton, Kendal, Blair and Johnson," and backing the personal measure of his ancient enemy, Martin Van Buren.[14] But he was a man of principle, and he would follow where principle led.

3

The issues between Calhoun and the Southern Whigs were clearly expressed in a straggling but bitter debate in the House in September and October. A few weeks after the message Caleb Cushing, the fluent Whig Congressman from Massachusetts, made an able bid for Southern support. The attack on the state banks, he said, was first an attack on State rights, and then an attack on property in general. "By destroying the banks, then, you will revolutionize the property of the country . . . you revolutionize society." With dramatic emphasis Cushing appealed to the South. "Will not the same desperado spirit, which strikes at one form of property strike at another? If it ravages the North, will it spare the South? Can law, order, property, be torn down at one end of the country, and stand untouched and unshaken at the other? Will not anarchy in half be anarchy in the whole? It seems to me," he concluded, "to become every part of the country, North as well [as] South, and not least of all the South, to guard well the conservative elements in the social organization of these United States." [15]

This powerful statement impressed many planters. But Calhoun thought differently, and Francis W. Pickens, his spokesman in the House, delivered the South Carolina retort. It might be to the advantage of Northern capital to rob labor of its full product, Pickens observed, but it was to the advantage of the South that labor receive its full product, for in the South labor and capital were identical. "When we contend for the undivided profits and proceeds of our labor," he cried, "do you not see that we stand precisely in the same situation as the laborer of the North? We are, to all intents and purposes, in the place of laborers. We are the only class of capitalists, as far as pecuniary interest is concerned, which, as a class, are identified with the laborers of the country. We must therefore join with

[14] Calhoun to Anna Marie Calhoun, September 8, 1837, to J. H. Hammond, February 18, 1837, Calhoun, *Correspondence*, 379, 367.

[15] Cushing in the House, September 25, 1837, *Register of Debates*, 25 Congress 1 Session, 885–887.

Northern labor in its resistance to Northern capital."[16] When later in the debate, Ely Moore rose to denounce some Northern Whigs who had lashed into Pickens, the alliance appeared complete.[17]

The axis between Moore and Pickens, between Martin Van Buren and John C. Calhoun, was firm, but brittle. Agreement was perfect up to a point, and thereafter disagreement was infinite. "I am an aristocrat," John Randolph once remarked in a brilliant summary of the Southern position; "I love liberty, I hate equality."[18] Calhoun's political line was the median between love of liberty and hatred of equality. Indeed his fear of radical democracy, with its equalitarian and majoritarian tendencies, remained second only to his fear of capitalism itself. He flinched even from the name. "The word democrat better applies to the north than the South," he said in 1838, "and as usually understood means those who are in favour of the government of the absolute numerical majority to which I am utterly opposed and the prevalence of which would destroy our system and destroy the South."[19] In leisure moments, he worked out an elaborate system of minority rule which promised to come into sharp conflict with the majoritarianism of his Northern allies.[20]

[16] Pickens in the House, October 10, 1837, *Register of Debates*, 25 Congress 1 Session, 1393–1395. John Quincy Adams was infuriated by Pickens, "a coarse sample of the South Carolina school of orator statesmen—pompous, flashy, and shallow," and by his speed, "delivered with an air of authority and a tone of dogmatism as if he was speaking to his slaves." Adams, *Memoirs*, IX, 399.

[17] After half an hour of thunder, Moore broke down as he had before and was carried home to be bled. His collapse came rather to the relief of Adams, who had been impressed by his "prepossessing countenance, a rather courteous deportment, . . . a good command of language," and appalled by his "whole system of insurrection against the rich." "If his strength were equal to his will," Adams decided, "he would be a very dangerous man. As it is, he is a very unsafe one." *Memoirs*, IX, 405–406. For Moore in the house, October 13, 1837, see *Register of Debates*, 25 Congress 1 Session, 1470, 1588.

[18] Bruce, *Randolph*, II, 203.

[19] Calhoun to R. B. Rhett, September 13, 1838, Calhoun, *Correspondence*, 399. Cf. J. H. Hammond's remark: "Circumstances had placed us in alliance (connection rather) with the Democratic party of the country, tho' we professed at the same time to be of a higher school of democracy, one of fixed principles and incompatible faith." Hammond to Calhoun, May 4, 1840, *Correspondence Addressed to John C. Calhoun, 1837–1849*, C. S. Boucher and R. P. Brooks, eds., 823.

[20] The administration was equally aware of the underlying differences. Frank Blair laid down the terms of the alliance in a series of editorials in the *Washington Globe*, September 7, 8, 10, 11, 1838. Taking as much care as Calhoun

The reasoning which justified this alliance with radicalism was indeed too subtle for most planters. Calhoun carried his own circle of bright young men—Pickens, J. H. Hammond, Dixon H. Lewis, R. B. Rhett—and a select group of politicians, including W. F. Gordon of Virginia, and William P. Taylor, the son of John Taylor of Carolina. But he failed to move the planting class as a whole, neither the Virginia school, with its real if less radical concern for State rights, nor the Southern Whigs, with their scorn for "abstractions." The Virginians dissented sharply on the subtreasury, and in 1840 Abel P. Upshur published *A Brief Enquiry into the True Nature and Character of Our Federal Government*, the classic attempt to reconcile the State-rights position with Whiggery—and thereby to rationalize the Harrisburg convention, which had just nominated William Henry Harrison and John Tyler.

But the illusion of Tyler, Upshur, Henry A. Wise and their associates that they could be Whigs for Jeffersonian reasons was quickly dispelled after 1840. Calhoun had observed correctly that the North could demand its price; and, when Clay unveiled the Whig economic program, the Virginia school, led by Tyler, woke to realities and left the party. Their confession of error was signalized when, after Upshur's death, Calhoun, a better logician, succeeded him as Secretary of State.

Even after the Tyler defection, however, the wealthy planters remained predominantly Whig. Two thirds to three quarters of the slaves were in Whig hands. And, as Calhoun had foreseen, those who threw themselves on the protection of Northern conservatism were steadily obliged to accept the Whig economic program. They had rejected Calhoun as a "metaphysician" and Tyler as an "abstractionist," and, being practical men, they bartered away their economic and constitutional advantages for the uncertain patronage of Northern business. They came, in the fifties, to decide that Calhoun had been right. But it was too late, the game was lost.[21]

---

himself not to call the Southerners "democrats," Blair emphasized that this union between "the Democracy of the North and the planters of the South" was for mutual safety against a common enemy.

[21] A. C. Cole, *The Whig Party in the South*; U. B. Phillips, "The Southern Whigs, 1834–1854," *Turner Essays in American History*; Simms, *Rise of the Whigs in Virginia*.

ASSIGNMENTS

I. Develop an expository defense of a judgment (a paper of 1500–3000 words). Choose a problem (preferably one you analyzed as an assignment following Chapter 5), state purpose and readers, marshall adequate evidence, and develop your argument to satisfy highly critical persons.

II. Write a critical evaluation of:

a mechanism, a process, or an organization
a musical performance
a director, a coach, or an executive
a painting or mural
a set of rules
a movie
an architectural design

III. Write a review of 500–800 words (name your readers) of:

a novel
a television play or campus theatrical performance (to be viewed and reviewed by your entire English class)
a new textbook
latest issue of a college magazine or professional journal

IV. Write a research paper based largely on published information:

(a) Choose a problem suggested by one of the reading selections in this book (for example: How much are colleges growing? How many people read science fiction? Was Stalin a Czarist spy? How many women will want careers in the next twenty years?). Develop a paper using material from this selection and at least five other different sources.

(b) Choose a problem suggested by one of your other courses. Get advice and approval of your subject from the instructor in that course and your English instructor.

Index